Derek Paul (handwritten)

WESTERN I

Bombay is the pulsating commercial c   ...uia, its chief
port, and point of entry for most visitors by air. Yet already one
senses authentic India: that heady diversity of colours, cultures,
languages, cuisine and easy tolerance amid bustling bazaars and
Victorian buildings.

Beyond Bombay, the hinterland of Maharashtra State offers
great cave-temples at Ajanta, Aurangabad and Ellora, the pilgrimage towns of Shirdi, Pandharpur and Nasik, Shivaji's rock fortresses, and the pleasures of Kolhapur, Ahmadnagar, Pune, Daulatabad's castle, and cool hill-stations such as Matheran and
Mahabaleshwar.

Vast Karnataka is worth weeks of exploration, beginning in its
pleasant capital Bangalore, spacious Mysore, hilly Mercara, coastal Mangalore, Jog Waterfalls, the immense ruined capital of
Vijayanagar, such wondrous Islamic cities as Bijapur, Gulbarga
and Bidar, and the splendours of Hoysala dynasty Hindu temples
in Somnathpur, Belur and Halebid.

Western India focuses on the Jain centre at Sravana Belagola,
the magnificence of Aihole and Pattadakal, Tipu Sultan's capital
Srirangapatnam, and the Shiva temple on Elephanta Island.

Intended for first-time visitors as well as for experienced travellers keen to understand the background to the vision, _Western
India_ provides a sympathetic and thoughtful companion to some
of India's most rewarding sights.

PHILIP WARD, FRGS, ALA, FRSA, has spent many of the last
35 years in Africa and Asia, including 8 years in Libya, nearly 2
in Indonesia, and has visited India many times. His latest books
include _Japanese Capitals, Finnish Cities, Travels in Oman, Ha'il:
Oasis City of Saudi Arabia_, and _Bulgaria_, which won the International Travel Writers Competition in 1990. He is the author of
The Oxford Companion to Spanish Literature, the Mexican novel
Forgotten Games, and such poetry collections as _A House on Fire_
and _Lost Songs_. His first book on India was _Rajasthan, Agra,
Delhi_ (1989) and his second _South India: Tamil Nadu, Kerala,
Goa_ (1991).

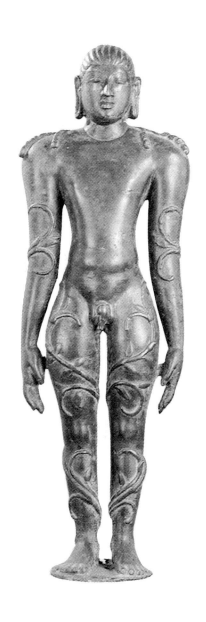

WESTERN INDIA

Bombay • Maharashtra
Karnataka

A Travel Guide

Philip Ward

Oleander

The Oleander Press
17 Stansgate Avenue
Cambridge CB2 2QZ
England

The Oleander Press
80 Eighth Avenue (Suite 303)
New York, N.Y. 10011
USA

British Library Cataloguing in Publication Data

Ward, Philip, 1938–

Western India: Bombay, Maharashtra, Karnataka –
(Oleander travel books; vol. 19)
1. India
I. Title
915.470452

ISBN 0–900891–32–7

Printed and bound in Great Britain

Contents

Acknowledgments

Since the journeys recorded in this book were undertaken over a period from early 1990 to early 1991, readers will allow the transparent device of conflating them into one seamless journey for their own ease of reading. The book can be used as a guide for a journey of several months or, by using the contents list and index, for a shorter journey cutting through parts of the itinerary, which connects to the north with my *Rajasthan, Agra, Delhi* and to the south with my *South India*.

For part of my time in India I was Writer-in-Transit as a guest of Exodus Expeditions of London, whom I thank for their willing collaboration. Mostly I travelled solo on buses, trains, auto-rickshaws, cycle-rickshaws, tongas, boats, coracles, lorries and on foot. No praise is too high for the efficient, patient and underrated punctuality and frequency of Indian transportation systems, not to mention their exceptionally good value for money.

I appreciate the kindness of John Updike in allowing me to reproduce a passage from his novel *S.*, H. R. F. Keating, for a passage from *Inspector Ghote, his Life and Crimes*, and Anita Desai, for a passage from *Baumgartner's Bombay*.

Among many friends, I have to thank Mrs S. R. Chitalkar at Pune's Hotel Amir and the rickshaw-driver Shaikh Husain; in Mangalore, Mr G. V. Narayana of the Cashew Development Corporation and B. Satish Kamath of Achal Industries; in Mudbidri, M. Adiraj, Supervisor of Sri Jain Math; and the staff of the private clinic called Alva's Health Centre in Mudbidri, whose emergency treatment enabled me to continue my journeys without delay; in Anegondi T. T. Guthi and Rama Deva Raya, in Hospet, Raja Achyuta Deva Raya; in Mundgod's Tibetan Colony the Abbot and my host Lobsang Chophel, and the interpreter Dakpa Topgyal.

In Bombay I enjoyed a lengthy interview in the home of the Zoroastrian High Priest Dasturji Dr Firoze M. Kotwal, and in Nagarhole, another with the Range Forest Officer, K. M. Chinnappa. Thanks again to Veena Chopra for teaching me the Hindi I needed for everyday use.

And my wife, Audrey, and my daughters Angela and Carolyn, have provided strength, support, sympathy and innumerable gallons of hot Indian tea, as well as that indefinable sense of calm intensity that is our home. A man who cannot write in such surroundings must be incapable of inspiration.

PHILIP WARD

Introduction

My intention while travelling the length and breadth of Western India from Bombay and Bidar to Bangalore and Mangalore has been to select solid information and personal impressions of places likely to interest a reader or traveller keen to experience at first or second hand the subcontinent's diversity of landscape, humanity, art, architecture and historical development.

Western India is here taken to denote the city of Bombay, and the hinterland of Maharashtra (though not the eastern part of the state around Nagpur, which is conveniently visited from neighbouring Madhya Pradesh), together with the vast state of Karnataka. It is a companion volume to my *Rajasthan, Agra, Delhi* (1989) and *South India* (1991) and will, I hope, appeal to the same wide audience.

The book opens in one of the world's truly great cities, Bombay, and stresses its growth, in particular as a treasury of Victorian architectures. Maharashtra is comparatively little known, except the world-famous sites of Ajanta and Ellora. Aurangabad has caves quite as spectacular, and in Pandharpur, Nasik and Shirdi, pilgrimage towns as fascinating as Benares. Hill stations such as Panchgani, Mahabaleshwar, Matheran, Khandala and Lonavla lure holiday-makers the year round. Hundreds of great fortresses dot the mountaintops, and I have selected Sajjangarh near Satara and Sinhagarh near Pune, to match the marvellous castles near Bombay such as Janjira and Bassein. Daulatabad and Kolhapur rank among the most magical of Indian towns, the former a huge pinnacled stronghold; the latter a royal town of palaces.

Karnataka is so immense that much of Western Europe could be lost within its borders. Natural wonders include parks and waterfalls. Artistic triumphs include the exuberant Hoysala temples of Somnathpur, Belur and Halebid. The great capital of Anegondi-Hampi could absorb one, like Pompei, for a week. The former enclave of Kodagu still seems spiritually isolated from surrounding lowlands. The Jain life of Mudbidri, the Tibetan Buddhist life near Mundgod, and the industrial activity of Bangalore: even the most jaded traveller will come across surprise after surprise, from Hampi Bazaar to Car Street in Udupi. The Hindu centres of Badami, Aihole, Pattadakal and Mahakuta give way, as one ventures northward, to the great Islamic cities of Bijapur, Gulbarga and Bidar. You may not see any other foreigners during your stay, but you will explore the most remarkable civilisation, threatened by the Vijayanagar Empire to the south and the Mughal might to the north.

The best months to visit Western India are during the height of the North American and European winter. While Finland's lakes freeze over, evening breezes bring merciful release to the busy streets and squares of Bombay. Try the months from the end of the November to the beginning of March.

You may have chosen a package tour to Rajasthan, Agra and Delhi. Packages are even becoming available to South India. But very few travel companies offer a package to Maharashtra and Karnataka as yet, which is why these itineraries emphasise self-help. If you have learned the ways of India on previous trips, this is your chance to break out on your own. So these routes rely on road transport, usually inter-city buses, and auto-rickshaws locally. In Bombay use buses within the city, trains to explore Bassein, and boats to Elephanta, Chaul and Janjira. I have included some rail journeys where they are recommendable, such as the Bangalore-Mysore run, or Badami-Hampi. You can hire private cars and drivers at state tourism head offices in Bombay and Bangalore and that way you may save time. But you spend a lot more money and lose daily contact with the throngs that give India its unforgettable verve and knife-edge excitement, its unexpected encounters with missionaries and wedding-parties, beggars and pilgrims. The car is not an Indian invention, and it consorts oddly with timeless landscapes.

Westerners often come to India for strange reasons, such as an answer to universal questions of life and religion. They visit Shirdi for the shrine of Sai Baba and Pune's Osho Commune. They meditate at the Hindu centre of Sringeri or smoke ganja on the beaches of Karnataka. Some come for transcendental realisation, some for a long winter holiday, others to practise yoga, often with vegetarian beliefs.

Every traveller is surely unique, and will benefit from India in a particular way which neither that traveller nor anyone else can predict. I found immense joy in Bidar, Anegondi, Badami, Bassein, and Kolhapur. Others would prefer the early caves of Bhaja, Bedsa, Karla, or the marvellous countryside around Jog Falls. I found invigorating ideas of rite and ritual in discussions with the Zoroastrian High Priest of Bombay and monastic debate among exiled Tibetan monks at Drepung Loseling. Others would enjoy the shrine at Ramdas near Satara, or Kumbh Mela at Nasik. You may feel that nirvana eludes you in India as elsewhere, and that spiritual experience is for Sundays, not blind gurus in noisy bazaars. But what you had been looking for might well appear before you in Western India, before the triple-faced Shiva at Elephanta, or in the Ibrahim Rauza garden at Bijapur. Your Eurocentric perspectives will be at least slightly affected by India's endemic poverty, its struggles against squalor and pollution. In the year that Czechoslovakia elected a dissident playwright President, India sent a gift of grain to the U.S.S.R. A land of contradictions continues to contradict one's expectations in a most ebullient, pulsating way.

It follows that I can offer no conclusions about what I have seen, thought, read and felt. India is at once complex and unique, both constantly in flux and at a deep level almost changeless, as Hindu teachings reiterate. You think you have solved the question, when the very question itself disappears into thin air. Not so much the Indian rope trick, as the Indian universal trick: that all is illusion. And yet . . . I listen to a tape of Ravi Shankar's music, I touch against my cheek the gift of a silk cloth from the Abbot of Drepung Loseling, and I open again photograph albums of Ellora. These are all real enough?

I suggest that you drop what you are doing and plan a visit to Bombay, then Maharashtra, then Karnataka, in roughly the order suggested in this book. Then you will return a person changed and deepened, wondering how you could have lingered outside India so long. You will never be the same again.

Illustrations

Photographs are by the Author and maps by regional tourist offices unless otherwise stated. One colour illustration for the cover was kindly supplied by G. H. R. Tillotson (Hoyasaleshwara Temple, Halebid, Karnataka) the others are by the Author: Rajabai Clocktower, Bombay, and a mural painting from Ajanta (Maharashtra).

1 BOMBAY

Early Bombay

The name 'Bombay' is a Portuguese corruption of 'Mumba' or 'Mumbai', a manifestation of the Hindu goddess Parvati. Parvati's consort, Lord Shiva, is worshipped at Elephanta Island in the bay.

Mumba Devi's temple at Bhuleshwar is the third dedicated to the patroness of the Koli people. The first was erected on a site near Victoria Terminus, and demolished during the Muslim invasions of Sultan Mubarak of Gujarat about 1320. Rebuilt on the same site, it fell victim to the restructuring of Old Bombay in 1737.

Topographically, Bombay as we see it today is a peninsula overlying a group of seven islands connected by reclamation from the sea: Parell-Sion, Mahim, Worli, Mumbadevi, Mazagaon, the tiny Old Woman's Island, and Colaba. Four centuries ago it was occupied by native Kolis and a Portuguese factory or trading post. Nowadays municipal limits stretch northward into Salsette Island beyond Tulsi Lake and Kanheri Caves to the east and Manori and Marve beaches to the west.

The Kolis, a fishing caste, settled on these islands about two thousand years ago, and still fish there today, bringing into port such delicacies as *bombil*, which became *bambolim* in Portuguese and bummelo in English. It is a small, silver fish with the scientific name *harpodon nehereus*, known popularly as 'Bombay duck', and is served as a snack in many Bombay restaurants.

Nowadays the Kolis, aboriginal Dravidian settlers of the coast around Bombay, find temporary refuge wherever they can, for their little fishing village in a much larger district called after them Colaba (with a Portuguese 'C' for the initial 'K') is a poor, crowded spectre of their first expansive domain. Their shacks of woven mats and simple fishing boats appear and disappear along the coast whenever municipal reclamation schemes decide to occupy their stretches of coast. Koli women twist their saris between their legs and racially are darker than most who came later. The term 'coolie' for a hired labourer has been associated in folk etymology with these Kolis, but both Tamil and Kannada have a word *kuli* meaning 'hire' or 'wages', by extension a person hired or given wages, and this correct vowel-form is supported by G. Oppert in *The Original Inhabitants of Bharatavarsa or India* (1893).

If you want to see rural Kolis today take the train to Andheri: one of their main villages is at Versova, 27 km north of Central Bombay, beyond Juhu Beach, west of the Aarey Dairy, and facing the attractive beach of Madh. Versova beach is not a pleasure-beach: you can take a hired boat over to Madh, or reach Madh by road via Malad (which is also a rail station) and then by road via Marve (ferry across to Manori beach is also available) then due south to Madh.

1

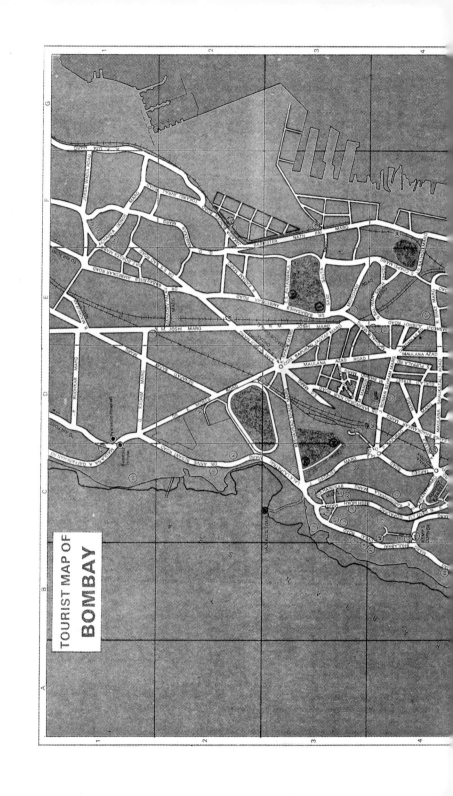

TOURIST MAP OF
BOMBAY

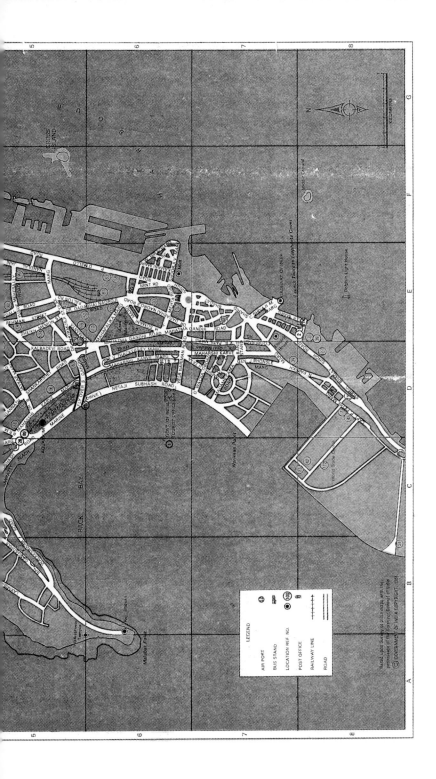

LEGEND

AIR PORT

BUS STAND

LOCATION REF. NO.

POST OFFICE

RAILWAY LINE

ROAD

I envisaged the islands having been colonised – ironic as it may seem to us today – by second-century Buddhists because they were quiet, out of the way, in a state close to nature. They must have regarded Kanheri as isolated, and apt for meditation. Within a few years Aryan Hindus had spread throughout Gujarat and Maharashtra, but no town was risked on these lowlying, swampy islands, and although Silahara Hindu rulers erected a temple complex to honour Walkeshwar on Mumba Devi Island near Malabar Point in the mid–11th century, we know of no permanent settlement until the Hindu King Bhima Deva founded a town on Mahim Island as a refuge from Muslims in Gujarat, who raided and finally took control of the islands in 1401, from their capital in Ahmadabad.

The Portuguese won control of the area in 1509, and would dominate the Indian Ocean until challenged by the Dutch and British in the 17th century. It was in 1534 that the Sultan of Gujarat made over Bassein port, with the islands of Salsette and Bombay, to the Portuguese, and in 1613 the Mughal Emperor Jahangir permitted the British to trade from their factory in Surat. By a dowry arrangement, Bombay was granted to the British in 1661 when Catherine of Bragança married Charles II, but the Portuguese Viceroy in Goa forbade the British to take control and only four years later did Humphrey Cooke seize possession as agreed by treaty. In 1668 Charles II leased Bombay to the British East India Company and Aungier began the process of land reclamation to connect the islands of Bombay, fortifying the area, building docks and a mint, providing a Company militia which later became the Indian army, and attracting a range of Muslim and Hindu settlers from the less safe surrounding countryside.

Of Portuguese rule, the vast majority of public works disappeared under the British, leaving only the gate of Bombay Castle and a ten-foot sundial within the castle, now closed to the public as a part of the Government Dockyard establishment. The dockyard was expanded by Lavji Nasirwanji Wadia, a Parsi shipbuilder who preferred Bombay to his home in Surat, beginning in 1736. He claimed that a teak-built man-o'-war made in Bombay would last five times longer than a ship made of English oak. The main landing-place was by the present Old Customs House, partly reusing stone from the Portuguese barracks of 1665. The front wing is dated 1714 and it became a customs house only in 1802. Admiralty House, near Cama Hall, at the end of Marine Street, is another ancient survivor, having served later as High Court and Great Western Hotel. The Mint, north of the castle, was created (1824–9) by Major John Hawkins in a style rarely seen in Bombay: neo-classical, with a delightful if unexpected Ionic portico. Bombay rupees had been struck as early as 1672 by the East India Company but this grand edifice promised coins of a better quality. Equally neo-classical is the magnificent Doric Town Hall completed in 1833 to designs by Colonel Thomas Cowper: eighty-seven metres long and thirty-three metres wide, with Corinthian columns within except for Ionic in the Medical Board's sector. Otherwise the Town Hall now accommodates the Bombay Asiatic Society (formerly the Royal Asiatic Society, Bombay) and other learned bodies. The Library has been disgracefully neglected.

As you look at Elphinstone Circle, remember that below it stood Bombay Green, one of those many verdant quarters that existed before Sir Bartle

Flora Fountain, Bombay

Frere's new plans. He laid out or renovated thirty-five roads across the jumble that was cluttering up Bombay, ensuring wide pavements and plentiful trees. He also made ample provision for those gardens in which polluted twenty-first century Bombay can breathe: Victoria Gardens, University Gardens, Grant Road's Northbrook Gardens and Elphinstone Circle Garden. When the British moved southward to reclaimed Colaba, the 'Native' or 'Black' Town became more congested, and gradually the jungle was tamed, then uprooted, and finally replaced with a chaos of buildings in areas named often for the trees once common in areas now urbanised: Bhendi from the bhend tree, Ambewadi from the mango, Kelewadi from the banana, Chinch Bander from the tamarind. To follow the curve of Bombay Fort's vanished walls, you can visualise the original gates. Apollo Gate stood where Old Customs House Road met Rampart Row, Bazaar Gate stood by the police station which was a sentry post at the gate, and Church Gate near the station. The walls – like the fragment which survived at least until my last visit near St George's Hospital behind V.T. – once ran along Raveline Street, Bastion Road, Outram Road and Rampart Row.

Worship in Bombay is a theme that you could never fully explore, for all the sprawling exuberance of dozens of Hindu temples for 70% of Bombay's population, the Buddhist shrine at Worli, the main Jain temple overlooking Back Bay near the Dhobi Ghats, two large Parsi fire temples in the jumble of lanes beyond Crawford Market, the mosques serving 15% of Bombay's population, the synagogues near Jacob Circle, in Byculla and Knesset Eliahu in the Fort area; the twenty or so Catholic churches such as the Holy Name Cathedral in Colaba and Our Lady of the Mount in Bandra, and such Protestant outposts as the Cathedral Church of St Thomas.

Central Bombay has a number of focal points: the St.Thomas Cathedral is on one of them: Elphinstone or Horniman Circle, on the former 'Bombay Green' obliterated in the 1860s to provide a majestic, imperial-style sequence of façades owing much to Italianate inspiration and English cast iron. St Thomas' has been here much longer; indeed it was begun in 1672 by Gerald Aungier, known – at least to the British – as 'the Father of Bombay', who in 1669 had succeeded the equally able and energetic Sir George Oxenden as President of Surat and Governor of Bombay. Aungier defended Surat against Shivaji and his Marathas but realised that the British factory would be far more effectively protected from an island base and insisted on creating the fort on Bombay island, now largely demolished and forgotten except for the name.

The church of St Thomas which Aungier began in 1672 was elevated to See status in 1833, when the present tower replaced the old belfry. I saw no Indians within: indeed St Thomas' is a shrine to the Raj and its heroes, with monuments to Colonel John Campbell who defended Mangalore against Tipu Sultan in 1787, to Major Eldred Pottinger of Herat, to Captain Hardinge who captured a French cruiser in 1808, and Governor Jonathan Duncan, who prohibited with the full force of law infanticide prevalent in Varanasi and Kathiawar.

Gerald Aungier died in 1677, but by then he had invited Hindu merchants to escape from Jesuit persecution in Goa, brought Parsis from Surat, Hindus from Gujarat, Muslims from the Gulf and Red Sea, and refugee Armenians. He encouraged each community to live according to its own beliefs, without interfering with its neighbours, and called together landowners to establish

6

their claims and titles. Other Governors might have expropriated land, but Aungier made sure that compensation was offered for Old Woman's Island, Colaba, the Fort area, and lesser forts at Mahim and Sion. Aungier himself thought Bombay's harbour after reclamation 'certainly the fairest, largest and securest in all these parts of India, where a hundred sail of tall ships may ride all the year safe with good moorage', a potent factor in monsoon time. Surat, the original English factory on the northwest coast, was abandoned in favour of Bombay in 1687 because Marathas had ravaged the town in 1664, in 1670, and were promising to ravage it again. Mughal tax-gatherers made heavy demands on Surat merchants to pay for Aurangzeb's campaigns to subdue Hindu India by the sword.

In 1687, the East India Company moved from Surat, nowadays a backwater on the Gujarati coast, to Bombay, and the fate of these islands was sealed: it would become to the West Coast as Calcutta would to the east – a place of magnetic attraction for jobs, careers, industries, enterprise. A causeway linked Bombay with Salsette in 1803, the marauding Marathas were overcome in 1817–8, and their lands annexed to create a majestic new Bombay Presidency. In 1830 the first tarmac road connected Bombay with the rest of India and a new steamship service linked Bombay with Suez; eight years later the causeway to Old Woman's Island and Colaba linked the last two of the city's islands to the shore. In 1853, a 35-km railway joined Bombay to Thana on Salsette Island, setting a precedent for the rest of India to be served by a rail system, and the year after Bombay opened its first cotton mill to process cotton earlier exported to Britain. In 1862 Sir Bartle Frere's reconstruction of Bombay began by razing the old Fort area and inviting major new designs for markets, courts, schools and university. In 1869 the opening of the Suez Canal shortened the sea route Europe-Bombay to only three weeks. In 1896–9 bubonic plague killed about 110,000, roughly an eighth of the city's population. The state visit by King George V and Queen Mary in 1911 was celebrated in the 1920s by the building of the Gateway of India, opposite the Taj Hotel, which had been founded in 1903 by the Tata family.

In some ways, despite two World Wars, Partition in 1947, and the founding of the Tata Institute of Fundamental Research (1945) now on a new reclaimed site in Colaba and Bhabha Atomic Research Centre (1957) at Trombay, Bombay still looks very much like the city that Sir Bartle Frere might have visualised in the 1860s, though the plethora of hideous statues of British administrators and generals have often been replaced by their Indian counterparts. But the population has rocketed to 13 million.

To enjoy the city at its best, visit in January, and spend a week roaming the bazaars and temples, the suburbs and historic Victorian centre: Elephanta in the bay and Kanheri in the Sanjay National Park. Use suburban electric trains and red double-decker buses. Above all, talk to the people and listen to them. They have extraordinary stories to tell.

The Gateway of India
My alarm exploded at my ear at 7 a.m. in a dingy cubicle at Oliver's Guest House, Walton Road, and after a quick dry brush of my teeth and a sluice under a dripping shower, I headed out into the warm, sunny January morning

7

towards the New York Snacks and Milk Bar, a hole in the wall not far from Taj. Next door the Nanking Chinese Restaurant confessed it was closed in large, halting English 'for Chinese New Year. This is Year of Horse.' After finishing breakfast, I booked a morning tour of the city with Ganesh Travels (our bus number MMK 4548) and sat on the corniche to watch Bombay rouse itself from torpor. Little schoolgirls barged ahead of each other into pick-up school buses, causing the first yelling stress of the day. 'Come to Elephanta', beckoned a tout: '25 rupees ordinary launch, 40 de luxe.' A snake-charmer set up his basket close by, uncovering a flute and a somnolent cobra. On the other side a coconut vendor began to slash nuts with a machete. Crows pecked and hustled at last night's crumbs.

'Hullo, mister, you want nice girl, beautiful girl, Indian Airlines, I bring her to your room.'

'Hello, Sir, Sir, you want good marijuana, good quality?'

Two Hindus sat clucking with sadness and surprise over the morning's paper. 'You know what?' 'Heh?' 'Ava Gardner just passed away.' 'Tsk'. Poor old Victorian Bombay. Like an aristocrat down on his luck who puts on the same old jacket because it's the only one he possesses, but is let down by its shabby collar, worn cuffs, creeping discoloration, Bombay drifts into helpless decay, lethargic, slow, an embarrassment to friends. The morning's *Indian Express* grimly records the total non-implementation of the first half of the Bombay Development Plan, 1981–2000, without holding out any hope for the second half. Land has been reserved for use by the Municipality, then left inactive. A landowner refusing to be named described how his plot at Goregaon was 'for 16 years reserved for a booster pumping station, then for the last ten years earmarked first for a public hall, then a welfare centre and library, none of which has ever been started.'

This decaying Bombay, hot, stifling, humid, polluted yet caressed at night by faint breezes off the sea distant as memories, has been best evoked by Anita Desai in her novel *Baumgartner's Bombay* (Heinemann, 1988), in which an elderly, Jewish, shabby ex-internee spends his last years among cats and the pressing tide of villagers who have ended up like human jetsam in Bombay, like Baumgartner himself. 'He had to avoid the gnarled and rotting feet of the man who always lay in a drunken stupor at this time of the morning, his head inside the shelter and his legs outside, like pieces of wood flung down, as well as the pile of cooking pots that the woman washed in the gutter so that they shone like crumpled tinfoil in the glare, and the heaps of faeces that the children left along the same gutter, and the squares of greasy paper from which they had eaten their food the night before.'

Bombay, the eternally tolerant and international, I salute you for inscribing Swami Vivekananda's words near the Gateway of India:

'Ye are the children of God, the sharers of immortal bliss, holy and perfect beings. Ye divinities on earth, sinner! It is a sin to call a man so; it is a standing libel on human nature. Come up, o Lions, and shake off the delusion that you are sheep – you are souls immortal, spirits free, blest and eternal.' Beside the full-length figure of the benign Swami (1863–1902), little boats roll and sway as in any tiny Cornish harbour: we might, were it not for rank sticky heat, be strolling around Mousehole. Tour buses in ranks disgorge chaotic swathes of multi-coloured tourists from all over India, Australia, Europe. Some stroll hand in hand to the Gateway of India, ironically photographed as a typical – indeed prototypical – Indian building, though it was designed by George Wittet to commemorate the 1911 visit to Bombay of King George V and Queen Mary en route to the Delhi durbar, and dates from 1924. Like the equestrian statue of the Maratha leader Shivaji nearby, it serves no practical function but stands like the Marble Arch in London as a yellow basalt symbol of its city.

Chhatrapati Shivaji stared defiantly over the Arabian Sea, as a white-uniformed figure in a Pandit Nehru hat poked his double-jointed fingers closer and closer into the face of a fat man in beige, perspiring with the effort of listening in silence to a rival who would not take yes, no, or maybe for an answer. Our location was Apollo Bunder, 'Apollo' misrepresenting the *palla* or sable-fish, one of the shad family or *hilsa*, and 'Bunder' denoting a wharf or quay, as found in the Iranian 'Bandar Abbas'.

Facing the Gateway of India rises the Taj Mahal Intercontinental, a five-star de luxe hotel with a good bookshop and all other expected facilities; it is an institution, a familiar meeting-place, and a landmark, and when I strolled around in jeans I excited no comment.

I was invited into the spotless Taj kitchens by the Executive Chef, Satish Arora, a brilliant innovator at home with traditional Indian cuisine as well as with international dishes. He cooks some four thousand meals a day in the Taj's restaurants. The Tanjore offers live sitar music with Indian dishes, the Golden Dragon Chinese regional cooking from Szechwan, and the Rooftop Rendezvous chic French cuisine. The Taj has eleven separate banqueting halls and regularly hosts business meetings for up to a dozen wedding receptions for nine hundred, with bands and horses. Among his range of specialities are Lobster Arora, Raan (lamb marinated in natural yoghourt, garnished with cucumber, beetroot, and onion), and the Goanese chicken dish called Murg Cafreal. The Taj's 24-hour coffee-shop is the Shamiana, with a barbecue in the evenings.

One can take tea here while staying – as I did – at one of the cheap guesthouses in Colaba, the area behind the Taj, from Arthur Bunder Road at one end of the long Mereweather Road, to Mahakavi Bushan Road at the other. If you have no reservation in Bombay, you can take a bus or cab to Whalley's Guesthouse at 41 Mereweather Road and, if unlucky, explore in all directions from there.

By the Gateway of India, an old man in homespun smiled at me: 'You are from England, sir?' 'Yes.'

'I am 62, sir, unemployed. Those were the good times, sir, when there was work for me, for everybody in Bombay, the British times. Please give one rupee, sorry sir.'

As embarrassed as the old man, I dug in my pocket and brought out a five-rupee note. 'Thank you, sir, sorry sir.' To what may we be reduced, after all, each one of us? As I wander round India, listening, looking, learning about possibly the most complex nation-state on Earth, I think about the essence of the bhakti movement. In the early 16th century, yesterday in terms of Indian philosophy, Chaitanya urged us toward 'the humility of grass, the fortitude of trees, and self-abasement for the sake of others.' Despite being caught up in

9

the struggle for work, the fight even to get on a bus, we should never forget Chaitanya's words.

Marine Drive
The Taraporevala Aquarium was a Parsi foundation of 1951. Its location on Marine Drive beside Chowpatty Beach is inspired: you might think that only salt-water fish are collected there, but denizens of fresh water can also be seen between 11 and 8, all adequately labelled but without teaching aids to make the visit useful for schoolchildren. Closing day is Monday.

After watching coral fish from the Laccadives, turtles and moray eels, stingray and catfish, somehow I felt no attraction to the fish-and-chips on sale nearby. Someone had scrawled on the wall 'There's no milk like cow's milk' and I photographed a colourful wedding-party, with bugles, trumpets and drums, as it wended its apparently haphazard route along Marine Drive, the band's splendiferous turbanned leaders like a company of itinerant major domos.

Nariman Point culminates in the National Centre for Performing Arts, with the Parsi-sponsored Tata Theatre (1981), designed by the American architect Philip Johnson, and the Jehangir Nicholson Museum of Modern Art. Parsis such as the Tatas, Naval Wadia, and Dr Homi Bhabha, have played a major part in the patronage of contemporary Indian art. One day the uneasy mix of European-style abstraction and Mughal-style particularity may throw up a genius, but in the meantime patrons such as Sadruddin Daya, unafraid to buy up whole exhibitions by younger artists, are making it possible for modern art to survive and experiment in cosmopolitan Bombay. Curving round Back Bay along Marine Drive you come first to Oberoi Towers Hotel, and then to Indian Airlines and Air India offices on Madame Cama Road corner.

If the buildings along Marine Drive look less majestic than Bombay Town Hall or less ramshackle than the tenements or *chawls*, that is because Marine Drive itself (officially Netaji Subhash Marg) was reclaimed from the sea as recently as the 1920s. Cricket pitches are located far enough from the sea for a watery six to remain the height of ambition, but youngsters aim for the heights of the stadium where the Indian team plays its international test matches in Bombay.

From Marine Drive you can see Government House, or Raj Bhavan, at one time consisting of only one bungalow and, with two others ('The Retreat' and 'The Beehive') was surrounded in the early 19th century by the jungle that was stripped bare of all but the holy banyan trees to make way for a steady influx of new bungalows halted for a while by an order in the 1850s. This was not the first Government House. In *Palaces of the Raj* (1973), Mark Bence-Jones evokes the charm of Parell, the original country retreat of the Governors from 1719 and their principal residence from 1829–85. Having been a Franciscan friary, and then a college of the Jesuits who were expelled in 1690, the house at Parell was believed to be accursed since a church had been desecrated to form the great banqueting hall. Worse still, the friary had been built on the site of a Hindu temple of Parali Vajinath, accounting for its name. In fact, Parell was unhealthy because of its proximity to a swamp, and a Governor's wife, Lady Fergusson, died there of cholera in 1882. It was virtually as airless as the Governor's House within the Fort, abandoned in 1829.

Mountstuart Elphinstone added side wings after becoming Governor in 1819, and replaced the ox-drawn carriages of earlier days with elegant horses. Lady Canning stayed at Parell on her first visit to India, enjoying the cypresses 'entirely covered with flame-coloured bignonia, like pillars of fire.' She compared the nearby Mahim woods with the hothouse at Kew combined with *The Swiss Family Robinson* and *Paul et Virginie*. Elphinstone was succeeded at Parell by Sir John Malcolm, who reduced hospitality to a single dinner and a single ball each month. During his Governorship a Persian envoy, on seeing the British ladies dancing a quadrille, suggested to Malcolm that the ladies should not trouble themselves any further on his account, imagining them to be a species of *nautch* girl provided for his benefit.

Following the fashion, the grand folk of Parell made their new homes on Malabar Hill's scented slopes, with verandahs open to sea-wind, so the Governor took the hint and moved from Parell to Malabar Point, leaving the house appropriately enough as a laboratory for plague research, so it remains as secluded from the visitor today as it was in those days of Elphinstone and Malcolm, Grant and Falkland, Frere, FitzGerald, and Sir Philip Wodehouse.

Chowpatty Beach

I have been fortunate enough to attend Bombay's crowded festivities one September, at the beginning of the new fishing season, celebrating Ganesha and allowing him to be accompanied by his father Lord Shiva and his mother Parvati on a day-long procession to Chowpatty Beach. The images are left to float away, then devotees walk into the waters as far as they dare.

But all the year round Chowpatty days and evenings attract tens of thousands of sauntering holidaymakers. They are not attracted by bathing, as at Miami Beach or Bournemouth, but by the social occasion. You relax with your friends, male and female, watch the lights go on in Marine Drive to form the brilliant 'Queen's Necklace', and choose snacks from the variety of stalls proffering ice-cream and bhelpuri, idli sambar and potato and onion dosas, coconuts and roasted chickpeas, sweet coloured water and pastries, samosas and even the occasional pan: a betel leaf filled with betel nut, lime and spices such as cardamom. Spat betel-juice has splattered on walls and pavements all over India from the earliest times, and the addiction endures.

Snake-charmers and contortionists, rifle-kiosk wallahs with blown-up balloons to puncture, donkey-men and tricksters: Chowpatty is a constantly-changing panorama of the human condition: children seem to grow up more quickly in Bombay and Calcutta than anywhere else, and I put their worldliness down partly to the ways of street and beach, where pickpockets come out as the lights go on, and drug-pedlars whisper tantalising prospects of marijuana to easy prey. Touts will offer you the delights of a taxi-ride to the 'cages' or brothels of Kamatipura, where girls for sale are protected by sturdy minders from unsuitable clients: they have to be protected because men outnumber women in Bombay by about 5 to 3, partly because men venture forth from their villages while keeping their families back home, where the cost of living is lower.

Other ingenious souls will attempt to relieve you of your money by short-changing and palming 'good exchange rate', procuring young boys, selling 'brown sugar' or heroin which arrived in India in the 1980s and has since claimed forty thousand known addicts, poking performing monkeys, or plain importuning for money, without any great prevarication.

You might see a Hindu priest dressed in white leading a tidemark ceremony to celebrate the annual replacement of the sacred cotton thread around the male Brahmin body, a symbol of the highest caste.

Not far from Chowpatty Beach stands Mani Bhavan, a museum commemorating the life and work of Gandhiji, at 19 Laburnum Road. Open from 9.30 to 6, Mani Bhavan accommodated Gandhi whenever he visited Bombay from 1917 to 1934. The room where he worked and slept can be seen: an evocative quiet moment in your Bombay life, and there is a museum of memorabilia.

Northwest of the race-course, along Lala Lajpatrai Marg where it runs into Dr Annie Besant Road, the splendid new Nehru Planetarium soars into the sky, a marvellously light pierced cylinder commissioned from the architect I. M. Kadri in 1977. As well as the regular shows at 3 and 6 (English) and 4.30 (Hindi), you can explore the exhibition of the cosmos. The planetarium closes every Monday.

Theatre, Music, Dance
Though plays have always been improvised, written and acted in India, dance drama and music have invariably proved more popular throughout the subcontinent. This is hardly surprising, given the divergence of languages and the universality of music. But every theatrical tradition is unique, and says much – often subtly – about local customs and mentality which cannot easily be surmised from travel alone. So I always try to visit a local theatre, whether in China, Bulgaria or Egypt. The Tata Theatre in the National Centre for Performing Arts at Nariman Point will usually have something exceptional. Hindi, Marathi or even Gujarati plays can be found at Birla Matusri Sabhagriha, New Marine Lines, and the Sahitya Sangh Mandir on Charni Marg. The Tejpal Auditorium, Gowalia Tank, provides theatre in Hindi, Gujarati and occasionally also English. For plays in English and concerts of Western music try Sophia Bhabha Auditorium on Bhulabhai Desai Marg. Try also Hanuman Theatre on Delisle Road for folk drama, Shanmukhananda Hall, Lokmanya Hall, Shivaji Mandir, and Rabindra Natya Mandir for evening entertainment. Large hotels offer dance performances aimed at a foreign audience, and consequently diluted for a brief attention span. Authentic Indian performances of improvised music tend to last for many hours, as virtuoso soloists inspire each other to heights of fantastic brilliance.

Malabar Hill
If you have time, explore the Jain Temple on Ridge Road, Malabar Hill. You should not introduce leather (whether bags or shoes or belts, or fashionable clothes) into any Jain sanctuary, for it is offensive to Jains. Jainism is the nearest religion to modern cosmological theory, for it teaches that the universe is infinite and uncreated by any deity. While Western scholars attribute the birth of Jainism to Vardhamana Mahavira, a contemporary of Gautama Buddha, who died in about 526 B.C., Jains themselves believe that Mahavira is only the last in a chain of twenty-four *tirthankars* ('makers of the ford, or river-crossing')

those beings beyond the cycles of creation, preservation and destruction held sacred by Hindus. Whereas Hindus pray for blessings, Jains regard their own tirthankars as beyond any human intervention, having achieved a state of being beyond the heavens in which gods and their released worshippers exist in a pure state beyond our powers of contemplation. The best that we can achieve in this life, therefore, is by a process of austerity and non-violence to rise to a higher stage of reincarnation, and later achieve salvation from the cycle of reincarnation in the holiness of the tirthankars.

Jains offer symbolic fruit and rice, and commune individually, without any communal worship, ringing the temple bell before departure to summon the deity.

Walkeshwar is a Hindu temple complex on the west slope of Malabar Hill. Legend says that the Banganga tank was opened up by an arrow fired by Rama when he stopped to rest on his way from his birthplace at Ayodhya on his way to Sri Lanka, to rescue his beloved Sita from the demon Ravana. Dating to 1050, the temple is dedicated to the 'Sand Lord' of the lingam. Rama is said to have moulded a phallic symbol of Lord Shiva from local sand, and around this the main temple was erected.

After seeing Walkeshwar you can stroll down the lane from Banganga Tank to see the Hindu burning ghat and cemetery down by the sea.

Then if you make for Babulnath Road, you will come to the Shaivite temple to Babulnath, up the steep hill.

Malabar Hill, catching sea breezes, is a favourite picnic spot for families. Kamala Nehru Park was laid out in 1952 in honour of Jawaharlal Nehru's wife: while parents enjoy the panoramic views over Bombay, children scamper up and around the enormous shoe, originating from the nursery rhyme 'There was an old woman.'

Vendors of popcorn and soft drinks congregate outside this as indeed any other park in India, beggars spread their palms or tug at your clothes, and touts approach you to change money: 'dollars, friend you have Deutschmark mebbe?' But compared with Calcutta, violence, robbery and pickpocketing in Bombay are relatively rare. Certainly I felt safe in the Pherozeshah Mehta Gardens, laid out opposite Kamala Nehru Park as long ago as 1881. Lads played football desultorily, not with the dynamism of Goan boys: the fanatics' sport in Bombay is cricket. A crocheted table-cloth was draped on the ground in front of me for my admiration; 'See, sir, only two hundred rupee, very good, all handwork, best price only.' A performing monkey is trained to grip a man's trousers until he is released by handing a coin to the monkey's handler. Sir Pherozeshah Mehta (1845–1915) was described by Lord Hardinge as 'a great Parsi, a great citizen, a great patriot and a great Indian', and like many Parsis rose above his communal origins to become a statesman passionately involved in the Indian National Movement, a practising barrister (1869–76) and a member of the Bombay Municipal Corporation. He supported Gandhi, and in 1911 was appointed Vice-Chancellor of Bombay University then founded the Central Bank, the first bank staffed wholly by Indians. In 1913 he founded the *Bombay Chronicle* and was sometimes known as the 'uncrowned king of Bombay.' This generous, wise and tolerant leader is aptly commemorated in such cool, well-tended gardens high above the urban din and dirt.

13

After leaving Mehta Gardens, the tour bus drives below and beside the Towers of Silence. It is considered disrespectful to the dead and living to approach a Parsi Tower of Silence, and actual admission is strenuously forbidden, even to relatives of the deceased.

The Parsi custom of neither burning nor burying their dead, but exposing them to be devoured by carrion birds, such as vultures, predates the origin of their religion over 2,500 years back, but was reiterated as a religious injunction by Zoroaster, who stated that the faithful must not defile earth, fire or water. It seems illogical that their air – an element which might be equally sacred – could be defiled by putrefying bodies, but if one were to judge religions by their decree of logicality, none would have survived.

A Parsi funeral traditionally took place at home or in a pavilion near the tower of silence of *dakhma*. Hereditary pall-bearers, usually four in number, would then bear the shrouded corpse on a stretcher waist-high into one of the seven circular enclosures thirty metres in diameter pierced only by a locked gate, and surrounded by high walls on which vultures would perch for their next grisly feast. The corpse is then placed naked and, once pecked clean by the carrion-birds, the bones are hurled into a central pit lined with charcoal and sand to filter rainwater and ensure it does not pollute the earth. Nowadays, some Parsis argue that the old methods are insanitary: neighbours complain that vultures drop rotting flesh on to roofs, balconies and gardens. Cremation is seen as a modern development objectionable only to the truly reactionary.

The 18th-century Mahalakshmi Temple is the next brief port of call on the city bus tour. Hindu merchants propitiate the Great Lakshmi, goddess of prosperity. Yes, she has answered the prayers of those who have covered her graven image, above tiger and demon, with bangles and necklaces. She gives her name to the racecourse which opened in 1878, after the old Byculla course was abandoned. The racing season from November to March occupies weekends and some Wednesdays, and Bombay has the kudos of hosting the national stud book at the Royal Western India Turf Club. The Bombay Turf Club was founded in 1800, and racing was fostered first by the British and then by the Parsi community: now Mahalakshmi races are crowded 'with all sorts', as a Bombaywallah sniffed loudly in my hearing, but the expanse of green in the heart of a vast city strikes one as welcome as Hyde Park in London or Central Park in New York.

Prince of Wales Museum
The Prince of Wales Museum of Western India (closed on Mondays, hours 10.15–6) is devoted to art, archaeology and natural history, while its counterpart in Byculla, the Victoria and Albert Museum (10–6), has departments of geology, agriculture and some natural history, as well as exhibits on the early history of Bombay. Within the Prince of Wales compound stands the newer Jehangir Art Gallery, and near the Victoria and Albert in the Victoria Gardens is the zoo, like the museum closed on Wednesdays. Don't be surprised to see the Victoria renamed the Veermata Jijabai Bhonsle Udayan: the Flora Fountain was renamed Hutatma Chowk but that too is ignored, like most of the new street names. Bombayites are much too fond of their past to replace it by arbitrary neologisms.

The Prince of Wales Museum was begun by 1905 by George Wittet and like his Gateway of India expands the Indo-Saracenic style.

Striking miniatures include leaves from a 17th-century *Khamsa* of Nizami and a ferocious contemporary Mughal 'Camel Fight', but the bulk of these treasures are from Rajasthan, such as the *Ramayana* scene (1649) painted by Manohar at Udaipur or the 18th-century 'Krishna bringing home the cattle at dusk' from Bundi.

Karl and Mehrbai Khandalavala's major collection of miniatures and drawings presented to the Prince of Wales is now shown in rotation. Chairperson of the Museum, he shakes his head over the 'flood of fakes' which drown the few genuine pieces still in circulation, and diminish the status of classic Indian art. Mehrbai shows a 14th-century Karnataka bronze of Hanuman as her household deity. Though a practising criminal lawyer, Karl spent all his spare time on collecting and studying Indian art, and his monograph on the Pahari School (1958) is still the standard work.

Church ivories from Goa date from 17th–18th centuries, and Indus Valley terracottas from the period between 2500 and 1750 B.C. The centre-piece below the dome is one of the stone sculptures for which the museum is rightly renowned: the 12th-century Shalabhanjika from Narayanpur, Karnataka. She is sinuous, graceful and imaginatively detailed, summing up in one image the passionate emphasis placed on the female figure from a 2nd-century Gajalakshmi (Pitalkhora, Maharashtra) here to the delirious eroticism of the early 11th-century Vishwanatha Temple to be seen at Khajuraho. Moti Chandra, Director of the Museum, has written a valuable guide to the *Stone Sculpture* (1974) in large format and a short but effective monograph on *Indian Art* (4th ed., 1987).

More miniatures follow, among them a Pahari work from Guler (1775), 'Abu Ben Adhem attended by angels', and the wondrous 18th-century 'Elopement' (cat. 53.86) from Bundi, light grey, dark grey and red. Don't miss the Nepali and Tibetan galleries, particularly a delicate 16th-century Tsong kha pa from Tibet. Dr Chandra has pointed out that the collection of sculpture is vitiated by several factors: when it was founded in 1909 it had no collection of its own and therefore relied on gifts and transfers from the Asiatic Society of Bombay, the Archaeological Survey of India based in Delhi, or the defunct Archaeological Museum in Pune; very little money was available; and in the early days scholarship was defective so that some less significant works were acquired. Thus it is that you come to Bombay for Gandharan sculpture, but not for Sunga, Kushana or Gupta treasures.

Pitalkhora's Buddhist caves date from the Satavahana-Kshaharata period (2nd century B.C.) and Vakataka times, during the 5th–6th centuries A.D. They were not excavated until 1953, when some works were removed for safe keeping to the Prince of Wales.

Ashoka's 3rd-century B.C. Buddhist stupa at Amaravati can best be seen at the site museum, the British Museum, and Madras Government Museum, but the Prince of Wales has some fragments that the local zamindar did not burn for lime. Much more valuable are the 2nd–3rd century grey schist reliefs from the Gandharan region centred on the modern Peshawar/Swat region of Pakistan. Hellenistic classicism blends with Buddhist serenity to yield works of high

15

spiritual value, such as 'The First Sermon and Turning the Wheel of the Law' and 'The Buddha with Disciples.' Elephanta Island's smashed Brahma and Durga have been rescued, and a replica of the 6th-century standing Shiva allows us to see an image now worshipped in the modern Mahadeva Temple in the suburb of Parel due north.

Don't miss the 7th-century Early Chalukya ceiling panels from Aihole in Central Karnataka: Vishnu, Brahma, and Shiva with Parvati.

Among the bronzes are an 8th-century Pallava Standing Vishnu from Nallur (Tamil Nadu), a 9th-century Western Ganga Bahubali from Sravana Belgola, and an 11th-century Pala Standing Vishnu.

When I began my suburban Bombay tour I had very little money left, having saved my airport departure tax in a concealed inside trousers pocket, so a bunch of three bananas and water from my screw-cap bottle sufficed for lunch, just before the Ganesh bus picked me up by Jehangir Art Gallery for a long afternoon.

I was sitting crosslegged on the pavement outside the Art Gallery just behind a gray-haired woman with a blue-green shawl who was selling ready-made waistcoats from an upturned black umbrella placed between her legs, when a nearly bald man with a furrowed forehead and blazing black eyes accosted me gently, as a puma will stroke its mate.

'May I ask for your ear, one moment, please Sir', he enunciated, so distinctly that he defied me to ask him to say it again.

'How can I help?' I responded.

'I am taking annual subscriptions on behalf of the League of Perfect Gentlemen.'

'I know I shouldn't be asking this, but what does the League of Perfect Gentlemen do?'

'We are holding courses for the edification of the lower classes, teaching how to open doors for others, how to drink tea not out of saucers, much of this kind of thing. Then it helps to assure the behaviour of our members from one year's end to the next. You know what is redicivism?'

'Recidivism?'

'Plus or minus'.

'It means going back to sin again.'

'You are correct, Sir. We check up on redicivism.'

'That sounds good.'

'You can be quite renowned that the gentlemen in our League has no such tendencies. One year, maybe two, all is perfect. For this we need many subscriptions.'

'I tell you what', I replied, bending my ear for a persistent kansaf-wallah to clean it with warm mustard oil, 'you pay my subscription to the League of Perfect Gentlemen, and I'll pay yours to the Suicide Club.'

Afternoon Tour
A three-hundred metre causeway crosses Little Bay to the Islamic tomb of Haji Ali, cut off from the mainland at high tide but at low tide visited by a stream of Muslims running the gauntlet of meek, squatting beggars awaiting largesse (or more frequently smallesse in the shape of copper coins), exchanged by

canny pilgrims, conserving all their banknotes but one, with discreet money-changers on the shore. There is a great press to beg at the beginning of the lines, before the coins run out, and many of the shriller, tougher beggars make sure to retain these favoured places.

Such is the romance of air travel that the bus visited Sahar International Airport to gape at the arriving and landing aircraft before calling at Aarey Milk Colony Observation Post, catching cool breezes at this height.

The Aarey Milk Colony was set up after World War II in a jungle area to provide standards of a model farm. Buffaloes are maintained in hygienic conditions and with veterinary care. Their owners pay a small fee, and collect some of the profit. Restaurants and cafes give these hilly gardens the air of a holiday resort. Aarey posts notices sternly prohibits picnicking, but families have brought their snacks and sit out in a circle on the lush lawns, laughing, talking, and chaffing, while kids dash around in the traffic-free environment, climbing trees and playing ball. Azaleas run riot. 'You are to come here directly!' scolds one sari-clad mother, but her two lads hide behind a tree, shoving and giggling. Views range across high-rise apartments to the sea, and you breathe more freely at this altitude.

Just south of the Aarey Milk Colony are the Jogeshwari Caves, but the main 6th-century Shaivite Temple is woefully eroded and if you are seeing the contemporary Elephanta shrine then Jogeshwari will disappoint, with barely-discernible figures; best-preserved are a Shiva playing dice with Parvati, and a Shiva Nataraja above the lintel.

Film City
The bus now passes the gates to Film City, where the major Indian film studios are situated. Madras may produce more films, if one totals output in the many languages of South India, but Bombay produces most of the Hindi-language films and with a nationwide audience exceeding 100 million paying customers every week, the stereotypical Hindi all-singing, all-dancing, all-violent movie is regrettably here to stay: the subcontinent's version of American 'soap operas'. Popular film music blasts out from the tour bus: it has often been released up to a year before the film itself to whip up a frenzy of expectation for the movie, and everyone makes a great deal of money, from the stars and playback singers, to directors and lyric-writers. The first kiss was permitted on an Indian screen in 1978, but the heady cause of realism has otherwise made little progress, and escapism remains the order of the day: idyllic love scenes, a black-dyed villain and a spotless hero assembled from any token Victorian melodrama. Films stars come and go, like the numerous movie magazines, but the massive industry churns on, with little interest in originality and innovation. If you collar an Indian director and challenge him to produce a film of high quality, worthy of the tradition of Satyajit Ray and Mani Kaul, he will reply that he is the slave of the audiences, who want only luxury, rich colours, and a simple story easily followed in which right overcomes wrong. If you ask one of the lower to middle-class bachelors or young married men who make up the bulk of cinema audiences whether he likes the film, he will answer 'what else is there? they only make one kind of movie.' On Pali Hill the guide points airily to the home built for Nargis, and each film star's home is indicated left or right to *oohs* and

aahs.

Bombay's extraordinary contrasts are exemplified by the ultra-modern Indira Gandhi Institute of Development Research close by a shanty-town without electricity or water.

Kanheri

The Sanjay Gandhi National Park, with tongas plying for hire at the entrance, incorporates a Lion Park; the lakes of Vihar, Powari and Tulsi supplying Bombay with some of its water; an outdoor movie set; the Trimurti Digambara Jain temple; and above all the hundred and one numbered caves of the Kanheri complex, sited on a forested black mountain (in Pali *kanha* means 'black') roughly 43 km from the centre of the city, yet almost a world away. If you want to spend more time at Kanheri, the nearest lodgings are in Borivli (10 km), which has a rail station, and on feast days and Sundays a bus service to the caves and back. On other days, you use one of the taxis at Borivli station.

Kanheri is summarily shown on a bus tour: only caves 1–3 are visited, number 3 being the major sight in the great monastic settlement. The first caves may have been excavated as early as the 1st century, when the Satavahana dynasty encouraged the study of Hinayana Buddhism, and the last date from the 11th century, when they were visited by three groups of Parsis from Iran, to judge from Pahlavi inscriptions.

Cave 1 is an incomplete vihara, with cushion capitals on both portico pillars. Cave 2 is a vihara with a panel of prayers to Padmapani similar to those in caves 41 and 90, and images of dangers affecting human life, from raging elephants and shipwreck to man-eating lions. Inscriptions date from the 2nd century (on the water cistern) and the 4th–5th centuries (close to the nine worshippers of Buddha).

Cave 3 is a temple or chaitya: the most significant cave at Kanheri and the last Hinayana chaitya hall, from the late 2nd century A.D. The sculptural and architectural styles remind one of Cave 8 at Karla. A hunting scene is carved on the front parapet wall. Mithuna couples in low relief are full-face, each pair caught solemnly as in a wedding video, with fleshy lips and humorous eyes.

Sri Sadashiv Gorakshar, Director of Bombay's Prince of Wales Museum, has pointed to Parthian influences in the face and hairstyle of these men and women, but lion-head earrings have Gandharan resonance, and at least one northern master must have been involved with artisans working over the centuries at the Kanheri complex.

The two standing Buddhas were added three hundred years later, and these figure-types, 22 feet high, with their associated bodhisattvas, form the most impressive feature at Kanheri. Octagonal columns with bell-capitals and pot-bases are ornamented with familiar iconography such as the Buddha's footprints, and worship of the stupa. Here the stupa itself is plain, but Cave 4 has a stupa with several Buddha reliefs. A standard suburban tour stops at Cave 3 because of the time factor, so if you want to spend a great deal more time at Kanheri, come on your own, or leave the tour here, and return on your own at sunset.

As befits a crowded working monastery, most caves are simple rooms for dwelling with a verandah, hall, and water-cistern, and many had ovens for

18

Kanheri Cave 3 (exterior)

communal eating. Following a path south from Cave 1, you come to Cave 4 with an elaborately-draped eleven-headed and four-armed Avalokiteshvara. The rest of the complex can be found along a path leading first north then due east from Cave 3, passing 32, 33 and 35 before reaching Cave 11, the durbar hall equivalent to Ellora's Cave 5. It has eight octagonal columns and Buddha figures in the shrine. Retrace your steps to Cave 9, which remains unfinished, and walk southward to the semi-circle of Caves 54, 53, 51, 50, 56, 60, 63 and 66, following the mountain's contour. Cave 67 or the Chitrasala is carved with excellent Buddha sculptures, including the Sravasti miracle. Caves 84–87, on the other side of the wooded complex, were excavated as a cemetery, and brick stupas dot the site. Inscriptions from the cemetery are among the earliest evidence for Buddhism in Western India, indicating titles for monastic teachers deceased at Kanheri, and proving the burial of servants as well as the deceased's family. Cave 89 depicts a variety of women's hairstyles, and a vivacious parrot pecking at a mango. Cave 90 is a masterpiece of sculptural composition centred on the seated Buddha while performing the Sravasti miracle: again the 5th-century date is corroborated by the Mahayana emphasis on the figuration of Gautama Buddha himself, with naga kings surrounding the lotus. Look for a marvellous image of Indra with his thunderbolt. The calamities of human life which we have seen in panels at Ajanta and Ellora recur here: death by elephant, cobra, lion, shipwreck, fire and armed robbery are among scenes reminding us of our perilous existence. Cave 97 is a lookout point, as is no. 101, at a height from which the fortress of Bassein is visible. An advanced latrine system has been worked out just above this cave. From Caves 102–9 there is a fine panorama over Tulsi Lake, and a series of great hewn tanks for bathing and laundry. A day at Kanheri, full of surprises, can be a relief from the noise, fumes, and overcrowding in Bombay city. Butterflies of a dozen species flutter, dip and settle like old men to a good book. The Bombay poet Dom Moraes memorably opened his poem on 'Kanheri Caves':

> Over these blunted, these tormented hills,
> Hawks hail and wheel, toboggan down the sky.
> It seems this green ambiguous landscape tilts
> And teeters the perspective of the eye.

The valley of Kanheri remains the home of some holy men, *sadhus* who congregate here to purify themselves by austerities in a manner which convulsed Osho to laughter. One sadhu at Kanheri when I visited the caves in the 1970s was a guru demonstrating tapasya, or self-imposed asceticism to the point of suffering. Gandhi's favourite tapasya was fasting, but Swami Lomasgiri of Kanheri concentrated all his suffering potential into standing, leaning on a swing year after year, awake or dozing, blackbearded, single-minded, patient yet unseeing the world of illusion around him.

ISKCON
Twenty years later I visited the white marble courtyard of the Sri Sri Radha Rasa Bihariji Temple. Milling crowds cheerfully paid over sums relatively large in Indian terms for cassettes and books in a dozen Indian and foreign languages devoted to the texts of the International Society for Krishna Consciousness, Hare Krishna Land, Juhu Road. The courtyard is overlooked by a white marble temple and waving palms. Unlike Osho Commune in Pune, ISKCON attracts hundreds of thousands of ordinary Hindus, who recognise the rituals and take benefit from a visit as from their local temple.

The society itself was founded in 1966 by His Divine Grace A. C. Bhaktivedanta Swami Prabhupada, one year after emigrating to the U.S.A. 'He had appeared in this world', as they say, in 1896 in Calcutta, and in 1922 became a student of Srila Bhaktisiddhanta Saraswati Goswami, rising to the status of disciple in 1933. His assigned mission was to spread Vedic knowledge in English and in 1944 he began the fortnightly magazine *Back to Godhead*, retiring from family life in 1950 at the age of 54. He devoted many years to translating Indian spiritual classics into English, before founding New Brindaban in the hills of West Virginia as a farming community now running to over a thousand acres.

In Brindaban, India, Srila Prabhupada's Krishna-Balarama temple and guest-

Courtyard of Krishna Temple, International Society for Krishna Consciousness

house opened in 1975, and three years later this Bombay complex opened, with a theatre, guesthouse and vegetarian restaurant, in addition to the temple. The ideology is that of Srila Prabhupada's interpretation of the Vedic scriptures, and in particular the *Bhagavadgita*, in which Krishna passes instructions to his devotee Arjuna. The method of realising Krishna-consciousness is by chanting the Hare Krishna maha-mantra or 'great chant': *Hare Krishna, Hare Krishna, Krishna Krishna, Hare Hare, Hare Rama, Hare Rama, Rama Rama, Hare Hare*, just as a 'young boy awakens his natural attraction for a young girl in her association.' Srila Prabhupada, in *The Science of Self-Realization* (1977), divides mankind into four classes: the *karmis*, who work for material profit; the *jnanis*, who try to escape the miseries of life and become immortal; the *yogis*, who want mystic power; and the *bhaktis*, who want nothing for themselves but only to serve God, identified with Krishna. Quoting *Bhagavadgita*, '*bhaktya mam abhijanati*,' that is 'only by devotion may one come to Krishna.' He therefore repudiated as worthless the other three types of yoga, though most would argue that their practice is interdependent. His Divine Grace, who passed away in 1977, prohibited meat-eating and caste-distinction. Like Maharishi Mahesh Yogi who rose to fame as a guru of the Beatles, Srila Prabhupada enjoyed quasi-divine status and a bevy of luxury cars. When asked about this, he replied 'God travels in a golden car. If the disciples offer the spiritual master an ordinary motorcar, it would not be sufficient because the spiritual master has to be treated like God.'

In England the Bhaktivedanta Manor, Letchmore Heath, Watford, accom-

21

modates ISKCON U.K. headquarters in an Elizabethan manor house. As at all ISKCON temples, the day begins at 2.30 a.m. with a shower, devotions in the temple, mantra-chanting, bhakti yoga classes, and a study of the Vedic classics. After breakfast at 8.15 the day's activities begin, and may include tending the dairy herd, making incense, cooking, cleaning, gardening and maintenance.

Juhu Beach

Sunset on Juhu Beach means that thousands of little stalls light up. While Ramada Inn and Palm Grove hotels dominate the skyline, the hubbub below takes on a scale altogether more human: children scream for rides in a pony-cart, or on camelback. Below planes departing westward into the Asian skies, performing monkeys leap and dart for a few paise. I drank delicious coconut water, and tills clashed and rattled, tinkled and rang around me to honour the goddess Lakshmi. A dark-eyed beauty slyly offered a boyfriend *bhelpuri*, the local popcorn, and beggars zigzagged like hummingbirds after nectar, staying still only long enough to sum up their chances of eventual success. Bombaywallahs wandered out vaguely to meet the tide. Kiosks proffered squeaky toy dogs, plastic planes, whirring wind-up helicopters from Taiwan, Krishna bows-and-arrows, and betel-leaves. Today's detritus, they hope, will be swept out to sea tomorrow, for if the tide doesn't tidy up, no-one else will. The beach is five kilometres long, but is at its most noisy near Ramada Inn, and if you want to be alone there is nothing for it but to aim briskly for the far distance.

Bazaars

Marvellous Bombay is of course most things to most people; film capital, business capital, and of course clothing capital. Fifteen million dollars' worth of clothes are exported every year from India, mostly from Bombay. Fashion Boulevard is Mahatma Gandhi Marg, where most shops sell hard, fast and cheap until eight or so every night. You can find an all-cotton T-shirt for less than two dollars, and any tailor can run you up a bespoke dress, suit or pair of trousers within 24 hours. At the boutique end of the spectrum, Tarun Tahiliani's Ensemble opened in 1988 displays and sells the work of nine leading designers, or you could try the arcades of leading hotels such as the Taj or the two-storey shopping block next to the Oberoi.

Nothing is more typical of Bombay than its many bazaars, which will absorb all the time at your disposal. The most imposing is Crawford Market, for food, but others have their own attractions. In Bhendi Bazaar Muslim traders congregate as in Lahore or Karachi, with Urdu street-names to point the way. Thieves' Market, or Chor Bazaar, is situated on Mutton Street, where you can pick up whatever has recently fallen off the backs of lorries, from unworkable horn gramophones and brass lamps to carved rosewood tables and antique pottery that may one day become antique in reality but at present is merely a clever fake. Look for a nearby perfume bazaar largely Muslim in ownership, the leather market in Dhaboo Street with a few real European handbags and a flourishing fake industry. Nobody should miss the tantalising jewellery market, the Zaveri Bazaar, off Abdul Rahman Street, where silver but mainly gold will glitter like any Aladdin's cave with bright lights to highlight the gorgeous

Upper storeys of Mangaldas Lane near Phule Market

reddish gold favoured by Hindu and Parsi women alike to suit their complexion. Stout, shrewd Gujarati Hindus dominate Zaveri Bazaar, summing up everyone who passes through their doors with a mixture of amused tolerance, patience ending in boredom, and a profound awareness of human weakness.

'You will find nowhere more competitive price,' shrugs one ineffable sales-man, haloed in a reflected chandelier, and bathed in red and golden glory. If you admit what you paid him to the jeweller next door, you will be pityingly patronised: 'Oh, well if you had come to me first only, you would have had much better price, we are stocking only the best here.'

Diamonds are a girl's very best bet in Bombay, because prices are way beneath Amsterdam levels, if you know what you're buying and haggle expertly. This is not a field for the dilettante: you must pay in foreign currency and obtain a special customs certificate, as with antiques, for nothing over 100 years old must be taken out of India – if in doubt consult the Archaeological Survey of India, Sion Fort, Bombay. Antique dealers outside the hotel complexes include Heeramaneck and Essaji on Battery Street and the Pundole Gallery by Flora Fountain. Roam Kalbadevi Bazaar for brass and copper, and Mangaldas Bazaar for textiles.

Regional handicrafts from all India can be found at the Central Cottage Industries Emporium on Shivaji Marg behind the Taj Hotel, at the Jehangir Art Gallery shop, and in leading hotels. For specialised Western Indian crafts, try Gujarat Handicrafts Emporium at Khetan Bhavan, J. Tata Marg. Many states are represented at the World Trade Centre on Cuffe Parade; Rajasthan Government Emporium is at 230 D.N. Road, Haryana products in the Air India Building, Nariman Point; Kashmir on P. Mehta Road, Kerala at 'Kairali', Nirmal, Nariman Point; and Bihar at Dhun-Nur, P. Mehta Road.

For books, major hotels can be relied on for some popular sellers, though Indian distributors are very selective and import only what is heavily discounted. I like best Taraporevala, and the throng of second-hand bookstalls between the Telegraph Office and Flora Fountain, where authentic bargains slump amid dross.

To purchase musical instruments, Sardar V. Patel Road offers a good choice: at no. 386 R. S. Mayeka and at no. 419 Haribhai Viswanath.

As regards music, you will find some cassettes of good classical Indian music, but most of the demand is for pop hits from the latest movie, interchangeable but in every case destined to be played at top volume and ignored. 'From loudspeakers in all corners of the smart new shop', notes H. R. F. Keating in his 1984 Inspector Ghote story *The All-Bad Hat*, 'music was pounding out at maximum volume. His attempts to make anyone behind the counter hear had so far come to nothing. At last he could stand the frustration no longer. He leant across the glossy counter, seized a young man behind it by the side of his silk kurta, and drew him close. "Please to stop all this noise," he demanded.' Needless to say, the remark is fiction. In Bombay nobody ever gets the volume turned down.

On the corner of Carnac Road and Dadabhai Naoraji Marg is Mahatma Jyotiba Phule Market, best known to previous generations as Crawford Market, designed in 1865 by William Emerson to the orders of Sir Arthur Crawford, Municipal Commissioner from 1865 to 1871. Its style is based on 13th-century

Phule Market, Bombay

Norman Gothic, and elsewhere the masons were – like those forebears – allowed some humorous freedom in the contemporary Gothic High Court nearby, where apes frolic and a wild pig taunts a tiger. But the reliefs on the outside of Crawford Market arises from half a world away: from the Ruskin-Morris axis in England, where agricultural toil was romanticised and the co-operative ideal had not yet found its despair in the future U.S.S.R. Worthy farmers are shown with faithful hounds. Its high-pitched roofs protect the market from Bombay's climate to some extent, but during monsoon times the windows are protected by blinds, above paving-stones brought from Caithness. John Lockwood Kipling (1837–1911) was the municipal architect responsible for the figures high on the exterior of Crawford Market. Father of the novelist Rudyard, Kipling had been trained in London, and moved in Arts and Crafts circles. His sister-in-law was married to the painter Edward Burne-Jones, and he brought to India the Ruskin-Morris ideals of anti-commercialism and pride in one's craft, whether painting, drawing, wood or stone. In about 1872 he drew a series of Bombay personages ('The banker', 'The dhobiwallah', 'The blacksmith') now preserved in the India Office Library and Records in London. Rudyard was born in Bombay in 1864, and a portrait of him by Sir Philip Burne-Jones (1899) hangs in the National Portrait Gallery. It was Rudyard, having returned to Bombay at 17, after schooling in England, who made the name of Kipling world-famous with his *The Jungle Book* (1894) and *Kim* (1901), but he laboured for years to earn background knowledge as sub-editor of the *Civil and Military Gazette*, the Anglo-Indian daily of the Punjab. If you want

25

to feel the texture of Anglo-Indian perceptions in the 1880s, Kipling's satirical *Departmental Ditties* (1886) and the stories of *Plain Tales from the Hills* (1887) cannot be surpassed.

You could look up at the glass-covered, iron-ribbed halls and down at displays of cascades of flowers, fruit, vegetables, and counters solid with meat, and imagine without difficulty that this is Victorian Bombay, coolies running with baskets on their heads, and each vendor with his own distinctive patter to lure your attention. Outside are pets such as overcrowded parrots going mad with claustrophobia and melancholy caged monkeys. Beyond is the Fish Market where the day's haul of pomfret, lobsters, prawns and squid are the subject of good-natured haggling in several languages.

Victorian Bombay
The School of Art where J. L. Kipling was Principal is now named for the Parsi philanthropist Sir Jamsetjee Jeejeebhai, and dates from 1877, sixteen years before the Anjuman-i-Islam School designed by James Willcocks.

You can make your way north to the Friday Mosque in Princess Street, or explore the maze of crowded streets with traditional buildings and a pulsating life which encourages you to sit in a wayside bar and watch the world go by with a yoghourt lassi in your hand.

Along Carnac Road, if you ignore the traffic din, you will come to the Gokaldas Tejpal Hospital (1877), designed in the neo-Gothic style by Col. J. A. Fuller, with medallions by Kipling senior; St Xavier's High School (1867); Elphinstone High School (1872, corner of Cruikshank Road) and the Roman Catholic St Xavier's College, followed by the Cama Albless Obstetric Hospital with Gothic windows and the Police Courts (1888) also with more than a touch of Gothic about them. Next come the Municipal Buildings (1893) completed by F. W. Stevens after his acknowledged masterpiece close by: the so-called VT or Victoria Terminus (1878–87), inspired by London's St Pancras by Sir Gilbert Scott.

I met Canadian backpackers with hours to spare before their train to Delhi who closed their eyes and *went to sleep* in this creation. One might as well go to St Paul's Cathedral for a spot of shut-eye. No: the statue above Stevens' Municipal Buildings represents *urbs prima in Indis* and VT is surely *locum primum in urbe*. Up to a thousand trains a day serve VT, and their 2½ million passengers fill virtually every train to double capacity. Long-distance trains usually leave between 6 p.m. and midnight to avoid midday city heat and humidity, so if you wander round the station at midday you will find much to marvel at. Red-uniformed porters squat by heavy-duty trolleys, surveyed by sculptured gargoyles and peacocks in a riot of Indo-Saracenic-Gothic fantasy which I could conscientiously guess to be Manueline-Sicilian Baroque if chal-lenged to name the architect, but as for being *English*? We are thought reserved, withdrawn, fastidious, shy, even austere – the very antithesis of this ferrocarrile Taj Mahal. If as a daily commuter you have to reach VT by grotesquely-packed trains, sweating, smelly and stifling, nothing could be more hellish. But for a traveller wandering around these platforms at ease, with no train to catch, no bedroll to rent, no mind-numbing thirty-hour journey to dread, VT is a treasure-house, a museum of humanity, with a great staircase beneath a dome more impressive than Covent Garden's Viennese staircase for *Der Rosenkavalier*. Stained glass allows ecclesiastical light into the booking-hall, a 14-foot image of Progress strides the dome like a grandiloquent sovereign, and every type of Indian passes through these portals, from a married Hindu lady with her red-spotted forehead, to so-called 'East Indians', or Catholics once resident at Bassein and Salsette. Here is a Parsi in neatly-folded *pughri*, a white turban; there is a Jain woman in red with gold jewellery. I overhear a conversation between two Bombay wallahs drinking tea at a stall: it is not in standard Hindi but a mangled form, with Gujarati, Urdu, Marathi and English words thrown in like Spanish ingredients in an *olla podrida*. No matter what happens, you are ready, but the ingredients are limited to a hotch-potch. English is one of the two official languages of Maharashtra, the other being Marathi, but Hindi as the lingua franca of Northern India has a firm if partial grip.

A friendly Parsi offered me a tea, and we spoke of the sectarian violence in Ayodhya that threatened to polarise secular India. The minority government of Chandra Shekhar had just resigned and he was worried about a Muslim backlash from the rise of Hindu fundamentalism. 'We have so many Muslim fundamentalists in the Middle East and Far East,' he worried. 'Even in England you have Salman Rushdie affair which is caused by these fanatical Muslims. Of course we fear Hindu fundamentalists will want Hindu state just to protect ourselves; this Ayodhya Babri Mosque is just symptom. They want to pull it down to stop the spread of Islam. If all Muslims had left for Pakistan in 1947 this would not have happened. Even educated Hindus say they want a Hindu state here, but what would that solve? We should end up with moderate Hindu against extremist Hindu, Hindu against Parsi and Christian and Jew . . . I tell you, sir, once you change India from secular state, nothing but trouble will be coming.' His short fat friend nodded in silence, his black eyes endlessly roaming the busy station.

From VT you could wander around the Bombay Gymkhana Club district, to Lady Ratan Tata Palace, the Scottish Kirk, and the Capital Theatre, then continue towards Apollo Bunder and the Gateway of India via Flora Fountain. The Telegraph Office (1869–72) was designed by James Trubshawe as the original General Post Office, but became too small and was replaced by a new Post Office (1909) designed by John Begg and located in Fort Street. It was based on the Bijapuri style, and strikes me as another of those imaginative successes that have made of Bombay an architectural portfolio almost without equal. If you can take exuberant eclecticism – the Taj Mahal-like Raudat Tahi Mosque (1973) in the largely Muslim Bhendi Bazaar, as well as the pinnacled Mumbadevi Temple at Phansi Talao ('Gibbet Pond') – then your architectural digestion is as good as maybe.

Flora Fountain (renamed Hutatma Chowk) was designed collectively in 1869 as a tribute to Sir Bartle Frere, who demolished much of the decaying Fort area in the 1860s and made sure that ample, spacious new buildings were constructed consonant with the city's expansion and importance in India and throughout the Empire. It takes its name from the Roman goddess of abundance, Flora, who stands in eloquent drapery white and shining, though many will remember it painted gaudily. F. W. Stevens was responsible for Oriental Buildings, and on Hornby Road look for Fort House, renamed Handloom

House, once the home of Sir Jamsetjee Jeejeebhai and close to the neo-Gothic Jeejeebhai Institute (1871). The Khadi Store, state-run, was formerly the suppliers to the British armed forces Whiteway and Laidlaw, and even now it resembles a large English linen shop in Manchester or Birmingham about 1935. It was slightly cheaper than the former Army and Navy Stores on Gandhi Marg next to Elphinstone College (1890) and the Sassoon Institute, with the timeless Sassoon Library designed by Colonel J. A. Fuller in 1870, and a statue of David Sassoon (of the Baghdadi-Jewish family) by Thomas Woolner. Birmingham Art Gallery shows a painting by Ford Madox Brown called 'The Last of England' (1852–5) whose pathetic emigrant was based on the departure of the sculptor Woolner in 1852, seen off by Brown's Pre-Raphaelite friends Rossetti and Holman Hunt. Brown himself intended to emigrate to India, but the sale of this picture for £150 cash gave him enough money to stay at home. Such are

David Sassoon Library, Bombay

the coils of destiny which loop around us like lianas, gripping us tight or letting go.

Opposite the Telegraph Office is the wondrous fantasy on Venetian Gothic created as a Public Works Office (1869–72), designed by Colonel Henry St Clair Wilkins, a visionary whose next great enterprise was the Secretariat (1874) farther along Mayo Road in much the same style: vast, long, spacious, polychrome, faced with fawn Porbandar stone and enlivened with red and blue basalts, which weather splendidly. Wilkins remembered Venetian aristocratic staircases and arcaded balconies, but expanded the scale to fit the new open spaces created by Sir Bartle Frere's *rimaneggiamento* of Fort St George, which once commanded the harbour. Though the stelliform fort has all but disappeared, we have an 18th-century engraving by Jan van Ryne of the main building and triangular bastions defending the walls reproduced in *The Forts of India* (1986) by Virginia Fass.

Next to the Public Works Office is Colonel J. A. Fuller's neo-Gothic High Court (1871–9), a riot of precipice and staircase, tower and vaulted corridor. You would imagine it as a fairy-tale setting for Grimm or Andersen rather than as a solemn court for English judges designed by a soldier! Fuller was called 'the leading constructional engineer of his day' and the unrestrained bravura of his giant central tower, with flanking octagonal towers surmounted by Mercy and Justice, can be enjoyed more perhaps by our generation, stunned blank by brutalist post-modernism, than by any generation before us.

Such amplitude of tone, gesture and elevation applies equally to Sir George Gilbert Scott's designs for Bombay University built between 1869 and 1878.

Statue to Sir Dinshah Fardunji Mulla (1868–1934), with the Rajabai Clock Tower

The eight-metre high Rajabai Tower in yellow sandstone takes its premise from Giotto's campanile in Florence, except for an octagonal lantern finishing in a pinnacle. The four clock faces have Florentine-style balconies below them, and at certain times it is possible to climb the tower, named for the mother of its donor, Premchand Roychand. Gilbert Scott (1810–77) is best known in Britain for St Pancras Station, the Albert Memorial, and St Mary's Cathedral in Edinburgh, but who is to say that his Convocation Hall and University Library are not more sweeping, substantial, and thoughtful works, deriving ideas from mediaeval French and Italian Gothic, it's true, but blending these elements with energy and fantasy into something majestically new? The Convocation Hall has whirling spiral staircases which remind one of Chambord, and a wooden gallery borne by cast-iron brackets. The hall was created at the expense of the Parsi philanthropist Sir Cowasjee Readymoney, of whom Thomas Woolner has created a fitting statue, serious and commanding, in the garden. Scott's fine library is on two floors, with spiral staircases and stained-glass windows within that nascent Arts and Crafts ideal which made all work a sacrament.

Beyond the great Secretariat I explored George Wittet's Science Institute, begun in 1911, the choice of Renaissance style justified by its homogeneity from halls, administration buildings and library to the College itself, the whole slightly dismayed by aged yellow basalt, which has worn less attractively than the neighbouring Secretariat's red and blue. The architectural tour has returned to the magnificent domed Prince of Wales Museum and the Scottish Kirk (1819) in a neo-classical style which served equally well for the Kirk in Madras.

A Dabbawallah's Day

Bombay has to feed its thirteen million people somehow. A quarter of a million or so frequent wayside stalls, and around 150,000 can lunch in restaurants, but although some commuters bring packed lunches from home, the institution of the hot lunch brought from home by dabbawallahs or tiffin-carriers has grown steadily more popular ever since 1885, when the Bombay Tiffin Box Suppliers Association was first formed.

A dabba comprises four tiny cylindrical boxes which nest airtight into each other, with rice in one, dhal in another, vegetables in a third, and possibly curds in a fourth: a handled lid is placed on the topmost.

A housewife prepares the meal early enough every weekday for the runners who collect these dabbas marked to show the local supervisor's name, the nearest rail station, the station of destination, and the worker's number. Dabbawallahs, who come mainly from Pune, earn about Rs 800 per month, of which Rs 5 are withheld as association dues. The tiffin box will change hands five or six times from home via Victoria or Churchgate to office, where it will be delivered at 1 p.m. and collected at 2. Laden trays 2' x 5' on the head might weigh up to 100 kg, but other dabbawallahs use push-carts, weaving through dense traffic. The whole miraculous system is run by eight hundred local supervisors, and 3,800 dabbawallahs, recognisable from their white Nehru-style caps, or traditional white dhoti or lenga and white shirt.

'Lavkar, lavkar' (*quickly, quickly* in Marathi) is the constantly reiterated dabbawallah cry as he summons the tiffin box from the yawning early-morning housewife, or the tardy diner delayed at his desk. Nobody must be allowed to inhibit the system's efficiency.

It is less generally known that bachelors may also benefit from the dabba service. Special dabba kitchens provide a hot lunch for Rs 7 daily, of which R1 goes to the dabbawallah.

The Parsis

None of the regular tours visits Framji Dadabhai Alpaiwalla Museum, Khareghat Memorial Hall, Khareghat Colony, N.S. Patkar Road., but if you are as fascinated by Parsi religion, history and customs as I am, you will find it amply worth the trek to this Parsi colony in south Bombay. The first Parsis arrived in Bombay from Iran in the 1670s, just a decade before the East India Company moved its western factory from Surat. Everywhere you go you will see the names of prominent Parsi families: Tata, Jeejeebhai, Readymoney, Cama, Wadia, Pestonji. It was the father of the Tata dynasty, Jamsetji Nusserwanji Tata (1839–1904) who built the Taj Mahal Hotel. F. D. Alpaiwalla conceived the idea of a public museum to demonstrate the range of Parsi cultural achievements, and bequeathed his fine collection to the Parsi panchayat, or community. Dr J. Unwalla contributed his own objects from early Iran, and in 1981 the museum was reorganized, though even now only a fraction of the great collection can be shown.

Many objects date from Achaemenid, Timurid and Safavid Iran, such as neolithic terracotta mother goddesses from Susa, combs, scissors and shoes from a Tower of Silence, together with an original astodan where the corpse's scavenged bones were laid. The Indian National Movement to achieve self-esteem and progress towards independence was led in the 19th century by a group of intellectuals, prominent among whom were three Parsis, Dadabhai Naoroji Dordi (1825–1917), Sir Pherozeshah Mehta (1845–1915) and Sir Dinshaw Wacha (1844–1936). Naoroji, who dropped his surname meaning 'coir-rope' in his youth, became the 'Grand Old Man of India', after achieving distinction in mathematics (he became a professor at Elphinstone College), business (as a cotton baron in England), and nationalism. He struggled against British exploitation of India economically, administratively and militarily. To prove his theory that Britain was draining India dry he wrote *Poverty and Un-British Rule in India* (1901). To Indianise the Indian Civil Service, he made it possible for Indians to be directly recruited in India as recently as 1922. To limit India's expensive military involvement, he protested against wars undertaken by the British in Burma and Afghanistan. In 1873 he was made Premier in the State of Baroda, but he was forced to resign two years later because of the Gaekwad's non-cooperation. In 1888 he met Gandhiji and 'became a real Dada to me', to quote Gandhi himself. He fought Central Finsbury as Liberal candidate against the Conservatives in 1892, and received 2,959 votes against 2,956, thus becoming the first Indian elected to the House of Commons. He left Parliament in 1895 and became President of the Indian National Congress in 1906, vowing to achieve full independence, but he died in 1917, three decades before his aim could be fulfilled. The Alpaiwalla Museum has a family tree showing the connections between Dadabhaiji and an ancestor granted land in India by Emperor Jahangir: the firman itself is also present.

The prophet Zoroaster himself (628–551 B.C.) is by an oddity of history by

Jamsetji N. Petit Institute, Bombay

far the least-known of the founders of the four great world religions spewed forth like some spiritual volcanic lava from the human mind's inchoate mass. In China, Confucius taught principles that are revered to this day, despite the historical aberration of Maoist dictatorship. In the Near East, Israel restored its nation's pride after the Babylonian captivity with the rebuilding of the Temple (520–16). In the foothills of the Himalaya Gautama Buddha was born about 576 and founded a faith that spread throughout much of Eastern Asia and still counts adherents in millions.

Zoroastrianism survived intact, and greatly influenced the Roman Empire through its connections with Mithraism, until the crucial battle of Nihavand in 641 A.D. when crusading Arabs seeking to spread Islam overcame King Yazdegerd III and his fifty thousand men of Khurasan, Rayy and Hamadan. Everywhere forcible conversion decimated the Zoroastrian community, whose survivors fled to the mountains of Kohistan or abroad. Estimates of Zoroastrians or Parsis today vary widely, but few remain in Iran as a result of scourges by Islamic fundamentalists, and even in tolerant India only some 115,000 survived in 1951. Nowadays it is feared that the community may be only eighty thousand strong and still dwindling.

Who then *are* the Parsis? Gushtasp Irani is sure that they are among the most innovative and energetic of men: Parsis built the first cotton mill, ran the first Indian printing press, pioneered railway construction, founded schools and hospitals and provided a clean water supply for Bombay.

Non-Parsis are prohibited from attending services in fire temples, but one can find out about these moving and historic ceremonies in books and articles, such as 'The Jashan and its main religious service, the Afringan', by Dasturji Dr Firoze M. Kotwal, High Priest of the Wadia Fire Temple in Bombay. The Dastur, or High Priest, is a genial bearded research-scholar of great warmth and courtesy, passionate about the need to preserve traditional Zoroastrianism against a modernist tendency to convert.

'We arrived from Gujarat in 936 A.D. as a small community in a few boats, yet now there are 60,000 Parsis in Bombay alone, and seven high priests for the whole of India: two in Bombay, 1 in Surat, 2 in Udvada, 1 in Navsari, and 1 in Pune to serve the 4,000-strong community there.' Continuity of race, religion, beliefs and customs are vital, according to the Dastur, though in print he has confessed that 'the second half of the 20th century has witnessed an unprecedented shortage of priests', and though Parsi families a few generations back would have numerous progeny (his grandfather had 18 siblings), the tendency now is to small families and a consequent decline in numbers: the Dastur himself has only three brothers and sisters.

One can easily visualise the Hindu tolerance of fire worship (fire representing best righteousness, truth and cosmic order), given the local Indian devotion to Agni, God of Fire. Five times each day the priest serves the fire, getting up at 1 or 2 in the night to ensure the fire never dies. In the small village of Udvada, Gujarat, a high priest tends the oldest fire in the world, more than 1,000 years old, and at Udvada since 1742.

Inside the Clubs

Providing you can find a member to propose you, you can obtain temporary membership at one of the great Bombay clubs. The first was the Byculla Club (1833) to be succeeded by the Bombay Gymkhana on Mahatma Gandhi Marg (1875), the Royal (now Bombay) Yacht Club on the harbourside near Apollo Bunder (1880) and the Willingdon Sports Club on Khadiah Marg (1917), the last-named being the only one not discriminating against Indians from its foundation.

The Bombay Gymkhana was established solely for Europeans, so gymkhanas or sports clubs were founded also for Hindus, Muslims, Catholics and Parsis, side by side along Marine Drive not far from Chowpatty Beach. The Willingdon was founded precisely with the pacific intent of bringing Europeans and Indians together in recreation as in their working environment.

Just as you might be driven around Dharavi to try to empathise with the deprivation of Bombay's urban poor, or take morning coffee in the privileged plush of the Taj Mahal Intercontinental, so you can saunter in the Paul Scott – Evelyn Waugh – Jim Corbett style of comfortable Europeanness after the dangers of the wild by swimming or playing snooker at the Bombay Gymkhana, or admiring the gardens or playing golf at the Willingdon.

I took a red double-decker bus downtown and, as I received my ticket from the bus conductor, watched in amazement as he flicked open the lid of his ticketbox, drew out the myriad stubs, and scattered them like confetti over the floor of the bus. I said to a Parsi businessman at my side, 'In Singapore they would have fined the man S$1,000 – about Rs 7500 – for allowing litter on his bus like that, yet here the man is littering his own bus.' 'I tell you my good sir, I have begged this BEST company many times to put litter bins on buses, but how can they put litter where no bin?' 'Possibly they might empty their boxes back at the bus depôt?' 'Possibly, impossibly, I would say probably improbably.'

Colaba and the Afghan Church

On Colaba Causeway I bought a Marathi audio cassette from a stallholder called Hasmukh Shah. Blind since the age of seven, he sells greetings cards by the use of braille on the back of a duplicate, knowing unerringly where each is kept. This charming man, exceptionally well-balanced, has a diploma in physiotherapy, and a politics degree from Bombay University, but he is kept too busy to do his master's degree because he spends all his spare time working on behalf of the handicapped.

Sometimes in Bombay I took a fleeting meal at Leopold's Restaurant or a vegetarian thali at Laxmi Vilas nearby on Naoraji Furunji Marg, off Shahid Bhagat Singh Road, behind Taj Mahal Intercontinental. Today I preferred the Apollo Restaurant opposite Laxmi Vilas, and sank down with my perennial sigh of exhaustion, after hours of being overwhelmed by India's gargantuan profusion. Sarah, taking a year off between 'A' levels and going up to Oxford, asked if she could sit with me to avoid being harassed.

'God my stomach's really been playing me up,' she groaned, 'I wish I were anorexic.' Sarah was dressed in a sari-like sackcloth, her long hair lank and undernourished, her hands fidgeting and voice twittering in an orgy of nerves. 'I saw a man bleeding in the street at Agra,' she blurted out.

'Have you no companions?'

'I started off with a girl called Gillian from Keele but she's laid up in a YWCA at Delhi.'
'?'
'Then I met a guy called Mark, UB40, he was *really* into Yogaville, you know that Swami Sachidananda place in Virginia.'
'Isn't that the guru who trained as a welder?'
'Yaah. Well Mark was told he was a reincarnation of a ship-breaker, so he's gone to Alang Beach to find himself.'
'And where are you off to?'
'I'm to some extent holed up hereabouts, because my credit card and pounds were stolen at Churchgate Station, and I'm waiting for my new Access.'

Sarah meekly allowed me to pay her rudimentary bill, while her bleak eyes obstinately tried to ignore begging children crowding around the entrance-door.

I took a taxi-ride to the Afghan Church along Shahid Bhagat Singh Road because I felt as vulnerable there as Sarah looked. St John the Baptist's is known as the Afghan Memorial Church because it is dedicated to British soldiers who fell during the Afghan War of 1835–42. As in St Thomas' Cathedral, we might be in England – Nottingham or Derby perhaps, with no Indian to disturb the illusion. Designed by Henry Conybeare, with a bell chamber and steeple by J. A. Fuller, the Afghan Church presents to an awe-struck but largely uncomprehending and diminishing clientele the neo-Gothic principles put forward by the precocious Augustus Pugin (1812–52) who pamphleteered against the 'degraded' architecture of his time in favour of the 'Christian' style, by which he meant the Gothic. If you close your eyes in the nave at St Augustine's Ramsgate or at St George's Cathedral, Southwark, and then suddenly look up, you will experience Pugin's vision expressed here in St John the Baptist's. The stained-glass windows by William Wailes count as a special glory, especially the west window, with a deeply-felt Christ Crucified and in glory. The spire pierces the tropical sky to a great height, making the church a notable landmark at sea. A melancholy European Cemetery (closed in 1763) at the southern edge of Colaba reminds one of the old saying that one might well survive only 'two monsoons' in Bombay, but this is chiefly a military cemetery, though it includes a mass grave for victims of the sunk *Castlereagh*. The old lighthouse dates from 1771 and its successor from 1874.

As for the main European civilian cemetery, it was located near the Hindu and Muslim graveyards in an area called 'the city of gold', or Sonapur, from the local saying about a corpse: 'he has become gold.' In 1961 the cemetery (closed since 1866 for new burials) was transformed into a children's park for the well-to-do, patrolled by a lathi-wielding guardian.

Taxis
The same taxi took me back past the docks to Elphinstone Circle. It is no use telling taxi-drivers an exact address, for they have no detailed town plans and in terms of 'the Knowledge' ingrained in every expert London cabbie they seem almost clueless, so you tell them the nearest landmark which they know, like Flora Fountain or Zaveri Bazaar, and they will drop you in the vicinity. Part of their well-documented helplessness derives from the fact that Central Bombay 'just growed', like Topsy. Shanties rise and are demolished almost like

the tide. Many lanes are culs-de-sac: mere spaces between shops or shacks which vanish when filled as though they had never been. Another problem with Bombay taximen is that most are illiterate in any language, so that useful signs are just ignored. Another is that they are overworked and make mistakes in mishearing, and that they are generally too bashful to query a foreigner's pronunciation. Another is that roads have changed names, and foreigners always find the new Indian names more difficult than the old British ones, yet most maps show only new names without equivalents. Yet another is that road names are used generously to cover a multitude of side alleys off that road.

Chawls and Shanties
But the worst problem is historical: anywhere north of VT and Azad Maidan – roughly Central Bombay – developed higgledy-piggledy because of multiple land-ownership, and the problem has crashed out of orbit to the point where every few square metres you could find a different owner, or set of owners, each with a more or less valid claim to a property or part of a property, beginning with large houses subdivided because of a growing family, then sold off to many families, who built also in the garden, then demolished perhaps to make way for the industrial tenements known as chawls. Once these were considered first-rate investments: many small apartments for low rents which would repay the cost of building in a few years and then show a clear profit after minimal maintenance. But the controlled rents in chawls have made maintenance ever more difficult to justify, and needy tenants have little to spare for upkeep, so the chawls become weekly more run-down, overcrowded, disease-prone and unhygienic. The wooden balconies once gaily-painted now peel and rot, but the privilege of living in Bombay, where jobs of a sort are sometimes to be had, will compensate any country cousin forced to abandon sterile land after a bad year in a countryside where no jobs exist bar farming.

The chawl was a socio-industrial experiment established by mill-owners in Bombay in the late 19th century who required their labourers to live near at hand without having to spend a great deal on housing or transport. But they were built for a much smaller population than that served today, with indoor latrines and taps far too few for such crowds. Moreover, many office-workers with extended families live in these chawls, which were originally intended for shift-workers, so sleeping space is even more limited than it used to be. Four, five, or six storeys high, a chawl may be safe from monsoon flooding at higher levels, but during the hot season these rooms can become almost unbearably suffocating. As few families can afford refrigerators, most food has to be bought daily, fresh, and usually consumed by the wayside.

Most of the shanties have no water or electricity, and the open drains present a constant and growing health hazard. Dharavi is reputed to be the largest single slum in Asia, and it grows at the rate of several hundred a day from those affected by famine, flooding, or failed harvests. Even if they were to save up for a deposit on a flat, there are not enough flats, either now or in the foreseeable future.

Mrs Henry Sherwood noted in her *Autobiography* (1854) that in her time, 'No one can imagine what the solitude of a large house in India is – when the heat and glare without renders it totally impossible to go abroad, and when no sound meets the ear through all the weary morning, but the click of the punkah within and the cawing of the crows without.' Perhaps if La Sherwood had been offered a few hours' rest in a room crowded with nine others sleeping, two talking, one cooking and one studying by a torch, she would not have been so critical of her solitude.

Sarah and her bewildered contemporaries might stand for a whole generation who treat India as they attempt to deal with love and romance: encountered too early, disaster is the likely outcome. The complexity of India's society, history, languages and religions, its art and architecture, its anthropology and its world views, are such that one's initial reaction is bafflement followed by withdrawal. Finding India is profoundly *not* like visiting Paris while studying French. A second reaction, if one persists, is an increasing fascination that comes from better understanding with a cautious parallel increase in sympathy. At this point one needs an antidote in the shape of Japan or China to make one realise that India is markedly different, not only from other Asian countries like Indonesia or Iran, but also from its neighbours such as Nepal or Sri Lanka. Finally, uncritical devotion gives way to critical affection, taking India on her own terms and trying to change oneself not into the painfully parodistic carica-tures of sadhus that young hippies become, with greasy hair and a superficial acquaintance with yoga terms, but into someone who can appreciate the context in which real Indians live real lives, in circumstances almost wholly different from ours in America or Europe or Australasia. It is at this point that one reaches a plateau where one can accept each Indian one meets as an individual from a definable background rather than as a stereotypical Hindu, say, Jain or Sikh. In a world governed almost exclusively by stereotypes each such encounter becomes worthwhile.

The Weight of Numbers
Bombay grows like tropical fruit: very quickly, and with easily sustained damage. Its population first exceeded 1 million in 1911, then rose slowly until the years of World War II when, from a figure of 1.69 million in 1941, 3 million in 1951 and 4.2 million in 1961, it shot up to 6 million in 1971, 8.2 million in 1981, more than 13 million today, and a projected 17 million by the year 2000. Nobody can stop the influx of at least 300–400 immigrants a day: nobody even counts them properly: no census can be complete with a mobile population paying no taxes and putting up shanty towns or slums, you might call them now, so far distant from the city centre that it takes these hopeful commuters anything up to four hours to travel in on perpetually overcrowded trains, filled not only to the doors and windows, but the roofs, and hanging off the edges. Deaths in local rail accidents occur daily, are expected, and go largely unre-ported and uninvestigated.

Where is the police force that could cope with such numbers? Wielding a lathi, whistling to keep traffic forever in motion, the policeman is a figure of authority whom few will consult except in dire calamity. Droves of beggars who infest each traffic lights like buzzing mosquitoes bare leprous skin or wave arm-stumps or leg-stumps. Women push deformed babies at passenger-windows (drivers are hardened) in the hope of small change, and scream an endless babble of hopeless pleading. They will of course not go back where they came from and are well-known: their best chance is metropolitan coins or small-denomination banknotes from those immeasurably wealthier than they, such as financiers, bankers, merchants, film stars. The contrast between outrageous wealth and starving poverty is never as visible as in shabby, decaying, Victorian Bombay, which manages somehow to reel from municipal crisis to monsoon flooding, power cuts to riots, mafiosi to rat epidemics, and yet survive, serene in tropical sunsets gorgeous enough to whisk you into daydreams and duskdreams.

Elephanta

Escaping from the heat, humidity and pollution of downtown Bombay can be achieved by visiting Kanheri Caves in the Sanjay Gandhi National Park, an excursion to Bassein (Vasai, in Marathi), a harbour cruise, a visit to the National Maritime Museum on Middle Island, a coastal battery owned by Western Naval Command (open only 2–5.30 on Saturdays and 10–5 on Sundays and holidays), or by the universally popular hour-long trip from the Gateway of India to the island of Gharapuri ('Fortress Island') for the caves known as Elephanta from a sculpture of an elephant now to be seen in Victoria Gardens, Bombay.

I bought my Rs 25 ticket for a launch departing at 8 a.m. and when the boat filled we left, ten minutes late with the usual fine disregard of seagoing men for landlubbers' sense of time. A party of vivacious schoolgirls on a picnic outing from Bombay entertained themselves and the rest of us with songs danced with grace and suggestive wriggles deducible from temple carvings at Khajuraho or a thousand popular Hindi movies.

The skyline as we chugged across the harbour silhouetted the old Taj Mahal Hotel, the Gateway of India dwarfed by the new Taj annexe, and Bombay Yacht Club. Grey-clad Indian Navy ships billowed above us like elephantine cliffs. The frenetic movement of the sari-clad teenage girls, dancing with and for each other using elaborate hand and arm movements did not disturb one taciturn Indian businessman, who turned the pages of the morning's *Times of India* with single-minded concentration.

Once on the jetty, I climbed the steps between twin heights of knick-knack stalls: silver, sea-coral necklaces, shell bracelets and thousands of bangles. Alternatively, as S. V. Vani's *Guide to Elephanta* so eloquently puts it, 'Coolies are available to carry you upside in armed chair.' At the top is a great Shiva Temple hewn from the living rock in the mid-sixth century by the Traikutaka dynasty or their immediate successors the Kalachuris. The conformation of the temple was governed to a great extent by the natural rock, and has three axes: the eastern courtyard faces one lingam shrine to the south, and another to the west, the third is the north-south axis from the main temple-entrance to the Maheshmurti, or Triple-Headed Shiva, one of the great masterpieces of Hindu sculpture, with a place of honour as resonant in India as Michelangelo's David in Florence, or Rodin's *Burghers of Calais* in the mainstream of French sculpture.

Other temples on Gharapuri are also dedicated to Lord Shiva, but the majesty of the central cave suggests royal connections, and a line of itinerant artist-craftsmen who would work in the west of Maharashtra, following patron-dynasties which conquered and established petty kingdoms. At Elephanta the absence of decoration on porticoes and capitals concentrates the worshipper's mind and soul on the huge panels. It is believed that the ceiling was completely frescoed, to judge by fragments and outlines still visible here and there.

Beginning from the right, the first panel depicts Shiva Nataraja, Lord of the Cosmic Dance, setting the universe in motion though remaining still within himself, his face nobly serene and detached, with smaller figures of his consort Parvati, his son Ganesh the elephant-headed, the legendary musician Tandu, Shiva's son Kumar, Vishnu on his garuda, Brahma and his swans, and the usual clutch of flying angels and ascetics. The lingam shrine (the lower part believed to be Brahma, the central part Vishnu and the upper part Shiva) has massive doorkeepers such as skull-bearing Yama and the god of fertility Varuna. Shiva slays the demon Andhaka on the west porch, his sword of wisdom almost vertical at the left having overcome the evil of ignorance, below flying gods and goddesses to whom the harmony of the universe has been restored.

Facing the Slaying of Andhaka is the marriage scene of Shiva and Parvati, Brahma officiating as chief priest and Vishnu attending to bless the pair. Policemen with lathis patrolled the main shrine, though they had missed the vandals by a matter of several centuries: one of Shiva's legs is missing entirely, and Parvati has lost both below the knee, but her face is modestly downcast, her breasts voluptuous, her waist tiny, her figure demurely small beside the tall, Aryan-like Shiva.

Crossing to the main three panels, on the right is Shiva Restraining the Descent of the River Ganges, once a celestial river. She, Ganga, consented to descend to Earth but her great force would have swept all before her unless intercepted by mighty restraint. Shiva offered himself as mediator, catching the flow of the waters in his tresses as we have seen at Mamallapuram (Tamil Nadu). The symbolic nature of Shiva's act is the power of concentration, capable of overcoming physical, emotional and sensual attachments.

The heart of Elephanta is Maheshmurti, in which Shiva appears with three faces: his destructive aspect on the left, his pacific, creative aspect on the right, and in the middle the calm, liberated countenance of Lord Shiva. Some scholars believe there may be a putative fourth face to be considered, remaining within the rock. The next panel is androgynous, in classical Greek terms, but in Hindu terms the perfect equilibrium between man and woman conjoined in one body, a divine unity, Shiva the active principle merging with Parvati the passive principle. Viewed from the right, however, the figure seems wholly female, with rounded breast and sinuous thigh; from the left, the figure appears entirely masculine, his face calm but austere, his waist manly. It is only when one sees the figure from the front that the union becomes clear, that one 'sees straight', a magnificent evidence of the dual nature of the body, a preternatural intuition of the fact that our mind is never wholly male or female.

Moving left again we find Parvati, defeated by her modesty in the cosmic dance, this time victorious over Shiva in a game of dice, symbolising the worshipper's need to throw in his lot for good and all with Shiva. Facing Parvati is unmoving Shiva in the act of pressing Mount Kailasa down on the arrogant demon king Ravana. The last great panel shows Shiva Yogeshvara, the Lord of Yogis, seated on a lotus in the act of concentrating cosmic energy within him.

Bassein

While Old Goa's evocative Portuguese colonial ruins attract visitors by the thousand, Portuguese Bassein (1534–1739) I found virtually deserted, as though the Portuguese had just decamped leaving the field uneasy. Women carried water in brass containers, and scrubbed colourful shirts and saris at ancient cisterns.

At Bombay Central I located a suburban train from Churchgate headed for 'Vasai Road', Vasai being the original Marathi form corrupted by the Portuguese. The fast train stopped only at Dadar, Bandra, Andheri, Borivli, Dahisar, Mira Road, Bhayandar, Naigaon and Vasai Road; its silent, impassive commuters could have been on the Piccadilly line. An advertisement above my head offered help for 'Nursing Aged (Rs 20), Sick (Rs 30), Holiday Home Neral (Rs 50), any operation (Rs 90) per day, Abortion (Rs 90).' A pall of pollution hung like a miasma over Bombay's shacks, clearing only briefly at the saltpans west of Bhayandar, and the misty Ulhas River south of Bassein harbour. At Vasai Road I hired an auto-rickshaw for the 11 km to Bassein fort. A brave new equestrian statue of Shivaji, Maratha champion and nationalist, dominates the desolate remains of the Portuguese mansions, thirteen churches, five convents and a cathedral attached to the Dominican convent. When the Portuguese captured Damão from Sultan Bahadur of Gujarat in 1534, they obtained Bassein in exchange for military co-operation against the Mughal emperors, and even now their stout walls and potent port gateway resist time's envy. A Christian population still survives, worshipping at our Lady of Grace,

Bassein. Ruined Portuguese church

Bassein. Fort walls and rusting hulks

attending Thomas Baptista Junior College and St Gonzalo Garcia Orphanage School.

Rough paths through the undergrowth lead from church to cathedral, from ancient well to mansion, forlorn, roofless, snake-infested, mournful in decay even as the graceful palms waft moving shadows over wall and portico. No guides, no caretakers, no guardians protect these precincts from looters who have stripped marble facings from churches, leaving brickwork and old plaster. A potbellied official came out from a building marked in Marathi 'Customs and Excise Office' wearing only a faded yellow towel and enamel basin at his midriff. Why do we need him in a semi-jungled walled city 45 km north of Bombay? Because a few hundred metres away a harbour allows small vessels to bring in passengers and cargo, possibly dutiable. Ferries ply along the river, though the rotting hulk 'URN 333' did not look as if it would be going anywhere. A fisherman on the sloping jetty threw out a desultory net, with a whining dog Bill Sikes would have recognised. At the harbour castle entrance, a bitch suckled four tiny pups beside hideous carcases of boats rusting in the idyllic calm waters. A stilt gazed studiously below the surface, without detecting a fish of note. I ascended the corner bastion to watch a ferry divide the waters into two. Then I walked through the knee-high undergrowth towards a wondrous arch and vault to melt the heart of Gianpaolo Pannini: its two left capitals hovering after their columns had been robbed away, its two right capitals missing like their columns. Bassein reminds me of Troy or Carthage in a way: it is piquantly romantic for what is no longer there at all, but left to the imagination, like the paintings of Monsù Desiderio or Samuel Bak.

Chaul and Janjira

As Bassein represents the Portuguese grip on the coast north from Bombay, so Chaul stands for Portuguese possessions immediately south from Bombay.

The Portuguese held Chaul harbour from 1522 to 1739, twelve years longer than they held Bassein. Chaul's walled city presents a melancholy picture of ruined churches and mansions, mostly robbed away by local builders. Chaul fell to the British in 1818, when they overthrew Peshwa Baji Rao, but there is little hint of the 'great trade' found there in 1584. The neighbouring village of Korlai has a fort with a Church of Our Lady of Mount Carmel and a Christian population silently hankering after a Portuguese destiny no longer theirs. From Bombay Chaul can be reached drearily by road, through Panvel, also the nearest railhead, or much more quickly and easily by daily ferry-boat between New Ferry Wharf and the village of Revas, a trip of 1 hr 40 minutes. A connecting bus gets you to Chaul in an hour.

South from Chaul (again much nearer and more convenient by sea than by road, which requires a spell on the Bombay – Goa highway, then back down to the coast) lies the fishing-village of Murud, with its sparkling beach and shrine to Lord Dattatreya. The enterprising Maharashtra Tourism Development Corporation has a splendid new holiday resort at Murud, from which you can charter a dhow for the short but spectacular trip to the sea fort called Janjira, actually a corruption of the Arabic Jazira ('island') Maharib or Muharaba. Arabic has two letters we pronounce as 'h'. Interpreted with the soft 'h', Maharib means a place of refuge or sanctuary, which fits in very well with this island stronghold; with the hard 'h', Muharaba denotes warfare, a battle, a struggle, which was the constant keynote hereabouts, first as traders from the Horn of Africa, possibly Somalis or Ethiopians or Zanzibaris, attempted to build an impregnable stronghold to protect their transshipped supplies, and then when pirates seized the island and lived off the booty from boarded vessels plying along the coast.

Janjira fort dates from 1511, when the slave-traders made their *feste Burg* and escorted Hajjis on their way from the Sultan of Bijapur's domains to the eastern Gulf ports and thence to Makkah and Madinah. Interestingly, the Marathas who proved so buccaneeringly successful by land made no inroads against Janjira, though Shivaji tried by sea in 1659 and his son Shambhuji tried tunnelling across in 1682. The African fleet, allied with Mughal ships from Surat and other friendly ports, drove away the Maratha threat. Sidi Sur-ul-Khan built a palace now ruined and abandoned, for Janjira is quite depopulated now, protected only by rusting cannon. I have travelled by dhow along the coasts of Oman, but there is no castle-island there to match the majesty of Janjira.

And if your imagination is fired by Janjira's banyan trees gripping the palace walls like monsters from outer space, or by its majestic lion seizing six minute elephants in claws, jaws and encircling tail on a somewhat alarming stone relief, you might wish to explore some of the other coastal forts of Maharashtra, northward in sequence Kansa or Padmadurga, built by Shivaji; the Sidi fort of Underi, Shivaji's Khanderi, and Arnala north of Bombay before Bassein. Southwards from Janjira lie Kanakdurg on the shore, Suvarnadurg another island fort, Gopalgarh and Bankot, renamed Fort Victoria by the British who captured it in 1790.

2 MAHARASHTRA

Early Maharashtra

Maharashtra dates in its present form from 1960, encompassing the city of Bombay, with over thirteen million inhabitants, and a dominantly Marathi-speaking hinterland that once formed a part of the Bombay Presidency, which included also Karnataka, Sind and Gujarat. In *Ballads of the Marathas* (1894), H. A. Acworth suggested that the name 'Maha-Ratha' derived from the words for 'great chariot', by extension a 'great warrior' who fought from a chariot. This would then have become Sanskritized as 'Maharashtra'. Others suggest that 'Maha-rashtra' means simply 'Great Region', but H. Dundas Robertson had the astounding idea that the name 'Marhutta' derived from *mar*, to strike, and *hutna*, to get out of the way, denoting 'those who struck a blow suddenly and at once retreated out of harm's way'. Folk etymology gets a bad name from precisely such a notion.

At first Maharashtra was inhabited by Dravidian tribes, but the coast was Aryanized in language and religion before the Persian conquest of the Indus Valley in the late 6th century B.C. Alexander the Great advanced, to be followed by Chandragupta and the Maurya empire which died with Ashoka in 231 B.C. Their legacy of Maharashtra fell to the Satavahana dynasty ruling from Paithan on the Godavari, south of Aurangabad, with ports at Chaul and Broach in Gujarat. But in 210 A.D. or thereabouts their empire was seized by the Western Kshaharatas (Bhumaka, 105–10 and Nahapana, 110–24) and the twenty-seven rulers of the Karddamakas, whose line became extinct about 300 A.D.

Little is known of the Chutus, who are believed by some scholars to have been a branch of the Satavahanas. The Vakataka dynasty which died out between 515 and 550 gave way to Kadamba rule in the south of Maharashtra and Kalachuri rule in the north. In the 6th century the Chalukya line established a steadily expanding empire from Badami in competition with the Pallavas of Kanchipuram and the Pandyas of Madurai, each temporarily gaining or losing some advantage. By 742, the Rashtrakuta prince Dantidurga had taken Ellora from the Chalukyas, and within ten years by shrewd Pallava alliances had become master of Deccan. The Chalukyas had disappeared by the end of the twelfth century, creating a power vacuum filled by the Yadava dynasty which reached its zenith under Singhana (1210–47), though some would argue that the best Yadava period was that of Ramachandra (from 1271), for it was in his reign that the Maratha mystic Dnyaneshvar completed his exposition of the *Gita* on the banks of the Godavari.

Three years later, in 1294, Ala ud-Din Khilji advanced on Yadava Devagiri, and took by surprise the fortress-town we now know by the Muslim name of

43

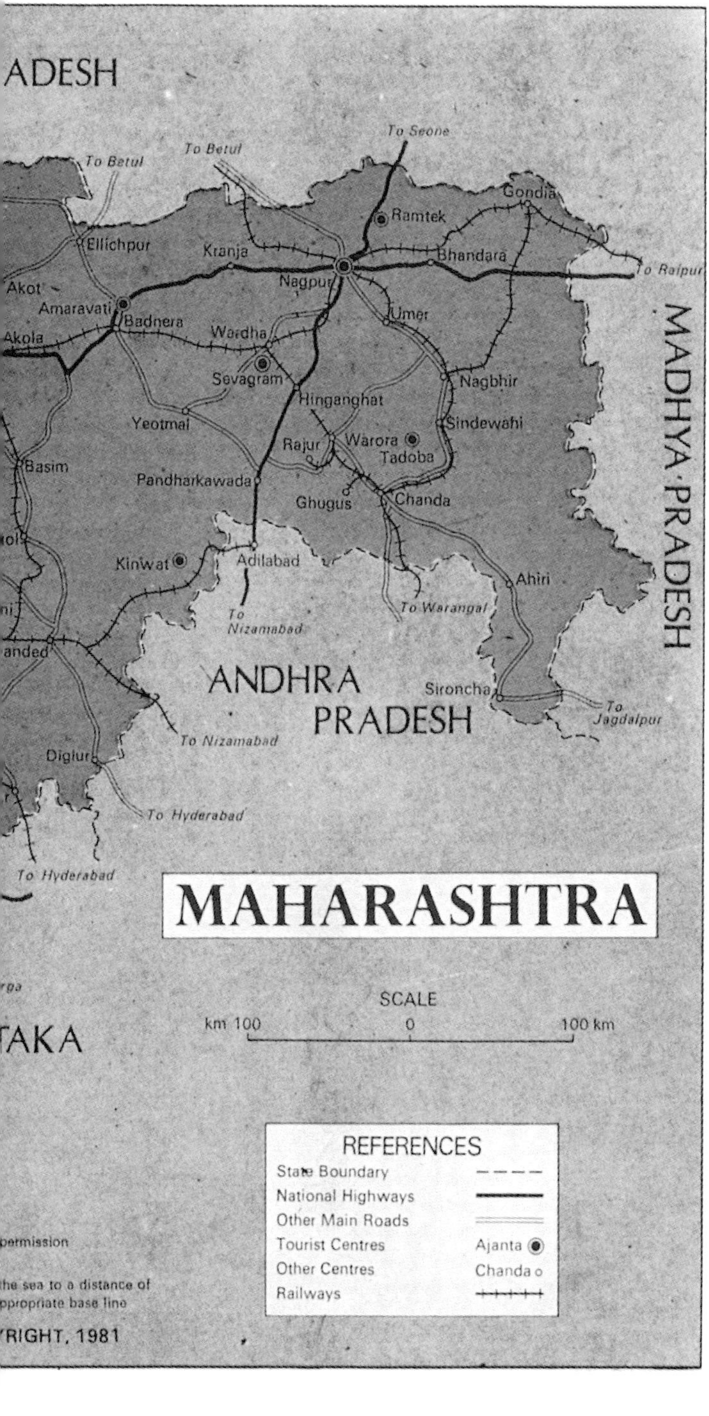

ADESH
To Betul
To Betul
To Seone
Gondia
Ramtek
Ellichpur
Kranja
Bhandara
To Raipur
Akot
Nagpur
Amaravati
Badnera
Umer
Akola
Wardha
Sevagram
Nagbhir
Hinganghat
Yeotmal
Sindewahi
Rajur
Warora
Tadoba
Basim
Pandharkawada
Ghugus
Chanda
Kinwat
Adilabad
Ahiri
To Nizamabad
To Warangal
anded
ANDHRA
PRADESH
Sironcha
To Jagdalpur
To Nizamabad
Diglur
To Hyderabad
To Hyderabad
MADHYA PRADESH
MAHARASHTRA
TAKA
SCALE
km 100
0
100 km
REFERENCES
State Boundary
National Highways
Other Main Roads
Tourist Centres
Ajanta
Other Centres
Chanda
Railways
permission
the sea to a distance of
appropriate base line
RIGHT, 1981

Daulatabad, given it by Muhammad bin Tughlaq in 1327, after which it became for a time the Tughlaq capital in place of Delhi. Following the Bahmani dynasty (1347–1527), a Hindu revival occurred under the Maratha leader Chhatrapati Shivaji Maharaj (1627–80), who became the Maratha national hero: a kind of Robin Hood, William Tell and Charlemagne rolled into one. A combination of shrewdness and valour earned him overlordship of the western Deccan against the Bijapur dynasty and Mughal powers in Delhi. After his death, however, Maharashtra became a conglomeration of petty fiefdoms. In 1687 Bombay became the leading possession of the British East India Company, but was made subordinate to Calcutta in 1753. In 1774 the first British war against the Marathas culminated in the 1782 Treaty of Salbai by which Salsette was ceded to the British. By the Second Maratha War the British obtained more territory and the last of the Peshwas, Baji Rao, was taken and pensioned off (1817–18) so that pacification of the whole region could begin. Modern secular laws were passed, courts established, and a new system of education set up. Cotton was grown to feed Lancashire's booming industry, and a phenomenal rise in demand occurred under Sir Bartle Frere (Governor, 1862–7) as the American Civil War disrupted cotton supplies from the South. Frere ensured that the great railway system was completed, and demolished the old city walls of Bombay to allow for its commercial expansion.

Maharashtra provided the seeds of nationalism with the anti-British exploits of Tilak, and of course Nagpur, in the east of the state, became the chosen site for Mahatma Gandhi's ashram in 1939.

Marathi is the language of 80% of the population, which is overwhelmingly Hindu by faith, but there are substantial minorities of Muslims centred on Aurangabad and often speaking Urdu, Buddhists, Jains, Christians (usually in the coastal belt and near Goa) and a steadily diminishing number of Parsis.

Neral to Matheran

Beyond Bombay, the Western Ghats look invitingly cool, misty and healthy. Two hours out of Victoria Terminus you arrive at Karjat on fast trains such as the Deccan Express, leaving V.T. at 6.45 a.m. or the Hyderabad Express, leaving at 12.35 p.m.

At Karjat you catch a local train for the 15-minute journey *back* to Neral Junction.

Indian hill railways appeal to us all, not only to railway buffs, because they exemplify ingenuity in tackling almost insoluble technical problems with elegant simplicity. The marvellous B-class 0–4–0 tank engines of the Darjeeling line represent one solution, the X-class 0–8–2 tank engines of the Ootacamund line represent another, but the four fully-articulated 0–6–0 tank engines of the Matheran Light Railway, built for the opening of the line up from Neral in 1907, are probably the most effective of all. This type of engine was designed by Sir Arthur Haywood at Duffield Bank in Derbyshire in the 1870s, and is still in full operational use over 80 years after its introduction, a magnificent tribute to appropriate technology, though coal quality is lower now, and the engines are without their original Riggenbach compression braking system. Matheran station is only 20 km from the lower end of the line, but the ruling gradient is more severe than the much longer Darjeeling line, the curvature

Matheran station. The narrow-gauge engine

sharper, and the technical achievement consequently much greater.

Departures from Neral for the two-hour uphill climb are at 08.40, 10.15 and 17.00 (plus an extra train at 10.15 between mid-March and mid-June), and from Matheran downhill at 05.45, 13.10 and 14.35 (plus an extra train at 14.35 between mid-March and mid-June), taking about 100 minutes. Two peculiarities of the trip are that it has its own booking-office, haunted by crows and pi-dogs, and that you cannot buy a return ticket, though virtually everyone who goes to Matheran will need one. I passed the time of day with Jibodhan Ramjit, Station Superintendent, who told me 'Ever since December there has been a sharp downfall in the passengers going to Matheran' and took with me tea and a sweet sticky cake. A notice read 'Passengers are requested to book all their luggage which will be kept in the brake van except walking sticks, umbrellas and tiffin carriers', and inside the Toytown-to-Arkville-style blue and cream first class carriage another read 'For your safety keep windows open during storm as otherwise bogies may get thrown.' Two porters industriously loaded cardboard cartons of liquor on the brake van, and one of them pointed to my neckhung camera. 'Beware monkey-thieves in Matheran', he called. The miniature train chuffed worriedly up the hill 'giveitago, giveitago, giveitago', and one hour later halted in relief at the first station, Jummapatti, where passengers leapt out (there is no toilet on the train) in search of equal relief. Goats grazed around the train, and vendors bearing ice-cream cones and Gold Spot performed their desultory sales pitch.

Twenty minutes later we reached the second station, which I transliterated as 'Vatar Pyp', not quite so exotic when interpreted as 'Water Pipe' because the pipe transmitting water between mountain and plain crosses the line at this point. We puffed slowly but triumphantly into Matheran station, with a retired locomotive on a plinth presaging what would happen to our own engine, given time, and I found a tablet praising the railway as the 'Brainchild of Mr Abdul Husain Adamjee Peerbhoy' (another Parsi), 'Financed by his father, the late Sir Adamjee Peerbhoy'. A monkey watched me emerge from paying my Rs 7 capitation tax on leaving the station precinct, and I remembered the warning about predatory primates.

I found a public garden holding the secret to Matheran's popularity on a monument to one Hugh Pointz Malet, Bombay Civil Service, Collector of Thana, who discovered this hill in May 1850. He came up from Chauk by the narrow steep footpath near One Tree Hill and returned to Chauk via Ram Bagh. Six months later he returned to Matheran, erected a small hut, cleared footpaths and in February 1851 built 'The Byke', then opened up a road from Chauk via Ram Bagh. Lord Elphinstone himself visited Matheran in 1855 and chose a site for Elphinstone Lodge, thus sealing the success of this new retreat from Bombay's humidity. Quiet hotels now dot wooded slopes: Regal Hotel, Rugby Hotel, Brightlands Resorts, and lower down Aman Lodge, with its own station, the Tourist Towers and Gujarat Bhavan, Lord's Central and the Alexander, the Bombay View and the Royal.

Wherever you walk, you soon come to a romantic precipice: Byron, Caspar David Friedrich, Berlioz would all have adored Matheran, from Garbutt Point, Panorama Point (following the railtrack), Chauk Point, Louisa Point, and around Charlotte Lake which lies just past the Silvan Hotel on Acharya Atre Marg. There are plenty of cafés and restaurants on Mahatma Gandhi Road, where the station debouches into the little town, but the greatest pleasure in weekday Matheran (avoid the weekends if you can) must be the serenity and silence of the woods, where monkeys leap and watch alertly for thrown scraps. The venturesome might like to try a footpath southwards from One Tree Hill, where Shivaji's Ladder descends into the plain. This is the path 'discovered' by Malet which had of course been well known to local people for centuries.

Lonavla
Khandala is a rail station served by only local trains, but all trains from Bombay stop at Lonavla, which is in any case much closer to the great caves of Karla, Bhaja, and Bedsa, and makes a delightful, cool stop in the Western Ghats on the way to Pune. Lord Elphinstone, Governor-General of Bombay, started the fashion for visiting Khandala and Lonavla in 1871, and since then these health-and-holiday resorts only 5 km apart have burgeoned with sanatoria, dams and new hotels, as well as an officially-sponsored rock climbing school at Karla, and a yoga institute near Walvan Dam, between Lonavla and Karla. Buses exist in Lonavla, but auto-rickshaws willing to wait for you make an attractive option, and are surely worth a small extra expense.

The first excursion might be to Lonavla Lake or Bhushi Lake, 1½ km from the town, one on each side of the southward road; the second to the Tungauli Lake and up to Rajmachi Fort, used by the Maratha warrior Shivaji in his campaigns. But the major reason for coming to Lonavla is the sequence of great caves, beginning chronologically with Bhaja (2nd century B.C.), continuing with Bedsa (1st century B.C.) and culminating in the glory of Karla, described by Karl Khandalavala as 'the finest Buddhist cathedral cave in India, nobler in its proportions and grandeur than even the great *chaityas* of Ajanta and the Vishvakarma *chaitya* of Ellora'.

Bhaja

To reach Bhaja, my auto-rickshaw driver Prakash Lakkandi turned right instead of left at the Karla turning, sailed over the level crossing at Malavli station, and chuttered beside the new town of Bhaja being built some way away from the present higgledy-piggledy village sprawling away from the shady square, where the auto-rickshaw stops. A footpath brings you (with a stream of noisy, helpful children) beside the rock-face and after ten minutes up a stepped stone path to the temple precinct.

Here you gaze across to the impressive fort of Lohagarh, and up to the forbidding heights of Vishapur, possession of which gave hegemony over the fertile valley. The entrance gate to the site is opposite Cave 12, the most exciting, with the first apsidal chaitya hall in the Western Deccan, quite demonstrably much earlier than the more beautiful example at Karla. The architect, a Buddhist monk from Northern India, was more at home with timber structures, and felt obliged to insert teak struts into the stone vault, possibly for aesthetic reasons but more probably out of nostalgia. Twenty-seven octagonal columns divide the temple into a curved central hall and an ambulatory; a stupa is set at the far end but in front of the columns, which slope gradually inwards,

Bhaja. The view across to Lohagarh fort

49

Bhaja. Indra on his elephant, a relief in Cave 19

as if to counteract expansion and contraction in timber! We know the monks were Hinayana, because the stupa shows no image of Buddha, and related to Sunga artists at Bharhut and Sanchi in Madhya Pradesh. The teak beams were painted, but so much of the colour has been lost that we cannot reasonably speculate about designs or motifs. A timber doorway once closed the entrance (the sockets can still be seen) but that too has of course perished. Three quite interesting monasteries (5, 6 and 11 in the official numbering) are situated left of Cave 12, and to the right the caretaker will show you numbers 13 and 14, 18, the tiny 19, and the large 20.

Cave 19 has two fascinating early sculptures in very low relief (the earlier, the lower, in general, in Western Deccan), which are still well preserved. One is Surya, the sun-god, with his chariot drawn by four horses, accompanied by a retinue and trampling in his full-pelt career the bodies of enormous demons; the other is Indra, seraphically astride his elephant Airavata which appeared when the ocean churned up. Two doorkeepers appear in equivalent low relief. Cave 20 is a stupa cave: five within, three outside behind four columns, then a further six outside in a slightly convex arrangement. Nobody came, nobody went . . . I felt as isolated as the first Buddhist monk-architect surveying his immortal work.

Bedsa

Bedsa too is almost never visited. East of Bhaja in the same long massif, it is approached by a fairly rough road south of Kamshet rail station; it lies north of Pawan Dam, and can be reached from Kamshet by bus or auto-rickshaw. From Bedsa, the hike uphill is just over 3 km, at the end of which you see wonderful belltop-columns surmounted by capitals consisting of horses with riders, clearly by a non-Indian sculptor, possibly an Iranian of Greek ancestry, or maybe a Parthian or Scythian. These foreigners living near the coast were known to have converted to Buddhism, because of donative inscriptions, including seven at Karla alone. 'Foreign' doorkeepers have been noted at the Pitalkhora monastery of the 1st century B.C., in the Ajanta area, that is contemporary with Bedsa. The women at Bedsa have long plaited hair, bare breasts, and Hellenistic-type faces, while the men wear only a loincloth and a fantastic turban, and seem more Greek than Persian.

This extraordinary sculptural and architectural achievement, forming the verandah to Cave 7, gives way to an apsidal chaitya hall of chaste simplicity, as though the effect is intended to draw one in with wonder, and leave one to meditate on the Void. Octagonal columns slope inwards, as at Bhaja, and the stupa is of Hinayana type, without a figure of Buddha. Cave 11 is a vihara, or monastic establishment, with nine separate cells opening off a vaulted room.

Karla

Returning from Bedsa and Kamshet towards Lonavla, you turn right at the Karla Hotel by the Bhaja crossroad, and drive to the foot of the cliff, where stalls provide offerings (for the Hindu shrines on the way), fruit, souvenirs and cold drinks. A vendor of ridiculous trinkets displayed on his T-shirt the legend 'Hot Love'. Every so often, due to the road's unevenness and potholes, the plastic pipe connecting the fuel tank had worked loose, and Prakash had to stop to fix it on again. He was still attending to this chore as I wriggled past a hectoring of guides and up towards wild songbirds, delirious with their own freedom. I felt with them a sacred knot of complicity as they rose on warm currents.

At the top of the steep stone steps I paused for breath about 110 metres above the green valley, and listened to the jangling bells and incantations within a little Hindu shrine that has sprung up outside the great Buddhist chaitya hall.

A few monastic establishments with associated cisterns surround the chaitya hall without distracting from its effortless dominance. It dates from Kshaharata dynasty's period of power in Western Deccan, in the 1st century A.D. and seems to face the earlier Bhaja across the valley as if in boastful emulation. Clearly, this monk-architect knew of the earlier chaitya hall, and was determined to outdo Bhaja in terms of size, ambition and sculptural decoration. This he achieved with a kind of arrogant ease, like the apparent triumph of Raphael explicable after the example of his master Pietro Perugino. The propylaeum reminds you of the entrance to Greek temples, and is faced by a rock-cut screen as on a French Gothic cathedral, except that this is of course hewn out of the living rock. Three entrances are surmounted by a pillared clerestory (the ecclesiastical terms from Christianity seem oddly appropriate), with a series of holes to support a timber musicians' gallery. Within, more representations of arched timber buildings appear above frontal elephants. Of course the Buddha figures carved higher up date from a later period, when Mahayana Buddhism had replaced Hinayana.

Karla. Vendor of trinkets near Hindu temple

Karla. Detail of mithuna couples on the verandah of Cave 8

Karla's chaitya has a three-aisled interior, except that the rows of columns meet in an apsidal curve around the back of a monolithic stupa with a dramatic wooden umbrella over an inverted stepped finial. The 37 octagonal columns have pot bases, inverted campaniform capitals, with inverted steps surmounted by wondrous groups consisting of elephants with a man and woman, he dhotied and turbanned, she bare-breasted, with foot-rings and a small belt.

The vault has teak timbers in place, just like an upturned boat in a shipyard awaiting repair. The mithuna couples on the door allowing access to the interior present an Asiatic-Greek appearance similar to the couples at Bedsa: vigorous, as godlike in stature as humans can be, and with a confident assurance in their full gaze that stems partly from their sculptor's towering genius. Nesting pigeons fluttered and splashed their droppings on the smooth floor.

Outside, one *simhastambha* or lion-column is capped by four lions of toy-like ferocity, like those green Chinese ceramic lions that mewl rather than roar from 'antique' shops in Hongkong. A matching *simhastambha* presumably stood at the right, but fell victim to the Hindu shrine to the goddess Ekvira.

As I explored the twelve-cell vihara next door, I noted that the wooden ladder I ascended by could have been drawn up by monks in case of sudden attack. Then the village women deserted the shrine, and the whole of Karla was left to me in the heat of the day. As I sank to my haunches, tired and hot with the exertion of climbing and walking, the enveloping coolness of the vihara proved yet again the practical wisdom of the monks, who chose this idyllic countryside for its beauty, peace, distance from big cities, and because within the cells or chaitya hall you are *never too hot*. Meditation seems a natural course of events, and darkness within an antidote to garish colours of earthly splendour.

Pune and Sinhagarh

Arriving by train at Pune station into the pandemonium of crowds, noise and shoving, beggars and vendors, my first reaction was to pick a hotel close by (the Ashirwad or adjoining Amir) and head out by taxi or auto-rickshaw to the grand isolation of Lion Fort, or Sinhagarh, silent, sparsely-populated yet only 18 km southwest of the straggling suburbs below Parvati Hill, past the Best Boot House, Girinagar, the Institute of Armament Technology (with its own sailing club on a nearby lake), then into Sinhagarh National Park.

It was at this point that my auto-rickshaw driver Nandu Pawar admitted he had never been to the fort, as his engine sputtered and died. The climb had been too much for it. I walked on, hoping to reach the stronghold 2,300 ft above the plain before nightfall. Nobody passed me in either direction: I strode out like a conquistador, or like a Maratha spy infiltrating the defences of the Bijapuri general. Known as Kondane until 1647, it was given its new name by Shivaji in 1647. A mediaeval foundation, it fell to Muhammad ibn Tughlaq in 1328, and to succeeding invaders of the Deccan such as Malik Ahmad of Ahmadnagar (1486) and the dynasty of Bijapur (1637). After Tanaji had taken it for the Marathas in 1647, it was coveted by the Mughals, and blockaded in 1701 for two years. The British pacified it in 1818, and since then it has slept, like a sprawling tawny lion, exposed to the fierce heat of midday and the searing winds of winter nights. Shaped like the foot of Italy, at its heel rears the Pune triple Gate, the Kalyan triple Gate beneath the ball of its foot, and a palace at its instep. By the Pune Gate I found an ancient bearded vendor of yoghourt in black pots made locally, and intercepted him as he was packing up his head-tray prior to descending to his cottage. A kestrel hovered above me like a harbinger of death, then I found that a dozen families *live* inside Sinhagarh, so carrion and scraps will be available for such clawed and beaked hunters. The rocky outcrop looks impregnable, fortified by forty-foot high basalt walls, but I had to remind myself that it has been captured many times: what men can defend, men can also attack. The well-water looks anything but salubrious, and the gaudy recent Tanaji Memorial is painted pink, yellow, pastel blue and bottle green, but otherwise living up here would seem almost idyllic – for a time. Tea-houses and hopeful-looking restaurants offer the visitor a domestic respite from the endless, breathtaking vistas on all sides.

Next morning, in Pune, I found the friendliest auto-rickshaw driver of all: Shaikh Husain, an English-speaking Muslim frequenting the courtyard of Hotel Ashirwad. He proved a valuable ally in discovering the less familiar aspects of Pune as well as the highlights. He took me to the Potters' Bridge, where small dark-grey or black pots are thrown by hand on the wide sidewalks, before showing me the evocative 8th-century underground temple called Patalishwar in the district called Shivajinagar, on Jangli Maharaj Road. Lord Ripon called Victorian Pune 'an uninteresting place, without a vestige of Eastern colour', a description so grotesquely wide of the mark that he cannot possibly have remembered Patalishwar, nor the three-storey mansion called Vishrambagh

Pune. Patalishwar underground temple

Pune. Vishram Wada

Wada in Budhwar Peth or 'Wednesday Market', an imposing Maratha palace transformed first into a Sanskrit College, then a high school and a law court. A circular Nandi shrine has been hollowed out into a square courtyard, which gives on to an underground temple to Shiva. On the external wall, a cross-legged ascetic once a wrestling champion, naked but for a diminutive loincloth, sunned himself in the pale morning light, while a lad in a white lungi conned a textbook. Pune's population of 1.6 million magically reduced itself to two, as I prowled the cave of Patalishwar, unfinished because of sudden cracks in the rock: even a Vishnu with protective naga king remains incomplete. A lingam reigns in the centre, and a Ganesh image behind.

Through a gap in the wall I came to the Hindu temple-tomb dedicated to 'Jangli Maharaj' himself: the King of the Jungle, an ascetic who died in 1818. Pipal and banyan trees, both sacred to Hindus, grew indulgently, amply, showering the serene hill garden with their equilibrium. A worshipper brought his palms up to his red-spotted forehead before a garlanded full-length portrait of the Forest Lord, and sped silently to the right, collected his sandals upright with a scoop of the foot, and left for what office, what plebeian duties?

If you have time for only one museum in Pune, then the Mahatma Phule Museum on Ghole Road must be outranked by the Kelkar Museum, but I had time for both. It is just that the Phule Museum is one of those depressing, deserted, decaying displays with yellowing notices and never-changing exhibits that plagues India like indelible ink. Nobody comes, nobody cares, and you have to invest a great deal of your own energy into enjoying it when the function of a museum is – in today's jargon – to be user-friendly. Showcases display handicrafts such as brocades from Benares, woodcarving, marble, lacquer, brass, copper and bidri ware, sandalwood, ivory and coconut shells. Stuffed birds and animals gaze forlornly: a lion from Gir National Park, a common babbler, a purple sunbird. Rooms are devoted to agriculture, geology, weapons, and a gallery of drawings by Prof. Dinkar Thopte. After taking Irani tea at the New Central Restaurant, we arrived at the Peshwa palace of Baji Rao I (1720–40), reminding me how recent is Pune's growth. It doesn't appear prominently until 1599, when it is recorded as a regency of Ismail, Nizam Shahi Sultan of Ahmadnagar, under Malaji Bhonsla, grandfather of Shivaji himself. Peshwa Baji Rao I laid the foundation of Shanwar Wada ('Saturday Palace') in 1730 and completed it in 1732. It remained the chief residence of the Peshwa rulers until their demise at the end of Baji Rao II's reign in 1817, when the Battle of Khadki ('Kirkee') resulted in Pune's surrender to the British, who had been invited to Pune as allies by the Peshwa.

Fire damaged Shanwar Wada so extensively on three occasions that very little can be seen above ground level within the massive walls and colossal Delhi Gate, with its anti-elephant spiked doors and two undamaged bastions. Shiver as you pass through the gate, for in the high balcony above you the Peshwa Narayan Rao was assassinated by his guards in 1773, only a few months after becoming ruler, and there too that Madhava Rao fell or was pushed to his death in 1796. Shaikh Husain showed me the site of the seven-storey palace, and the Thousand-Jet Lotus Fountain. Attractive lawns and shady trees make a pleasant garden of the stronghold, outside which youngsters play cricket, and old men watch and chat. So much for Pune before the British.

If, like me, you are intrigued by Victorian architecture and its almost unrestrained fantasies in Maharashtra, Pune does not rival Bombay but has its own modest attractions, such as the University in grey Italian Gothic (1866), situated in the new Government House, the official residence of the Governor of Bombay during the monsoon season from the time of Mountstuart Elphinstone, designed by James Trubshawe in bizarre emulation of Queen Victoria's Osborne House on the Isle of Wight. The drawing-room has a minstrels' gallery, and the ballroom speaks eloquently of those gracious times when the British dammed the river 'for boating'. The British found Mahabaleshwar much cooler, but during the heavy rains it was dangerous, and Pune became the natural choice: much higher than Bombay, and much flatter than Mahabaleshwar. Sir Robert Grant, Governor from 1834 to 1838, when the Old Government House situated across the Mula river, east of the confluence of its tributary the Pavana, used to walk along a certain path every day after dark, and on the day he died here a Hindu sentry observed a cat emerge from the house after dark and stroll along the same path. A believer in the transmigration of souls, the sentry told the rest of the Hindu staff what he had seen, and from that day onward they believed that the soul of Sir Robert had entered the cat. Which one, of course they did not know, because it had been noticed after dark, so whenever any cat emerged from Old Government House after dark, the sentry smartly and dutifully presented arms. The Old Government House in the suburb of Dapodi later became a Public Works Department Store, but by the 1930s it had fallen into disrepair.

Sir Bartle Frere, Governor from 1862 to 1867, built the new Government House near a pass or *khind* dedicated to Ganesha, and so it was called laconically Ganesh Khind. Frere's magnificent Italianate concepts, executed with such nonchalance beginning with the long drive up to a porte-cochère, came to an abrupt halt with the collapse of the Bombay cotton industry at the end of the U.S. Civil War, and Frere was chastised in the House of Commons for his 'extravagance and insubordination', a charge levelled again at his successor Sir Seymour FitzGerald, who lavished £500 on a ballroom chandelier.

Sir Bartle and Lady Frere are shown in portraits in the city centre Council Hall, opposite the Daftar (Records Office), with its Peshwa archives. 1867 saw the completion of St Paul's Church, the two Sassoon Hospitals in English Gothic and the red-spired, red-brick Ohel David Synagogue financed by Sir David Sassoon, who erected his own tomb here in the grounds. Bats roost in the timbers outside and parrots in the clock. I found a bent old Jew in a skullcap who waved away in disdain 'the Jews who have gone to Israel', leaving only three or four men, far short of the congregation of ten men required for an active synagogue. Sir Henry St Clair Wilkins and Major Melliss, who had designed the Sassoon Hospitals, were also active elsewhere. Melliss designed the District Courts, again linking Gothic with a kind of tropical exhilaration; Wilkins designed Deccan College, and beyond Pune Engineering College (Gothic, 1859), the grey stone riverside mansion called Garden Reach, commissioned by Sir Albert Sassoon (1862–4) and subsequently owned by the wealthy Parsi philanthropist Sir Bomanji Dinshaw Petit.

Across FitzGerald Bridge from Deccan College you can visit another charming Victorian-period palace, the Agha Khan's Palace called Yera Wada (1860), across the river from Bund Gardens and the Osho Commune. Yera Wada became notorious for the house arrest of Gandhiji, and a memorial is maintained to him and to his wife Kasturba, who died here.

India is rightly sensitive to the needs of its tribal peoples and nomads, resisting 'il gran turismo' which would distort their way of life forever. But because the tribals are so numerous (7% of India's total population) they are studied at the Tribal Research and Training Institute at 28 Queen's Garden, Pune, where a Tribal Cultural Museum (10–5.30) can be visited on the second floor. In Maharashtra, the tribals totalled 2.8 million in 1971, and 5.1 million in 1981. The steps are decorated with stone carvings from the Marai people, Waghdeo, Bahiram and Danteswari.

In the evening I enjoyed the excellent dramatic qualities of the Marathi play *Chimangani* at the Tilak Smarak Mandir on Tilak Road, the alternative being *Ghasiram Kotwal* at Bal Gandharva Rang Mandir on Jangli Maharaj Road. Apart from the numerous movie theatres, plays and dance can be seen also at Nehru Memorial Hall on Ambedkar Road and Bharat Natya Mandir on Sadashiv Peth.

Next morning Shaikh Husain awaited me outside Hotel Ashirwad. We plunged headlong into the traffic to find the International Book Service in the Deccan Gymkhana district, where I stocked up with *16 Modern Marathi Short Stories* (Kutub Popular, Bombay, 1961 but still in print thirty years on) and Dilip Chitre's *Anthology of Marathi Poetry* (Sadanand, Bombay, 1967), the only translations I could find from Marathi literature. The morning paper told how, at Shivajinagar, Judge S. G. Mutalik had acquitted Chiman Dahya Solanki of burning his wife to death. Solanki had suspected his wife Lalita of having relations with her maternal uncle, and poured kerosene on her, lighting a match and setting fire to her. On her deathbed, Lalita had told a judicial magistrate that her husband had set her on fire.

We drove along one-way Lakshmi Road past shops selling saris, gold and jewellery, and the Commonwealth Building now housing the Life Assurance Company of India and Shaikh Husain stopped outside Poona Automobiles. 'Go inside', he pointed: along a narrow alley I came to Belbagh, an oasis of quiet (except for crows and cockerels) with a wooden temple to Vishnu and Lakshmi, and lateral shrines to Ganesh and Shiva.

I browsed among the spices, fruit and vegetables in Phule Market (formerly Ray Market) and then made for the Raja Dinkar Kelkar Museum, one of the many important private collections of Indian art, crafts and antiquities, and one of the few thrown open to the public, in a historic mansion still occupied by the founder's family. D. G. Kelkar himself died in 1990, but the museum remains open, 8.30–12.30 and 3–6. Objects come mainly from Tamil Nadu, Maharashtra, Karnataka and Gujarat, and date generally from the 18th–19th centuries. A wooden temple door from Paithan (Mah.) and windows and a cupboard from Patan (Guj.) exemplify the intricate skills of local craftsmen. Vajris, or metal skin-scrubbers, have decorative handles and rough soles. Here is a door from Jaisalmer inlaid with ivory, a five-armed, five-headed Hanuman, a magnificent standing bronze Rama (South India, 13th century) and a charming Rajasthani toy consisting of a brass cart pulled by a horse with a cannon on its head. The first floor consists of the Mastani Mahal, carved at Kothwal and moved here in its entirety with brown walls painted in black and white elegantly, befitting the dancer who captivated Baji Rao I. A delicate painting of Mastani on glass depicts her as ethereally pale, with blushing cheeks, her modesty covered by gauzy, transparent chiffon. Hubble-bubbles, Mughal paintings, betel-leaf plates, drums and priceless sitars worthy of Ravi Shankar exemplify the range and quality of the Kelkar Museum. The second floor exhibits the spectrum of lamps, from a Nepali 18th-century sun lamp and a contemporary brass Mughal lamp from Delhi, to an ingenious 19th-century lamp for poison-testing and a South Indian acrobat lamp. Fine trays, dishes and cups are inlaid in bidri style, and textiles include blouses from the Banjara tribe of Kutch, Gujarat. The third floor is a treasury of toys, my favourite being a bronze elephant with canopied seat. Of the 3,000 leather puppets in the collection, the changing display during my visit consisted of a mounted sequence of scenes from the puppet-play *Hiranyakashyapu*, on a demon king who married Kayadhu, a princess of Jambhasur.

Shaikh Husain and I explored the beautiful gardens of Saras Bagh not far from the traffic node called Swargate, then lunched at the popular Rasraj Restaurant, sheltered from the two o'clock sun by its rush roof. We then ascended Parvati Hill by ninety numbered steps to the Peshwa Museum (8–12, 3–8) and the Sri Ganapati temple installed by Balaji Baji Rao, also called Nana Saheb Peshwa, in 1749. Sparrows pecked sacrilegiously at offered coconut fragments. A watchful policeman with lathi was stationed by the portal of Sri Kartika Swami, an idol installed here in 1766 of whom it is whispered (and fully credited by men) that 'if a lady takes darshan she will become a widow', that shameful, almost hopeless state which in the past drove thousands of women to *sati*.

Then I tiptoed barefoot in the unassuming tomb of Nana Saheb (1721–61), a Hindu swastika drawn on its marble. His impassive portrait hung above the tomb and eight portraits of Peshwa personalities around as if in a gallery.

We descended from Parvati Hill, and cruised passed buses marked PMT. 'Pre-menstrual tension?' I enquired. 'Pune Municipal Transport'. 'Ah, Perpetual Moving Trouble.'

Litter-bins in Pune are inscribed 'Throw it in the bin. Because it's your home', making me think irresistibly of Oscar the Grouch in *Sesame Street*, whose home really was the trash-can.

Shaikh Husain dropped me unwillingly, as a father leaves an infant at his first kindergarten, at Koregaon Park, north of the railway line from Pune to Sholapur and south of the confluence of the rivers Mula and Mutha, and at the entrance I asked about a guided tour of the Rajneesh Ashram, which had recently been renamed the Osho Commune International, 'osho' being a Japanese word for 'the enlightened one'. During his last years, Bhagwan Shri Rajneesh had been attracting more and more followers from Japan.

He had been born Rajneesh Chandra Mohan, into a Jain family in Kuchwada, Madhya Pradesh, in 1931. Educated at Sagar University, he taught philosophy for a time at Jabalpur University. He began his career as a travelling orator and guru in 1966, and two years later he had fully evolved his theory of sexual liberation anathema to orthodox Hindus and traditional ascetics but highly attractive to young westerners. 'If you want to know the elemental truth about

Pune. Osho Commune. A devotee in maroon robes buying flowers

love, the first requisite is to accept the sacredness of sex, to accept the divinity of sex in the same way as you accept God's existence – with an open heart.' Equating love, sex, and religion seemed headily suited to the year of *Hair* in the theatre, *2001* in the cinema, and student revolutions in France, Japan, Italy, Britain, West Germany and the U.S.A. It is from these countries, rather than from India itself, that Rajneesh continued to draw his disciples. In 1970 he announced a change of name to Bhagwan, which might be translated 'godhead'. He drew from all the occult and esoteric writers, notably from Taoists, Zen Buddhists and Gurjiev, Tibetan masters, Tantric tradition, and modern 'liberation psychologists', such as R. D. Laing. He railed against the narrow, hypocritical Christian churches and found nothing in orthodox Islam, but much in the Sufi mystics. He rejected many Hindu accretions, but prized Krishna the dancer, Kabir the mystical poet, and the vision of the Bauls.

He represented a threat to established religion wherever he roamed, for he created a personality cult that attracted especially the questing and the weak-willed, whom he constantly derided for misunderstanding him, for asking stupid questions, and for being as greedy for immediate spiritual success as are their contemporaries for a quick kill on the stock market. Indeed, Bhagwan demanded that all his disciples be rich, for like celibacy poverty was a crime against nature. If poverty brings misery, and happiness is the goal of religion, why should seekers not become as wealthy as humanly possible? He parodied the American dream by acquiring ninety-odd Rolls Royces, deserving that notorious epigram: 'Jesus saves, Bhagwan spends'. He taught rebellion against every government and every system, parodoxically even his own, though in practice he could feel bitter towards apostates such as Hugh Milne (*Bhagwan: the God that Failed*) and Sally Belfrage (*Flowers of Emptiness*). I suppose he provided the kind of father figure that South African blacks found in Nelson Mandela or Iraqi children in Saddam Husain. You don't resist such figures: you are rushed headlong in their flow-tide. Bhagwan preached constantly, sometimes up to four hours a day, for much of his life, providing enough raw material for six hundred edited books in thirty languages, audiotapes, video-tapes, tarot cards and the fortnightly newspaper *Osho Times International*.

At the entrance to Osho Commune at 17 Koregaon Park I asked for a tour. 'You have to have an AIDS test', a young American told me in a Californian accent, and 'you can't take any notes or photographs.' 'Why?' I asked, 'and then again, why not? I don't want to make love, I just want a tour. Is there a charge?'

'We don't take money,' replied the maroon-robed Californian, 'just tokens.' 'How do I get tokens?' 'You buy them.' 'For money?' 'Yes, of course.' 'Isn't that a trifle illogical?' 'You're being very aggressive, you know. There's no need to be negative.'

'But I thought Osho taught everyone to be a rebel.'

'O.K., you don't have to take an AIDS test if you're only taking a one-hour tour.'

Young aspirants to join the ashram, mainly Americans and Europeans in their twenties or early thirties, were being led meekly for their AIDS test, while a young German girl called Greta in the world (Osho gave everyone their own fresh name when he met them and hers was Kunji) told me not to take notes or pictures, because the press is generally hostile, and journalists have to be specially vetted before being taken round. Greta told me that Pune ashram was founded in 1974, and remained active until 1981, when 'forces hostile to the teachings of Bhagwan' suggested that he might avoid house arrest by voluntary exile to the U.S. At that time five thousand disciples had congregated in Pune, with an estimated fifteen thousand more scattered around the world, even in the Soviet Union, where interest in Bhagwan elicited visits from the KGB. The residents of Antelope, Oregon, were persuaded by various means to welcome Bhagwan to the area, and 4,000 disciples soon renovated a ranch, and the forty retired persons of Antelope moved out.

John Updike, in the novel *S.* (1988), his brilliant yet gentle satire on Rajneeshpuram in Oregon, his 'Ashram Arhat' in Arizona, has evoked this hilarious mix of greenbacks and sannyasins in a form letter sent out to enquirers . . . 'Demand for places and our limited facilities is such that we must ask a minimum deposit of ten thousand dollars (U.S.). In addition there are fees totalling eight hundred dollars monthly to cover a modest portion of the unavoidable expenses of your food, housing, health and accident insurance, lecture and darshan fees, and supervised meditation. Sannyasins are of course expected to practice worship in the form of constructive labor for twelve hours a day, and either to bring with them sturdy boots, a sleeping bag, a sun hat, and appropriately colored garb or else to purchase such supplies at the Varuna Emporium . . .' Osho has claimed over and over again that paradox and uncertainty lie at the heart of all we think we are, so the religious paradox of 'get rich to get well' seems no stranger than the rest.

Bhagwan became a multi-millionaire through the welcome gifts of his adherents, and Rajneeshpuram soon witnessed the acquisition of more than ninety Rolls Royces, and a cohort of women who ran the ranch in his name, chief among them Ma Anand Sheela, his personal secretary. A great banner which floated above him in public lectures read 'Surrender to me and I will transform you, that is my promise'. But he apparently surrendered to the organisers of Rajneeshpuram, who were indicted by the U.S. Government on such counts as drug offences, financial fraud including tax evasion, arson, alleged murder, and poisoning up to 750 citizens of a nearby town to win an election by disabling potential antagonists. Bhagwan was arrested and deported in 1985 after pleading guilty to immigration, fraud and other specimen charges. After a year's wandering in the hope of finding refuge in, among other nations, Uruguay, Bhagwan finally returned to Pune and became as successful as before, with a new team of confidential advisers. He advocated no structured religion, refused to appoint a successor, and named a 21-person group to run his ashram after his passing on, which was not to be mourned.

Greta said that the original orange robes were discarded in favour of free choice, but he then changed the attire to loose-fitting maroon robes. I found entrepreneurs outside the commune offering beautifully-made robes of a suitable style on offer at about US$7. I obediently followed in Greta's footsteps, listening to her fluent and well-rehearsed explanations on a familiar theme. She had practised transcendental meditation for the last two years and now in ten minutes achieves a level of regular, profound and consistent experience that took her many hours at first. 'You can do it on your own,' Kunji told me, 'there is no need to enter a group if you own the tapes.' A German girl embraced a young American man, their arms around each other, palms and fingers spread out for maximal contact. Two Japanese girls chattered excitedly, released from the social constraints afflicting them back home in Yokohama. 'We have no alcohol and no drugs,' stated Greta, but the loose maroon robes could conceal most substances known to man, and there are no body checks on entering the commune. Nobody seriously denies that sexual orgies take place, for that is one kind of release that Bhagwan constantly advocated and practised, but many other kinds of release from inner stress and repression are practised too, many possibly beneficial to some. 'Whirling Tonight' in the Buddha Hall, read one notice. For evening meditation, white is worn. Gardens are cultivated, flowers held close to the face, all senses primed for action. The commune runs its own travel agency, bank and bookshop, where a very active trade was being carried out by efficient European staff. I bought for cash, without much difficulty in spite of the fact that officially no cash purchases are possible, a copy of *Beyond the Frontiers of the Mind*, a selection from Osho's works printed by Tata Press in Bombay and published by the commune's own Rebel Publishing House from an address in Cologne. Kunji told me that a Hamburg police chief comes here once a year 'to recharge his batteries', but there is accommodation for only a few hundred pilgrims here, and most visitors live in hotels and guesthouses outside the ashram. It is not easy to predict what will happen to the commune now that its pivot is no longer present in the flesh, but presumably many will return to refresh themselves from the fount of their original inspiration. Where societies impose rigorous norms as in orthodox Islam, orthodox Judaism, orthodox Catholicism, Osho preached the sacredness of the individual.

'Everyone,' he taught, 'is born a rebel because everybody is born to be an individual in his own right. Everybody is born not to be in a drama but to live an authentic life, not to be a mask but to be his original face. But no society till now has allowed people to be themselves.' It is a tribute to the city of Pune that so outspoken a critic of conventional religions should be sheltered and given room when he was not allowed the democratic right to air his views in the U.S.A., any communist country, Greece, Switzerland, England, Ireland, Canada, Antigua, Holland, Germany and Italy. Uruguay and Jamaica both allowed Bhagwan to settle there, but pressure from the U.S. Government changed their minds.

As I was led back to the commune entrance under Kunji's watchful eye, I mused aloud 'Why would 600 books be necessary if it could all be expressed simply, as Bhagwan said? If it cannot be expressed simply, how can it be reduced to 600 books?' She shrugged. 'And why can I not take a photograph of the gardens, say, or pilgrims in their maroon robes?' 'It is not allowed.' 'Can I buy a postcard of the grounds or of Osho's quarters?' 'No, just a portrait of Osho himself.' 'But I have that on the cover of the book I just bought. Well, thank you for your time and trouble.' 'I don't think you have an open mind. You want always to criticise.' 'It is *because* I have an open mind that I always want to criticise. One day you may also feel you wish to criticise. On that day, you will acquire an open mind too.'

Everyone will derive their own conclusions from their own visit to Osho Commune. I certainly felt a spirit of warmth; expensive seeking for quick solutions in such notions as 'alchemical hypnotherapy', 'vibrational harmonising', and crystals; and a feeling that young people here can derive certain types of satisfaction that they feel to be lacking in their own job-oriented home environment. For Indians locked hopelessly within a caste system they might abhor, Osho Commune presents an opportunity to escape at least for a time, and mix with wealthy young Westerners.

A Train to Sholapur

If at Pune you suddenly felt the urge to be surrounded by teeming humanity, voluble, jocular, shouting and pushing, accompanied by bedrolls, briefcases and bulky luggage clothed in canvas, I can recommend second-class compartments of the Hyderabad Express. I first bought a ticket to travel, then asked Mr B. Lal, Chief Ticket Inspector, how I could obtain a seat reservation. 'Look for Mr Rajab Khan, Platform 4.' At 4.20 I joined the queue where Mr Rajab Khan was ticking off no-shows, and he sold me a seat numbered S/5 31. When the train arrived at 4.55, I found that the seat was occupied by two ladies, 3 babies, and five shopping bags with clothes, food, and sundries. I silently exposed my ticket to their affronted stare, and felt indecent. A smiling man examined my credentials to the seat, gently expostulated my need to the incredulous squatters, and waved along the corridor to equally congested seats. Owing to the innate Indian respect for law and order, especially as expressed in a firm baritone, the ladies collected their belongings, inanimate and human, and shoved through the crowd in a manner reminiscent of Canto XIV of Dante's *Inferno*:

> Supin giacea in terra alcuna gente;
>   alcuna si sedea tutta raccolta,
>   e altra andava continuamente.
> Quella che giva intorno era piú molta,
>   e quella men che giacea al tormento,
>   ma piú al duolo avea la lingua sciolta.

> (Some lay supine on the ground, others crouched on
>   their haunches, while others roamed restlessly around.
> These last were the majority; those that lay still the
>   fewest, but the most vocal in their sound.)

Apart from the lower cost, travelling second-class in Indian trains has two main advantages. One is the greater mix of passengers to observe and engage; the other is that windows are open, whereas in first-class they are often closed and smeared with days of dusty travail. The 263 km by train from Pune to Sholapur was due to last for 5½ hours, so I was lucky to be allocated a window seat and even luckier to find a congenial companion – as far as Daund – in Vijay P. Bhujbal, a security guard with the Co-operative Bank there, and a choirmaster at the Church of Christ in the Australian Baptist Mission. He belongs to the State Reserve Police, called out in case of riots, and for pleasure shoots fish in the Bhima river from a tree, firing when it is hot, between February and May, and the fish emerge at the surface more frequently to breathe.

Asked about the communal controversy over the Babri Mosque in Ayodhya, Vijay predicted that the only real solution was a new benevolent dictatorship on the Indira Gandhi model. 'The many strands of partisan prejudice on all sides are bringing confusion and unhappiness,' he opined. 'We are looking for one good, strong man or the military itself to tackle the threefold problems we have, that is population growth, spread of corruption, and lack of proper hygiene.'

At Kedgaon he indicated the Mukti Mission Hall founded in the 19th century by the Brahmin Pandita Ramabai Mukti. She converted to Christianity and translated the Bible again into Marathi, Maharashtra has 5% Muslims and 1% Christians: Vijay regretted the slow expansion of the Christian faith. 'These people', he spread his palms out generously to encompass the trainload, 'have no self-respect, no creativity, no efficient administration. They made good slaves and bad masters. That is why we prospered under British rule. They were good masters, fair, just, vigorous, got many things done. We have none of their style today.' I modestly disclaimed any part in the Raj. Above me, four men were playing cards on one berth, and on the upper berth a tiny dark woman breastfed her infant. Opposite, in my view, a portly guard off-duty till we came to Sholapur snored amid the deafening arguments of two women, each clutching a boy of six or seven who alternately howled and sulked.

Vijay beamed at me: 'I have never seen anyone so calm when their seat was not free. No Indian, no foreigner would ever behave like that.' 'Everywhere a smile will achieve more than a curse,' I answered with the sententiousness expected by a choirmaster, 'and if I count to ten, I have lost interest in anger before I reach seven and a half.' I did not say that the only chance a Western man has to observe Indian women in close-up would be in precisely such situations, which I wanted to be worked out without my arrogant intervention. I prefer not to interfere, and to watch them in all moods from coquetry to petulance, taciturnity to slumber. Cackling and gabbling, restless and candid, they seem totally incapable of controlling their children: no cultural pattern farther from the Japanese could be imagined.

I lost Vijay in the colossal racket of Daund station, where a reviving Nescafé partly compensated for the loss of my forthright friend. Two hours later, at Kurduwadi, I leant out from the window to buy a two-minute omelette from a vendor with a loaf of bread and a kerosene stove. He cracked a couple of eggs into a strangely distorted frying-pan, tossing them like a pancake when half-done: the omelette actually caught fire some of the time before being rescued, folded inside a slice of bread, and passed through the window. I bought a mango-juice packet from a boy on the train, and a pack of five bananas wrapped in old newspaper. At the station bookstall I bought the Central and Western Railway timetable, and turned to the regulations. 'One TV set/one tricycle for child/one musical instrument is permitted to be carried as personal luggage per passenger', but if each passenger availed, as the saying is, even balancing his euphonium on his TV set while sitting aside a tricycle too small for him, the whole service would collapse. There are further pitfalls for 'unbooked dog'. 'Unbooked dog in first class or A/C class will be charged 60 kg × six times the luggage rate for entire journey, minimum Rs 50/-. Unbooked dog in II class A/C chair car will be charged 30 kg × six times the the luggage rate for entire journey, minimum Rs 50/-.' If I had a dog weighing 60 kg that insisted on travelling first class and refused to book ahead, my instinct would be to disown him to any inquisitive ticket inspector. But then, presumably even the largest inspector would back off, gibbering and failing to implement the injunction 'Dog will be removed to break-van for remaining journey.'

Sholapur
We arrived in Sholapur exactly on time at 10.45 p.m., and I staggered, slow and heavy with fatigue, to the nearest hotel, the inaptly-named Maharaja, where clients incessantly kept ringing room-bells for service, and I emerged from a fitful sleep to find what I thought to be a bottle-smashing party was in fact no more than a waiter in the corridor putting bottles down and picking others up.

I woke at seven to orange sunlight muscling in through barred windows, and pondered with relish the day ahead, and then the rest of my uncertain life, mysterious of course like yours, eccentric, so many sparks from a catherine wheel. I admired old balconied houses near the Maharaja, then ambled into breakfast at the Rajdhani ('our cook has not come') then at the Hotel Vikram Palace, 29 Railway Lines, the dearest inn in town, at Rs 176 for an air-

Sholapur. Old houses near Hotel Maharaja

conditioned single-room. The morning paper announced the Prime Minister Mr Chandra Shekhar's amazement that despite forty years of planning, thousands of Indian villages were still without drinking water and 60% of the population lived in abject poverty. I swallowed my hot coffee guiltily, paid for it, and hailed an auto-rickshaw for the fort. Once the walls of Sholapur extended four km around the old city but, as the population rose, walls were hacked down in 1872–3 and now only fragments remain. But the fort has been splendidly preserved by turning it – like Pune's Shanwar Wada – into a public garden, here with a zoo (chital and Assam monkeys) and an aviary (doves and peacocks) as well as trim hedges and tall, dusty palms assailed by pollution from the dense traffic outside. The outer wall dates from the 14th century, but the impressive inner wall with its four massive square towers from the 17th. I emerged from the gardens to walk round the citadel, and found the First Church of Sholapur in full Marathi voice, past a stall purveying Bibles and

66

prayer books, Biblical pictures, cassettes and videotapes. But the citadel wall stopped short by a dam, with a well from which fair dusky maidens were drawing water, and bare-chested men were dipping in the dam by stone steps. The fort is surrounded by water on all sides; it never really woke up from its bad dream of surrendering to the British under General Pritzler in 1818, the year he took Sinhagarh. A very small salmon-pink, pastel-green, pastel-blue Hindu temple is set gingerly beside the waters.

The Coastal Road

In *South India: Tamil Nadu, Kerala, Goa*, I described the sea voyage from Bombay to Goa. The land journey through Konkan, the coastal strip west of the Western Ghats, has its own appeal, if you do not object to the switchback effect of crossing ridges and valleys. Leaving Goa, laterite walls hem fields in such a way as dry-stone walling protects the Derbyshire Dales, but this is a land of coconut palms and patient oxen. Water buffalo are led uncomplaining to their labours. At the police outpost of Patradevi, cockerels competed in their racket and in their earnest foraging with rampant crows. 'Please ignore touts' said a Goan notice, implying that Maharashtra has none to be ignored.

Our bus honked its dogged way through Kudal, Kankavali, and Talera, where no warring dynasty had left its mark. Rural India, timeless and traditional, wakes at dawn and goes to bed at dusk as it has always done. The cycle of the seasons, the monsoon, credits and moneylenders, festivals and weddings: these are the talk of farmers and tenants, wives and children. North of Talera a potter stood with his clay bowls and dishes beneath a weeping banyan, his cart in the shade. By twelve noon our bus from Mapusa was entering Hatkamba, with its vistas towards a gently undulating brown horizon, its sturdy groves of green trees, and its blocks of cow dung drying in the midday sun. We lunched simply off boiled rice and talis at Hotel Alankar, just outside Hatkamba. Nocil's few white houses dozed in the siesta at three while the agrochemical factory produced fertilisers, then at 3.40 I made out a straggle of women washing in the river south of Kajati, and spreading their white clothes and bedlinen on the bank. Four o'clock and school was out at Kajati: girls in fresh white blouses and blue skirts crossed a dyke from their school to the main road between ricefields.

S. N. Pendse's novels of liberation, progress, and feminism are the 20th-century equivalent of H.N. Apte's neo-Dickensian Marathi novels which brought secular realism and humanist values into a literature then steeped for better or worse in vague religious sentiment. Pendse set his Marathi novels on the coast of Konkan roughly midway between Bombay and the port of Ratnagiri, around Dapoli and Bankot. Heavily regionalised, like the Sicilian works of Pirandello, Lampedusa, or Sciascia, the novels of Pendse act out inexorable destiny amid red, rocky landscapes where tenacious trees are buffeted by sea winds, monsoon torrents wash away carefully-tended soil, and its dry dusty season becomes furnace-hot. Social conflicts arise because the vested interests, such as Anna Khot's in *Wild Bapu of Garambi* (1952; translated by Ian Raeside, 1969), are challenged from time to time by forces such as Bapu Samal for social change, female rights, and liberation from caste controls. There could be no

Talera. A village potter with his wares

better preparation for afternoons wandering around the villages near Dapoli, where you will come across many folk like Bapu's father Vithoba.

'. . . There would be two or three village feasts every year, and then Vithoba was always well in evidence. He would pour out the water, churn milk, turn the crusher to make sweet fillings, and draw the powder-designs: rangolis. He was best at serving rows of guests. Every so often the women might forget a helping of chutney and pickles, but Vithoba? Never!'

The bus to Bombay dropped me off at Poladpur, home of a leprosy hospital, where I picked up a minibus to ascend the last 28 km to Mahabaleshwar.

Mahabaleshwar
Every hill station in India differs from the rest: in Maharashtra, Matheran may lie only 80 km east of Bombay, but as a hill station its proximity to the city is offset by its lesser altitude (around 2500 feet) compared with the average 4500

feet of Mahabaleshwar. Lonavla and adjacent Khandala provide alternatives nearly as close to Bombay as Matheran, and are generally not so crowded. The season at all these resorts runs from October to May, with much higher density at weekends. Don't think about Mahabaleshwar in the rainy season; it averages between 200 and 300 inches a year, while neighbouring Panchgani averages about 75 inches.

A Colonel Lodwick, later General, takes the palm as the first European to climb these hills. Clambering around, the story goes, with a walking-stick and one dog, Lodwick felt so exhilarated that he sent a letter extolling these cool and scenic heights to the *Bombay Courier*: now his prescience is rewarded with a monument on Lodwick Point, a western lookout from which a pathway leads 13 km southwest of the town to Pratapgarh, one of the magnificent hill-forts associated with Shivaji.

Sir John Malcolm took the hint and in 1828 established a sanatorium for the sick and a resort for the healthy by acquiring the land from the Raja of Satara in lieu of other territory. 'Boy' Malcolm, as he was called, relished hunting for tiger and other game so much that the new town was originally named Malcolmpeth in his honour.

Jonathan Duncan, Governor of Bombay from 1795 to 1811, had been a splendid choice for the job: of an upright, careful, incorruptible character not prone to display or arrogance. Sir John Kaye's *Administration of the East India Company* speaks of Duncan's having been 'Brahmanised by long residence in India', a condition familiar to many old India hands. Mountstuart Elphinstone, Governor of Bombay from 1819 to 1827, saw to the codification of the laws and fostered education, emphasising the rôle that Indians must be given despite the paternalism then fashionable. Where Duncan had been a plain man of simple tastes, Elphinstone loved the classics, Italian and even Persian poetry, tempered always with a bout of pig-sticking and days out hunting in the field.

Malcolm provided the same curious British contrast. 'We had glorious hunting and shooting – thirty-one hogs slain in the last two days by the spears of our party'. Yet he would spend most of every day from public breakfast to social dinner cooped up to wrestle with roads and telegraphs, tax-collecting and economic reform. This bluff, humorous, energetic, just and high-spirited man who once served as a Persian interpreter found the leisure to write a *Sketch of the Political History of India since 1784*, a *History of Persia* (2 vols., 1815), and *A Memoir of Central India* (2 vols., 1823). To this soldier-poet we owe the foundation of Mahabaleshwar, with detached summer villas called Locksley Hall, Brighton Park, Barchester, Glengarry or Ivanhoe.

Roads are connected by rides: Duchess Ride between Strawberry Gardens and Duchess Road; Lamington Ride between Blue Valley Road and Satara Road, with 'coolie paths' between.

Old Mahabaleshwar nestles around the source of the holy Krishna River, with a temple to Krishna known locally as Panchganga ('Five Rivers', the others being Gayatri, Savitri, Koyna and Yenna). A gnarled, crouching Hindu of about sixty-five with glittering black eyes and a slender stick three times his bent height, waved me towards the temple. The earliest shrines here must date back to prehistory, but Krishnabai in its present form is attributed to Singhan, a Yadava king ruling from Devagiri in the 13th century, then restored first by Chandra Rao More of Jaoli in the late 16th century, later by Shivaji himself in

1635, by Shahu (1670–1709) and lastly by the 19th-century banker Parashuram Angal.

My friend Z. R. Irani had no time for local myths, but interpreted the old legend, as the crouching figure repeated it in hope of baksheesh. On this site many yugas ago Lord Brahma was performing ascetic self-mortification or yagna with the gods Vishnu and Mahesh, and his junior consort Gayatri, but forgot to wait for his senior consort Savitri. When Savitri arrived, her fury knew no bounds, and she transformed them into rivers, but not before they retaliated, turning her into a water-course as well. Vishnu became the river Krishna and began to flow east, Mahesh became the Koyna and started to flow south, Brahma became the Yenna and started to flow east then south, and the Gayatri and Savitri flowed westward from the sources even now called Gayatri Point on the way to Arthur's Seat. It doesn't matter that the Krishna doesn't have its source here at all, or that the river Solshi descends Blue Valley eastward from Helen's Point. What matters is the sonority of the ancient names, the resonance of myths that tower above the actual waterfalls like yeti-anecdotes above a Tibetan village. Fear and trembling are part of the human condition: they put us back in our place, humbling us properly as vassals in the dominion of the ecosphere. Malcolm did more than recognise a watering-place, with spring flowers at Lingmala more sensational than Grampian heather: he recognised a mountain sanctified by its glorious beauty, from the 2500-foot drop at Elephant's Head to the awesome sunrise from the huge bare rock called Wilson Point, highest point in the town justly named 'The Place of Almighty God'.

Not far from Krishnabai Temple is Hanuman Mandir said to be a resting-place of the saint and mystic Rama Dasa in 1635, the Sri Rama Temple, and the Mahabal Temple sponsored by Raja Shahu's banker Parashuram Angal. Lord Shiva is worshipped here in the form not of a carved lingam but a natural rock about a spring. These temples in Old Mahabaleshwar are reached from a turning right off Elphinstone Point Road approaching from Duchess Road, after passing Dingley Dell on your right.

Believe it or not hunting is still licensed, and leopard, tiger and panther are all reported in the vicinity from time to time, not to mention wild pigs and sambhar. Meandering horse-rides along well-trodden paths cut across motor roads here and there, but generally remain unspoilt.

When Pune becomes impossibly hot in May, everyone tries to get away to Mahabaleshwar. During the Raj a versifier calling himself 'Momos' pointed up the contrast between the two towns:

> The Ladies of Mahableshwar
> Have strawberries for tea,
> And as for cream and sugar
> They add them lavishly;
> But Poona! oh, in Poona
> Their hearts are like to break
> For while the butter's melting
> The flies eat up the cake.

The Ladies of Mahableshwar
In wraps and furs delight,
And often get pneumonia
'Neath blankets two at night;
But Poona! oh, in Poona
The gauziest wisps appal,
And ladies sleep (they tell me)
With nothing on at all.

The Ladies of Mahableshwar
In such sweet charms abound
That doctors say their livers
Are marvellously sound;
But Poona! oh, in Poona
They nag and scold all day,
And contradict their husbands
Until they fade away.

In Raj days before the car came to Maharashtra, the journey from Pune was taken by train as far as Vathar, then uphill by tonga or carriage drawn by horses owned mostly by Parsis, who changed animals at Panchgani, while the travellers rested under casuarinas in fresh breezes. Servants would be sent on to set up their tent encampment and unpack. Government bungalows could be used only by senior officials, and the local hotels were generally considered at that time *infra dig.*

I stayed at the Grand Hotel, among quiet gardens behind Madhu Sagar, where I tasted various brands of honey. Jambul honey is collected in March (their leaflet recommends it against 'cough, cold, diabetes'), Hirda honey in April (to treat 'constipation and gas'), and Gella honey in May ('for eyes and brain tonic'). Madhu Sagar also markets jams made from local strawberries, raspberries, pineapple, mangoes, oranges and apples, and runs a beekeeping museum.

The Grand is in fact extremely modest and quiet, being current holder of the Best-Kept Garden prize in Mahabaleshwar. 'Kindly observe these timings' suggested the notice-board: Bed tea 6.30–7.30, running hot water 7–10 a.m., breakfast 8–9.30, lunch 12.30–2.30, evening tea 4.30–5.30, tombola 7–8.30 and dinner 8.30–10.30. My room no. 10 with its own verandah would have been perfect except for the perpetual din of loud pop music from loudspeakers arranged so that peace was made equitably impossible throughout the grounds.

I headed past the Hotels Shalimar and Satkar uphill towards the bazaar, that pulsing heart of all Indian towns. A muaddin called the Muslim faithful in the distance, then beyond Paradise Hotel and Shreyas Hotel (Vegetarian) I came upon Treacher's the Chemist's, Wines, Provisions by the bus station. A cordial colonel with a moustache invited me to the Hindu Gymkhana Club (there is a Parsi equivalent) for cards, lawn tennis, skating, billiards or table tennis, but I denied my English inheritance as a games-player and bought instead postcards of Yenna Lake and golf-course, sunset at Bombay Point, and a dizzying view from Pratapgarh.

In the bazaar generous stall-vendors offered sample channa (nuts) and chikki (a sweet sticky with popcorn) to tempt purchase of a bagful. Women on their haunches sat motionless by shallow round baskets of tiny strawberries and raspberries nearly black in hue.

'Here, mister, fine quality walking-stick cherry wood only seventy-five rupees.' Could I have been walking that slowly? At last I reached Zavare Rustam Irani's Imperial Stores, originally built for service familes when Mahabaleshwar served Britain's garrison town of Pune. Inside the store I found the old address: 92 Dr Salim Road. Parsis like Zavare may be in a diminishing minority, but Maharashtra can be considered their last refuge in a world inimical to the faith of Zarathustra. His great-grandfather Gilan Irani fled from Bandar Abbas in Iran, bringing with him his son Sorabji, who settled first in Pune, then moved upstation. Zavare's father Rustam Sohrab Irani flourished, so now Imperial Stores is the best supermarket in town, strategically placed for bus stand or bazaar. I took a Chinese meal in the Meghdoot Restaurant, which also offered Gujarati and Mughlai cuisine, then chatted in the Petit Club with the Librarian, while youngsters played table-tennis in the next room. Yellowing

Mahabaleshwar. Bazaar

newspapers have a sparse readership, and the bookstock is seldom replenished, but an air of dogged good humour and denominational tolerance dignifies this home of books. The budget for book purchase in the 1989–90 financial year had been set at Rs 20,000, or well under a thousand pounds, to cover not only newspapers and magazines but new books in English, Marathi, Gujarati and Hindi. It is hardly surprising that the Petit Library, founded in 1901, still stocks Green's *History of the English People*, Kipling's *Stalky & Co*, Lord Lytton's *Ernest Maltravers* and Debrett's *Peerage* for 1874. The Parsi founder, the Hon. Bomanji Petit, would have been touched that his foundation still existed ninety years on, but might well have been disappointed that its progress had been so hampered by shortage of funds, space and modern techniques such as air conditioning or bibliographical control.

Next morning I found Christ Church (1842), with its stained glass blinking in deft morning light, and the mosque, the Mahabaleshwar Club (1882) of which the library forms a part, and the Wheat Rust Station off Sassoon Road.

I enjoyed boating on Yenna Lake, but the serene pleasures of hiking and riding I shall never forget: finding that Reay Villa is now the Savoy Hotel, finding that Arthur's Seat (named for Arthur Mallett, whose wife and child drowned in the river below) had collapsed in 1973, climbing to Connaught Peak, with its view over Yenna Lake and Krishna Valley. I discovered Morarji Castle, where Mahatma Gandhi stayed in 1945, near the Red Castle, nowadays Bharat Lodge Hotel. Between the golf links and Yenna Lake I found cemeteries for Hindus (north side of Temple Road) and Parsis (south side). I even managed to identify Mount Malcolm, the Old Government House (off Satara Road) built in 1829 but converted to a private estate in 1868.

Pratapgarh

From Mahabaleshwar, you can trek across country to Shivaji's hill-fort of Pratapgarh; by groaning bus it can take an hour to cover the 22 km by road to the foot of the outcrop. The story begins at a hill-fort called Shivner 80 km north of Pune, near the town of Junnar. It looks like any rocky outcrop now, from the dusty main road, but it was a Hinayana Buddhist centre in the early centuries A.D. and you can see dozens of hermit cells on the eastern face to this day. The fort was assigned in 1599 to Shivaji's grandfather Maloji of the Bhonsla dynasty, and it was here in 1627 that the future Maratha leader was born. A curtain wall protects Shivner on three sides: on the western flank it is shielded by four gates and a moat now dry. Within the walls three tanks supplied fresh water to a besieged defence, and a mosque dates from Mughal occupation in the 1630s when Aurangzeb, governing Deccan for his father Shah Jahan, felt obliged to seize independent sultanates such as Bijapur, Gulbarga and Bidar. Aurangzeb had already taken other hill-forts such as Purandhar (32 km SE of Pune) and Sinhagarh (20 km SW of Pune).

So whether you have a chance to see Shivner or have to be satisfied with the above description, Pratapgarh will evoke the hundreds of forts that Shivaji built or strengthened to dominate the road system of his empire, even to the extent of levelling hills nearby if they looked as though they might threaten his imposing eyries. Shivaji lived in thrall throughout his life to a double oath: to win back what he considered Maratha lands for the Marathis against usurping

Mughals from the North; and to reinstate India's native Hinduism against what he believed to be the alien intrusion of Islam. Another great fort, Rajgarh (Royal Fort), rises 50 km SW from Pune and formed Shivaji's rocky capital and military headquarters from 1648 (when he was crowned there) until his death here in 1680. In 1670 he was crowned 'Lord of the Umbrella' or Chhatrapati, a quasi-divine epithet, but by then he had become widely detested by his enemies for his demand of 25% tribute: the dreaded *chauth* of revenues due from subject lands. Where his levied *chauth* was denied him, his troops arrived like so many claps of thunder, pillaging and seizing goods and chattels in lieu of money 'owed'. If you visit Rajgarh nowadays you walk (or are carried on dolis) up the 1400 steps in the afternoon, and then have to stay the night, to avoid the heat of the day, in a modest rest-house.

Pratapgarh is much easier of access, however, being close to Mahabaleshwar with its comfortable hotels and with only 500 steps much easier to climb up though, as it wearies in noon heat, it is best conquered in early morning or mid-afternoon, when the light is gentler, and you can pick out distant ridges. A double bank of fortifications is supported by corner bastions. The rounded main gate, or maha darwaza, towers up with vertical slits. The Tomb of Afzal Khan (1969), with a pantiled roof, is situated below the fort, and commemorates the Muslim general of Bijapur induced here by Shivaji under feigned truce then murdered by Shivaji's treacherous steel claw or 'wagnakh'. Muslims hold a memorial service every January or February (depending on the Islamic calendar) at the darga of Afzal Khan. Pandit Nehru not only unveiled a statue to Shivaji in 1957, but was indirectly responsible for the new road that year leading to the foot of the fort through thick forest.

The lower fort has a temple to Bhavani (a local name for the goddess Parvati) which Shivaji built in the religious emergency of being unable to visit the Bhavani temple at Tuljapur, in the last decade of the 17th century. Pratapgarh's windswept Bhavani temple possesses a pair of lantern pillars as rugged and unexpected as Gaudi improvisations in Barcelona.

On the northern and western flanks the foot rises sheer above vertical precipices of more than seven hundred feet. To the east and south, by contrast, the slopes are forested as if Birnam wood had camped near Dunsinane. The upper fort has a temple to Mahadeva, as Lord Shiva is known here; you can still see vestiges of residential buildings and barracks for Shivaji's army against Muslim foes. I had brought with me as a kind of atmospheric talisman a hymn of creation from the Rigveda. Possibly the martial Shivaji would never have learnt these words, in a Vedic language related to classical Sanskrit much as Homeric Greek relates to classical or Attic Greek as written by Plato or Sophocles. But as I hear the verbal majesty of the *Odyssey* on reaching Ithaca, so I respond at Pratapgarh's windy, rocky heights to the first verse of the hymn as much as to the last, with its poignant admission of human ignorance in the face of cosmic creation. We think we 'know', but as the boundaries of knowledge extend ever farther, all our past religious, scientific and philosophic theories flee behind us like the Earth behind Voyager to Saturn.

Nasad asin, no sad asit tadanim;
nasid rajo no vioma paro yat.
Kim avarivah? Kuha? Kasya sarman?
Ambhah kim asid, gahanam gabhiram?

Pratapgarh, near Mahabaleshwar

Nothing then was or was not;
neither air on Earth nor Heaven.
What was concealed? Where? In whose keeping?
Was there first water, unfathomable, deep?

. . . . .

Iyam visrstir yata ababhuva;
yadi va dadhe yadi va na:
yo asyadhyaksah parame vioman
so anga veda, yadi va na veda.

Whence this creation came,
whether it was begun or not,
he who in the uttermost heaven surveys it,
he only knows, or else he does not know.

I sat on the brink of a precipice and envisaged the astonishment of painters
like Turner or John Martin at such a majestic expanse of crags and more softly-
rounded mountains misting in the distance pink-grey. Martin would have added
a horde of tiny people, disproportionately diminished to enhance the sublime
grandeur of the landscape. Turner would have feverishly limned every subtly
shifting hue, knowing in his heart the frustration of the greatest artists that
nothing will ever really *do*. Nothing can replace the physical frisson of sitting
here, on the rugged heights here at Pratapgarh, or at Rajgarh, as if one were

a hostage to marauding Marathas but no – I recalled that when in 1664, Shivaji attacked Surat, that prosperous Mughal seaport with its British, Dutch and French factories, many townspeople were tortured before death. Shivaji's way did not include the expensive maintenance of hostages.

Panchgani
The first hill-town you reach from Mahabaleshwar on the Pune road is Panchgani, an idyllic mountain retreat far from the noise of Pune and the endless metropolitan hustle of Bombay here in Krishna Valley, where the waters of Dhom Dam keep farms and rice-fields irrigated all the year round. The climate is dry, bracing and cool, though the views are not as spectacular as in Mahabaleshwar, except from Tableland with a panorama of Panchgani itself, Parsi Point to reveal the sweep of the valley, and Sidney Point, from which the distant town of Wai can be observed at the foot of these high ghats. Panchgani is a healthy setting for expensive schools, and for the Moral Rearmament Training Centre established here in 1965 by Rajmohan Gandhi, nephew of the Mahatma, which incorporates model farms with Maharashtra's first pure-bred Jersey herd and experimental tree-planting.

At Wai, the heat of the plains takes your breath away, but banyans lining the roads give shelter and shade to the slow traffic, such as bullock-carts, pedestrians, or cyclists. The Krishna Irrigation Project has visibly enhanced crop levels in recent years. Then the bus breathed a sigh of relief as it made its final jolt off the minor road from Wai and on to the major highway linking Pune with Satara and Kolhapur.

Satara
A comfortable eight-hour busride from Bombay Central bus station, Satara lies a good way from the nearest rail halt, called Satara Road, on the Pune-Miraj section of the South-Central Railway. The town itself is a typical Maharashtran hill town, dominated by a great fort, in this case Ajinkyatara (1192), open to the public except for the Low Power TV Relay Centre inaugurated in 1988. A spectacular vantage point, Ajinkyatara has little within it, so I headed out by auto-rickshaw for the majestic Sajjangarh Fort, wrested at the end of the 17th century from Maratha control by the Emperor Aurangzeb, who was content to take the strongholds one by one, by a process of attrition.

Sajjangarh towers on its rocky outcrop like a fabled Arthurian fortress, and created a formidable challenge for besiegers. The first gateway is reached at the 137th step (there are no doli-bearers for the infirm), the second gateway at the 177th, and the third at the 227th. Sajjangarh is now the home of Ramdas Swamiji temple, and next to it is shown the Swami's original home, with memorabilia of his times with Shivaji, from their first meeting in 1649 to the guru's initiation of the soldier-king in 1674 and Shivaji's abandonment of his regalia in 1679. 'Ramdas' simply means the servant of Lord Rama: the poet-saint's given name was Narayan Suryaji Thosar, but he received a vision of Lord Rama after his father's death, refused marriage, and began the life of meditation and wandering that produced three books of a new Marathi *Ramayana* and the 205 verses addressed to Mind which he called *Manobodha*, translated in an English version available at the temple.

The former royal family is descended from Shahu, Shivaji's grandson, whose dignified Palace or Rajwada is now a complex of law courts and Range Forest Offices. Shahu's wooden Durbar Hall, with a throne-podium at one end, has silent fountains and low scribes' desks, unoccupied while I was there because of a government holiday. Inquisitive faces peered down at me from the former zenana, on the upper floor, but I sidled away from old Maratha ghosts, to visit the small Shivaji Museum (10.30–5.15, closed Mondays), with a hero stone and cannon in the front garden, facing the bus station.

The British took Satara in 1818, but by then it had witnessed siege and massacre, successful defence and overnight betrayal in common with all the other hill-forts of Maharashtra. Shivaji took Satara in 1673 after a long siege, and his son Raja Ram made it his capital in 1698. The following year Aurangzeb determined to eradicate Pryagji Prabhu and his Maratha hordes for all time and pitched camp on the north and north-east. His forces under Tarbiyat Khan invested the fort from the east, Shirzi Khan from the south, and the Emperor's son Azam Shah from the west. Pryagji's position seemed lost, and yet . . .

And yet Shivaji's man Parshuram Trimbak had from beyond the lines procured the treachery of Aurangzeb's own son, and ensured supply lines into Ajinkyatara. Mining operations under Tarbiyat Khan took nearly five months; the first mine partially succeeded, causing some rock to fall inwards and bury some of the Maratha defenders, including Pryagji who – however – was pulled out alive to great acclamation. The second mine exploded rock over two thousand of the attacking forces and Azam Shah no longer guaranteed a lifeline

Satara. Rajwada, now a law court

of provisions. His plans for surrender were accepted by Pryagji and the Emperor, who never learned of his son's treason, and renamed the fort 'Azamtara' in his son's honour. The Mughals held their new prize for only a very few years before it was fittingly lost again by treachery. On two giggling young girls from Bombay all such dark associations were lost in the generous Maharashtran afternoon sun. Chipmunks raced along cracked, overgrown walls in emulation of their inconsequential chatter. I listened in my mind's ear to Olga's opening aria from Tchaikovsky's *Eugene Onegin*:

> Zachem vzdikhat', kogda shastlivo
> moyi dni yuniye tekut?
> Ya bezzabotna i shalovliva,
> menya rebonkom vsye zovut!

> Why sigh, when full of happiness
> my youthful days flow gently by?
> I am carefree and playful;
> they call me still a child!

Mahuli

Five km east of Satara stands a complex of temples of no great antiquity, but characteristic of sanctuaries set in rural tranquillity: it is near Mahuli that the Krishna joins the Yenna. They are of 17th–18th century date, and honour the chhatris or cenotaphs of the former royal family of Satara, who come from Shivaji's stock. The oldest temple is that to Sangameshvara, Shiva as lingam at the confluence of two or more rivers (1679), and the largest to Vishveshvara, Lord of the Universe, Shiva as lingam (1735). Others are dedicated to Rameshvara and Bholeshvara, and all bear the distinctive elements such as towers with fluted domes, with two-storey mandapams. Separate pavilions sacred to Shiva's mount Nandi are likewise towered.

Mahuli hill-fort (like Gingee in Tamil Nadu) has three summits of varying height: Mahuli takes the palm, with Bhandargarh to the south and Palasgarh to the north slightly lower, their basalt sides sheer and black like enormous panthers. Mahuli seems to have been left alone by victorious besiegers, unlike Bhoj's 12th-century Panhala fort, which the British chose to destroy in 1844. The mosque here at Mahuli persuades some scholars that the fort is of Mughal origin, but these heights must have surely been defended long before Muslim incursions south from Delhi.

On my way from Mahuli I heard the piping double whistle of the greenbacked, orange-breasted Indian pitta. Sambhar, camouflaged by the denuded brown hills in the distance, grazed for safety in groups, sniffing air for the slightest danger. On telegraph wires crested larks presented their song to the narrow strip of road in a wide barren landscape.

Kolhapur

I could cheerfully have spent a week roaming Kolhapur, yet it seldom appears in any book devoted to aspects of India, presumably because it has neither the world renown of Ajanta nor the population of Bombay; it lacks the eccentricity of Pune's Osho Commune or Panchgani's MRA utopia. Yet for lovers of Indian antiquities its museum preserves precious relics from the prehistoric and historic site of Brahmapuri, and for lovers of Indo-Saracenic architecture it preserves some of the most remarkable achievements of 'Mad' Mant, of the Royal Engineers.

First to Brahmapuri Hill, which as the name indicates is the place where local Brahmins are cremated; nearby in the Rani's Garden, the ruling family were cremated. Excavations on Brahmapuri Hill have produced finds from Satavahana times, including contemporary Roman Empire artefacts, such as a 2nd-century copper Perseus and Andromeda of Alexandrian workmanship now in Kolhapur's Town Hall Museum. A local bronze 'Family riding an elephant' there provides a dazzling insight into trade routes suddenly juxtaposed, like objects in Nara's Shoso-in from trans-Asiatic silk routes. We know of Kolhapur's existence as early as the 3rd century B.C., after Chalcolithic man had cleared jungles in the first half of the first millennium B.C., just as we know of other towns in Maharashtra at the same period: Chaul and Sopara on the coast, and inland Karad, Ter, Kalyan, Junnar, Nasik, Nevasa, Paithan, and in the north of the state Prakash, Bahal, Pitalkhora, Bhokardah, Kaundinyapur, Paunar, and Pauni. Interestingly, of all these ancient sites only Ter (ancient Tagara) on the river Terna in Osmanabad district and Brahmapuri have yielded imports other than coins and bullae. A Satavahana-period house in Brahmapuri has provided as many as 37 metal objects, including Indian hanging lamps, toy carts, vessels of various kinds, and a figure of Poseidon, or Neptune, whose trident appears today at pilgrimage sites all over India as sadhu-borne emblems of Lord Shiva.

Kolhapur's first mediaeval temple is that devoted to the town's tutelary goddess Amba Bai, in Hinduism an aspect of Durga, but in prehistory the mother goddess herself. A priest within called it Maha Lakshmi. Some of its 10th-century foundations survive, but the tall tower is of 18th-century date. The outstanding feature is the panelled ceiling of the columned mandapam: Vishnu as overlord of the eight directions, from north clockwise Kubera, Ishana, Indra, Agni, Yama, Nirriti, Varuna and Vayu. Kolhapur became the capital of a princely state when it was given to Shivaji's younger son Raja Ram in 1689, and only lost capital status to Satara for a time in 1698.

Modern buildings festoon Kolhapur deliriously, because as in Madras, Calcutta and Bombay, nobody really knew how to design buildings that would be appropriate for India, with its eclectic heritage of Hindu, Buddhist, Jain and Islamic traditions; its extremes of climate from Darjeeling to Pondicherry; and its necessity to house modern services such as city administration with utilities such as airconditioning, electricity, and gas. Many designers have taken a course that begs the question, and end up confused; many more have opted for one end of the spectrum, and avoided trying to solve questions at the other end. Le Corbusier's Chandigarh says 'we must modernise'; Major Mant's New Palace at Kolhapur (1881) says 'we must compromise'. Nobody really knows what to do, even now. Meanwhile, we can see the 17th-century Old Palace, now law courts and police station, and find out how much of that (and of Dig and Mathura) inspired Charles Mant in his New Palace, completed in 1881 as the culmination of his Indo-Saracenic career which began in Kolhapur with the Public Library (1875), the Hospital (1878) and the High School (1880).

Kolhapur. Mahalakshmi Temple

The New Palace, still occupied in part by the former royal family, houses a museum in one wing nowadays, and there is a canteen, aviary, and beside the small lake a small zoo with antelope, emu, and spotted deer. Of course one removes footwear in all Indian temples, but Kolhapur requires the removal of shoes before entering both the Town Hall Museum and the New Palace Museum. In the current controversy dividing India between higher castes and the lower castes, for whom the Government hopes to assert positive discrimination in the job market, a major place of honour belongs to Sir Shahu I Chhatrapati (1884–1922), and his tutor, Stuart Fraser of the Indian Civil Service. Sir Shahu gave up the chance of an English university education to devote himself to the people of Kolhapur and to diminish the influence of the Karkan Brahmin priesthood, a task begun by taking into his own service educated non-Brahmins, building a leper asylum, mixing with all classes and castes, and arranging loans for poor peasants hitherto at the mercy of moneylenders. Such enlightenment preceded Gandhi's teachings, and gave hope to all Untouchables. He was succeeded in 1922 by Rajaram II, by Shivaji V (1942–6) and by Shahaji II (1947–83). The Durbar Hall still has its throne in place, its zenana gallery, and its stained-glass episodes from Maratha history captioned in English. An old-fashioned trophy gallery displays stuffed green pigeons, black rhino, brown bear, silver fox, Malabar squirrel, and bison.

By contrast, Charles Mant's Town Hall of 1872–6 – a mad quail preserved in aspic – recalls Venetian Gothic in taste, and remained a stylistic cul-de-sac: you cannot envisage any way forward from this bold experiment. You might be lucky enough to see wrestling in a stadium holding 20,000 people: Kolhapur's

Kolhapur. New Palace

total population does not currently exceed 300,000. East of Kolhapur a temple to Kotitirtha Mahadeva, an aspect of Lord Shiva, is picturesquely set in water. Back in the town I met a crowd emerging from a cinema, and wondered how many of them realised what they owed to Kolhapur-born Vanakudre Shantaram (1901–90), whose career spanned the era of Indian silent movies from 1913, social issues of the 1930s (when a feminist film help to promulgate an anti-dowry law in Bihar), his own silent movies from 1927 and within a year three talkies in Marathi. In 1934 his *Amrit Manthan* was made bilingually in Marathi and Hindi, urging nonviolence among India's many communities. His *Admi* depicted the tragedy of prostitution, while *Shakuntala* (1943) proved not only commercially successful, but became the first Indian film commercially released overseas. In the English-Hindi *Dr Kotnis-ki Amar Kahini*, Shantaram himself played the title rôle: a young Indian doctor working in China in 1939 to help war victims. The decline of Shantaram came with the trivialisation of the Indian film industry into violence, stereotypes, and banal song-and-dance routines: he too succumbed to such trends, but he will be remembered among dance enthusiasts for *Jhanak Jhanak Paayal Raje* on the Kathak dancer Gopi Krishna.

Arun Kolatkar, born in Kolhapur in 1932, has experimented with a range of poetic modes, including the bhakti style of the 17th-century Marathi poet Tukaram, whom he has translated. His best work that I have read is the occasionally sceptical *Jejuri* (1976), centred on a pilgrimage town 50 km south of Pune where the Dhangar tribe, largest of fifty nomadic tribes in Maharashtra, worship Lord Shiva in his aspect as Khandoba. Though they range mostly round Jejuri, the Dhangar move their sheep to the Sahyadris after the monsoon, returning to drier lowlands just before the rains. Some Dhangar have settled in and around Jejuri, mostly as farmers or weavers of woollen blankets.

Kolatkar has this epigram on Jejuri; the Chaitanya he names is a 15th-century Bengali saint worshipped by some as an incarnation of Lord Krishna:

'Sweet as grapes
are the stones of Jejuri,'
said Chaitanya.

He popped a stone
into his mouth
then spat out gods.

The Shalini Summer Palace (1934) on the edge of Rankala Lake has been worthily transformed into an hotel in the Ashok chain: I took a pot of tea in the Maharani suite (Room 212), basking in the lake view from its marble balcony. Stucco ceiling, four-poster bed, luxury bathroom, all for little more than a standard double room would cost at a Hilton in the U.S.A.

It was 8.45 a.m. on a Sunday morning and the bell was tolling for the nine o'clock service at All Saints' (1881), where Mr Peters of the Bible Study Group was talking to the minister. I studied the memorials: Col. H. N. Reeves, Political Agent, Kolhapur (1840–9); C. H. Candy, died in Kolhapur at the age of 74 in 1925; Col. Charles Wodehouse, Five Years Political Agent at Kolhapur. The minister confidently numbers the Christians of Kolhapur at 8,000 even today, and the Catholic Church of the Holy Cross next door swaggers dissonantly apart, yet close enough to huddle from the dreaded polytheists, those

Hindus . . . The Jesuit Fathers run St Xavier's High School near the New Palace.

My auto rickshaw-driver Vijay Khalkar from Pulevari took a cascaded glass of tea with me in the shadow of a banyan, then we found one of the leather-sandal manufacturers, New Rashtriya Leather Works, to inspect grades of quality: Kolhapuri chappals are famous throughout India.

As the great fort of Sajjangarh is to Satara, so the fort and hill-station of Panhala is to Kolhapur: 18 km away, so close enough for a half-day excursion, or a picnic lunch. Nearly 3,000 ft above sea level, the fort is always cool, and dates back to at last 1192, when Raja Bhoj II ruled there until 1209. The Adil Shahi dynasty of Bijapur conquered Panhala in 1489, but Shivaji seized it briefly in 1659 then again in 1673, relinquishing it to Mughal forces only from 1690 to 1707, when it reverted to the Marathas. As always in Maharashtran forts, full use has been made of the natural scarp, which is defended by a manmade wall at Panhala more than seven km long and three gates, of which two survive, the British having destroyed east-facing Char Darwaza (Fourfold Gate) during their siege of 1844. You can approach also by Tin Darwaza (Threefold Gate) in the western wall, or by Wagh Darwaza on the northern flank, both protected by guardrooms and massive doors. Inside, the older palace survives only in foundations, but the newer exists in two storeys. A massive Ganga Kothi was for storing grain, like two other storehouses in the citadel.

Pandharpur

The largest pilgrimage in Maharashtra is that to Pandharpur on the river Bhima, where processions from all over the state converge at the temple of Sri Vithoba, an aspect of Vishnu with two hands at his waist. There are four main pilgrimages in the year, of which the most important culminates on the 11th of the Hindu month of Ashadh (June-July). The temple is of 12th–13th century Yadava date, roughly contemporary with Yadava Devagiri to the north, but most of its present appearance is of the 17th–18th centuries, and hence of Maratha date. Its Late Deccani style decorations and domes are modified by Mughal-type many-lobed arches and lotus-based fluted columns.

The eleventh day of both waxing and waning moons is a day special to Warkaris, who pray and fast then, and are allowed only one light meal 'to keep body and soul together'. The Warkaris are a *bhakti* or devotional sect of Hindus drawn from all levels of society, who practise their religion while remaining within Hindu society and accepting its norms. To become a Warkari, S. V. Dandekar prescribes that each person 'should act according to his own caste and stage of life. But in the Kali Yuga (that is the present age) more is needed. So the way of devotion and remembrance of the names of God have been given in addition.' But a Warkari's most important duty is the twice yearly pilgrimage, for *wari* means 'coming and going' and the physical journey involving dedication and some degree of discomfort (even if you travel to Pandharpur by train instead of accompanying the palanquin on foot) must be undergone to enable the worshipper to acquire merit: without the pilgrimage – as G. A. Deleury remarks (*The Cult of Vithoba*, Pune, 1960) – there can be no Warkari.

Every Warkari while on pilgrimage is considered a *santa* or saint, and the company of saints travelling to Pandharpur includes all past saints, who are carried in palanquins represented by their traditional clogs or *padukas* fashioned in silver. The Pandharpur legend grew up around the figure of Pundalik, a prodigal son who repented his evil ways and became a model of filial respect. When Vishnu called for hospitality in the guise of Vithoba, Pundalik could not be distracted from massaging his father's feet longer than was needed for him to throw a brick for Vithoba to stand on, and Vithoba, instead of chastising the son for scant hospitality, so far appreciated the son's devotion to his father that the god can be found to this day, standing on that brick, in the leading temple of Pandharpur. Pundalik, on the other hand, is worshipped in an 18th-century shrine in the river Bhima and became an example of saints still worshipped in the Warkari tradition, from Dnyaneshvar and Tukaram, up to the recent sannyasi Gaj Maharaj (1876–1956), who traversed the villages of Maharashtra to preach against untouchability, idolatry, alcohol and meat-eating. It is worth mentioning that the great Kshatriya leader Shivaji was a devotee of Sri Vithoba, who is thus as closely identified with Maharashtra as Sri Murugan is identified with Tamil Nadu.

The saint Dnyaneshvar is the author of the Gita commentary called after him *Dnyaneshvari* (*c*. 1290) and lyrical poems; because he came from Alandi, the main palanquin procession to Pandharpur begins at Alandi, but others come from Amaravati, Paithan, Saswad, Mahuli, and indeed from all over Maharashtra, much as the Muslim Haj receives pilgrims from all over the Islamic world. Only Ramadasa of all Maharashtran saints seems to have no particular association with Pandharpur. The songs and hymns of the saints have influenced Marathi literature so strongly that secular literature seems to have been stunted, and even Marathi films have been strongly predisposed to subjects connected with the saints. There have been Prabhat Studio film-biographies of Tukaram, Chokhamela, and Eknath, as well as Dnyaneshvar: their effect on actors and audience alike has been salutary, to the point where some actors carried out holy actions for the rest of their lives, so great was the impact of their work.

The sacred singer Tukaram (1598–1649) was a devotee of Vishnu-as-Vithoba, worshipped at Pandharpur. Tukaram spent some years as a grain merchant before renouncing the world. His thousands of religious songs or *abhang* could be heard as prayers perhaps, as visions in part, but however unfashionably naive they seem now, there is no doubt that they provided a great stimulus to the rise of Marathi consciousness under Shivaji.

Tukaram addresses Vithoba thus in one *abhang*:

> As a young bride gazes at her mother's home,
>   And must be dragged away;
> So my soul will always gaze at you,
>   That you and I shall meet today.

> Just as a child will scream, and cry and moan,
>   When its mother leaves it be;
> Just as fish is trawled up through the foam,
>   So, says Tuka, is the loss with me.

Pilgrimage in India from Tirupati to Badrinath, from Rameshwaram to Dwarka, from Madurai to Prayag, is a central fact of Indian life which western visitors often miss, for the places they visit (Udaipur, Ooty, Goa, Kashmir) tend to be scenically interesting or architecturally magnificent, without the spiritual dimension. But India runs on religion the way a truck runs on diesel, and if we are to figure out how India works beyond the intricacies of bureaucracy or modern industry, it is to Pandharpur (or Jejuri or Shirdi or Nasik) that we might come, since although a hundred thousand Warkaris might descend on the Bhima riverside twice a year, for much of the time the town is a quiet backwater of only 70,000 residents, unlike the permanent teeming hordes of Banaras, which only dull the senses by their huge numbers.

Hinduism holds sacred the number seven, with seven sacred rivers, seven sacred mountains, and seven sacred sites. The rivers are Ganges, Yamuna, Godavari, Saraswati, Narmada, Kaveri and Sindhu. The mountains cited in the *Mahabharata* as holy are the Raivataka, Vindhya, Sahya, Kumara, Malaya, Sri Parvata, and Pariyatra. The sacred cities are Ayodhya, Mathura, Maya (Hardwar), Kasi (Banaras), Kanchipuram, Avantika (Ujjain), and Dvaravati (Dwarka).

In fact, virtually all India's rivers and mountains are holy to local people and, as for sacred cities, there are more like seven hundred and seventy seven. Every place associated with saints, miracles, or the gods is considered holy, and perhaps we should do better to enter into the spirit of Hinduism and its early heresy Buddhism, and regard all life actual or potential as sacred, a view easily assimilated in Himachal Pradesh, for example, within sight of Nanda Devi, or at many Keralan places such as Guruvayur or Trichur. Wherever a rishi or guru treads, his footsteps make that passage holy, across fields, or on dusty paths across the length and breadth of Maharashtra.

Ahmadnagar

Muhammad III (1463–82), of the Bahmani dynasty of Deccan, died a victim of drink at the age of twenty-nine, and his son and later successors became pawns in the hands of unscrupulous ministers such as Malik Hasan. Hasan was the *éminence grise* behind the throne of Muhammad's twelve-year-old son Mahmud (1482–1518), who was held virtually a hostage until he caught Hasan in notable treachery and had him strangled by the Governor of Bidar. Malik Hasan's son Ahmad Nizam al-Mulk plotted with Yusuf Adil Khan of Bijapur (Karnataka) and Fathallah Imad al-Mulk of Berar, nowadays comprising the districts of Akola, Amaravati, Buldana and Yavatmal in north-eastern Maharashtra. In 1490 they assumed royal dignity and independence from Bidar, now in Karnataka. Qutb al-Mulk of Golconda in Andhra Pradesh followed in 1512, and Barid al-Mulk of the Barid Shahi dynasty broke away, leaving the Bahmani dynasty moribund.

The Portuguese seemingly left the Nizam Shahi dynasty to its own devices: the only state to reap such peculiar advantage. Presumably the Portuguese considered Ahmadnagar too far off to cause any great disturbance, yet it forms a significant node in communications west to Junnar and Bombay, south to Pune, and north to Aurangabad. Water for drinking and irrigation is assured by the river Sina. An insignificant settlement was overcome by Ahmad Nizam Shah in the early 1490s. We now see a typical Islamic town in Maharashtra full of 16th-century mosques and mausolea, the home of the unreliable historian Firishta, or Muhammad Qasim Hindu Shah Astarabadi (*c.* 1570-*c.*1630), whose

Gulshan-i Ibrahimi appeared in two recensions in the first decade of the 17th century.

The great age of Ahmadnagar ended in 1599, with its capture by Akbar's Mughal forces. Chand Bibi, wife of Ali Shah of Bijapur, was killed in the siege and her octagonal tomb is shown 9 km east of the city. Shah Aurangzeb died here in 1707 and his temporary resting-place is shown at the Alamgir Dargah. The Marathas then seized the city, and in 1803 it was taken by Wellesley in the Second Maratha War.

In Ahmad's reign, which ended in 1509, he devoted himself to building new mosques for the propagation of the faith in a land surrounded by a tide of Hinduism. The Qasim Mosque (1500–08), simple and unostentatious, does not bear comparison with the Lutfullah and other later Safavid mosques in Iran, but possesses its own austere integrity which those who know the early mosques of Jordan, Syria and Iraq will recognise as following the original architectural impulse, before grandiloquence took hold. We owe to a Turkish soldier, one Rumi Khan, the mosque called Makkah after four stone pillars allegedly deriving from that holy place; the Makkah mosque was probably started in the reign of Ahmad but completed rather later.

Ahmad Nizam Shah's mausoleum has a charming façade and a relatively well-preserved walled tomb well worth a quiet half hour. His successor Burhan I (1509–53) achieved little in the way of monumental architecture, though he encouraged a Shi'a college and mosque, the Husaini, with a dome and a madrasah clearly evidencing its Persian origin. Husain I (1553–60) initiated a major series of public works, in particular the fortress east of the city, with twenty-two great bastions around the walls, and the Farhad mosque. An account of his reign with his consort Khanzada Humayun is told in an unfinished Persian poem to be found in the Bharata Itihasa Samshodhaka Mandala (Pune). Twelve of the original 14 paintings survive: folio 58 illustrates the dohada theme, that is the blossoming of a tree at the touch of a woman both beautiful and chaste, a concept as old as Sanchi. The MS does not describe the king's death, so it may have been cut short in 1565, around the period of the small Damadi mosque, whose minarets begin to acquire greater decoration and finely carved stonework.

Husain was succeeded by Khanzada as regent, but in 1569 Murtaza I, her son, imprisoned her and his younger brother Burhan II, who escaped and fled to the comparative safety of Akbar's court in 1583. Burhan II served as a general in two unsuccessful campaigns against Berar (1585 and 1589) but with the aid of Ibrahim II of Bijapur he won back Ahmadnagar from his own son in 1591 in his early thirties. We can see him at this period in an exquisite miniature to be seen in Paris (Bibliothèque Nationale, supplément persan 1572, folio 26). A patron of learning and the arts, he had a splendid library pillaged by the Mughals when they seized the city in 1600 from the luckless Ahmad II. The sandalled ruler is offering gold to a prosperous courtier, and is the first Deccani portrait I know to show a face in three-quarter view. Two Ethiopian slaves – then much in demand throughout Deccan – are in attendance; the man waves a scarf in a fanlike movement seen also in the Pune *History of Husain* mentioned above, while the boy presents pan to the ruler. Similar Ethiopians, costumes and accessories are found in a miniature from the Polier collection now in the Staatliche Museen, Berlin, where an effeminate, drowsing prince is taking his 'Siesta' beneath a spreading plane tree. The Ahmadnagar prince concerned may be Murtaza II, placed on the throne by the *éminence grise* Malik Ambar in 1602 and put to death by the latter's son; Fath Khan, in 1630. The whole ambiance is so strikingly removed from Ahmadnagar today, shabby, dusty, and come down in the world like a sadhu covered with penitent ashes, that it demands a real imaginative effort to invoke hereabouts these gold ornaments, girdles and armbands, this opulent court life with black African slaves, these elegant maidens occupying their abundant leisure with garlands, songs and the long afternoon of the soul. But dusk fell in Ahmadnagar three hundred and fifty years back, and that fact can be adduced as an extra melancholy charm. The Amar Hotel seems mildly surprised as you turn up at the reception desk, and book in for an air-conditioned night's sleep.

Aurangabad

Routes from Bombay are via Nasik and Yeola or via Pune and Ahmadnagar. Regular low-priced tours (starting at 7 and 8 a.m.) go to Ajanta Caves and there is a packed day in the city, environs and Ellora (starting at 7.30, 8 and 9 a.m.) which includes Daulatabad Fort, the mausoleum called Bibi-ka Maqbara and Aurangabad's Caves, a historic watermill 3 km from the city, and the second tomb of Emperor Aurangzeb at Khuldabad, the first being at Ahmadnagar. I recommend the Ellora tour if you are pressed for time, but really Ajanta's extraordinary atmosphere calls for an overnight stay, preferably at the nearby Forest Rest House (reservable on tel. 4701), run by the Divisional Forest Officer, Osmanpura.

Aurangabad received its present name from the Emperor, whose wife Begum Rabi'a Durrani is buried in a Taj Mahal-like mausoleum commissioned by Prince Azam Shah, who briefly succeeded Aurangzeb in 1707. Just as Ahmadnagar is preëminently a 16th-century city, Aurangabad experienced its zenith in the 17th century, since when it has dreamed ineffectually of empire. Mughal power declined, so the city found itself a marginal addition to the territories governed by the Nizam of Hyderabad.

As Khidki, 'The Window' – towards Devagiri and Pratisthan – the city paid tribute to Ala ud-Din Khilji in the early 14th century, then fell to the Bahmani dynasty in 1347. When the Bahmani kingdoms disintegrated it came under the sway of Ahmadnagar, but avenging Mughal forces in the reign of Jahangir put it to fire and sword in 1612. Only slowly rebuilt, it was renamed for the illustrious, fanatical Mughal general who dreamed of annihilating Hinduism from Delhi south to Deccan.

We can divide our exploration of Aurangabad into the period before 1682 when the Mughal city walls were quickly thrown up to deter Maratha attacks, and the more settled period thereafter, ending in 1720 with the apotheosis of Shah Ganj Masjid, surrounded by shops on three sides in the great bazaar. In the Deccani heartland, Shah Ganj pronounces, Islam is overlord. The minarets declare 'La ilahu ill' Allah': there is no other god but God. From then on we have a British cantonment, as at Pune, Marathwada University, colleges and schools, a silk mill and offices, banks, and hotels, but secular architecture has nothing here to match the exhibitionism even of Kolhapur, much less Bombay.

Malik Ambar, the Ethiopian power behind the Nizam Shahi throne, was responsible for the Friday Mosque (*c.* 1610) with a usual ablutions tank in the courtyard and accommodation on three sides, much of it shaded by a great banyan. Aurangzeb enlarged the mosque at the end of the 17th century. Malik Ambar also sponsored another stone mosque inside Makkah Gate, which possibly antedates the Friday Mosque, and Naukonda Palace (1616), ruined now but still impressive with its hammam or bathhouse, public and private palaces and zenana or women's quarters. Mosque enthusiasts will urge auto-rickshaw drivers to Lal Masjid (1655) or Red Mosque, so called from its coat of paint over basalt; and Market Mosque (1665; ask for Chauki Masjid) with its double-minareted gateway and five onion domes.

The last great monument before Mughal fortifications gave Aurangabad its present form is the Mausoleum of the Empress, which emulates the greatest Mughal building in India, Taj Mahal, built in 1623–43 to honour the memory of Aurangzeb's mother Mumtaz Mahal by his father Shah Jahan. Begum Rabi'a, Aurangzeb's first wife, was immortalised here in 1678 by the architect Ataullah in a mausoleum which obviously has never had the acreage of praise devoted to it that its more illustrious predecessor rightly commands from every visitor. Dome and openwork screens are in marble, but elsewhere marble is intercalated with stone and brickwork in harmonious proportions. One finds oneself guiltily condemning Aurangzeb for parsimony, when one realises perfectly well that a good Muslim does not prize elegance and wealth above purity, simplicity, or humility. Thus the name of the deceased is properly not recorded on a grave-stone. But by what rationale can one justify the lack of humility shown by raising a memorial that will outlive wind and weather?

Bibi-ka Maqbara is open from sunrise to 10 p.m., but its floodlit evenings and dawns are so sparsely inhabited that I should never saunter there in the glare of day. On Fridays it is free; otherwise the admission ticket is a mere 50 paise. At 8.20 all but the ticket-vendor and as hopeful torch-holder had left the mausoleum. I found the central pool drying up, a dog lapping round the deckling edges, and sad cypress coaxed presentiments of death. The four corner towers loom out of proportion with the mausoleum below infinite stars; then the clicking whir of crickets brings the wanderer down to earth again, where peacock feathers splay the ground. Whisking chipmunks neat in shape and movement bring one up sharp, as before a sergeant-major: 'back straight, eyes straight, keep alert, man!'

Aurangzeb's court – as befitted a man devoted at least to the outward forms of Islam – may have banished painters and all but the most orthodox Muslim craftsmen, but master architect Ataullah did what he could despite declining standards in the craftsmen surrounding him, and despite decreasing funds in the treasury for grand works. If you compare it with the contemporary Badshahi Mosque in Lahore, almost military in its strength and solidity, Bibi-ka Maqbara seems appropriately feminine and alluring, though standards of course dropped in the forty years since Taj Mahal first amazed the world. For one thing, this mausoleum is scarcely more than half the size of Agra's jewel, which dissipates the orderliness of pinnacles and domes: at Aurangabad confusion results from enrichment, and a sense of formality and stiff organisation based on a known model inhibits our enjoyment – better perhaps to see Taj Mahal *after* this successor so that one's eye is innocent in Aurangabad and can respond more generously to this gate in the southern wall, these three spacious pavilions, this perennial canal leading to Rabi'a's tomb. There, in the crypt below where I stood barefoot, paraffin lamps burned to illumine fine tracery in marble. Coins and a couple of banknotes had been dropped on to the silent cloth-covered tomb. I shall never know the magic of solitude at Taj Mahal, but here I stood in a darkened tomb, with an empty mosque nearby, and nobody breaking into my reverie.

My rickshaw stopped at Modern Pan stall for betel-chewers where I changed rupees to pay the rickshaw-wallah then he drove me back to my Hotel, the Aurangabad Ashok on Dr Rajendra Prased Marg. Meals there were delicious but the service proved incredibly slow, and I generally ate at the Highway Garden Restaurant on the other side of the road, opposite the cheaper Hotel Raviraj. Highway Garden made a pleasant open-air change from air-conditioned hotel restaurants.

The following morning I began to walk around the walled city Aurangzeb called his own, starting from the Paithan Gate, roughly at the south. The bazaar around it hummed, and I took breakfast near the little Ashok Hotel. Much of the walling has been taken down or left to disintegrate with the passage of time, as though Aurangzeb will gradually be forgotten if we wait long enough. Constructed in the 1680s, the walls stood roughly 4½ metres high, and extended for a perimeter of nearly 10 km, with some parapets loopholed for musket defence and crenellated. Before reaching the western or Makkah Gate I crossed a bridge over the river Khan to find the water mill or Pani Chakki (1695), with a Mughal garden and a shrine commemorating a spiritual mentor of Aurangzeb called Baba Shah Muzaffar, who belonged to the Chishti Sufi sect. I had with me Niccolao Manucci's *Storia do Mogor* translated by William Irvine, and recently edited by Michael Edwardes as *Memoirs of the Mogul Court* (Folio Society, n.d.) which is devoted to the reign of Aurangzeb, from his accession in 1659 by usurpation up to 1700, seven years before he died. His life had been a strenuous failure. 'He had crushed the heretics; he had tortured and slain infidels; to the end of his life he had striven in person against unbelievers; and he had extended to the sea the great empire received from his father, only to witness, with his own eyes, the unmistakable symptoms of its dissolution.' What would Aurangzeb have thought when at Partition in 1947 the majority of the Islamic faithful of India left the country of their birth, to be replaced in Deccan and elsewhere by corresponding numbers of Hindus?

Continuing clockwise around walled Aurangabad, from Makkah Gate to Delhi Gate I visualised the magnificent Qila-i Ark, or citadel of the fortress, where Mughal courtiers and their descendants spent the more or less restless years of exile from their preferred homes of Delhi or Agra. Their lives were spent in secrecy, concealing favourite indulgences of sex, drugs and alcohol from their puritanical Emperor, whose fury at the prevalence of drink at his accession led him, in Manucci's words, to say in a passion 'that in all Hindustan no more than two men could be found who did not drink, namely himself and Abdulwahhab, his chief judge or qadi. But with respect to Abdulwahhab', interposes the Venetian, 'he was in error, for I myself sent him every day a bottle of spirits which he drank in secret, so that the king could not find it out'.

Only a single archway of the former citadel remains; a minister of the Nizam of Hyderabad cleared the wilderness which had arisen and found fountains and reservoirs and ruined buildings despoiled for their stone. Outside Delhi Gate a few minutes' walk will bring you to the tomb of Pir Ismail, another monument commemorating a teacher of Aurangzeb; then retrace your steps and continue around the city clockwise to the Jalna or eastern gate, then back to Paithan gate.

I had ordered a double omelette and pot of coffee for 6.30 the following morning at the Highway Garden Restaurant but nobody had arrived twenty minutes later so I turned the corner and found Food Wala's Bhoj restaurant open for breakfast. Two businessmen with large gold watches and new European suits were opening and shutting Samsonite cases in a flurry of important activity before catching the plane at Chikal Thana Airport. 'I am urging you finally to complete, sign and seal this very day itself', gesticulated the Delhi-wallah in the brown suit, 'once we are losing this final opportunity, how we will get it again?'. The Delhi-wallah in the grey suit waggled his head with the wisdom of a man who knows the difference between down and up.

'Why I am waiting here?'

'Less haste, more speed.'

'You want I should drop at rail station?'

'For why? I have own car.'

As usual, my head swam with the certainty that the words I overheard were English, but the language flitted off at a tangent: an Indish that most visitors could easily take for a delirious English one might blurt out under the influence of malaria.

I caught an auto-rickshaw to the caves north of the city, carrying a powerful torch and Carmel Berkson's monograph *The Caves at Aurangabad* (Mapin, Ahmadabad, 1986), a perfect repudiation of sceptics who class Ajanta and Ellora above Aurangabad on hearsay alone. In reality, all the chaitya and vihara halls cut in Maharashtra's rocks possess their own value as spiritual, artistic, archaeological and architectural masterpieces, more or less complete, more or less damaged, but each evocative of Buddhist times when India received the Middle Way and Jataka tales according to the Hinayana or the later Mahayana monks and abbots, saints and laymen. For Hindus, generally speaking Buddhism is a protestant sect to be classed along with Jainism. Hindus swiftly laid claim to the caves, adding here at Aurangabad for example a Brahmanical cave south of Cave 6, while at Ellora Caves 13–29 glow with the Hindu pantheon's exuberance, and Caves 31–33 derive from Jain devotees.

Aurangabad Caves 1–5 are grouped west of the main track up to the Sahyadi Hills, and Caves 6–9 east, the groups lying about 1½ km apart.

All date from the 6th century, apart from Cave 4, which is a first-century B.C. Hinayana chaitya, rectangular with a monolithic stupa. All the other caves are viharas of Mahayana Buddhism and are located roughly 60 km from the capital Pratisthan, where the Satavahana empire carried out domestic and maritime trade until the 3rd century A.D., to be succeeded by the Chalukyas. As always, trade introduced political and religious notions new to towns and villages on its routes. Pratisthan, now Paithan, lies on the Godavari river, and conducted river traffic as well as commerce along roads connecting the ancient ports of Barygaza (Broach, in Gujarat), Sopara and Kalyan with Nasik, Pitalkhora, Ellora, Khidki (now Aurangabad), north to Ujjain, east to Varanasi, and south via Tagara (now Ter) to kingdoms in modern Andhra Pradesh and Tamil Nadu.

Buddhist monasteries became both places of retreat, and wealthy landowners prospering with donations of gold, goods and lands from worshippers, much as Hindu temples prosper today. The old Hinayana asceticism of Cave 4 had given way by the 6th century to a comfortable standard of living, with food grown on monastic lands and acquired by barter or payment, silk robes, oil for lamps, and a supporting staff of architects, painters, storemen, sculptors, labourers, and administrators. And the donors need not have been specifically Buddhists, but ecumenical Hindus choosing to lodge with the monks on journeys or to 'keep their options open' by seeking Buddhist blessings on pilgrimages as well as by following older Vedic rites. Such tolerant behavioural patterns are observable all over India today. In 6th-century Mahayana, monks and nuns were supported by communities of lay people, who provided services, goods and money sufficient to assure continuity to monastic life and practice.

The *guha* was originally a simple hermit's shelter hewn out of the rock to keep the elements at bay, with a movable rush mat or rolling boulder protecting the solitary from wild animals if not from roaming bandits. When a teacher attracted disciples, a larger hall was excavated within malleable types of rock, as here at Aurangabad, with simple cells off a common central hall: this became a vihara. In addition, a chaitya hall was developed, with a stupa to symbolise the presence of Gautama Buddha; its farther end was apsidal, its roof vaulted, and its interior columned for grace and strength: this is the characteristic Buddhist cave temple, just as the vihara is the cave monastery.

The monks would have learnt, taught, disputed and prayed, studied logic, grammar, painting, sculpture and the tendentious subject of what might be portrayed (the Mahayana school favoured physical portrayal of the Buddha, while the Hinayana rejected it), astronomy, mathematics and medicine. The cardinal emphasis of the new Mahayana doctrine was that anyone might practise the same teachings as Gautama Buddha, become a bodhisattva, and then possibly after numerous reincarnations achieve Buddhahood itself. The bodhisattva, a being who deliberately postpones his own opportunity for nirvana in order to help the rest of mankind, might be monk or layman. Despite his belief that all appearances are illusory, he strives to work compassionately in this world for the betterment of others. In Mahayana-age sculptures, the compassionate woman appears as a bodhishakti, stirring or reviving the impulse to worship the fertility principle or mother goddess, nature elements such as Earth, Sun and Moon, and objects of local cult worship. Tantric esotericism grew up in this world of intellectual and mystical ferment, drawing on Vedic ideas, yogic practice, and Mahayana rebellion against the more ascetic Hinayana philosophy. Tantrism occurs at Aurangabad in such features as the diamond sceptre (*vajra*) or the mandala form of some caves so shaped for circumambulation of the stupa. It is from this Indian Tantric tradition that the varieties of Chinese, Japanese, Mongolian and Tibetan Buddhism eventually derived, and anyone visiting a lamasery in Lhasa or a Japanese monastery of the secret teachings will do well to have soaked in the atmosphere of Aurangabad and Ajanta, Nasik and Ellora, as a chronological foretaste.

The chronology at Aurangabad is 4 (2nd–1st century B.C.), 3, 1 (both 5th century), 5, 7, 6, 2, 8, 9, but the two complexes are too far apart to follow this chronology on foot. Caves 1–5 are placed together, and caves 6–9 at more than 2 km walking distance. So they are described in convenient numerical order here.

Cave 1 is a vihara intended to surpass Cave 1 at Ajanta but the artisans gave up after completing the portico and verandah, because they found the rock too soft and porous. Yet what a magnificent array of sculpture survives! A full-breasted shalabhanjika on a column is one of the many fertility symbols: a nymph whose touch enables a tree to flower. By contrast the seven past Buddhas on the south porch wall seem pedestrian. Each column has its festoon of unexpected delights: a loving-couple in a lotus medallion, dwarves, and flying figures in a whirl of fantasy. The portico has two Buddha panels with Avalokiteshvara and Vajrapani. At the south he sits on a lotus in dhyana mudra, that is with both hands on his lap, palms upward, one upon another; at the north he sits in the mudra of turning the Wheel of the Law.

Cave 2 at first sight looks like a straightforward square sanctuary, with a simple portico. But the quality of the 6th-century sculpture is high, from the central Buddha turning the Wheel of the Law to the guarding figures beside the open doorway. Left is a standing Avalokiteshvara, the compassionate bodhisattva representing the community of monks or sangha; right is the coming Buddha, Maitreya, representing the law or dharma.

The spectacular Cave 3 has a columned verandah, a columned hall with a square central space and three chambers each at left and right, and a superb shrine with Buddha flanked by Avalokiteshvara and Maitreya, with worshippers kneeling in the round, against the walls, some with their hands at prayer and others presenting garlands, all gazing in wonder at the perfect Trisharana, or triple jewel: the wisdom of Buddha, the law of the dharma, and the community, or sangha. Their heads are at different angles, their body ornaments and hairstyles vary, but their expressions remain serene, detached from the world, engaged on a plane that we cannot share. Nothing in Classical Sumerian Egyptian, Greek or Roman sculpture prepares us for this encounter: it is unforgettable, like our first meeting with Mona Lisa or the Demoiselles d'Avignon, Michelangelo's David or Rodin's *The Kiss*. Something has been contributed here at Aurangabad to the way in which artists see the world. The rest of Cave 3 is charming, distinguished by fine carving of loving couples on the mandapam columns, but comes as an anti-climax.

Cave 4 is an impressive, though incomplete, chaitya, with a stupa which the devotee circumambulates clockwise and in origin it may be the earliest cutting in these rocks. The ribbed-vaulting style extends in time from this 2nd century B.C. foundation to Cave 10 at Ellora, nine hundred years later: a remarkable sense of continuity beginning at this period, which coincides with Cave 10 at Ajanta and reaches its apex of harmony at Karla's Cave 8 in the 1st century A.D.

In 1977 a seated Buddha on a lion throne was released from a landslide by the Archaeology Survey, and shown to be in the mudra of turning the Wheel of the Law: its two protective bodhisattva figures have been damaged but the faintly-smiling Buddha himself has suffered minimal harm.

Cave 5 has a Buddha in meditation or dhyana mudra of the 5th century, refined and classic: with just a touch of asymmetry to lure the eye into a close examination. Structurally, this cave may have formed part of a vihara complex, but too much is missing to make any assertion sure.

Caves 6 and 7 are obviously related, chronologically and structurally, within the 6th century building programme, but aesthetically Cave 6 appears to be later, when the creative spirit had lost some momentum. The south square column in the porch shows a consort of a bodhisattva Tara, standing under foliage, and the north square column shows Tara with Vasudhara and Hariti. Beyond these columns we approach the inner sanctum between a standing Namasangiti Manjushri and a standing Vajrapani Lokeshvara, showing Tantric accretions to Hinayana thought. The sanctum has a seated Buddha, with Avalokiteshvara and the Buddha-to-come Maitreya. A passage around the sanctum will bring you to two more manifestations of Buddha in small rear sancta: on the left an Amitabha or Western Paradise Buddha, and on the right a Vairochana or Primordial Buddha. Do not miss traces of original ceiling paintings in the mandapam: cream, blue, white and red are discernible. Eight side cells were

Aurangabad. Cave 7. Dancing Tara with deities of music and the dance

used for meditation: try sitting cross-legged in one and returning in time to the ferment of new ideas in the 6th century, when Mahayana was spreading and the spirit of dance was being reintroduced at a period of Tantric or esoteric challenge to the severely ascetic Hinayana doctrine now in full retreat.

The place of women in the world suddenly became an issue: Tara as a female aspect of Shiva and a female consort of Avalokiteshvara was thrust into Hindu-Buddhist cosmology and religious thought: in Cave 7 she became a perpetual female presence, despite the Buddha's original proscription of dancing. Buddha seated on his lion throne, his hands turning the Wheel of the Law, must be one of the delights of Kalachuri sculpture, but even he is overshadowed by vivacious goddesses in sensuous poses and lively mandapam panels portraying the 'Eight Perils of Existence': fire, slavery, illness, shipwreck, wild animals, snakes, marauding elephants, and pregnancy with a difficult labour. All these are being conquered by Compassionate Buddha, Avalokiteshvara, who is also depicted on the right. Within, panels of Tara and her attendants emerge from the dark vestibule as your eyes gradually become accustomed to the grey. The repressive morality inculcated by Judaism, Christianity and Islam has no place in Hinduism and Tantra-influenced Mahayana Buddhism where sexuality is acknowledged as a true and intrinsic part not only of our daily lives but also as a necessary constituent of religious experience.

Quite apart from the surprise of the Tara figures as earth goddess and female principle intermediate between male figures at the front of the cave and the Buddha enshrined within, Cave 7 is exceptional for the delineation of hair and headdresses on Taras and attendants, with jewels, crescent moon, flowers, all individualising the previously abstract. More audaciously still, the Buddha shrine itself has been infiltrated by Tara, goddess of the sacred dance and music, with a group of seven dancers or musicians representing the seven-note scale, or *saptasurabhuta*. One plays a clapper, one drums, and the tambourine, one the flute, indicating the prevalence of percussion at this period, and characteristic of all other periods of Indian music.

Cave 8 has a totally different emphasis: its incomplete state allows mental reconstruction of the stages from initial excavation to the hollowing-out of main halls and meditation cells. Here six monastic cells are visible, and a number of bas-reliefs are worth attention, but a sudden crack in the rock shows why the enterprise was halted.

Cave 9, on the other hand, returns us to the Tantric view of woman's centrality in religious life, as well as the conventional Buddhist figures, with a four-armed attendant on the Buddha, the only many-armed figure to be seen in this cave-system. Three unfinished sanctuaries must have been abandoned because of faulty rock.

A recent small excavation south of Cave 6 should be visited for the Syncretistic Cave which proves yet again the urge towards tolerance and multiple worship seen all over India from Kaniya Kumari to the Himalaya region.

Two sons of Shiva (Virabhadra and Ganesha) flank the standing 'seven mothers': Brahmi, Maheshvari, Kumari, Vaishnavi, Varahi, Indrani and Chamunda, facing a seated Buddha, with the goddess Durga on the adjoining wall, to the right of Buddha. We shall see Virabhadra again at Ellora, where he possesses eight hands, and at Elephanta. Virabhadra was created by Shiva to assert his right to be worshipped by Daksha, a son of Brahma, who offended Shiva by instituting a sacrificial rite solely for Vishnu. Shiva therefore in anger created from his mouth Virabhadra, with a thousand heads, a thousand eyes, a thousand feet, wielding a thousand clubs, a thousand shafts. According to the Vayu Purana he held a conch-shell, a discus, a mace, a battleaxe and a blazing bow. If you want to relate to the Indians' mental world of heroes, gods and cataclysmic warfare between them, conjure in your mind the figure of Virabhadra shining with terrible splendour, decorated with the crescent moon, clothed in a tiger's skin, dripping with blood, his colossal mouth equipped with fearsome tusks.

At this apparition, accompanied by thousands of powerful demigods, mountains heaved, Earth quivered, winds roared, and seas churned. Daksha, quivering in terror, surrendered and acknowledged the supremacy of Shiva. Of course, the whole legend arose from the agelong conflict between supporters of Vishnu and Shiva, and Vaishnavites were quick to change the ending to one in which Vishnu came to Daksha's aid and seized Shiva by the throat to reverse the likely outcome. How restful it would be if all antagonism could be resolved by such literary means!

Ajanta
I descended from the hills above Aurangabad, keeping the Islamic Bibi-ka Maqbara in view at the beginning, and took a waiting auto-rickshaw to the bus-station for the next departure to Ajanta, 105 km away.

An adventurous, pale-cheeked spinster in a cotton blouse of brown square, prim and posed as in a faded sepia photograph of Aunt Maude, pent up within her all the bravura of self-congratulating hardship, until I said in a stage whisper 'I imagine you're having the time of your life.' She dimpled with all the skittishness of an adolescent.

'I came into a legacy, and decided that I should travel around India until I had spent every penny.'

'I too resist the thought of building societies legally making off with large amounts of money I invest in them. Travelling in India always seems a legitimate revenge.'

'I hope we meet again, young man. We obviously have many things in common.'

'Victoria Wood and Julie Walters, Elisabeth Schwarzkopf, Kathleen Ferrier, Lynn Seymour and Antoinette Sibley.'

'Janet Suzman and Glenda Jackson, Jane Austen and Emily Dickinson.'

'I hope you never find out what your limits are', I yelled, running for a comically overcrowded bus.

'Thank you,' she called out, 'but I don't expect we have many'.

Two Americans I had met the night before had chosen to take a Matador Taxi (yellow and black) without giving, one supposes, too much superstitious credence to the fact that 'matador' means 'killer'. I had pointed out to them when asked that by taxi they could make a detour to the 12th-century Vaishnavite temple at Anwa, and see the old town of Ajanta, 8 km from the caves, walled and moated in 1727.

Our bus rattled and clanked across flat scrub landscapes, almost featureless during the dry season. Deccani villagers wore freshly-laundered white hats like those worn by the late Pandit Jawaharlal Nehru. Crows alighted on the ground, prospecting for scant food. A cloudless blue sky presaged heat and clarity. We passed through the town of Sillod, deserted in early afternoon inertia.

Ajanta itself is a site unexpectedly verdant, which is one of the reasons why it was selected, and quiet (another reason); even the touts with precious stones, semi-precious stones, slides and postcards remain cooped up in the car park while you clamber along a narrow (but perfectly safe) path to the caves. These are the most spectacular Buddhist murals anywhere in the world except for Tunhuang's Caves of the Thousand Buddhas in Kansu province, China, and the Japanese cycle of wall-paintings in the Horyuji Kondo destroyed in 1948.

The caves had been forgotten until 1819, when a small group of British officers stumbled on the caves in this isolated ravine while out hunting, but it was not until 1845 that James Fergusson drew scholarly attention to the uniqueness of the site in his *Illustrations of the Rock-cut Temples of India*. Ideally, one should approach Ajanta's art and architecture chronologically. The first group of caves, dating to the 2nd–1st centuries B.C. in the period of Hinayana dominance, consists of numbers 8, 9, 10, 12 and 13, roughly central. The later Mahayana group in which Buddha is depicted as opposed to the aniconic precepts of Hinayana, consists of nos. 6, 7 and 11 (*c.* 450–500), 14–20 (*c.* 500–550), and 1–5 and 21–29 (*c.* 550–650). The famous paintings are to be viewed in the light of the fact that Italian restorers were responsible for extensive touching-up, a mixed blessing which many visitors seem to ignore completely. Some caves even now are usually closed for 'conservation', which may include conjectural repainting of questionable value. Should we allow the paintings to fade, authentically, or should we retouch in an approximation of what some second-rate artist might think of as appropriate?

The types of structure at Ajanta, already familiar from the smaller complex above Aurangabad, are the chaitya, generally a large vaulted hall with an apsidal end, divided longitudinally by two colonnades into a broad nave and two aisles; and the vihara, a central hall surrounded by square cells cut into the rock, where monks might live and meditate.

The scarp over the Waghora river rises 250' high, and was occupied by Bhil tribesmen at one time; they blackened the paintings with their fires. Iconoclastic Muslims descending from the north did not know of the site, which had been abandoned during the 7th century in favour of Ellora. Caves were cut beginning with the ceiling and working downward. The process of cutting into the basalt, carving, and painting were long drawn out: several decades were spent on any given cave. The planning was meticulous, and the finishing to a high order of technical skill.

One of the presiding geniuses was King Harishena (*c.* 475–510), of the Vakataka dynasty, not himself a Buddhist, but described in Cave 17 as 'that moon among princes protecting the Earth'. Harishena had a Buddhist prime minister called Varahadeva who became patron of Cave 16. The painters were not monks, but guild-painters accustomed to work on secular palaces for the Vakataka rulers, though in the interests of accuracy one must remember that traces of paintings occur for example in Cave 9 and Cave 10, both contemporary with the original excavation, in the last centuries B.C. without Buddha figures and overlaid with later Buddha figures and attendants.

It is likely, to judge from an interpretation of Dandin's *Dashakumaracharita*, that after the death of Harishena and the disruption of the Vakataka empire due to the ignoble actions of Harishena's successor, the aged Varahadeva managed to restore peace and stability from about 520 A.D., when a new series of painted monasteries was begun.

Visitors should carry a good torch and acquire Mitra's cheaply-priced local guide to Ajanta at the ticket office open daily 9–5.30, but for the armchair traveller I shall try to convey a little of Ajanta's majesty and fascination. Local accommodation can be had at Fardapur, 5 km from the caves.

Caves 9, 10, 19, 26, and 29 are chaitya halls or temples; the rest of Ajanta's caves takes the form of monasteries of various ages and in various stages of completion. Later viharas also enclosed a shrine for independent worship.

Caves 1 and 2 (as well as 16 and 17) are illuminated at a small charge; officially no more than twenty persons are allowed entrance to these caves at any one time, so rather than wait outside, I suggest you continue to another cave. Cave 1 is the first or last: as the most splendid vihara, splendidly painted, it may be left till last, for a notable climax. Its painters must be those of the generation after 16 and 17, and belong to the same guild, but they have introduced such innovations as shading, increased the use of stylisation, and used black hair as a surrounding to the face, enhancing plasticity. A high-relief Buddha in the inner shrine is shown in the mudra of teaching the law in Sarnath deer-park. If the identification of the Hindu god Indra beside him is correct, the intention will have been to indicate willing subservience of the Hindu pantheon to the Mahayana world-view around 500 A.D.

The porch is missing, so our first view is of colonnade similar to that of Cave 19, a chaitya hall. Bludgeoned from childhood with views of Greco-Roman architectural orders, it is difficult for a Westerner to appreciate the enormously wide range and complexity of columns, square, fluted, octagonal, round, all compounded below an intricately-carved capital below a painted ceiling. This whole cave, like all the others, was excavated by an army of artisans and labourers with pickaxes and chisels. The distant model must have been timber architecture, because mimicry of timber features occurs quite late, and possibly Perso-Median influences (from the 7th century B.C.) were brought here to the Deccan by craftsmen fleeing the destruction of the Achaemenid Empire. Cave 1 has a central hall 65 feet square, illuminated by natural light (focussed beyond it on the Teaching Buddha) with small cells on all three sides. The doorways are carved with serpent deities (the naga-king was worshipped at Ajanta before Buddhism), couples in dalliance, and musicians.

Mural paintings on the main hall walls, beginning left of the main doorway, illustrate some jataka tales, that is stories concerning former lives of Buddha. Shibi jataka tells how the Bodhisattva saves a pigeon from a hawk, compassion overcoming ferocity. After the conversion of Nanda (Buddha's cousin), the Samkhapala jataka ingeniously conjoins the naga-Bodhisattva legends by show-ing the Bodhisattva as injured serpent-king rescued by the commoner Alara who offers his animals to the hunters in lieu. Episodes from Mahajanaka jataka show King Mahajanaka shipwrecked, tempted, and ultimately renouncing the world. On the rear wall, twin aspects of Avalokiteshvara guard the antechamber to Buddha's sanctuary: that on the left is the Lotus Avalokiteshvara known as Padmapani, a celebrated icon of Indian art combining elegance, plasticity, delicacy, perspective and spiritual beauty with great economy of line and colour. Indeed, if we are to believe the colours surviving decades of conservation at Ajanta, ochre, green and brown seem to have dominated the palette, a curious range omitting such obvious choices as red, white, and blue. It seems plausible that red darkened to brown, and blue yellowed to green, White has in some cases been restored to its pristine value, as in the complex Vessantara murals in Cave 17.

Painted pavilions and palaces are known from the *Mahabharata*, so the murals at Ajanta postdated the origins of Indian mural painting by at least 1400 years. *Kama Sutra*, predating the Gupta-Vakataka era, had laid down six principles of painting which would have been known to guilds active at Ajanta. Forms must be represented appropriately; structure and proportion must be accurate; action and feeling must be suggested; a quality of grace must imbue the work; an effect of similitude, *not* exact realistic imitation, must be achieved; and finally, the painter should use brush and colour properly. Moreover, unlike Western painters, or Chinese or Japanese painters of the classic periods, Indian painters were expected to have understood the art of the dance in order to express mobility, grace and feeling in paint. Such a mastery is evident in the Bodhisattvas in Cave 1, probably painted during the rule of Pulakesin II, who died about 642.

The apprentices would have prepared the rough rock surface by covering it with earth and cowdung strengthened with animal hair or chopped straw to a depth of an inch or more, smoothing it off, and covering it with a layer of lime plaster. When this had dried, artists outlined the figures in cinnabar red, and underpainted in a terra-verde roughly similar to Italian practice before 1400. The master artists would then have applied colour finished with highlights and in later caves also shading; the whole would then have been burnished to a fine sheen.

With my powerful torch I illuminated the Avalokiteshvara murals which form an extraordinary triptych with the great stone Buddha behind them, then the Mahajanaka stories with their elaborately realistic view of great royal courts of the time: their costume, jewels, and interior decoration. It resembled my first incursion into Pharaonic tombs below Thebes. In darkness a single shaft of light can irradiate the distant past as though we inhabited it still: a ravishing of the senses that enriches our existence forever afterwards. We can be intoxicated with another dimension of time in another land as certainly as by any opiate and more enduringly.

A pair of sumptuous lovers – ochre and green, hands roving, eyes lost in dreams – seated on the east wall of Cave 1 may have nothing directly in common with Buddhist thought but allows us to respond to the early sixth century in the courts of Northern Deccan much as the treasures of Tut Ankh Amun demonstrate the splendour of regal life in the Valley of the Kings in the 11th century B.C., redated according to *Centuries of Darkness* (1991).

Cave 2 was painted slightly later than Cave 1; its two 'Hariti Shrine' walls, with the paintings of Caves 16 and 17, form the aesthetic culmination of Ajanta art, between about 475 and 550. Ceilings play a great part in Western art from the Sistine Chapel to Tiepolo's Würzburg, but in Indian architecture they

Ajanta. Cave 2. A 5th-century Hariti and Panchika

are predominantly sculptural, as in Jain temples at Dilwara, or the elaborate
mandapams of South India. But in Caves 1 and 2 the ceilings are divided into
dozens of bands separating geometric patterns, scrolls and lotuses. Though
smaller than its neighbour, Cave 2 possesses similar features: a seated Buddha,
teaching in Sarnath deer-park, fills the innermost sanctuary, with a seated
Buddha on each side. Small cells for monastic privacy lead off from the main
columned hall, and jataka stories are painted around the walls: clockwise, these
are the Hamsa tales, the birth stories, the Vidhurapandita tales, the conversion
of Purna, and the rescue of Purna's brother from shipwreck. There are 547
Jataka tales in the six volumes translated from the Pali and edited by E. B.
Cowell (Cambridge, 1895–1907), told by Gautama Buddha to his pupils in the
forty years between Enlightenment and the 'putting off of his body'. They are
allegories, some would say, of the Middle Way, of Karma or Cause and Effect,
demonstrations of the Eightfold Path, indications of the Four Noble Truths.
His last words are 'All compounds are perishable'.

As Buddhism lost its momentum in India, as its disciples escaped north into
Himalayan fastnesses from Hindu or Muslim hordes, the mute messages on the
walls at Ajanta endured in their fragile state century after century. The Hamsa
jataka shows the Bodhisattva in the form of a goose seized, then released at
the command of the King and Queen, who listen to his sermon. After the birth
scenes, Mayadevi is shown leaning against a pillar: she is beautifully moulded
in a translucent dress and elegant jewellery. A shrine on the right shows a
sculpted Kubera, keeper of earthly treasures, with his consort Hariti, and a
procession of devotees. The right wall portrays the Vidhurapandita tale in

which a naga princess is seen on a swing, followed by a court scene, a game of dice and Vidhurapandita's march to the serpent kingdom. The story of Purna's conversion by Buddha occurs in episodes such as Purna's rescue from shipwreck, and his sandalwood monastery.

Caves 3, 5 and 8 were viharas never completed; neither was the late–5th century Cave 4, clearly intended as the largest and most majestic at Ajanta. Part of the hall ceiling collapsed and three cells unfinished, but the main doorway has finely carved married couples (mithunas), tree spirits (salabhangi-kas), and flying spirits (gandharvas). Cave 6 is a two-storeyed vihara, with a beautifully-carved shrine door and frescoes over cell doors discovered in 1935. Elephanta-like columns here and in Cave 7 date both to the late 5th century. Cave 6 is painted and Cave 7 carved with the miracle at Sravasti, where the Master multiplied himself. Cave 8, closed to visitors, is a vihara of the earliest or Hinayana group, like the chaitya hall known as Cave 9 (around 100 B.C.) in a style we shall recognise at Nasik. Rectangular with a curved vault and a pyramid-topped stupa, Cave 9 is divided into a nave and twin aisles by fourteen octagonal columns, with a further eleven at the further end. Look for superim-posed paintings: left of the doorway a Hinayana-period scene showing a naga king and attendants (correlating the new Buddhism with local animism) has been partly superimposed by a pair of monks, probably of Mahayana age, to judge from contemporary Buddha figures higher up. As you retreat from Cave 9, look up at the great window with its ribs deriving from timber models.

Cave 10 bears the graffito 'John Smith, 1819', one of the earliest recorded British vandals. The earlier series of paintings in this 2nd-century B.C. chaitya hall is a frieze protected by shutters, and curtains at a lower level, to keep out the strongest light. Wherever Buddha figures are superimposed, you may be sure they are of 5th–6th century workmanship. The left wall retains a scene showing royal worship of Buddha in the guise of a bodhi tree; the right wall has the Sama tale, in which a king kills Sama (Bodhisattva) with an arrow, the resurrection of Sama, and his reconciliation with the king. In the Chhadantha jataka, a Bodhisattva as a white elephant is killed by Chullasubhadda the favourite queen of the king of the king of Varanasi in revenge for the elephant's favouring his other wife when Chullasubhadda was his second consort. The tusks were brought to vengeful Chullasubhadda to prove that the white elephant had been killed and, when she cradled them in her arms, she realised the enormity of what she had done, and died of remorse. The pillar-paintings in tempera are later than the wall-paintings, and possess a kind of extravert knowingness that I find disconcerting. For instance, a standing Buddha with two disproportionately tiny monks is being surveyed by two gnomelike flying guardians who seem to be sheltering under his royal umbrella. Buddha's serene and compassionate expression accompanies the varada mudra, granting a wish. He is enclosed in a green gold-rimmed aureole and stands on a lotus.

Cave 11 is contemporary with Cave 10, but was remodelled in the 5th century so badly that it was left unfinished; 12 and 13 may be slightly earlier still, but their façades have fallen in, revealing square halls. You can see 2nd-century rock-cut monastic beds in the seven tiny cells of Cave 13. Above it is Cave 14, an incomplete vihara. Cave 15 is a vihara and 15a, accessible by a flight of steps near Cave 15, survives only in a front wall. Spend no time on these but make straight for Cave 16, a spectacular vihara making a pair with Cave 17, which antedate Caves 1–2 by 15 to 20 years as regards their paintings. The excavation and carving could not have been completed before *c.* 505–10, taking as one extreme our knowledge of the slowness of Indian guild-artisans, and at the other a donative inscription to King Harishena of the Vakataka dynasty, who was overthrown around 510.

Welcoming elephants and the Waghora valley's presiding naga-deity are carved before you arrive at Cave 16. Its main difference from Cave 17 is that the Buddha trinity (teaching Gautama flanked by Bodhisattvas) has no ante-chambers. Clockwise, the paintings show the Hasti jataka, in which Buddha incarnate as an elephant hurls himself over a cliff to provide food for starving travellers; the Mahasadha jataka shows Buddha resolving ownership of a child (a tale which reverberates into the 20th century in Brecht's *Caucasian Chalk Circle*) and of a chariot; Nanda's conversion with a moving portrayal of Nanda's wife, the fainting Sundari; the teaching of Buddha; the Sravasti miracle; and a sequence of scenes from the childhood and youth of Buddha, culminating in his wandering through the streets of Rajagriha. The ceiling seems to sag in the centre like a canopy.

Cave 17 has probably the finest paintings of all, and luckily their state of preservation corresponds to their high quality. Due to the demand for entry, visitors are limited to 15 minutes which is not really enough unless you are quite sure what you are looking for. The verandah's painted ceiling shows six figures with a total of six hands: a medallion with fine foliation here is a motif repeated on inner ceilings. Above the doorway are loving couples below eight seated Buddhas. At the left a royal couple drink wine, and then offer alms to the populace; at the far left a Wheel of Life indicates a Buddhist view of the ages of man. On the left of the central entrance flying Indra is surrounded by his attendants; on the right heavenly maidens possess all too earthly attributes, and farther right Buddha is seen subjugating the elephant sent to trample on him by his cousin Devadatta, who resented Gautama's fame and objected to his theological unorthodoxy. The interior late 5th- or early 6th-century frescoes narrate jataka stories that would have been as familiar to Buddhists then as New Testament scenes are to Italians of the Renaissance. The visitor will see these marvellous creations, so long protected from the ravages of strong light if not from over-zealous restoration, in clockwise order beginning at the hall doorway with tales of compassion: the Chhadantha jataka and then the Mahak-api jataka, which tells how Buddha in his incarnation as a monkey rescues a peasant from a ravine, only to be attacked with a rock, a crime for which the 'evildoer' receives immediate pardon. Devadatta stories reflect an early schism within Buddhism, but stories attacking him were interpolated into the canon later: Devadatta is never mentioned in the *Digha* and twice only in the *Majjhima*. Interestingly the 5th century A.D. Chinese scholar Fa Hsien mentions the existence of those who followed Devadatta and made offerings to three previous Buddhas, but not to Gautama. It seems likely therefore that followers of Gautama will have invented vilificatory incidents to denigrate Devadatta's name.

The whole left wall is a fascinating chronological creation portraying incidents in the life of Bodhisattva incarnate as Prince Vessantara, giving away the

Ajanta. Cave 17. A 5th-century mural scene from Vessantara jataka

miraculous elephant with the faculty of bringing rain, being forced by into exile with his family, living as an hermit, giving his children to a brahmin, redeeming his children, and being pardoned by the king his father.

Farthest on the same wall is a triple frieze with scenes from the Sudasama jataka, in which Gautama in his incarnation as a lioness persuades Prince Sudasa to give up cannibalism. Past the inner shrine we come to the Matiposhaka and Sama jatakas, the former delightful with elephants in a variety of attitudes, and the latter depicting the Bodhisattva as a pious youth bearing his blind parents in slings from bamboo poles carried on his shoulders. The great Simhala frieze facing the Vessantara cycle concerns the Bodhisattva incarnate as a beneficent horse protecting Simhala and his merchants from shipwreck off Sri Lanka, from being devoured by ogresses, and from being seduced by a demon in the form of a lovely woman. Scenes of splendour in the royal palace give these secular painters every opportunity to show sinuous female forms, jewels, and even hairstyles which immediately convey a vision of life and manners nearly 1500 years ago. The sequence ends with tales in which the Buddha as a compassionate stag offers himself to a palace chef in place of a pregnant doe.

Cave 19 is a magnificent chaitya hall, with a ribbed horseshoe-shaped window over a porch intricately carved with scrollwork, bands and foliation, leaving no surface plain. Within, a Buddha is carved in front of the stupa, proving Mahayana age. The naga-king and his naga-queen outside the cave reminds us of the local serpent cult. King Harishena's is the regnal period, but the donor may have been a dignitary called Gandhakuta, who also paid for Cave 17. If you consider that the interior carvings were created by masters after artisans had chipped away inner rock, the planning must have been awesomely accurate, and though most paintings are faded and chipped away almost beyond repair, it is possible to make out how they were designed on walls and ceilings, using Cave 17 as analogy.

Caves 20–25 were late residential halls, no. 20 being distinguished by charming bracket figures on its pillars, and no. 23 by fine lotus medallions, while no. 24 has a complete verandah and main door, giving a clear insight by its very incompleteness into the manner of its excavation from living rock.

Cave 26 (with its adjunct misleadingly numbered 27) is the fourth chaitya hall, and has several figures of Buddha around the stupa. Its huge dimensions emulate those of Cave 19, but it is incomplete, and sketchy chiselling in some places give the dizzy impression that the sculptor has just left for the day. On the far right, just inside, Buddha is tempted by Mara and his beautiful daughters; on the far left he reclines in serenity, pondering on the sadness of a world he no longer inhabits as he enters Nirvana. Below are wailing disciples who have lost their guiding light; above are apsaras and other heavenly beings rejoicing in their freedom from the cycle of rebirth. The stucco technique applied here will be found again at Ellora, but the paint has largely flaked off. Caves 28 and 29 are by contrast difficult of access and less interesting. I found wild bees nesting above several of the caves, but not in sufficient swarms to endanger the visitor. The swarms of touts on emerging from the archaeological enclosure are another matter: one insistent dealer thrust a small rough amethyst into my hand, 'Come, come, just two minutes to my shop', he shouted, two feet from my ear. 'Rahul my name, come quick, your bus not going back yet.'

Ellora

The bus to Ellora rocked over potholes and lurched at the jagged asphalt-edge every time another vehicle passed: even with adequate suspension, a vehicle does not easily tolerate such indignities, and ours had a suspension worn to a frazzle.

But of course one is intoxicated with the wine of Ajanta's beauty: its zenanas of gorgeous damsels, half-naked, always and perennially seductive beyond dreams of real women. A graduate of Kurukshetra University in Punjab felt as joyfully inebriated with love and wonder as I (who had never imagined in my youth I should leave Middlesex, never mind see Ajanta) and we chaffed each other with tales of our adventures. 'I studied Italian art with Pietro Scarpellini', I bartered. 'Na,' he haggled, 'I studied Sanskrit under Professor B. Prakash, but English too we had very much in our courses and spare time itself. I am most ardently enamoured of what your Bird of Avon sings: "Who robs me of my reputation steals trash, but stick and stones are another thing entirely".'

Not to be outdone, or not far, I riposted: 'He who steals my pound of flesh had better not be a vegetarian, because the quality of brisket is not strained.'

'You can lead a philosopher to a classroom, but you cannot make him think.'

'I come to cremate him, not to praise him. What for our burning ghats? Friends, Hindus, countrymen and all those who support V.P. Singh, let me be having your undivided attention just one moment, please.'

'Under the spreading banyan tree, the dhobi-wallah sits.'

'He should be thinking of Lord Shiva, but he's squeezing dead some nits.'

I found something appealing about our camaraderie, approaching Ellora, for while Buddhist Ajanta has no perceptible record of friendly syncretism, Ellora possesses Vajrayana Buddhist caves (numbered 1–12) of around 550–750, Shaivite Hindu caves (numbered 13–29) 600–870 A.D., and Jain caves (preëminently Digambara) of roughly 800–1000 numbered 30–34. Ellora is only 29 km from Aurangabad, and 3 km north of Khuldabad village. You can stay at Kailash Hotel ('with rooms, cottages and 24 hrs. hot water') a few minutes walk from the main caves complex, with its Heritage restaurant and Caveman's Bar. More evocative of small-town Maharashtran life, if noisier to that extent, is the choice at Khuldabad: Local Fund Travellers' Bungalow (reservations by phoning the Executive Engineer, Zilla Parishad, Aurangabad, tel. 5511) or the State Guest House (Khuldabad tel. 26).

Unlike Ajanta, Ellora was never forgotten, and these monuments of Chalukya and Rashtrakuta age span nearly five centuries in time and 2 km in length. They lay on familiar trade routes, and were recorded in awestruck tones by ancient, mediaeval and modern travellers, not least in that subtly evocative if generalised expedition to the Kawa Dol in the Marabar Hills described by Forster in *A Passage to India*, where the air 'felt like a warm bath into which hotter water is trickling constantly, the temperature rose and rose, the boulders said "I am alive", the small stones answered, 'I am almost alive".' We stand after all in a desert, dry for many months of the year, and occasionally forgotten year after year by monsoon rains, so that the few perennial rivers are not replenished, and drag their listless waters into the insatiable Ganga.

Ellora is a Tantric centre, abandoning the Mahayana emphasis on Buddha's compassion in favour of more active magical and even occult practices, such as spells and rituals which would have horrified the contemplative founder. The female principle enters Buddhism as *shakti*, the Chinese Yin, and re-emerges from prehistoric mother-goddess worship endemic in the subcontinent. Hindu sculpture at Ellora centres on the phallus, potent symbol of Lord Shiva, though Durga/Parvati as his female complement is figured on many sculptured panels, and Lords Brahma and Vishnu appear too, convincing all worshippers of whatever sect that Ellora rises to universal significance. Topographically, where Ajanta's rockface drops virtually sheer, Ellora's slope is more gradually inclined, allowing complex entrance halls to open out into remarkable shrines.

Avoid the temptation to head straight for the glory of Kailasanatha (Cave 16) which faces the entrance road, but turn right for the late 6th- and early 7th-century Buddhist complex numbering from the far end. Cave 1 has no sculpture and was believed by some writers to have served as a storehouse or granary. The next three buildings are viharas; Cave 2 is the most interesting, with gigantic Bodhisattvas protecting the entrance gate and shrine. Twelve ornate pillars with ribbed cushion capitals support the roof. The right-hand porch shows the miracle at Sravasti, and the general ambiance will recur in later Chalukya-style Hindu caves numbered 21 and 29.

Cave 5, which reminds me of the durbar hall at Kanheri, with low benches like those in Kanheri's Cave 11, has columns like those we have just seen at Ellora's Cave 2. Caves 6–9 form a complex excavated simultaneously, 6 comprising a main hall, two lateral celled halls, antechamber and sanctuary. The best features include a series of sculptured brackets with mythical beings; the left-hand Tara image, the consort or female aspect (depending on your theological preference) of Bodhisattva Avalokiteshvara, figured elsewhere, notably in Cave 5; and Bodhisattva Vajrapani, distinguished by the thunderbolt in his crown. The Tantric meditator concentrates on five circles (the cardinal points and the centre) and the wrathful form Vajrapani stands at the 'east', where anger must be conquered. Just as all Sikhs own a knife and an iron bangle, so all Tantric Buddhists own a *vajra*, or thunderbolt symbol, with ornate curved prongs at each end, as a reminder of personal potential. Cave 9, visited through Cave 6, bears on its façade a wondrous Tara with snake, sword, elephant, fire and shipwreck: dangers facing man in this existence.

Cave 10, conventionally dedicated to Vishvakarma, patron god of architects, has a roof mimicking timber construction, with angles supporting the beams, and a Buddha sitting beside the sacred bo-tree properly seen only when sitting at Buddha's feet, as all his worshippers sit and have always sat since the 7th century. If you connect amorous scenes with Hindu monuments such as Khajuraho, the chaitya hall called Cave 10 will stun you with its ravishingly sensuous loving couples on the inner side of the parapet on the inner gallery. It is the only large-scale chaitya hall at Ellora.

Cave 11 is wrongly named 'Do Thal' (two storeys) because its lowest floor was buried; like Cave 12 it is actually a 'Tin Thal' or three-storey structure of the 8th century. The strangeness of these viharas to my Western secular mind nudged me to an awareness that the self cannot be eluded, but by a process of discipline and wild anticipation it can be distracted to that we enter a parallel existence, which one might call 'as if'. Ellora's Buddhist centuries are one 'as if'; the massive and elaborate Hindu centuries provide another alternative to locking ourselves into a given space-time mechanism; as a historical novelist I wrote *Forgotten Games* about the contest between Cortés and Moctezuma, but as a geographical novelist I located their encounter in a Mexico of the mind that might once have existed in actuality, and now really does. I think of great Aztec courtyards whenever I pass through the courtyards of Do Thal and Tin Thal which are actually rock emptied into thin air; it seems miraculous that the teams of artisans would not have been allowed to use the open spaces in front of the rockface as a courtyard and build walls around them but no – that would have been too simple for the pious mind, which requires labour and service, as in Pharaonic Egypt. Cave 11 has Buddha in a teaching mudra, and Cave 12 Buddhas in a meditation posture and touching the earth. The grandeur of these two viharas must relate to some competitive streak, for great Hindu caves were being excavated at this period, and masons paid by Buddhists must have been told not to let the Bodhisattva down . . .

Cave 13 might have served (like Cave 1) as a storehouse but with nos. 14, 15 and 16 we are impelled as in some stone drama towards inevitable climax, from Ravana's Cave, to the Ten Incarnations, and ending with Kailasanatha, Lord Shiva's heavenly-earthly mountain, brusquely termed by Percy Brown 'not only the most stupendous single work of art executed in India, but as an example of rock-architecture . . . unrivalled'. He likens it to the Athenian Parthenon and the Javanese temple-mountain Borobudur; like both, it is surrounded by other works, related yet overwhelmed by comparison.

Cave 14 may be named for Sita's captor Ravana, but it is dedicated to Lord Shiva, who dances the tandava, a dance form invented by his attendant Tandu. Other scenes on the side walls figure avatars of Lord Vishnu: the boar incarnation of Varaha was drawn by William Simpson in January 1862 and is reproduced in *Visions of India, the sketchbooks* (1986), with an introduction by Paul Theroux, who calls Simpson the Kipling of watercolourists, for the two men shared sympathies not with pink, princely India, what I might call 'the Jaipur touch', but with common streets, hills and bazaars. The first panel portrays lion-conquering Durga as she struggles with a buffalo; her trident represents the might of Shiva, her consort. The second panel shows Lakshmi on her lotus being bathed by elephants. Vishnu as the boar is shown saving the earth personified as the goddess Prithvi: in the Hindu mind the earth goddess is symbolised by the cow, yielding to everyone the desired milk. If Vishnu had not held up the earth, it would have been overwhelmed by the great deluge caused by the demons, prefiguring the Deluge in monotheistic mythologies. The fourth panel depicts Vishnu seated between Sridevi and Bhudevi.

The shrine doorway is defended by the river goddesses Ganga and Yamuna. The right panels figure the Virabhadra aspect of Shiva, the seven mother goddesses with their infants, Ganesha, Kala and Kali, Shiva spearing the thousand-headed demon Andhaka, Ravana shaking the sacred mount Kailasa, dancing Shiva, Shiva playing dice with Parvati, and Durga slaying the buffalo demon.

Cave 15 is dated to the period of the Rashtrakuta sovereign Dantidurga (*fl.* 735–750) and must have been begun as a Buddhist monastery to judge from its similarity to Caves 11 and 12: Buddha himself appears on capitals of the first floor. Visitors concentrating on Kailasanatha at the expense of Cave 15 make

Ellora. View down from the main shrine of the Ten Incarnations of Vishnu

a mistake, for it takes several hours to appreciate the subtlety, vigour, variety and energy of these Rashtrakuta sculptures, spiritually emotional perhaps in the way that Rodin's works will appeal later to secular emotions. From its Buddhist origins, Cave 15 was transmuted into a delirium of Shaivite worship, with a relatively minor Vaishnavite sequence on the right wall: interestingly, the cave is locally known as the 'Ten Incarnations of Vishnu' or 'Dasavatara', and the Vishnu as lion-man or Narasimha destroying the demon Hiranyakshi, who forbade his son Prahlada to worship Vishnu.

The upper floor has a sanctum at the far end. A great pillared hall with sculptured panels has familiar iconography, clockwise: the spearing of Andhaka by Shiva, Shiva Nataraja, the dice-game, the marriage of Shiva with Parvati, Ravana disturbs them, Shiva rescues Markandeya from Yama, Shiva accepting the river Ganga in his hair, Shiva's son Ganesha, two guardian-figures before

107

the sanctum in which are figured Parvati and Lakshmi, then Subrahmanya, Shiva emerging from the lingam, Shiva destroying the demon Tripura, and finally the avatars of Vishnu, including Krishna raising Mount Govardhana, Vishnu on the serpent, Vishnu on Garuda, the Varaha scene, the Trivikrama scene, and the Narasimha scene.

The Rashtrakuta monarch Krishna I (756–73) ordered the Kailasa Temple (Cave 16 is the conventional numbering), but it was completed by his successors. In the *Indian Antiquary* of 1883, a contemporary inscription is quoted on the 8th-century temple: 'On seeing it, the greatest immortals in their heavenly chariots are moved to amazement, saying 'this temple to Shiva is self-existent; such beauty exists in no human work of art; the architect-builder failed to complete another such enterprise, asking himself in astonishment, "How was it that I could have achieved this?".'

Imagine the great cathedral-ship of Chartres rising above the flat furrows of northern France having been instead *revealed from within a mountain-range*. Rather than piling stone on stone, like any Christian church, Ellora's Kailasa emerged cavity after cavity: to create it, the builders first conceived their own gods carved in relief on panels, and then found them within. A quarter of a million tons of dark volcanic rock must have been removed from the site, leaving the rear wall of the manmade trench more than a hundred feet high, with two mighty trenches three hundred feet along linked at their inner edge by a third trench 175 feet long. This left an apparently monolithic mass isolated from the mountain from which artisans and sculptors would first removed huge masses of living rock, then carve out scenes from Shaivite myth. Yet in addition to this inspired gouging, from which would emerge 'the largest and most splendid rock-cut monument in the world' in Dr J. C. Harle's respected view, the original architects devised a complex entrance wall incorporating a double-storeyed gateway with an upper gallery; a free-standing bull pavillion, a pair of monolithic columns and a pair of elephants; and around the flanking walls panels with Shaivite gods and goddesses whom we recognise from preceding temples as Lakshmi and Ganesha, Parvati and Shiva, as well as the river-goddesses Ganga and Yamuna.

Shrines and galleries were hewn from the rock, many two storeys high, and most decorated elaborately with the most ardently-inspired figures of the day. The workers were predominantly Dravidian in training, and unlike its surrounding temples, Ellora's Kailasa represents the northernmost locality of a frenetic energy known from Mamallapuram and Kanchipuram, though understandably influenced over the decades by an awareness of earlier Rashtrakuta temples such as Cave 15.

As in the Sistine Chapel, the impact of the ensemble humbles at first view: where does one begin? Probably, within the main temple, which has reminiscences of the best Early Chalukya Shaivite temple architecture at Pattadakal, especially on the inner pillars of the Virupaksha Temple dateable to 745. Krishna I is known in fact to have brought Pattadakal under Rashtrakuta hegemony, so the same craftsmen may well have worked at both sites, and scenes from both *Mahabharata* and *Ramayana* echo style, technique and detail from Pattadakal. Look for example at the drama, vivacity, even distortion as gods and heroes, demons and animals enact their pulsating, world-shaking histories to which every Indian is heir.

Ellora. 8th-century temple of Kailasanatha

In a bout of creative anguish, the sculptor will hack and hammer away at the rock behind to force his mythological figures almost into the round: to make them literally dance in the case of Shiva Nataraja, or to enable their fight to break loose from the restrictions of the bland, blank volcanic rock at the back. Dravidian style requires the distinction of images from their surrounding architecture, a feature rarely seen in northern styles.

The great Kailasa temple itself is pyramidiform, with three storeys beneath an octagonal dome. It stands in that powerful multi-dimensional Hindu mode not only for itself and the rock from which it came but for the physical Himalaya far to the north, and the spiritual paradise of Shiva; its roof was once covered with traditional chunam (lime plaster) to mimic surf on a shore, snow on a mountain, or rushing waters foaming down a waterfall. Edges of symbolism blur with reality, as in the rest of Indian society, then as now, here as elsewhere. Sir James Mackintosh, visiting Ellora in 1810, said that the temple 'beggars all description and . . . must be one of the most stupendous and magnificent of the works of man.' E. M. Forster, a King's man not given to hyperbole, noted in his diary at sunset, 'More amazing than anything in a land where much amazes. Supporting cornice of blackened monsters-elephants, griffons and tigers who rend. The great mild face of a goddess, doing cruelty, fades into the pit-wall.'

If all ancient Hindu art and literature had been lost, the future archaeologist could reconstruct most of it from sculptured scenes from the *Mahabharata* and the *Krishna Lila* on the northern side of the main temple, and the *Ramayana* on the south, with magnificent large-scale lower panels of Shiva, Ravana and Parvati.

The lateral shrines seem to be later: the largest is Sri Lankeshvara, 107 feet x 60 feet, accessible by a stairway at the end of the portico, with its own Nandi image in the west wall. Loving couples entwine in eternal self-absorption on the outer parapet wall, commingling sensations of physical sex with religious exaltation natural to Hinduism.

Cave 17 is dated to the late 6th century and is thus considerably earlier than Kailasanatha, yet its architecture is serenely harmonious, as though a solution had been found which needed no alteration, but only embellishment to produce the later masterpieces at Ellora. Caves 18, 19 and 20 have no outstanding merits, but Caves 21 and 22 are worth inspecting; the former is the Rameshwara, with superb sculptures of the goddesses Ganga and Yamuna, erotic loving couples, and Shaivite scenes including the marriage of Shiva to Parvati, their dice game, the dance of the universe, and fierce protective guardians of the shrine. Cave 22 is dedicated to 'Shiva of the Blue Throat' or Nilakantha, whose lingam is found in the 8th century shrine. Cave 25 depicts Surya and the sungod in his seven-horse chariot; after Cave 27 we come to a ravine, then immediately to Dhumar Lena (numbered 29), and the last Hindu temples, known as Ganesha Lena and the Jogeshvari group, facing each other across the ravine. The most significant is Dhumar Lena, for its close association, in some minds, with Elephanta and Jogeshwari on Salsette Island, mainly because it follows a technique transitional between cutting into the solid rock, and carving out of the rock; one stands in the cruciform hall and feels transported back to the era when such enterprises seemed novel, yet natural. Karl Khandalavala dates Dhumar Lena to the 8th century, though others have postulated a date as early as the mid–6th century, when the Kalachuris were patronising new temples. The aesthetic quality of Elephanta is so much higher than Ellora's Dhumar Lena, however, that one would be tempted to point to the fading of a great tradition through time.

Jain caves beginning with no. 30 are of ninth-century manufacture, even to the paintings in Indra Sabha (Cave 32), which are contemporary with the Kailasanatha paintings. The first you come to, Cave 30, is called 'Little Kailasa' for its mimicry, yet all the passion and invention seem to have vanished; we are left with a simulacrum, like a plaster model of the Sanchi stupa, say, or Aurangabad's interesting but pallid Bibi-ka Maqbara compared with Agra's sublime Taj Mahal. Cave 31 is actually a minor adjunct to 32, which is the best Jain cave in Maharashtra, unnervingly incomplete on the ground floor yet ornate and animated on the upper floor with finely-worked pillars, inspired sculpture, and traces of more than one stratum of painting, the first possibly coeval with the excavation.

On the rear wall of Cave 32 rise Parshvanatha and Gomateshvara, the former a smaller likeness of the image which towers above Sravana Belagola. Also known as Bahubali, Gomateshvara is a son of Adinatha and is considered by some one of the Jain tirthankars: he is always shown standing, to fulfil a vow, with the white-blossomed madhavi creeper climbing his legs. In Hindu myth he overcame his step-brother Bharata in the struggle for the kingdom of Paudanapura, but renounced the throne to become an ascetic, always an honoured practice in India. His grateful step-brother thereupon constructed a golden effigy of him 2,000 feet high in a forest, and it was that image that inspired the figure here at Ellora, as well as the much more famous later version, fully sixty feet high, at the Jain sanctuary of Sravana Belgola, in Karnataka, towering above the village, in 1028. The ceiling of the higher mandapam preserves some painted fragments, mostly of flying angels and couples usual in such ninth-century ceilings.

Facing Cave 32, or Indra Sabha, is the Jagannatha Sabha numbered 33, with three celled halls open to a courtyard on the ground floor, and a pillared hall on the first floor. Cave 34, at the far end of the mountain's cape, is a small shrine with fine images of Mahavira in the shrine, Parshvanatha and Gomateshvara on the lateral walls, and Matanga and Sidhaika. Like Teotihuacán or Pagan, Ellora survives as an enduring complex testifying to man's indomitable creativity in the face of nature's harshness, expressed in steep mountain sides, tropical jungle, or arid desert. Man's evil, his brutality, and his capacity for destruction (recognised as an aspect of divinity in Hinduism) meet their match in these stone verities.

Khuldabad
The road southeast back to Aurangabad touches two towns of deep historical and religious significance to Deccani Muslims. The first is Khuldabad (the Heavenly Abode), a mere five km from Ellora and twenty-two from Aurangabad, and the second Daulatabad, another six km on the road south.

Clearly once a large and imposing town, Khuldabad seems almost preserved in early 18th-century amber if one takes as its focus the simple, austere tomb of Shah Aurangzeb (1707): its porch and gateway are additions of 1760, and Lord Curzon added the marble screen. Aurangzeb, unwilling to be a burden on the state, paid for his mausoleum with money earned by selling white caps he had quilted, and the walls surrounding the town were ordered by the same Shah. He chose this final resting-place partly because the ground was hallowed by the dargah of Sayyid Zain ud-Din who (died in 1370), a Muslim *pir* or 'saint'. In Iran, 'dargah' literally means 'doorway', but throughout India it has the sense of a shrine-tomb, and here Zain ud-Din is venerated in a simple dargah with two gates inlaid with bronze, silver and brass built in his honour long after his death.

Nearby are the tombs of Azam Shah (Aurangzeb's second son), his wife and daughter; and the dargah of Sayyid Burhan ud-Din who died in 1344.

Burhan succeeded Muntajib ud-Din, who was dispatched as a Chishtiyyah mystic missionary to Deccan by Nizam ud-Din Aulia with seven hundred disciples from Delhi. Nizam's mausoleum is described in my *Rajasthan, Agra, Delhi* (1989). Burhan's is said to possess hairs of the Prophet Muhammad's beard, which are believed locally to increase in number annually. I was also shown by a friendly local Muslim stumps in the pavement said to be the remnants of solid silver trees which waxed marvellously after the saint's death but were hacked down and sold to pay for the shrine's upkeep. The shrine doors are said to incorporate silver from these trees. Burhan's successor was the Zain ud-Din whose shrine-tomb we have already viewed.

To the right of Burhan's tomb are the tombs of Nizam ul-Mulk Asaf Jah I, founder of the royal dynasty of Hyderabad, and his son Nasir Jang.

Westward I found the mausoleum of Bani Begum, an 18th-century work commemorating the consort of one of Shah Aurangzeb's sons. Like the Aurangabad Bibi-ki Maqbara, this garden tomb is sheltered by a wall with domed kiosks, and charming pavilions echoing the Persian identification of paradise with the eternal stone garden enlivened with running water and flowers as a symbol of mortality. A similar effect is given by the Red Garden or Lal Bagh, created by Khan Jahan late in the 17th century, and deriving its appellation from its red porphyry.

On the sudden apparition of a rickshaw-wallah, I gratefully accepted a ride to the dargah of Malik Ambar (1626), Ethiopian minister to the last Nizam Shahi ruler, with the tomb of his wife Karima. Irrationally I felt as though rulers come here to die; it reminded me of the city of the dead at Thatta, near Karachi. The rickshaw-wallah sucked a boiled sweet as he watched me disappearing in the direction of Abu 'l-Hasan Tana Shah's tomb, burial place of the last Sultan of Golconda. The ever-resourceful if sacrilegious British turned Nizam Shah Bairi's tomb into a bungalow, but no such indignity damaged the Ahmad Nizam Shah dargah, where the remains of the founding Shah of Ahmadnagar (1490–1509) have their last resting-place. The square domed mausoleum has corner kiosks, the whole on a platform as though the shadow of the Shah wanted to view his surroundings. A migrant stork flew overhead, and a couple of mangy pi-dogs sniffed at the air in a kind of routine hope blended with the steadfast view that little good comes from rickshaw-wallahs or their burdens.

I managed eventually to locate the earliest Muslim dargah in Khuldabad: the 14th-century shrine to one Sayyid Bakhsh, west of the town. A Muslim woman was sitting out with her tiny daughter, sharing a piece of unleavened bread in total silence, while crows with glittering eyes and wings like elbows watched from all points of the compass ready to pounce on lost crumbs.

Daulatabad
'Abode of Good Fortune' or 'Success' or 'Victory', the city was known in pre-Muslim times as Devagiri, 'Hill of God', presumably because early Hindus assumed in their Vedic nature-worship that the great natural granite outcrop (at 183 m a good 100 m taller than Trichy's rock) must have been thrust up by a divine hand. Like Ajanta and Ellora, there is no doubt that Buddhism achieved a temporary hold over this region, for we have 1st-century B.C. Buddhist rock caves to prove it. Natural it may be, but Devagiri's conical rock stronghold has been adapted by many successive rulers, notably by the Yadava Hindu dynasty and the 14th-century Sultan of Delhi, Muhammad bin Tughlaq.

The Yadavas were a loose confederation of tribes which decided on Devagiri as their capital and over the centuries by a process of political deals and military strength based on Devagiri's apparent invulnerability kept their lands and powers intact, first as feudatories of the Western Chalukya dynasty and then independently from 1183, with the collapse of that line. The earliest Yadavas had hewn away the irregular face of the conical rock to create a sheer smooth vertical face between fifty and sixty metres high, above a moat dug 10 to 15 metres into the rockface, with a causeway permitting access across the moat. A Hindu town on the eastern slope has been demolished by Muslim conquerors who reused the stone.

The Delhi Sultans coveted the wealth and power of Yadava Devagiri and in 1294 Ala ud-Din, nephew of the Sultan Jalal ud-Din Firuz Shah Khilji attacked Ramchandra, Raja of Devagiri, and succeeded in overcoming resistance, returning to Delhi with gold, silver and jewels as the price of Ramchandra's ransom. Ramchandra was appointed Governor subject to Delhi, but his son Shankara defied Delhi's demands for tribute and was put to death in 1313 by Kafur Hazardinari acting for the Delhi Sultanate. Infuriated by the Hindu refusal to lie down and sham dead, Sultan Qutb ud-Din Mubarak Shah Khilji (1316–20) marched personally on recalcitrant Devagiri, and created the Friday Mosque (1318), the first Muslim monument in the town. It had no minaret, so that function was performed by the so-called Chand Minaret (1435), actually a victory tower and military observation post overlooking the north-east. It resembles closely Mahmud Gawan's madrasa at Bidar (1472), based in turn on the Khargird madrasa in Khurasan.

But Devagiri assumed major national importance only from 1327, when Ghiyas ud-Din Muhammad bin Tughlaq, dissatisfied with his new Delhi capital called Tughlaqabad, precipitately decided that Delhi lay too far north for his ambition to conquer the whole of India. We know from Chinese history that new emperors would often choose to move their capital, and this influences Japanese imperial tradition too, but the only transfer consisted of court and attendants. In the case of Muhammad bin Tughlaq, the plan was to move the entire population of Dehli. One of the greatest plays in Kannada is Girish Karnad's second work, *Tughlaq* (1964), in whose first scene the new Sultan announces to a throng:

'Your surprise is natural, but I beg you to realise that this is no mad whim of a tyrant. My ministers and I took this decision after careful thought and discussion. My empire is large now and embraces the South and I need a capital which is at its heart. Delhi is too near the border and as you well know its peace is never free from the danger of invasion. But for me what is more crucial is that Daulatabad is a Hindu city, and as the nation's capital it will come to symbolise the bond between Muslims and Hindus which I want to foster. I invite you all to come with me to Daulatabad' . . .

At the end of Scene Six, Muhammad's idealism has become monomaniac tyranny:

'Every living soul in Delhi will leave for Daulatabad within a fortnight. I was too soft, I see that now. They only understand the whip. Everyone must leave. Not a light must be seen in the windows of Delhi, not a wisp of smoke must rise from its chimneys. Nothing but an empty graveyard of Delhi will satisfy me now.'

Daulatabad. View down from the heights of Ghiyas ud-Din's fortress

114

Seven hundred miles had to be traversed, while famine stared the travellers in the face. Of course the enterprise failed, and Shah Muhammad was compelled to leave his new stronghold for the north again, where insistent Mughal raids increased in scale and intensity. His Governor, Zafar Khan, rebelled in 1347 and became the first Bahmani Sultan, retaining it as a northern garrison, just as Shah Muhammad had retained it as a southern fortress. So Daulatabad never became the effective capital of a united India, though it became the Nizam Shahi dynasty of Ahmadnagar's capital in 1600. The Mughal Shah Jahan too regarded Daulatabad as a key to domination of South India, and his general Mahabat Khan besieged it successfully in 1633, but lost it to Nizam ul-Mulk in 1757, three years before it was occupied by Maratha forces.

It is a great, almost rock-climber's ascent, steep, adventurous, with constantly changing views across the plain. The fortress we enter is principally that of Shah Muhammad's time: a citadel for a world-conqueror protected by three lines of defence on the east. The outermost wall 5 km long sheltered the population at large in a town now as abandoned as Cairo's City of the Dead. The second wall enclosed an area 1.2 km x 0.4 km known to Lahawri as Mahakot (Great Fort) and the third encloses the Balakot, with a magnificent entrance gateway, re-used Jain caves, a broad stairway hewn in the rock leading to a Mughal *baradari* (a pavilion usually with 12 pillars) built for Shah Jahan's visit in 1636 and another flight of a hundred steps leading to the eyrie, defended in its turn by cannon. The multiple stout wooden doorways are spiked against elephant charges, and an iron barrier at the end of a long tunnel is recorded as having been heated to the point where no attackers could touch it; eventually smoke emanating from it would choke invaders.

Near the third gate is the Chini Mahal, or China Palace, where Abu 'l-Hasan, last Qutb Shahi ruler of Golconda, was imprisoned by Aurangzeb from 1687 to 1700. Close to it is the cannon called Qila Shikan, 'Fort-Breaker', adorned with a ram's head and inscribed in Persian 'Storm Creator'.

After all the day-trippers had whirled away in their dust-clouds to Aurangabad, I sipped tea and dunked Very Nice biscuits in a tumbledown shack of limited pretensions, to enjoy that quiet, that radiance of twilight, those clouds of birds flocking home to roost, that easy content one feels in having achieved yet another lifetime's ambition. Many never reached Daulatabad from Delhi; many died here starving or ill; many never reached Delhi on the disillusioned trail back north. But you and I? We made it, after all.

Yeola

Bus passengers from Aurangabad to Bombay or Daman deserve a rest at Nasik, and so I decided to get a ticket to the pilgrimage city, and stop overnight. My bus parped and blared its ramshackle way out of Aurangabad bus station at 7.15 a.m., loaded not only to the doors and gangways, but piled up on the roof so that we could have been mistaken by a distant vulture for a double-decker. Rickshaw-wallahs pedalled gamely ahead, neither getting out of the way nor looking behind them in the belief that Lord Shiva would keep them safe for another day's acrid pollution. The Holy Cross Auditorium, army barracks and Christian barracks left behind, the bus eventually entered the Deccani plain. Above the dusty plateau as we headed west I made out to the north Daulatabad citadel above a band of trees, above a rocky fastness.

In January the plains are dry and almost featureless, the occasional listless acacia tenacious in its hold on life from one monsoon to the next, but luckily India's economic base is rapidly expanding from agricultural dominance to the industrial and service sectors. It's just that on the way to Yeola one might almost have stepped into the pages of Jeannine Auboyer's *Daily Life in Ancient India from 200 B.C. to 700 A.D.*(1965), and indeed the newspapers were not full of factory-openings or cultural events but of a self-immolator, Rajiv Goswamy, in agony after having set himself alight in the cause of high-caste prejudice against *harijans*, an act actually applauded by Pritish Nandy, editor of the *Illustrated Weekly*. The ancient caste system, ingrained as the *Mahabharata* and enshrined as the family deity, seems to be immovable, implacable, and virtually innate in the Hindu soul. To remove its tentacles in the interest of modernity would appear to involve fatal damage to the body and psyche of Hindu man.

At Yeola the bus-driver decided to stop in the bazaar for a coffee, and I roamed around with a jackal's inquisitive nose, eyes and ears. An outdoor barber's hut invited passers-by to partake of a quick haircut; other shacks had been knocked together in the shade of a spreading banyan tree for shelter against unrelenting sunshine, and there old men sat with glasses and little cups to survey champing goats, snuffling pigs and a shiny new bicycle recently arrived from Bombay. A Hindu shrine attracted no attention: it wasn't the time of day. W.S. Caine's *Picturesque India* (1899) noted that then Yeola was 'a town of some importance, well worth visiting, with a large silk-weaving and gold twist industry, employing 7,000 persons of both sexes. A very superior yellow silk cloth, called *pitambar*, and fine silk pieces with borders of silver or gold are made at Yeola.' At that time, Pune was also carrying on a flourishing trade in gold and silver thread, particularly for the sari borders called the *shikar* or hunting pattern.

A dhoti-clad ancient wizened of countenance and barefoot produced a passport-size photograph from his greasy wallet. 'See him, look him,' he beamed through his wrinkles at me, displaying a serious-minded young man in a western suit, probably scared stiff but with a kind of nervous arrogance necessary for self-esteem. I beamed back, clueless but intrigued.

'My son,' cackled the ancient, like the middle witch in the Scottish play. I feared we were to hear news of Birnam Wood's proximity to Dunsinane. He pointed with a bony index finger at the picture. 'My son, famous professor at your University, United States, Master Choose It.' 'University of Massachusetts?' I volunteered. 'Achcha', confirmed the bent one, 'Master Mastic.' 'He teaches mathematics at Massachusetts.' A vigorous shaking of the head indicated that I had gleaned the nub of the matter. Nothing is more likely than my crony's assertion. Indians have excelled at mathematics for centuries, and in our own Srinivasa Ramanujam has been described by Julian Huxley as the greatest mathematician of the age.

I recalled Jawaharlal Nehru's remarks on Ramanujam's genius, from his period as a clerk in Madras Port Trust to years at Cambridge, where he 'did work of profound value and amazing originality'.

Nehru continues in *The Discovery of India* (1946): 'Ramanujam's brief life

Yeola. Barber's shop, coffee shop, shrine to Shiva

and death are symbolic of conditions in India. Of our millions how few get any education at all, how many live on the verge of starvation; of even those who get some education, how many have nothing to look forward to but a clerkship in some office on a pay that is usually far less than the unemployment dole in England.'

The ancient of Yeola, demonstrating the artful way that Dame Fortune can fiddle statistics, must have felt isolated not only from his distinguished son, living in New England on a comfortable salary, but from his friends and neighbours whose close-knit families have stayed at home, in traditional occupations, speaking Marathi and living at peace – in general – with a fairly large Muslim minority and a smaller neo-Buddhist minority paying obeisance to the views and objectives of the late Baba Sahib Ambedkar, a social reformer and political leader appealing to lower castes.

Nasik

Legend tells how the elixir of immortality, disputed between gods and demons, was eventually carried off by the gods, who let four drops fall to earth from the *kumbh* or chalice. These drops fell at Hardwar and Prayag (now Allahabad) on the Ganga, at Ujjain in Madhya Pradesh, and at Nasik. A mela or festival is held roughly every four years according to astrological convention in each of these cities in turn, when the Sun enters Capricorn and Jupiter is in Aries. The purpose of pilgrimage to these holy sites is to wash away one's sins in holy water in an attempt to break free from the endless cycle of birth and rebirth. At Prayag in 1990, 6 February was deemed highly auspicious; such an occasion – affirmed the astrologers – would not recur until 2233 A. D. Nasik's pilgrimage came round in August-September 1991, Ujjain's turn in 1992, Hardwar's in 1993, Allahabad's in 1994, then the cycle begins again. The preëminence of Prayag is due to the belief that the present era, or Kali Yuga, began there when Brahma offered a sacrifice at the confluence of the spiritual river of wisdom Saraswati and the visible sacred rivers Yamuna and Ganga.

You can tell a Hindu saint or mystic from the charlatans, according to my new friend Ram Das, by the fact that the genuine mystic never converses with a non-Hindu. But he will emerge for Kumbh Mela at the four holy sites, attending the Great Hindu Congress for 'State of the Faith' meetings in enormous marquees, and demonstrating by public example how to perform the rites. Some holy men take no monastic office, but sit in perfect stillness to give *darshan*, that is to say 'a sight', which in temples will refer to holy images symbolising deities, yet applies in the case of living saints or mystics too. As you saunter through the pandemonium of barefoot sadhus blackened with endless exposure to India's pitiless sun, you come across squatting astrologers with almanacks and beads. Some cannot read, so the almanack becomes a tradesman's sign, like an old-fashioned barber's striped pole, or a pawnbroker's three balls.

Figures in the *Indian Express* suggest that as many as five million sadhus roam the country, begging for their precarious livelihood. Devotees acquire merit, it is tacitly assumed, by providing food and water as these mendicants reach their village: it is the villagers who provide hospitality to most of them.

Rama's Kund is a place to sit on your haunches and wait for sadhus, perhaps even for ordinary pilgrims from every walk of life, for no millionaire is too proud to forget his mortal obligations in a society revealing such contrasts between rich and poor. A rich Bengali in freshly-laundered khaki shorts, and flannels, escorted at a discreet distance by his bodyguard, approached the waters of Godavari, made his offering, and prayed. A prancing sadhu, high on ganja, glaring through telltale bloodshot eyes, tinkled with ankle-bells and let out a stream of abuse at the Bengali. His body, naked except for a grimy loincloth, had been tattooed with the sacred name of Lord Vishnu; his hair was matted and congealed with ash and cowdung.

'I am Ram Das', murmured a gentle voice in my ear, 'you are from which country?' I told him, half-turning, 'but I have not much attachment.'

'That is ideal, sir, the loosening of attachment. I too I worship each and every morning to try to loosen my attachment. I try to read some part of Chandogya Upanishad.'

'Asking his way from village to village, certainly he will reach Gandhara', I interposed, quoting that Upanishad. He smiled broadly. 'And do you "go into the forest", Ram Das?'

He made quandaristic movements of his neck and head which I was free to interpret in any way I chose. 'I think I still have my eyes bandaged. I am not even released to search for Gandhara.'

'And would you recognise it if you saw it?'

'If it exists, then I might not recognise it. If it is only a part of my own senses, then I should recognise it, perhaps. But you would not recognise my Gandhara at all. You would be thinking, what nonsense is this Ram Dam telling me?'

'I should assume that your Gandhara was real to you, but I should not wish to share it with you, and I do not wish to persuade you that my own Gandhara is more real than yours, or better.'

The third stage of life in India is the withdrawal from daily routines; the fourth and last is the solitary way 'into the forest' of the man who renounces the world, except for begging in it, and devotes his life to meditation towards release from suffering, becoming a sannyasi. The largest assembly of such sannyasin – for they do not always seek solitude – is the duodenary Kumbh Mela at Prayag, otherwise known as Allahabad. But there are hundreds of thousands of other *tirthas*, or holy places, throughout India, from Kaniya Kumari (haunt of the Divine Virgin) to Himalaya, haunt of Lord Shiva, from which sacred Ganga descends to the plains and the Bay of Bengal. Ganga is India's *suranadi* or divine river par excellence, but here at Nasik flows the sacred Godavari, and it too will reach annihilation by merging in the Bay of Bengal. A Hindi booklet on sale at the bathing ghats relates in its English summary that at 'Asthi Vilaya Tirtha people drop the bones of the dead which desolve in water within 3½ hours. The following great people have been dropped in the Asthi Vilaya Tirtha after their death: Mahatma Gandhi, Jawaharlal Nehru, Lal Bahadur Shastri, Dr Rajendra Prasad, Kannamwarji, Lohiya Maharaj and Mama Dandekarji.'

'Do you want to drop your bones here, friend Das?'

He regarded me half-humorously. 'I am for Varanasi, friend. My home is Lalganj, near Mirzapur.'

'What do you come here to find, if great Varanasi is so close to your own home?'

'I have come to the third stage of life. I have seen Hardwar; when I came back my office they said, "take promotion Ram Das". I have seen Ujjain; when I came back my office they said, take one more promotion. But if you go to Nasik-Panchavati, we think we shall not be seeing you again. My wife she is well provided for, my daughters they are both married, my son he in States M.I.T. Listen, Ram, I say. You go to reach back to find these places where the Vedas call.'

We read together the booklet. 'This holy place is very old and references are found pointing out its importances in all the Four Yugas. It was known as Padmanagar in Krita Yuga, Trikantak in Treta Yuga, Janasthana in Dwapara Yuga, and Nasik in Kali Yuga.' The yuga-system of chronology is not found in the Vedas, and first occurs in the great literary epics, being described by the monkey-god Hanuman. A maha-yuga, or 'Great Yuga' consists of 4,320,000 years, and 2,000 maha-yugas or 8,640 million years comprise one kalpa, equating to one day and one night of Brahma. Krita Yuga consisted of 1,728,000 years of eternal righteousness, a golden age without hatred or fear, when all castes fulfilled their functions, and all prospered without religious divisions. Treta Yuga consisted of 1,296,000 years during which virtue declined by a quarter, and men performed religious acts with a view to reward, depending on ceremonies and rites; asceticism decreased. Dwapara Yuga comprised 864,000 years during which virtue declined by a half with respect to Krita Yuga, the Vedas multiplied, increasing dissension among sects, truth and goodness diminished, giving way to unworthy desires and the proliferation of natural calamities and human diseases.

In the Kali Yuga, which we inhabit today, a period of 432,000 years has seen virtue reduced to a quarter of that in Krita Yuga. Rites and religious practices fell into disuse, sectarianism spread, crime and disease became ever more prevalent: so did anger, revenge, and intolerance.

Ram Das held his nose between two fingers and snorted, then coughed. A banana-seller in a pink shirt narcissistically touched back his straight black hair and put an elbow akimbo. 'One bunch three rupees, mister.' I bought a bunch and shared them at the water's edge with Ram Das, opposite a low concrete islet almost entirely filled with a hideous low-relief orange-red Hanuman figure trampling the demon.

Lord Rama is supposed to have spent part of his exile from court in the vicinity, with his brother Lakshman and his bride Sita. Most shrines are of the 18th century, when Islamic domed roofs influenced Maratha design. Ram Das took me to Sri Lakshmi Narayan Temple (1756). I waited outside while he made offerings and pondered the life and teachings of his namesake, the Maharashtra mystic Ramadasa who was born in 1608. He lost his father when he was only seven, then five years later ran away from home, practised penance at Takli not far from Nasik from twelve years, culminating it is said in the realization of God. He wandered for a further twelve years, after which he built a temple at Chaphal on the river Krishna and influenced the anti-imperialist Hindu leader Chhatrapati Shivaji Maharaj. Ramadasa wrote the influential *Dasabodha* and extended a chain of monasteries across Maharashtra where, he assured devotees, one could realise God even in this existence, and such a realisation is the summum bonum of human life and conduct. Everything in this world is holy *except the mind of a person not wholly devoted to God*. This accounts for the ideas of reverence which you find attached in Maharashtra to mountains and rivers, the lingam and the yoni, trees and cows. It accounts for the wide-ranging acceptance Hindus give to shrines and temples of other faiths. The ninefold devotional way begins with *sravana*: listening to the glories of God, reading the Sastras, and meditating on them; *kirtana*, or singing God's praises; *smarana*, or remembering God's name; *padasevana*, or service at the feet of God; *archana*, or worship of God; *vandana*, or obeisance to God; *dasya bhakti*, or the becoming of God by whole-hearted service; *sakhya*, or friendship towards God by repudiating any act or relationship which will damage the devotee's attachment to God; and finally *atma-nivedana*, or surrender to God by uniting with him through the mediation of the guru.

Nasik. Pilgrim bathing area of Panchavati

So I spent less time at Nasik looking at temples than at people, and wondering about the devotional stage reached by these pilgrims, each doggedly offering gifts of rupees or fruit to images representing the gods, at Nasik usually Shiva and his aspects. Shiva as the God of Skulls, the terrifying Kapaleshvara, is worshipped at a six-hundred-year old temple reached at the top of fifty steps. The greatest temple is Kala Rama ('Black Rama' so called from the colour of the figure within), an enclosure 260 feet by 120. The shrine within measures 92 feet by 65 and dates from 1782. The Rameshvara Temple, on the east bank between the river and the Kala Rama, has a lingam, but the most interesting feature of this Maratha-period temple is its mandapam roof, with grotesque animals. Rama's Kund, an artificial pool in the river, is said to be the site where Rama performed the funeral rites of his father, King Dasaratha of Ayodhya. Rama's chief temple has been called Panchavati, or 'The Five Ban-

121

yans', and this has given its name to a whole district: it is closed as you would expect to non-Hindus.

I stayed at Hotel Sachin 3 km outside Nasik on the Bombay-Agra highway, but you could lodge at the Hotel Samrat near the bus stand if you wanted somewhere more central, or at the Green View Hotel if you wanted to stay on the road to Trimbak, outside the hubbub of Nasik's pilgrim inns and hostels.

Trimbak ('The Three-Eyed') refers again to Lord Shiva, described in a hymn as 'Trimbak, the sweet-scented increaser of prosperity' and lies 30 km from Nasik, from which devotees travel to pay homage to the source of the Godavari and Shiva at the temple to Trimbakeshvara, which resembles Sundar Narayan at Nasik and was built in 1730 by Baji Rao Peshwa at a cost of nearly a million rupees, a fantastic sum in those days. You are allowed to look into the temple from a vantage point to see the impressive courtyard and shrine. A flight of some 700 steps leads up to a tank fed by the Godavari's source; the persistent are rewarded by stunning views.

A hill outside Nasik called Sunar Ali gives a wonderful view of the city and its winding river: the Old Fort or Junagarh may look modest, but it dates from Aurangzeb's time: that is to say the 17th century.

The Old Bazaar lives up to its name: no supermarkets for the traders of Nasik in their wooden huts, purveying bicycle parts and rice, ironmongery and cheap saris, plastic bangles and umbrellas against the crushing sun. *Chandni* and *The Italian Job* were showing at Nasik cinemas.

If you feel that New Delhi has nothing to do with the India that you came to see, and Goan beaches even less, then Nasik will provide pungent aromas, cripples in search of a cure or a few assuaging rupees, and a kaleidoscope of colours and shouts to convince you that authentic India can never change. It is always as idiosyncratic at Nasik as you thought: the priests get richer, and the pilgrims feel more devout for spending their time, energy and money on the pursuit of unworldliness. Bathing ghats, scattered kunds, thronged bazaars, busy temples and immortal river swirl with a vivacity no city in Europe can rival, unless you count Istanbul part-European.

Ten km from Nasik on the Bombay road you come to a memorable complex of twenty-four rock-cut Hinayana Buddhist monasteries and temples of chaitya hall and vihara type, a chaitya having a stupa at one end of an apsidal hall usually with a nave and two aisles separated by columns, and a vihara being a monastery with cells opening off a central courtyard, often preceded by a portico or verandah. The chaitya hall was by far the more significant building type in the Western Ghats area in a radius of 320 km or so from Nasik. Their sequence from the second century B.C. to the second century A.D. is: Bhaja, Kondane, Pitalkhora, Ajanta Cave 10, Bedsa, Ajanta Cave 9, Nasik, Karla, and lastly Kanheri which we have seen close to Bombay. Scholars estimate the order of their excavation from the rock by the degree to which the example follows wooden construction, beginning with the horseshoe arch at Bhaja's Cave 12 6 km from Karla, and ending with Kanheri's Cave 3, in many ways an imitation of Karla's Cave 8, but even there an atavistic attachment to timber reverberates for all to see.

Nasik Cave 18 of Satavahana date (1st century B.C.) recalls the superseded wooden style of earlier Hinayana monasteries. Outside, the arch preserves bas-reliefs of auspicious animals and emblems, and similarly low-relief architectural features such as cornices and railings. Compared with the complex and beautiful exterior, within the chaitya hall all is austere, fastidious, gifted to the Lord Buddha at a time before images of him were permitted. Caves 17 and 20 are viharas connected with the chaitya hall by staircases, of which that on the right no longer exists. The Buddha images were added in the Vakataka period, that is the 6th century, as occurred in the case of the chaitya panel in the rear wall of Cave 10, which is otherwise of Kshatrapa age, 2nd to early 3rd centuries A.D. Nasik Cave 3 resembles Cave 10 in its pot-like octagonal column bases on the verandah, with an inverted-pot capital giving a mirror effect, as at Caves 17 and 20. The actual doorway is surrounded by an imitation decorated wooden doorway protected by sculpted guardians. A great hall opens into nineteen modest cells for monks, with beds carved in the naked rock and not much else to distract the mind from Nirvana, unless you consider the female figures worshipping at the far end. Few of the Buddhist caves here at Pandu Lena are as spectacular or well-preserved as the adjacent 17–18, the nearby 20, or the imposing 3 and 10, but when you realise how many people visit Ellora and Ajanta without considering Nasik, it seems careless to pass from Bombay to Nasik without taking their very brief detour south of the main road.

Shirdi and Sai Baba
A mere 23 km from Nasik lies the little town of Shirdi, which has become a place of pilgrimage for miracle-seekers, though Sai Baba wrote no books and behaved in a peculiar way charted by Arthur Osborne in *The incredible Sai Baba* (2nd ed., 1972). Originating from Andhra Pradesh, Sai ('saint' in Persian) Baba ('father' in Hindi) came to Shirdi and lived there for nearly fifty years, until his death in 1918. Even his death did not stop the flow of pilgrims – in India it rarely does. It is not decorous for a European like myself to comment on the cult of Sai Baba who is hardly known beyond India's frontiers: I leave comment to Professor K. R. Dikshit of Pune University. In *Maharashtra in Maps* (1986) he writes of Shirdi, 'unlike the traditional and age-old religious places, this attracts tourists of a different genre who believe more in the miraculous powers of the late Saint, and would like to be their beneficiary, than the class that derives satisfaction in being the devotee of God and would like to imbibe an infinitesimally small fraction of the divine virtue. Regardless of the Cult, the place is flourishing with its hotels, mostly restaurants, and guides, not to talk of smart alecs who lurk around watching for an opportunity to make quick bucks.' Like Fatima, like Lourdes, Shirdi too has succumbed to the fast-miracle tourist trade.

3   KARNATAKA

Early Karnataka

'Karnataka' as we know it today is an invention of 1956, when demarcation ruled where Kannada-speaking majorities lived, by and large. Before, it had been known as 'Mysore State', but then it acquired territories belonging to Madras, Hyderabad, and Bombay, which shifted their own boundaries as Tamil Nadu, Andhra Pradesh and Maharashtra. New Karnataka is shaped like a boomerang facing east, with its two major cities close to the throwing hand at the lower edge: Mysore, now overtaken by the new industrial capital Bangalore. Its coastline, from Mangalore north to Karwar, divides Kerala from Goa. The vast plateau rises from the west and south and tips north and east, so that rivers and streams empty into the Bay of Bengal. The Kannada-speaking Dravidians form the majority, but there are pockets of Urdu-speaking Muslims (about 9%) throughout the state, 15% Indo-Aryan Konkanis and Marathas in the north and west, and 12% Dravidian Tamils and Telugus in the south and east.

Palaeolithic men inhabited the river valleys, and used stone tools, then Neolithic copper tools enabled men to settle and flourish in permanent sites at T. Narsipur and Hemmige (Mysore), Hallur (Dharwar), Piklihal and Maski (Raichur) and in Bellary taluq. Neolithic Karnataka, about 2500–1000 B.C., was characterised by ancestor worship and burial in pits, sometimes below the family hut. Iron was introduced to these smaller Dravidian people by Aryans from the north, about 1000 B.C., characterised by megalith structures over burials. The Mauryan dynasty pushed into ancient Karnataka: the story is that Chandragupta of the Mauryas ended his life here as a Jain monk in 297 B.C. but even if that is legend, we have a historic edict of Ashoka at Maski near Raichur dated to the middle of the 3rd century B.C.

We know that the Satavahanas reigned from the 2nd century B.C. to the 2nd A.D. because of coin finds (including Roman coins of the period) and their typical white painted pottery. They were succeeded by the Kadambas in the north of Karnataka (4th to 6th centuries) and the Gangas in the south (4th to 10th), the latter becoming subordinate to the rising Chalukyas of Aihole (from about 450) and Badami (from the 6th to the 9th). The Rashtrakuta dynasty rose in 753 and fell in 973, having created the Shiva temples on Elephanta and the Kailasa temple at Ellora. The Chalukyas came to power again, until 1189, when the Hoysala dynasty emerged to dazzle their contemporaries with their many magnificent temples, at the same time as the Chalukyas of Kalyani and the Yadava dynasty of Devagiri in Maharashtra. In 1336 the Vijayanagar Empire was founded, roughly simultaneously with the Bahmani dynasty first of Gulbarga, then of Bijapur. Vijayanagar collapsed in 1565, by which time the

Map of Karnataka

Adil Shahis had become established at Bijapur. In the North, the Muslims, Marathas and British vied for power while in the south the Wadiyar dynasty held Mysore, except for the interregnum of Haidar Ali and Tipu Sultan.

Karnataka became a byword for peace, stability and progress in South India in the 20th century, and Bangalore has steadily assumed predominance in science and technology, particularly in electronics and aeronautics.

Bangalore

A Sikh I met beside Ulsoor Lake looked me up and down as though estimating my worth as a confederate, and exclaimed conspiratorially, 'Between us, I think Bangalore is quite a dull stick. Not a patch on my Lucknow,' and I fear that I must sigh and agree with him. As a touring centre, it has advantages: 100 km SE are Kolar Gold Fields (visits on Mondays, Wednesdays and Saturdays); 60 km NE are Nandi Hills, with a Tipu Sultan fort and good trekking; 21 km S is Bannerghatta National Park (closed on Tuesdays); and 120 km SW are the Shivasamudram Falls on the river Kaveri.

But Bangalore is a modern city, with good employment opportunities for scientists and businessmen, but lacking the irresistible charms of Bidar or Bijapur. As the centre of the silk industry, it has a Department of Sericulture, and open farms on the road to Mysore; an aquarium on Kasturba Road for anyone keen on marine life; and an Industrial and Technological Museum next door to the Government Museum.

The city dates from as recently as 1537, when the Vijayanagar kingdom made a grant of land to an ally called Kempe Gowda, who invited craftsmen and merchants to practise their skills in an area protected by four strategic watch-towers. Haidar Ali and Tipu Sultan strengthened the town in the 18th century, and the Wadiyar dynasty of Mysore – restored by the British after Tipu's death – enlarged it and the British moved their main cantonment from Srirangapatnam to the much higher and healthier Bangalore. The cantonment area, spread out and amply endowed with parks and gardens, encouraged the building of classical bungalows, and later in the 19th century taller buildings with steeper roofs covered with Mangalore tiles and with 'monkey tops', or pointed hoods over the upper part of windows. Some believe that these were created to keep out monkeys, others that they provided perches for the rascals to foregather. Even now these streets retain their evocative names: Cunningham Crescent, Leonard Lane, Alexander Street, though their residents nowadays will be prosperous civil servants or high-ranking military men.

The five-hour sightseeing trip by bus includes Ulsoor Lake, Bull Temple, Tipu's Palace, Lal Bagh, Cubbon Park, Government Museum, Vidhana Soudha, Arts and Crafts on M.G. Road, and in season also the National Park. I suggest hiring an auto-rickshaw and seeing 'Boom City', the fifth largest in India, at your own speed. The traffic is much lighter than in Bombay or Madras, and you can see far more than the bus tour, spending longer wherever you feel inclined.

The place to start is the Kempe Gowda town, bounded by Kempambudi Tank on the west, Ulsoor Lake in the east, Bellary Road in the north and Lal Bagh in the south, and within that small rectangle (the whole of the modern city covers 130 sq km) the southwestern quarter. After Kempe Gowda had built temples to the god of power, Anjaneya, and the god of good fortune, Vinayaka, he created Basavangudi, the temple to Nandi, Shiva's bull mount. On the way to Bull Temple I stopped at the Ganesha Temple to enjoy a bridegroom's offerings, prayers, and solicitations among a crowd of well-wishers and a strident band dressed in white. A huge draped Ganesha filled the shrine almost to overflowing. At the top of the hill a massive garlanded black and shiny Nandi bulged in its own shrine, overwhelming a small lingam shrine at the back. Its modern gopuram rose swathed in scaffolding. Much more fascinating was the underground Sri Gavi Gangadhareshwara Temple where, every 14 January they said, a ray of light passes between the horns of a Nandi outside the temple and lights the idol inside. I have never met anyone present at that precise moment, but then, I have never met anyone I could believe who has seen the Loch Ness monster and my credulity threshold is quite high, even in Kempegowdanagar. I explored three levels of excavation in the cave, finding a black stone Hanuman decked in red and sporting a bathroom towel. A mynah bird loudly questioned my credentials at the gate, where an ancient bearded scribe in a worn dhoti rummaged in his plastic briefcase for a grubby clipboard. My driver then demanded twice the agreed fare to continue, so I paid him off with a patient shrug to his evident anger and took a grinning rival's vehicle to the Fort, opposite a Hanuman Temple with Dravidian gopuram and dome, lottery tickets being sold beside at a rate normally connected with hot cakes.

This is not Kempe Gowda's original mud fort, but a much stouter and taller oval construction made by Haidar Ali in 1761. The facings and decorations have largely vanished, so we can only faintly visualise the original fort, which fell to Cornwallis in 1791, but my first surprise was a pair of elephants over a Shiva lingam in the forecourt: quite what the Muslim Haidar Ali would have made of this I cannot claim to know.

Much more interesting, within a short stroll, is the Summer Palace within the former fort precinct begun by Haidar Ali in 1781 and finished ten years later by Tipu. Designed as a two-storey building, with a large open courtyard, its fluted wooden pillars are connected by finely-proportioned cusped arches as you would expect in a Muslim court. Walls and ceilings were once painted and gilded, but nothing remains. The zenana on the sides had ceilings lower but richly ornamented.

Haidar Ali was also responsible for the Lal Bagh ('Red Garden') but its charming iron-and-glass conservatory dates from 1889, when the foundation stone was laid, according to a portentous plaque, 'by H.R.H. Prince Albert Victor Christian Edward of Wales.' The botanical gardens have trees captioned in Latin and Kannada, shady garden benches on which city workers sleep, and an enchanting Japanese garden compels nostalgia for Kyoto. Bangalore's Horticultural Show filled the Conservatory, and I enquired of a ruminative judge what flowers flourished best at this height at this latitude (3000 feet a.s.l.). 'Really whatever perennial you put in, it will grow,' he assured me. 'Roses, celosia, cockscomb'. But then so do pipal (the bodhi of Buddhism), believed by Hindus to be inhabited by the trinity of Brahma, Vishnu and Shiva. At Anuradhapura in Sri Lanka a pipal has been dated by dendrochronology to 288 B. C. and the finest specimen in Lal Bagh lifts its weary, haunted boughs in a gesture of sempiternal fatigue. 'I would die if I could, but...'

BANGALORE

Scale: 1:57,000

0   0.57   1.14 kms

REFERENCES

Agricultural University C2
Raman Institute B2
Kempegowda Tower D4
Golf Grounds C3
All India Radio C3
Central Telegraph Office C3,4
Legislators' Home C4
Russel Market C3,4
Dept. of Tourism
Government of Karnataka A7
General Post Office C4
S.J Polytechnic C4
High Court C4
Parade Grounds A86
Government Museum C4
Visvesvaraya Industrial &
  Technological Museum C4
British Library C4
Max. Muller Bhavan C4
Cauvery Arts & Crafts CD4
Public Utility Building D4
Karnataka State Tourism
  Development Corporation C4
Mayo Hall B7
Football Stadium D4
Kanteerava Stadium C4
Public Library C4
Cauvery Bhavan/Indian Airlines C4
Bangalore Bus Terminus B4
City Market B4
Corporation Offices C4
Unity Buildings/Air India C4
Handloom House C4
Town Hall C4
Ravindra Kalakshetra BC4
Priyadarshini Handloom House C4
Fort B4
Tippu's Palace B4
Kempegowda Tower B5
Gavi Gangadareshwara Temple B5
Gokhale Institute of Public Affairs B4
Bull Temple B5
Indian Institute of World Culture B5
Jayanagar Shopping Complex BC6

Map of Bangalore

MG - ROAD

1 Govt. Museum & Venkatappa Art Gallery
2 Visvesvaraya Industrial & Technological Museum
3 Institution of Engineers
4 Aquarium
5 Bowring Institute
6 Air India & Unity Bldg.
7 British Library
8 Public Library
9 S.J. Polytechnic
10 Max Muller Bhavan

★ Accommodation

Bangalore. Lal Bagh. The 19th-century Glass House

The Sri K. Venkatappa Art Gallery is named for a court painter born in Mysore in 1887 who died in Bangalore in 1965. His low sculptural reliefs of 'The Parting of Shakuntala' and 'Shiva Tandava' exhibit that quandary of taste and fashion bedevilling all Indian artists, weighed down by a public having certain basic iconographical expectations and unconvinced by modernism, abstraction, or any reference to Western trends. So his Ooty or Kodaikanal landscapes fit into one genre, and his bird-paintings in the Persian style fit into another: of an integrated artistic personality there is only a chameleon's tongue visible. The first floor continues the stylistic hotch-potch from the frankly retrogressive to the pseudo-Western, such as C. P. Rajaram (1927–61) and his obsession with Henry Moore (even his titles read 'Head' and 'Mother and Child'). In the same complex the Government Museum (1866), old-fashioned in presentation, nevertheless possesses much more interesting work, such as 10th-century Buddhas from Pala district (Bihar), a 5th-century Dhanvantri of Gupta style from Mathura, and splendid stucco Gandhara heads of the 4th–5th centuries. Best of all is a Hampi 15th-century procession to war in high and low relief, figuring a shrewd parrot in a cage, and a prancing steed. Dancers and musicians of Hoysala origin show typical verve. Don't miss the exquisite drapery of Venugopala (12th century) and 10th-century Chola Bhairava in very high relief. In the other ground-floor gallery finds from Arikamedu (Pondicherry) include Chinese celadon, and Italian pottery imports dateable to around the time of Christ. On one side the upper floor is depressing with stuffed birds; on the other side fine Rajput and Mughal miniatures are so execrably lit as to be hardly visible. The Deccan school is represented by conventional portraits of seated sultans, expressing their refinement by holding poetry books, and

130

sniffing roses in garden landscapes they have themselves created. I forebear to criticise the gaudy, golden, glittering 'Mysore' style which has no more connection with aesthetic quality than Madonna and Child oleographs heaped on Roman street stalls.

Hungry, thirsty, leg-weary and exhausted after all-night diarrhoea, I sat and chatted with a guava-seller and foolishly bought a plate of the offered slices, before hailing a driver to the West End Hotel, opulently set in acres of grounds, and priced in US dollars ($75 for a standard single and $95 for a superior double) for the businessman in a western suit and lavish expense account. Between the golf course and the race course, the West End dates from the turn of the century, and is owned like Bangalore's Taj Residency by the same Taj group that operated Bombay's own fabled Taj Mahal.

Across the road I asked a policeman if I might enter the Bangalore Turf Club, and was escorted into the Jockeys' Stand, where the track was being watered for the Bangalore Derby held on the last Saturday in January. One paper predicted a win for Delage ('hat-tricker in Classics; looks unbeatable') with a second place for Alberetto ('looks fit and well; will put up a fight.') The flat-racing seasons in Bangalore are October-January and May-July, with meetings on a number of Fridays and weekends.

The Maharaja's Palace was begun about 1865, but has undergone a series of understandable changes since it was designed for a British merchant, and later adapted by the Maharaja of Mysore. Outlandishly mimicking Windsor Castle in comic Gothic towers and skyline, it finds a recent sequel in the nearby

Bangalore. Maharaja's Palace

Windsor Manor Hotel (1985), a charmless pastiche. I was advised that the best restaurants in Bangalore are the Chinese speciality houses off Mahatma Gandhi Marg, and there I ate slowly and carefully, of bland dishes, before exploring arts and crafts in the Cauvery Emporium and Sudarshan Handicrafts Emporium.

Victorian buffs will want to admire Sankey's Public Offices, now the High Court (1864–8), St Andrew's Kirk, St Mark's Church and the layout of Cubbon Park, all around 1864, as well as the earlier Raj Bhavan and neo-classical Bangalore Club, and the bungalows which many suppose gave the city its name. In fact, etymologists trace 'Bangalore' to the lowly bean, or 'bengalu', said to have grown here in great profusion.

The most celebrated modern landmark in the capital of Karnataka is Vidhana Soudha (1952–6), a very large granite range occupied by the State Legislature and State Secretariat. It reminds me too much of Washington Official Style in its equating of impressive with enormous, but I believe it goes down well with movie moguls and oil millionaires. And speaking of movies, the bored hordes of Bangalore have more than a hundred cinemas to select from, concerts at Gayana Samaj, and plays at Ravindra Kalakshetra. The only decent bookshop I could find was Higginbotham's on M. G. Road, but there are sidewalk-vendors of secondhand books and magazines in the vicinity also worth a glance.

By Shivajinagar bus station, I stopped to watch gullible passers-by parting with precious rupees. Govindraj squats by his parrot-cage, while his feathered assistants Mohan and Gundu unwittingly indicate your future by picking a card with a number, which Govindraj immediately interprets. 'Look for a very good stranger coming to your house, bringing many benefits. You will have safe journey. Money it will come, and you will get married and have many sons.' I thanked him for these insights, meekly handed over the agreed two rupees, and forebore to explain that the reason he assumed I was single was that I have never worn jewellery of any kind, not even a wedding ring, but I have been blissfully married (with two beautiful daughters) for 27 years . . .

The Train from Bangalore

Numerous buses ply between Bangalore and Mysore, but I chose the business-man's train, the 7.30 a.m. *Kaveri Express*, which leaves from the old station (platform 7), far across the bridge from the modern station – or across the tracks if you want to risk an accident. A waiter brought an excellent coffee and a hot omelette in two small sandwiches packed inside a banana leaf within an old Kannada newspaper. In my reclining chair I watched the sunlit, flat, fertile landscape slip past: vegetable plots, coconut palms, grainfields, areca palms: we could be in Kerala. John Mathai, a Keralan from the Small Industries Development Board, assured me that smaller industries were thriving in the penumbra of Bangalore's high-tech prosperity. West of Mandya, the ricefields appeared polished, manicured, painted a brilliant green well irrigated amid banana plantations. We stopped unaccountably for ten minutes at the drowsy station of Byadarahalli, where a woman sold oranges from a basket at 2 for Rs 3. John Mathai tisked: 'In Trichur they are only 25 for Rs 7.' A beautiful view of walled Srirangapatnam caused me to stand by the open door as we trundled past the dreaming ruins, then we rolled into Mysore at 11.30, having taken 4 hours to cover 140 km.

From Ooty to Mysore

My bus for the 160 km-ride via Gudalur from Ooty to Mysore chugged out of the bus stand north of Hotel Ritz promptly at 9 a.m. We passed strands of green terracing, then at 9.40 the Pykara Hydro-Electric Project before entering forests and beginning to descend a few minutes later near Liddellsdale Green Tea Factory to Nadurrattanam, where we all alighted so that the driver could take his tea at a wayside café. Above the café buzzing with four busloads of urgent feeders, brown terraces ranked back like raked seating in a theatre. Two scientists from Bangalore were enjoying a severe, loud conversation on the difference between academic qualifications from Edinburgh and an Australian university. A woman who had just attended to her two-year-old son's toilet behind a wall now playfully tossed the gurgling infant above her outstretched arms as if he were shouting laundry.

Ten minutes out of Nadurrattanam we came to Frog Hill View, then after six hairpin bends to Mudumalai Forest View. The steep roads are so narrow that downhill traffic has to reverse to permit uphill traffic to pass. Mudumalai itself (covered in my *South India*) can be visited by permission of the Wildlife Warden, Coonoor Road, Ooty, or Tamil Nadu Tourist Offices throughout the state, who will book advance accommodation. Nagarhole National Park is the biggest of Karnataka's wildlife reserves, at 400 sq km equalling Mudumalai in area. It is contiguous with Wynad (Kerala), Mudumalai, and Bandipur Tiger Reserve in Karnataka. This means that much the same wildlife can be seen in any of the four sanctuaries: the Indian bison known as gaur, leopard and occasionally tiger, sambar deer, both common and bonnet langurs, mouse-deer and the spotted deer or chital.

Bandipur Tiger Reserve accommodation and local transport can be booked in Mysore at either Project Tiger itself in the Government House complex in Nazirbad, or at the Divisional Forest Office. At Bandipur you can explore by elephant, but best is to sit silently on a tree-platform as animals come to drink at perennial pools. This allows better sightings than boat trips on the river Moyar or noisy jeep-runs. Entry into Bandipur is currently only possible in the mornings before 9 and in the afternoons from 4.30 to 6, but check these times before setting off. The best months for Bandipur and the other reserves are November to May: I have found December, January and February equally satisfying, but I cannot speak for June. Locally, they affirm that each reserve makes excellent spotting throughout the year, and I can well take the assurance on trust.

Gudalur is the town in the plain that glitters up at you from Frog Hill View, but how different the shambles at close quarters! One ramshackle hut displays 'TV and VCR For Hire' near the Catholic Syrian Bank Ltd., Tip Top Hairdresser, and Mummy Daddy Readymades. The main road to Mysore now transects Mudumalai Sanctuary, and we swish majestically through bamboo groves, watching for fugitive chital or wild pig, but catching a glimpse only of a screeching peacock, its fantail horrifically mauled, probably by a young leopard at a waterhole.

A fleeting golden oriole announced our arrival at Theppakadu Reception Centre, then five minutes later we reached Kakkanhala checkpoint just within Bandipur National Park.

Ten minutes out of Bandipur we reached the hotter plain, where women were carrying on their heads earthenware pots filled with water from a tank, and yoked oxen ploughed wide, rich fields. Gundlupet Forest checkpoint is patrolled by police anxious to stem the tide of smuggling rare birds, animals and timber from the threatened sanctuaries. Indian timber is vanishing both as a result of legitimate felling and racketeering by gangs who can command thousands of dollars for a single tree: rosewood, teak or sandalwood. The Conservator of Forests, Dr K. A. Kushalappa, told me in Mysore that a whole range of solutions was being tried in different regions according to local needs and preferences, often consulting the wishes of the inhabitants instead of laying down a national strategy. It is all a matter of common sense and consensus. For instance, the ten thousand Soligas inhabiting seventy small village settlements 110–150 km southeast of Mysore scrape a meagre living from fruits and berries and hunting small animals in woodland. Dr Kushalappa's plan is to consign to the Soligas custody of forest plantations on local state-owned land. The Forestry Department will plant grains, jackfruit, tamarind and gooseberries, which are particularly prized by Soligas, and the crops will be farmed and sold by the Soligas, who are being rehoused in new houses of brick-and-tile, though some retain their old mud-and-thatch homes. The alternative, already experienced by many tribes throughout India, would have been extinction or absorption into wider, less tolerant societies where land speculators and central-government large-scale plans dominate, intimidate and threaten to annihilate the fragile identity of minorities.

Mysore

The bus rolled into Mysore bus station at 1 p.m., and I headed for the hotels nearby, finding a cheap room at the comically-misnamed Hotel Ritz for under US$6. I was anxious to sniff the air for an aroma of R. K. Narayan's affectionately-depicted 'Malgudi', which as everyone knows by now is really Mysore. But, as Narayan says, 'small town life is the same everywhere: if my books have universal appeal it is because everyone knows a small town.' Garrison Keillor's Lake Wobegon, Hardy's Christminster, Clarín's Vetusta (Oviedo): they all partake of their own particularity and of the paradox that they are the whole world to a tiny proportion of the world's population, and totally ignored by everyone else. Narayan, an active 83 in 1991, takes two years to write a novel 'and every time everything goes wrong'. He smiles easily, a man obviously fulfilled, an author acknowledged worldwide as an authentic Indian master of the English language. Since 1935 he has produced fifteen novels, beginning with *Swamy and Friends* and ending (so far) with *The World of Nagaraj* (1990). His autobiography *My Days* (1975) needs a sequel and fifty years in Mysore have yielded enough anecdotes to enable him to fill several volumes. His stature is recognised by the University of Texas, where he recently spent a period as Visiting Professor, and he is an Honorary Member of the American Academy and Institute of Arts and Letters. As a writer he is an astute craftsman, achieving a brilliant, natural flow by means of a realism tinged with wish-fulfilment, a melancholy born of compassionate awareness. Sir Compton Mackenzie described *The English Teacher* (1946) as 'a wonderfully painted miniature of India wherein we can meet characters as vivid as Jane Austen's, and move through landscapes as delicate as Corot's.' If I were to compare Narayan with anyone else writing today, I should hover between William Trevor and Isaac Bashevis Singer. His guile and naïveté commingle with delicious audacity.

A Dravidian language unlike the Indo-European languages of the north such as Hindi, Kannada nevertheless incorporated many Sanskritic elements because of diplomacy, religion, commerce and military contacts. Kannada seems to have split from Tamil around the fourth century, when the first distinct Kannada inscription was recorded. A ninth-century book mentions thirty-six previous Kannada poets, and the tenth century saw a quickening renaissance of Kannada letters, especially with Jain authors such as Pampa and Chavundaraya.

Sarvajna, who lived early in the 18th century, was a wandering poet composing two thousand verses in *tripadi* metre, each verse of three lines, his subject matter including attacks on hypocrisy and superstitions intended to educate and inform the commoner.

Basavanna or Basaveshvara (1106–67) wrote Shaivite epigrams or *Vachanas* in an idiom comparable to Jayadeva's slightly later Sanskrit *Gita Govinda*. His followers followed the path of Heroic Shiva or Virashaiva, abolishing distinctions of sex, caste and class, and living together in revolutionary egalitarianism. Though a highly-placed minister of state in the court of King Bijjala at Kalyani, he denounced Hinduism's barriers, and announced that all should be unity within the heart of the devotee of the 'Lord of the Meeting Rivers', that is Shiva. Basavanna's first guru lived at Kappadi Sangama, a meeting-place of three rivers, which Basavanna took also metaphorically.

> Why care how long a rock takes
> to be worn by the waters?
> Why care how long I have worshipped
> when my heart is inconstant?
> Valueless, helpless as a phantom
> I guard hidden gold,
> O Lord of the Meeting Rivers.

Kannada literature has the same position in limbo as Telugu and Malayalam: flourishing within its own boundaries but virtually unknown outside, so that all there have perhaps an exaggerated idea of their own worth, or perhaps outsiders denigrate them in ignorance, prejudice, or both. R. K. Narayan and other regional writers who choose to express themselves in English can reach a vast audience and test themselves against rigorous criticism. Kannada writers have no such criteria: they are judged by peers naturally biased towards their own background, culture, and language.

By 1790, printing presses had been introduced by Portuguese, British and other missionaries to publish the Bible and other works in Kannada and the other regional Indian languages, and this factor and burgeoning literacy and the growth of trade led to a steady stream of books in Kannada. K. V. Puttappa is a major Kannada writer of verse plays and epic novels whose magnum opus is the *Sri Ramayana Darshanam*, an epic poem inspired by Valmiki's *Ramayana*. Puttappa, writing as 'Kuvempu' was Vice-Chancellor of Mysore University where English was the compulsory medium of education yet, he told me, 'no more than three or four per cent knew English well enough, and so many failed just because they could not master the language of instruction. What would

Map of Mysore

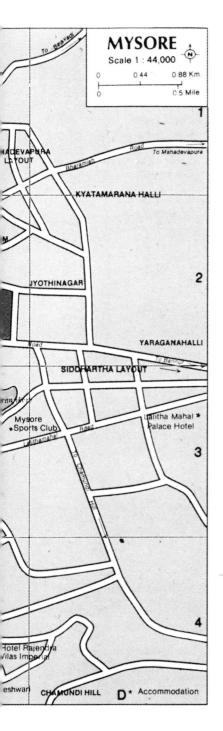

MYSORE

Scale 1 : 44,000

0   0.44   0.88 Km.

0   0.5 Mile

1

HADEVAPURA LAYOUT

Road To Mahadevapura

Bharamah

KYATAMARANA HALLI

M

JYOTHINAGAR

2

Road

YARAGANAHALLI

To Bangur

SIDDHARTHA LAYOUT

Mysore Sports Club

Lalitha Mahal Palace Hotel

Road

Lalithamahal

3

To Chamundi Hill

4

Hotel Rajendra Vilas Imperial

eshwari   CHAMUNDI HILL   **D** * Accommodation

REFERENCES

Bannimantap B1
St. Philomena's College B1
St. Philomena's Church C2
Mission Hospital B2
Ayurvedic & Unani College B2
Medical College B2
Department of Tourism B2
City Railway Station B2
Railway Offices B2
Karnataka State Tourism
    Development Corpn. Offices B2
Mysore Tourist Centre B2
K.R. Hospital B2
Chamarajendra Technological Institute,
    Cauvery Arts and Crafts & K.S.T.D.C. Office B2
Mysore Bank B2
City Bus Stand B2
Central Post Office BC2
Govt. Guest House C2
Clock Tower Square B2
Ridge House C1
Town Hall C2
New Statue Square B2
Devaraja Market B2
Indra Bhavan B2
Jaladarshini A2
C.F.T.R.I. A2
Cosmopolitan Club B2
Crawford Hall A2
Chamundi Guest House B2
Jaganmohan Palace B2
Central Bus Stand BC2
Lok Ranjan Mahal C3
Zoo C3
Chaluvamba Park B2
Mysore Sports Club CD3
Lalitha Mahal Palace D3
Oriental Library AB2
Maharaja's College AB3
Law Courts A3
All India Institute of Legopaedics B3
Govt. Silk Factory B4
Sandalwood Oil Factory A4
Rajendra Vilas Imperial C4
Hotel Metropole B2
Lakshmi Venkataramanaswamy Temple A1
Idga B1
Regulated Market B2
Taluk Offices C2
Central Police Station BC2
Manasa Gangothri (Mysore Univ.) A2
Indian Airlines B2
Maharani's College B2
Telegraph Office B2-3
K.R. Circle B2
Janatha Bazaar BC2
Exhibition Grounds C3
Chamundeswari Temple C4
Maharaja's Mysore Palace B3
Municipal Office B3
Central Library B2
Chaluvamba Hospital B2

you think if I asked American or English undergraduates to learn Kannada or Bengali just because the available books were not in English? You would say rubbish and quite so. Result is that I introduced Kannada as a language of instruction for undergraduates in Mysore and yet all those so taught passed and only 30% taught in English. You see my point? I am both practical and patriotic.'

The late D. R. Bendre, writing as 'Ambikatanaya Datta', was the greatest lyric poet of modern Kannada; the most eminent novelist is the rationalist and realist K. Shivarama Karanth, awarded the Jnanapit Prize for his novel *Mukajiya Kanasugalu;* the leading short-story writer of the older generation is Masti Venkatesha Iyengar, writing as 'Srinivasa'. Fifty collections of poems emerge every year in Kannada, and some poets deserve translation, among them K. S. Narasimhaswamy, Chandrashekhara Patil, Siddalingaiah and A. K. Ramanujan.

Some say that the name of Mysore derives from 'Mahisha', the demon slain by Shiva's son Karttikeya, and 'ur', a town; others that the first syllable refers to a local fertility goddess, one 'Mais'. It was once called Hadinadu.

But antiquity is unknown here, for Tipu Sultan demolished the old city in 1793 to make way for an open, spacious garden city with parks and wide streets that lend Mysore the perennial advantage of relative peace and tranquillity. Traffic moves smoothly and swiftly; broad pavements are safe. Scents of musk and sandalwood, jasmine and rose petals add to the relaxation of the town, where incense is made in family workshops, some of which welcome visitors to see the sticks being made.

The regular sightseeing car or bus (depending on bookings) in Mysore starts at 8.30 and returns at 8.30 p.m., calling at the Jaganmohan Palace art gallery, the zoo, the silk emporium, Chamundi Hill, then after lunch the Amba Vilas Palace, St Philomena's Church and Srirangapatnam (Daria Daulat, the mausoleum and Fort Ranganatha Swamy Temple), in season the Ranganathittu bird sanctuary, and ending at the illuminated Brindaban gardens. This is excellent value for those limited to one full day in Mysore, but doesn't do justice, of course, to the city's life, which needs at least three or four days at a more leisurely pace.

Amba Vilas Palace

The eclecticism of Bombay's great Victorian public buildings seems to triumph by a cumulative process: a kind of architectural indoctrination, a wearing down of one's initial resistance. In quieter Mysore, Amba Vilas obtrudes grotesquely, out of scale. I queued patiently at the entrance (10.30–5.30), paid Rs 2 for a ticket and Rs 1 to leave my camera, doffed my footwear, then followed the patrolled line of visitors in what Italians would call the unique sense, past eleven cannons which were once used to herald the beginning of Dussehra.

Amba Vilas Palace is the third on this site, the first dating from the fourteenth century, the second completed for occupation in 1801 and almost totally destroyed by fire in 1897, and the latest – hastily designed by the great Henry Irwin – took from 1897 to 1912, but the new façade was begun in 1932 and the interior was further embellished into the 1940s. It is unsatisfactory aesthetically, because the muddled amalgam of Hindu and British features never achieves a new synthesis. Amba Vilas is neither successfully Indo-Saracenic, nor Rajput.

Mysore. Maharaja's Palace

It borrows ideas from Delhi's Red Fort and Hoysala temples, drags a campanile from Florence and copies intricate Mughal interiors: it even attempts to implant domes from Agra's Taj, but the whole is unconvincing, even unnerving when you come across marble from near Jaipur and local soapstone figures. One even sniffs a touch of Buckingham Palace in the side elevation. Illumination by 41,500 permanent light bulbs occurs during the annual Dussehra celebrations, on Sundays, and government holidays. The present maharaja lives at the back and still owns Fernhill Palace in Ootacamund, which he leases out as a hotel.

The first hall is the Idols' Passage or Gombe Thotti, in which are shown the Hindu images worshipped by the royal family during Dussehra; here too is a model of the ancient wooden palace. Thirty-six royal standards are carried solemnly during the procession. The golden howdah used to bear the maharaja, but nowadays it carries the effigy of Chamundeshwari, borne by a luxuriantly-caparisoned elephant on Vijayadasmi, tenth and last day of Dussehra. The celebration is for the conquest of the demon Mahisha by the goddess Chamundeshwari, who brings up the rear of the fantastical procession of infantry, cavalry, tableaux, musicians and jesters, winding its way through the broad avenues of Mysore along Ashoka Road to the Banni Mandapam off the Bangalore Road and back to the palace. The royal durbar has been replaced by a ten-day music festival in the durbar hall, but the son of the last maharaja continues to hold a private durbar.

A painted corridor on three sides of the Kalyana Mandapam is decorated with oil paintings showing aspects of the Dussehra processions of 1934–45 by artists of Mysore such as S. N. Swamy, Y. Nagaraju and S. R. Iyengar: the figures shown include Ibrahim Khan in mural 3, the archaeologist R. Shamshastri in mural 14, and Hollywood's Sabu the Elephant Boy in mural 24. Mural 18 differs in representing the myth of Sri Rama before Chamundeshwari in the presence of Mysore personalities.

The Kalyana Mandapam or Peacock Pavilion is an octagonal royal marriage hall with a dome supported by triple iron pillars, by Walter Macfarlane of Glasgow and a stained-glass peacock ceiling also from Glasgow. The decorated balcony is a purdah gallery permitting royal ladies to view.

The portrait gallery is dominated by two paintings of Sri Krishnaraja Wadiyar IV as a child in 1885 executed by Ravi Varma, and a third of the adult Krishnaraja in 1933 painted by Y. Nagaraju. It is worth dwelling on this ruler, for during his thirty-eight year reign Mysore became a model state. Throughout his minority, from 1895 to 1902, his mother Maharani Kempananjammanni Vanivilasa Sannidhana acted creditably as regent, but Mysore saw its greatest age from 1912–19, when Sir M. Visvesvaraya acted as Chief Minister (or Diwan) and from 1926–41, when that position was held by the great Sir Mirza M. Ismail. Visvesaraya supervised the building of the dam called Krishnarajasagar, the University, the Bank of Mysore, a technical institute, Bangalore Engineering College and a Chamber of Commerce. Ismail laid out the Brindaban gardens, founded Mysore Medical College, and factories for porcelain, sugar, steel, cement, paper and aircraft. Maharaja Krishnaraja himself played the violin, preferring duets with his private secretary Evan Maconochie, and kept two hundred polo ponies and many dogs. A man of simple tastes, he knew and admired Gandhiji, just as his predecessor Chama Rajendra had given hospitality to Sri Aurobindo. He was responsible for the Lalitha Mahal Palace and the Rajendra Vilas Palace at Chamundi Hills, and enjoyed the genuine devotion of his people, who saw him in that peculiarly Indian fashion as a god-king-man-ascetic inhabiting several worlds simultaneously, as happens throughout *Mahabharata* and *Ramayana*. If we can see everything and everyone in more than one scale of time or space, then we open our minds to the possibility that all is *maya*, illusion, and we pursue that possibility of detachment which distances us from self-absorption in pain, grief, dread.

The chair room exhibits a pair of silver chairs, a pair of Belgian crystal chairs and two glass dressing-tables. Its ceiling is of Burmese teak carved by craftsmen from Shimoga. A hunting trophies room displays the shooting prowess of Maharaja Sri Jaya Chama Rajendra (1940–74), who was keen on the chase, despite his enormous bulk resulting from glandular problems. He would listen to Wagner on records in the evenings while at Bandipur, and read very widely. He was called upon to hunt when tigers or wild elephants threatened villages in those forests of Karnataka under his authority, but otherwise left alone the elephants whose numbers had fallen during his reign to a mere six thousand. Most trophies here were taken at Bandipur, all in the days before it was declared a national park.

The Indian elephant population is now estimated at barely twenty thousand, a figure requiring conservation at its present level, despite the encroaching of villagers for timber, the poaching of ivory by smugglers, and unrestrained grazing by 80 million cattle. Forty years ago, Project Elephant has estimated, Indian forest cover amounted to 20% of the land; in 1991 the figure is scarcely

10%. Deforestation has caused the remaining elephants, hungry and deprived of their traditional homelands, to wander into areas where villagers are often terrified, never having been threatened before. The task of settling the elephants into reserves to be accepted as sacrosanct by local people will prove difficult and costly to achieve, yet the present budget for containing the problem is barely £1½ million per annum. Given the financial muscle of ivory poachers and timber rustlers, wildlife protection officials and the police are likely to be tempted by bribes.

The armoury shows weapons from the 17th century: the Nimcha and Sanva swords used respectively by Haidar Ali and Tipu and the iron claws used by Shivaji against the Bijapuri general Afzal Khan. A five-bladed dagger would rend the flesh horribly, and each blade is believed to have been tipped with poison too.

The Durbar Hall is a ceremonial space centred on the golden throne, which legend credits with a previous existence at Hastinapura, as a Pandava possession in the era of *Mahabharata*! Chroniclers suggest that it lay buried and forgotten until revealed by a sage to Harihara I, founder of Vijayanagar, who used it until it came to Srirangapatnam in the 17th century, and thence to Mysore. Another story describes how it was given to a Wadiyar sovereign by Aurangzeb around 1700. At any event, one can believe that it comprises more than 280 kgs of gold (Kolar Gold Fields in Karnataka is incidentally India's only large gold-mine) and has an early 19th-century golden umbrella with festoons blessing Sri Krishnaraja III in Sanskrit invocations, and atop the *huma* bird which is said never to touch the ground, a story which grew up in Europe around the swift.

The west wall has early 20th-century paintings by the brothers Ravi and Raja Varma, the Mysore artist Sri Silpi Siddalingaswami, and a composite portrait of 1926 by Y. Nagaraju of four generations of Mysore rulers beginning with Krishna Raja III. Opulence gives way to vulgarity in the carved frames between marble pilasters ringed by a marble architrave. Sandalwood spandrels above the doors depicting Hindu divinities are ingenious, but lack the creative spark we find in Hoysala art. The colonnades are connected by Mughal-style arches, the whole facing the open space in front of the hall so that a multitude may see their king enthroned. Nowadays the multitudes traipse through the hall, sometimes mistaking over-indulgence and stylistic incoherence for authentic splendour. Doors plated in silver grate on the nerves, like the voice of a singer long past her prime who insists on demonstrating her talents.

I felt unmistakable relief to enter the Maharaja's Residential Museum in the old, admittedly shabby palace of the early 19th century. I bought a cold drink outside while queueing for a Rs 2 ticket, then breathed easily in the human, domestic scale of the Karikal Thotti, the Old Palace, with its silver throne made for Sri Krishnaraja III, silver chairs and silver palanquin. A Bohemian glass couch is even more splendid than the crystal chairs on show in Amba Vilas, and the chandeliers glitter with old Viennese charm. Sri Krishnaraja IV's private office has an antique telephone and solid desk. Best of all is the gallery above, with evocative sepia photographs showing scenes from the Dussehra procession of 1935.

Temples in the fort compound area were left alone by Tipu Sultan when he razed old Mysore, contradicting received ideas about his so-called Muslim fanaticism. Gandhiji once called Tipu 'an embodiment of Hindu-Muslim unity', a fact exemplified by his appointment of the meritorious, whether Hindu or Muslim, to public office and by his careful preservation of old Hindu shrines such as Kodi Bhairava Swamiji Temple outside the fort wall, Sri Lakshmi Ramana Swamiji Temple (c. 1500), and Varaha Swamiji Temple with a finely-carved doorway traditionally believed to come from a Hoysala building in Shimoga taluq.

Jagan Mohan Palace
Jagan Mohan Palace (1861) is situated a little to the west of the Amba Vilas, and now accommodates the art gallery named for Sir Jaya Chama Rajendra, after having been used as a residential palace until 1915. It was he – ruler of Mysore State since 1940 – who made the gallery over as a public trust in 1955, and gave the Ravi Varma paintings which somehow seem to set the mediocre tone and disappointment felt by the connoisseur here in comparison with museums in Madras, Tanjore, Bombay, Delhi and Calcutta. The problem is that Mysore was never an artistic centre, unlike the princely states of Bundi or Bikaner. In his catalogue, James Cousins pinpoints the issue by noting that 'the 19th century was a period of progressive degradation in Indian art, particularly painting. European impacts failed to do more than produce a mediocre amalgam of Indian subject-matter and European methods.' This is no place to speculate on all the reasons, but they include a readiness to copy and imitate the best of past art, a lack of confidence felt by Indian artists, a scarcity of connoisseurs and patrons interested in innovation, the absence of dynamic major galleries, the poverty of the artists and their public at large, the conservatism of Hindu iconography, the Muslim veto on portraying living things, and a fascination with the rise of international movements such as Victorian realism and the portraits of F. X. Winterhalter on the one hand, and Impressionism, Expressionism and surrealism on the other. India was disadvantaged in these ways and many more, and weaknesses grow like weeds in Jagan Mohan Palace.

The ground floor is devoted to western and oriental decorative arts, including a French musical calendar clock, furniture, porcelain, glass, and an undated ivory palanquin. Two galleries are devoted to portraits of Mysore maharajas which belong more to the history of Mysore than to the history of art; a third has portraits of westerners such as Wellesley, Gladstone and Dalhousie. The first floor has contemporary Indian watercolours, Ravi Varma's sentimental evocations of Hindu myth and history, S. L. Haldenkar's symbolic and highly popular 'Glow of Hope', and the charmingly symbolist 'Giriji in Penance' by Kamala Shankar Singh, showing a modest girl with eyes downcast. Nepali and Tibetan paintings for religious meditation stand apart from the insipid generality. On the second floor, the Ranga Mahal section has murals, oils and musical instruments.

Opposite Jagan Mohan Palace stands a restaurant cunningly titled Hotel Hillton to avoid legal wrangles; it bears little resemblance to its eminent near-namesake, for the staff consists of two cooks, three waiters, and a rotund Hindu cashier wiping his brow at frequent intervals whose day is divided between supervising clients' bills and kicking away inquisitive pi-dogs and scrawny crows.

It is both Brahmin and military, in Indian parlance, that is to say veg and non-veg, and I devoured an omelette, chicken, chili and peppered rice and chapatis washed down with two orange drinks.

The zoological gardens in Mysore are situated near the racecourse, on the way to Karanji Tank and the lovely domed Karanji Mansion. Opposite the zoo, visit Sri Lakshmi Fine Arts and Crafts emporium. Browsing in the bazaars of Mysore is a constant delight, not so much for the goods themselves, though they can be spectacular, as for the shoppers: those beautiful Mysore women in stunning saris, and those handsome men in white kurtas and white pyjamas, or stylish Western suits. Karnataka Silk Industries Corporation has a shop in Visvesvaraya Bhavan or RKR Circle and a factory on Mananthody Road. A general gift store for those in a hurry is Kaveri Arts and Crafts Emporium on Sayaji Rao Road. But the best sight for photographers is Devaraja Market north of New Statue Square and Vinoba Road. Vinoba Road has a small Folk Art Museum across Jhansi Lakshmibai Road from the State Tourism Development Corporation.

Chamundi Hill

As Mysore, like Udaipur, is a city of palaces, one should make sure of seeing two palace hotels, for the price of a pot of fine Mysore coffee. One is the white Summer Palace called Lalitha Mahal designed by E. W. Fritchley in 1930 and run, without any great flair or sympathy for the grand building, as part of the state-owned Ashok hotel chain. A dome based on that of St Paul's Cathedral in London sets the scale for a great yellow and green hall, and massive chandeliers. Stained glass, princely staircase, wide verandahs: it is all so romantically imposing that I expected a gowned Meryl Streep or Jeremy Irons in immaculate black tie and tails to emerge from the pastel blue royal suite. Equally aristocratic is Rajendra Vilas Palace Hotel on Chamundi, with rather better food and much cheaper rooms. It looks like an Italian mansion and was created in 1939 to give Maharaja Krishnaraja Wadiyar IV a taste of serenity when Dussehra threatened to overwhelm him with noise and bustle.

Chamundi Hill is named for the patron goddess of Mysore, and is supposed to protect the town below through her mediation. As an incarnation of Durga, she overthrew the rampaging demon Mahisha and her temple was founded by the ruling Wadiyar dynasty in recompense.

Ascend Chamundi Hill by road (the taxi winds about 12 km) or preferably on foot, direct up 4 km of steps, giving you a foretaste of the climb at Sravana Belagola. More than halfway up Shiva's bull Nandi mounts guard over Mysore in the shape of a great granite monolith five metres high carved in 1659. Once at the summit, you are allowed inside Sri Chamundeshwari from 8.30 to midday, and from 5 to about 8.30 p.m. You can find sustenance in pilgrim cafés near the temple, and this is obviously a very good idea. Don't try to use the half-hourly buses back to the central bus stand: they are terribly overcrowded.

The temple itself is of no great antiquity in its present form, being a hotch-potch of additions since the 17th century, entered by a pair of gopurams, of which the outer is very recent, like the tower sanctuary. It is for the magnificent panorama that the climb is worthwhile. As I sat and rested, a tawny dog the colour of pocked sandy earth curled round itself, tucking its wary head into its

Mysore. Chamundeshwari Temple

mangy body, licked its weary chops once, and closed its eyes. The sunset, as usual, ravished the horizon in roseate aquamarine and, as usual, everyone ignored it for more mundane concerns. Crows fought over a sliver of roti: the losers glared balefully at the victor.

I took a cab back to Hotel Siddhartha at 73 Government Guest House Road, but found their restaurant to be vegetarian. I booked a 13-hour bus tour for the following day to Belur and Halebid, then strolled across to the Hotel Sandesh restaurant nearby for a sweet lassi, maize and chicken soup, fish and rice with a papad and pistachio ice-cream, all for four US dollars. During the night I woke at 1.30 with mosquito-bites, at 3.15 with more mosquito-bites, and at 5.30 on the muaddin's sonorously amplified call for dawn prayer. The morning *Hindu* headlined elections in eight states and the Union Territory of Pondicherry. Soviet troops had been ordered to fire on troublemakers in Armenia and Azerbaijan. Breakfast at the Siddhartha consisted of grape juice, toast and jam, and a cup of tea, then the bus calling at Mysore hotels picked me up at 7 a.m.

Sravana Belagola

Stopping and starting at one hotel after another in no apparent order, the bus wove its cat's cradle of a route through the streets of Mysore, picking up two Madrasi businessmen here, a Delhi wife and husband there, a Bombaywallah yon, until we arrived back at the bus station at 8, and the guide disappeared again for ten minutes. My Buddhist training – elementary as it is – allowed me to close off the wells of irritation boiling up below the surface, and to relax. A ragged ancient crouching in a stone coffin-like receptacle by the side of the road appeared to be pouring kerosene over his feet, but he was presumably just taking a home-made shower in a horse-trough. The driver's cab bore a sign 'Contraband articles strictly prohibited. Passengers shall carry such goods at their own risk', which seemed an ambiguously-worded exhortation. At last our oddly-assorted busload moved off into the horn-parping morning, and we passed the three-doored west front of St Philomena's 19th-century neo-Gothic pile and headed north – except that we had barely sat down, passed the Agricultural Research Station and storks hunting frogs in the padi-fields, before the driver stopped for his half-hour breakfast at Hotel Triveni in Srirangapatnam which we did not leave until 9 a.m.

Repetitively inane Hindi pop music blaring throughout the bus, nobody could either think or make themselves heard in conversation. At a wayside shrine our Hindu guide left the bus to make a quick puja to Sri Ganapati, elephant-headed son of Lord Shiva, and bright-eyed infants scrambled on board with their wares, offering 'one orange one rupee' and informing me wisely 'London is the capital of your country'. The way blooms with coconut palms, and the fertile red earth will yield whatever you wish to grow, the flat expanse being easily ploughed by the slow oxen as they slurp boustrophedon, as if slowly writing Linear B. For a state the size of West Germany, Karnataka seems endless, with little traffic and few towns. Its agricultural importance can be judged from its very name 'black earth', 'Karu Nadu', though much of the land now looks impoverished by overproduction and shortage of fertiliser. At the little bazaar in Kikkeri I saw black pots and durian fruit for sale, beside piles of spice.

Kikkeri has one ruined Hoysala temple of 1111, a Hindu shrine to the local goddess Kikkeramma who accepts no animal sacrifices, and a very fine Hoysala to Brahmeshvara erected in 1171 with convex outer walls, and a marvellous verandah ceiling with nine carved lotuses. Unfortunately the forty deities have been badly mutilated.

Then ninety minutes out of Srirangapatnam we caught sight of Vindhyagiri, the great hill of the town, and soon parked in the immense car park at the foot of the mountain. We had arrived at one of the most sacred shrines in the Jain world. Sravana Belagola means the white pool of the ascetic, but the town has also been known at different times as Dakshina Kasi, Gommatapura, Surapura, and many other names. Legend takes the area back to remotest antiquity but the scholar S. Settar has found no inscription earlier than 600 A.D., when the district would have been even more isolated than it is today, forested and inhabited only by wild animals and those who came here for intense solitude, to die in peace in an area connected in Jain lore with a saintly monk called Bhadrabahu. During the 3rd century B.C. Bhadrabahu predicted famine and persuaded the Mauryan emperor Chandragupta to leave his capital in the Magadha area (southern Bihar today) and make for the south. On Chandragiri, smaller of the two hills here, a so-called 'Cave of Bhadrabahu' commemorates this story, though the conversion of a natural cave into a Jain temple cannot be dated before the 11th century, when a devoté called Jinachandra carved an inscription. Its porch is of the 17th century.

To visit Sravana Belagola at your own pace, in a hired car perhaps in order to cover on the same day the Jain centre of Kambadahalli and the Hoysala temple at Dodda Gaddavahalli, go first to Jinanathapura (north of Chandragiri), then into the town, then up Chandragiri, and finally up Vindhyagiri, watching the sunset from the summit.

Jinanathapura is 1½ km to the north, with a beautiful Hoysala-style Jain basti or temple dedicated to Santinatha and dated to 1117; its scrollwork and turrets are among the loveliest of all Hoysala achievements; its solitude further recommends it.

The matha or monastery is locally believed to date back to Chamunda Raya's time (about 981 A.D.), but the first written record is as late as 1131, 28 years before a reference to any urban settlement. The town grew as Benares and Nasik grew, by the pressure of pilgrimage, and the present great matha is of 17th–19th century age. Its 17th–18th century frescoes deal vigorously with episodes from the life of Parshvanatha, with the tale of Emperor Bharata, that of the Jain Prince Nagakumara, and such events as the annual festival in the town, and a durbar scene from the reign of Krishnadevaraya Wadiyar. Painted yakshis (female divinities) over the door-jambs are comparable with frescoes at Hampi. Jain bronzes are mainly of 19th-century date, but at least one is considered to be authentically of the 10th-century Western Ganga era.

Nearby is Bhandari basti, originally completed in 1159 by Hullamaya, a Jain general of the Hoysala ruler Narasimha, who acted as his treasurer or 'bhandari'. Its front hall was extended in 1527, and even later are the main entrance, gopuram and the free-standing pillar or manastambha facing the temple. The finest features are a 12-armed Indra dancing in the upper panel of the elaborate doorway, and the earliest Jain tirthankars in Karnataka, accompanied by their attendant deities.

Chandragiri is reached by a path and 192 steps north from the pool or tank which forms the navel of Sravana Belagola, though we cannot be sure that this is the original white pool or 'belagola' after which the settlement was named. The smaller granite hill of Chandragiri possesses a sacred enclosure with four main bastis, the largest being the earliest, possibly of the 10th century in Western Ganga style, certainly with 12th-century Hoysala additions. Scholars are unsure whether inscriptions referring to Chamundaraya are contemporary or later. Certainly Ganga workmen were chosen, and Dravidian elements were required of them, and we know from the pedestal inscription that the image of Adinatha, 1st tirthankar of the present age in Jain tradition, is by the foremost sculptor of the age: Gangachari. Known as Vardhamanachari, he is also credited with the yaksha-yakshi of this temple. In Jain iconography, all tirthankars are shown with identical features, except that the first, Adinatha, has long hair: they are distinguished by their attributes and vehicles. Serpent canopies halo the heads of the 7th (Suparshvanatha) and the 23rd (Parshvanatha). Individuality appears in the details of lion-faced fishes, elephants, gandharvas (flying divinities, often playing musical instruments) and I particularly enjoyed a seated, full-breasted maiden with one braceleted hand on the ground and the other holding a flower as if to penetrate with a melancholy smile the ephemeral world of the senses. Her vibrant, sensuous presence again invites us to ponder the ambiguity of religious art and its relation to the physical world. Here is a young woman in bloom, with beautiful hair and a rich necklace, enough to distract any monk from an ascetic life.

Chandragupta basti (probably 12th century) has splendid towers, images of Parshvanatha (central sanctum cell), Padmavati yakshi (west) and Ambika yakshi (east), a Sarvahna yaksha image, and a pair of superb perforated stone screens executed by Dasoja in the 12th century. These narrate the story of the saint and kevala Bhadrabahu (one of the spiritual stages below tirthankarhood) as described by the early Kannada poet Shivakotyacharya in his prose work *Vaddaradhane*. As a boy, Bhadrabahu was identified as a future saint and scholar by muni Govardhana, who took the child away to be educated and do penance according to his years and understanding. Eventually, Bhadrabahu achieved kevaladom, when Govardhana surrendered him leadership of the Jain community and attained samadhi, or self-willed death at the time considered appropriate. Bhadrabahu then wandered, seeking alms in the city of Ujjain (Madhya Pradesh), whose pious emperor Chandragupta sought him out and accepted srava-kavrta. When the saint received premonitions of a twelve-year famine in the north, he urged Chandragupta and his followers to leave Ujjain together with two thousand disciples. By the time the large procession reached Chandragiri (or Kalbappu as it was then known), Bhadrabahu felt near the end of his mortal life, and we can visualise him now, surrounded by just such Digambar Jains scattered over the area today. He urged his sangha to continue south, under his appointed deputy, but Chandragupta could not bear to leave the place hallowed as the last resting-place of Bhadrabahu, and survived him there for twelve years. The Jains say that Bhadrabahu was reborn as the god Amitakanti and Chandragupta as the god Sridhara.

Next door is the 'Badly-Lit' or Kattale basti, of interest for its ambulatory and its seated Adinatha in the sanctum with a pedestal inscription dating it to 1118. Finally on Chandragiri we come to the 11th-century granite Parshvanatha basti with the tallest lamp-pillar hereabouts, dated to the 17th century, and the tallest image except for the famous colossus of Bahubali. The tirthankar is 14½' high on a lotus pedestal, with reliefs illustrating an encounter with his enemy Kamatha.

Vindhyagiri

So-called in popular parlance, the Large Hill at SB was always called Per Kalbappu in the chronicles. The temptation is to head for the great Gommata monolith at the summit, as one makes for the leaning tower at Pisa, but like that impulse it should be resisted. For Vindhyagiri has two ponds, four pavilions known in South India as mandapams, five fortified gateways intended for times more turbulent than our own, and no fewer than eight temples. Sparse of vegetation, the hill has become a living Jain body, almost breathing with the ascent and descent of thousands of pilgrims, many of them non-Jains. Jainism is an offshoot from Hinduism, but retained such Hindu gods as Isvara, Varuna and Kali, at a stage lower than tirthankars, and Hindu demigods such as yakshas, yakshis, kinnaras and gandharvas attained their own dedicated temples in the 14th century. The worship of Brahma himself appears at Sravana Belagola in the 17th century, though the lowest mandapam on the hill dated to the 10th century called 'Brahmadeva' has been replaced by a modern structure. Some 600 steps ascend 470 feet to the summit, but for the infirm a wicker-chair contraption called a doli held by four bearers will make the pilgrimage possible. The first archway was erected in the 15th century and the second in the 18th. The Silver Gate (repaired in the 18th century) gives access to the outer fortress, and just to the right we encounter a small 17th-century temple dedicated to all 24 tirthankars with a relief of them on a stele in the sanctum. Much more impressive is the granite triple or Trikuta basti of the early 14th century commanding a marvellous view. Its central sanctum has a fine 4½' high image of Adinatha.

West of Trikuta basti is an open pavilion with an 11'-high 'Pillar of Abandonment' or Chagada Khambh presumed erected about 983 to celebrate the renunciation (by fasting) of life and possessions by Chamundaraya. Its exquisite Western Ganga scrollwork reminded me of Roman craftsmanship at Leptis Magna. West again is the Cennanna mandapam and temple of 1667 with a disproportionately tiny shikhara, with a manastambha, or Jain lamp-pillar, and associated ponds.

Next we ascend to the Akhanda or Monolithic Gateway, so-called not on its own account but for its monolithic pair of cells. Over the lintel Lakshmi presides with anointing elephants, and a finely-judged surround of lions and crocodiles; this is a splendid Western Ganga masterpiece of about 988, but the cells with reliefs of Bharata and Bahubali must be after 1130. Opposite rises a boulder called Siddhara Gundu, with eight rows of saints, possibly representing those who achieved samadhi at SB.

The next doorways are Kanchigubbi and Gullekayi Ajji, through which we come to the 14th-century Siddhara temple, with commemorative columns dated 1398 and 1432, and the Wadiyar Mandapam, built to commemorate the redemp-

Sravana Belagola. Gullekayi Ajji sculpture

tion of mortgaged temple property in 1634 by Maharaja Chamaraja Wadiyar of Mysore. Even more interesting is the Gullekayi Ajji Mandapam, with its 12th-century pillar, a yaksha image on the upper floor, and an image of an old woman with sari and blouse which must be later, stylistically. The legend tells how Chamundaraya, immensely proud of his colossus, determined to inaugurate it by pouring over it thousands of gallons of milk. To his consternation, his milk covered only the giant head of Bahubali, and when he sought advice, ministers pointed to an old woman who had been standing aside with a single egg-plant containing a few drops of milk. The priests brought the old lady up to the head of the colossus and when she inverted her eggplant or *gulla* milk gushed forth and covered the entire figure in milk. Chamundaraya prostrated himself, realising that she must be none other than the yakshi Padmavati, which is why among Jains as well as among Hindus she is revered to this day. An old woman in white – herself an incarnation of Padmavati? – humbly laid red blossoms between the goddess's ankleted bare feet.

Scientifically measured at 58' 8", the mammoth white granite figure of Bahubali towers over the town of Sravana Belagola. It was completed in 981 at the behest of the Ganga general and poet Chamundaraya, and named 'Gommata', the handsome one. The general served Digambar or 'naked' Jainism much as the Mauryan emperor Ashoka served Buddhism, and this colossus bears artistic comparison with the two much taller Buddhas at Bamiyan in Afghanistan, once painted red and gold but now as nakedly brown as the cliffs in which their protective niches have been hewn.

The figure depicted in dove-grey granite (almost white in moonlight) has emerged from the hill itself, naked as the Digambar Jain ascetics who have sat in lonely penance across the centuries, or stood like him so long that *madhavi* creepers (Gärtnera racemosa) have climbed up his legs, in the artist's imagination, and he does not stir when cobras emerge from carved anthills at his enormous feet.

In legends as early as the 9th century, Bahubali is the son of the first tirthankar, Adinatha, and brother of Bharata; he has been chronicled by many authors from the Rashtrakuta saint-poet Jinasenacharya to Anantakavi (1645). A new colossal image was carved in 1973 at Dharmasthala, South Kanara, so his tradition remains vibrant today. Renouncing the world, King Vrsbanatha divided his lands between his sons Bharata (who will rule from Ayodhya, connected with Rama) and Bahubali (who rules from the mythical Paudanapura). Bharata set out to conquer the world and did so, returning home at last with the Divine Disc which carries all before it. But when the Divine Disc cannot pass the palace doorway, Bharata realises that he has not subjugated every kingdom. His ministers hurry up to explain that his brother Bahubali resists when everyone else has surrendered. Aghast, Bharata attempts to convince Bahubali that he is surrounded on all sides and cannot survive if attacked. Bahubali then humbly bows before Bharata and explains that while all his other victories were welcome, he himself cannot submit against the will of their own father. 'So if you cannot agree that I should rule, you must bring out your hordes against me.' In this dilemma between fraternal duty and the kshatriya code of honour, Bharata calls for war, but the elders on both sides urge that innocent blood should not be shed, and a duel should be fought between the

Sravana Belagola. The great anointing festival in progress

two royal brothers. In eye-to-eye contact, an encounter in a lotus pool, and in a wrestling match, Bahubali is thrice victor, upon which the enraged Bharata commands the Divine Disc to annihilate his brother. The Disc circumambulates Bahubali instead, respectfully distant, at which Bharata falls at his feet and begs forgiveness. But Bahubali abdicates instead, restores Bharata, and renounces the world, standing motionless until the madhava creeper twines round his limbs and he becomes kevali, or enlightened. It is this eternal moment which we respect at Sravana Belagola, at midday or midnight, near the summit of Vindhyagiri. We have made some kind of pilgrimage and have achieved some degree of understanding, whether of love or loyalty, respect or wonder.

Every twelve years the head and body of Bahubali are anointed from atop specially-made scaffolding in a ceremony called mahamastakabhisheka (1982, 1994, 2006), but a great millennial anointing took place in 1981 to re-enact the original consecration by Chamundaraya. First of all 1008 brass pots of holy water were poured over the statue to a chorus of bugles and drums, trumpets blared and urns of coconut water and sugarcane juice were emptied over Bahubali's head, neck and shoulders, then an ocean of milk, a snowfall of rice-powder, turmeric, mahogany-coloured sandalwood liquid, and finally eight scents mingling in a flow of ashtagandha in a delicate pink. Finally a gentle cascade of flower petals floated down the immense granite saint and cries of hundreds of thousands of spectators irradiated the sky.

A lesser-known figure of Bahubali, rather smaller and dating from 1432, was erected at the Jain centre of Karkal, and if you take an inland circuit between Udupi and Mangalore you can see not only Karkal but also 15 km farther south the major Jain site of Mudbidri, ruled by a Jain dynasty called Chauta or Chettiar. I mean no disrespect to the towering images of Bahubali at SB and Karkal, but my favourite Karnataka figure of the Jain saint is a Rashtrakuta bronze of the 9th century, oakfirm, broad-shouldered, serene and still: it is under 50 centimetres tall and awaits you in the Prince of Wales Museum, Bombay.

To Belur

Dazzled with the effects of sun, fatigue and emotion, I closed my eyes for the fifteen minutes it took the bus to reach the busy little town of Channarayapatna, as Kolatur was renamed in 1600 when Lakshmappa, ruler of Hole Narsipur, conquered the town and gave it to his son Channaraya. The fortress was held in fief for the Sultans of Bijapur, then taken by Hole Narsipur and controlled by them until 1633, when Chamaraja Wadiyar VI of Mysore besieged it and overcame local resistance. Suffering under repeated Maratha attacks, the fort was strengthened by Haidar Ali. Another quarter of an hour brought us to Udayapura, one of a thousand such farming villages in Karnataka, and half an hour later we rolled, dusty and parched with thirst, into the small town of Hassan, past the rail station, coir emporium, Sri Prabhat Military Hotel (as elsewhere, 'hotel' usually denotes a restaurant without accommodation), tele-phone exchange, TB & Polio Clinic, and finally Hotel Amblee Palika on Racecourse Road, where a cheerful waiter rushed obligingly from table to table, and provided cold drinks, half a chicken with vegetables and fried rice, all within the allocated forty minutes. Cold beer is available, for Karnataka is not a dry state. You can lodge here, or at the government-owned Hassan Ashok with a lackadaisical restaurant at twice the price.

A frequent public bus service connects Hassan with Belur and Halebid from a stand near the cheap Sathyaprakash and adjoining Dwaraka Hotels. Hassan lies 40 km from Belur, which is 16 km from Halebid, but that distance is deceptive, for local roads are poor and the journey more uncomfortable and longwinded than it should be. The route seems half-desert, half-grassland, with weaver-bird nests looped around thorny mimosa bushes and rare sandalwood trees increasingly vulnerable to poachers. Casuarina, cassia, mango: the trees sound as tropical, as exotic as they look. Buses hoot, cars are made to swerve on to the road-edge as our behemoth cavalierly commandeers the centre; only oxen plodding with age-old resignation are allowed to maintain their course.

Despite the fact that, unlike Somnathpur or Halebid, the Hoysala temple at Belur is still active for worship, non-Hindus are graciously welcomed within much as non-Catholics are permitted inside the Vatican's Sistine Chapel: the greatness of art should supersede all religious differences. Belur temples and sculptures are all created in the same grey-green chloritic schist which is relatively soft from the quarry, but hardens with age.

The Hoysala dynasty responsible for Belur had their administrative capital at Dvarasamudra, now known as Halebid from 'hale' (old) and 'bidu' (capital), and held sway in south Karnataka as near contemporaries of the Pandya dynasty in the south and the Kakatiya dynasty in the north. The great Hindu temples of Belur and Halebid were both begun by Maharaja Vishnuvardhana, the former to celebrate his conversion from Jainism to the Vaishnavite sect of Hinduism. The Belur temple was begun in 1117 and completed in 1141, and the Halebid temple begun about 1121 and completed during the reign of Narasimha I, possibly in the 1150s, though records show that sculptors may still have been working on some figures during the iconoclastic Muslim invasion of 1310, after which Harihara I of Vijayanagar repaired it and restored its endowments.

'Belur' is a corrupt form of Velapura, so called from its grove of vela or babul trees, *acacia arabica*, the suffix 'pur' or 'pura' denoting a settlement. The mud and wooden houses of old Velapura have long vanished, leaving only the mighty temple, a contemporary of glorious Wells in England, and Glastonbury, of gargoyled Amiens in France, and the grey ship of Chartres, all small towns subordinated to the 12th-century propensity to build high and nobly for posterity. The story has it (but this is a Jain tale) that frequent earthquakes damaged and delayed Vishnuvardhana's vision of a temple to Vijaya Narayan. Eventually, he sought guidance at Sravana Belagola, where Jain priests exacted restoration of their grants, since which time no great natural disaster has struck Belur.

Chennakeshava Temple is named for the beautiful ('chenna') long-haired ('keshava') form of Vishnu, as is the later Hoysala temple we shall see at Somnathpur. It may be viewed in three main parts: the adytum or garbhagriha, known also as a cella or sanctum sanctorum, with the principal image; the vestibule or sukanasa; and the hall or navaranga, known as a mandapam or pavilion in much of south and western India, here diamond-shaped with three entrances. Perforated stone screens dividing the external pillars date from

Belur. Dancer in Hoysala style

the time of Ballala II, late in the 12th century, and achieve a pinnacle of aesthetic beauty justly compared to the figures at Khajuraho in their blaze of sensuous rhythm. The entrance gopuram on the east has a tower of Vijayanagar age. Within the walled courtyard are two ancillary 12th-century shrines: the Andal monument in the northwest corner, and the Kappe Chennivaraya shrine to the south.

When it comes to a description of the main temple, a rueful visitor might well emulate the Turkish ambassador who in 1433 'dared not attempt to describe the beauty of the temple, lest he should be accused of exaggeration.' The great architect is unknown, as they were by and large in Gothic Europe, but many of the sculptors have identified their names on their creations: twelve different artists at Belur, and fourteen at Halebid.

Eight horizontal friezes skirt the temple. Near the foot runs a chain of 646 elephants symbolising stamina, then in sequence above them a cornice of mythical beasts, half gryphon and half lion, which symbolise strength and courage; an elaborate series of scrolls; a beadwork cornice; niches with alternating yakshas and yakshis, pilasters dividing a row of exquisite female figures; a madhava creeper decorated with miniature lions and tiny figures; and finally double columns dividing figures set in panels. The most attractive frieze is that of women, each unique as women are, each private yet sensuous, elegant yet inaccessible, ineffably proud yet on a plane with everyone else, communicating yet enigmatic. But even these masterpieces are overshadowed by the extraordinary madanikas, the bracket-figures swiftly and vigorously carved in the orig-

Belur. Sculptural brackets in Hoysala style

inally soft stone which has hardened and darkened to an appearance of bronze. These royal maidens, whether princesses or concubines, demigoddesses or dancing girls (their humanity bridges a multitude of interpretations), are framed in a canopy of branches and flowers, servants shown respectfully tiny at their side. One madanika of proportions we recognize much later in Rubens holds up a round mirror in her left hand, gazing at it lost in centuries of admiration, naked except for a girdle, a rich headdress, necklaces, armlets, bracelets and anklets. Another grasps a tame parrot, fettered by her splendour. A third lounges with legs crossed, gazing abstractly to the right as she plaits her luxuriant tresses. A fourth dances to the music of the 12th century, her left leg raised and elegant fingers poised, on a flat dance floor whose rim is discreetly inscribed to the greater glory of her sculptor.

Each doorway has its own magnificence: guardians and fantastic lions, sea-monsters at the side, and Vishnu visions on the lintel. Non-Hindus may not enter the sanctum sanctorum, but its entrance is well worth the journey to Belur. Guardians in exotic costume protect the opening, and above the lintel Vishnu is accompanied by a radiant Lakshmi flanked by sea-monsters. As a boy I bought André Malraux's *Le Musée imaginaire de la sculpture mondiale* (1952) and Sir Herbert Read's *The Art of Sculpture* (1956), but neither of those luminaries mentioned either Belur or Halebid. It is time to set the record straight, and propose that these sculpture galleries count among mankind's most impressive achievements.

How extraordinary that the temple to Lakshmidevi at Dodda Gaddavahalli, between Hassan and Belur, should be almost totally lacking in external sculpture, even if the sixteen columns in the mandapam are profusely decorated. Look for the pair of malevolent demons guarding a sanctum, skeletal except for the grinning face with bulging eyes.

Halebid

Your day among the Jains and their converts ends in glory, as it began, with the 12th-century capital of the Hoysalas at Dvarasamudra, still showing traces of its 9-km walls at many points, and earth ramparts here and there, such as on the east side of the access road to the temple and indeed on both sides of the main road connecting Belur with Hassan. There are three small undecorated Jain temples between the tank called Dvarasamudra and the royal palace site. The two main Hindu temples are also located very close to the pool. The less important is the Kedareshvara, named for the great lingam of Shiva worshipped at Kedarnath in Uttar Pradesh, its sculptures less inspired than those by the great masters who worked on the Hoysaleshvara Temple several decades earlier, in the mid–12th century, and more or less continuously until the time of Ballala III, troubled by Muslim incursions.

It was begun before 1141, because that is the date of its consecration, but the sculptures bear no earlier date than Narasimha I (1141–73) and the earliest votive offerings on the inner wall are grants by a queen of Ballala II who was still alive in 1177.

The temptation is to concentrate on the multiplicity of details, but we must set that achievement in its architectural context. An inscription shows that it was designed and constructed by a certain Kedaraja, master builder, under the supervision of the chief officer of public works, one Kedamalla. It probably was intended to be completed by a superstructure of roof and tower, either never brought to fruition or removed for unknown reasons. Percy Brown, in *Indian Architecture (Buddhist and Hindu)* (Bombay, 1942) states that Hoysaleshvara 'is the supreme climax of Indian architecture in its most prodigal manifestation . . . As a monument to the phenomenal concentration, superb technical skill, ingenuity, imagination, and profound religious consciousness of those concerned in its creation, it has no peer.' Dvarasamudra may have disappeared almost as dramatically as Troy or Carthage, but its most glorious temple survives as a testament to the mind, spirit and manual dexterity of its great men, such as Devoja, named at the back of the Nandi pavilion as the artist of the west doorway: the same master had previously worked at Belur.

Structurally, Hoysaleshvara is a pair of identical temples connected only by their adjacent transepts. Unlike Dravidian temples, which are square or rectangular, it is star-shaped, with a double sanctuary and double mandapam. Each sanctuary has one central chamber and three lesser chambers, the whole raised on a platform five feet high echoing the plan of the buildings above it. Inexplicably in this shrine to the symmetrical, the two Nandi pavilions differ considerably in size, the one facing the east doorway of the southern temple being very much larger than its northern counterpart. The larger is 16 feet long, recumbent like Nandi on Chamundi Hill, and carved in a pot-stone impregnated with hornblende. The smaller is of talc also impregnated with hornblende.

The temple is dedicated to Lord Shiva, but the ecumenical quality of Hoysala art, typified by the Jain Bettiga's conversion to Vaishnavism and subsequent tolerance of all faiths, allows these artists to depict incarnations of Vishnu such as Krishna playing the flute, and Brahma on his vehicle the goose, as well as Shiva dancing and fighting demons. Indeed, we might be present at a joyful reunion of the entire Hindu pantheon, each deity manifesting himself innumerably. A mystic might claim that all these visible signs emanate from the one invisible god in the heart, but such a claim would be unhistorical, thrusting the rich diversity of Hindu myth and legend into a monotheistic straitjacket. If each tree and blade of grass bears within it a divine spirit, the number of divine presences must be infinite, which is oddly enough my own conclusion as I suddenly realised that I had walked round the neverending friezes and had begun a second circuit. I remembered a battle scene from the *Mahabharata* from having glimpsed it on my previous circumambulation; this is how the myth of reincarnation must have first appeared among men. It is true that the friezes have *no point of departure*.

Although as always it is hazardous to generalise, we might remember the suggestion by Betty Heimann in *Facets of Indian Thought* (1964) that the Indian 'thinks in a circle or a spiral of continuously developing potentialities, and not on the straight line of progressive stages . . . Indian terms can overlap or mutually cover each other like the overgrowth of plants in the jungle . . . the Indian term grows, as it were, from inside, and expands in layers of petals.' So dance, sound, as in temple music, or religious mantras, which can be superimposed or internalised, play a much bigger part in Hinduism than does the reading of texts. While Christian theology is taught mainly in libraries and books, Hinduism is received as a body of disparate, simultaneous and non-sequential *awareness* to be absorbed, rather than a body of doctrine to be learnt. The Indian – insofar as he is not influenced by Western ways of thinking – lives synchronically, in a multi-dimensional world. *Avidya* or ignorance is believed to consist of separate perceptions, whereas *vidya* or true knowledge is understood to consist of a synoptic sense of the whole, as might be observed in Buddhism on a *tanka*, where the cosmos is seen both as a single entity and at the same time in all its disparate parts. But in Hinduism the manifestation of Brahman in a mountain or an island barely hints at the unsayable reality which inadequate Western words try to express as 'God', 'Nature', 'Spirit'. We cannot imagine the endless reservoir of fullness and emptiness *at the same time* which is possibly one part of one Indian view of Brahman. A traditional Hindu will consider that what you and I consider real is entirely illusion, and the whole spectrum of what we consider unreal partakes of indescribable reality. An ultimate heresy for him is separateness: to break down barriers leading to separateness, the ascetic will try to purify his body of gross essences, leaving only what is refined. For the hermit, withdrawal from the transient forms of daily life is a first condition of achieving higher states of consciousness. During puja, the profane offering, the fruits of the earth, blend with the divine in a new fusion recreated anew in every sacred fire, in every sacred feast, in every religious festival. It is a heroic gift of Nehru – audaciously high-principled – to make of his people (or that eighty per cent who are of Hindu persuasion) a secular body constitutionally tolerant, liberal, and egalitarian. Some might argue that the rising tide of the Bharatiya Janata Party's Hindu sectarianism is a response to communal realities rather than the even-handed pacification advocated and practised by the Congress Party since Independence. But from the frightening perspective of Partition the drumming-up of Ayodhya Ramacentrism appears to represent a threat to that secularism which distances religious fervour from weighty matters of state deserving a balanced solution. These friezes appear to have been carved at the beginning of the world, and will outlive its end. In the west, art became bourgeois and familiar with easel painting and the rise of the middle class. Nothing like that happened in Indian mediaeval art, so we are infinitely distanced from Rama and Sita riding in hieratic procession, as we are from saints, sages, and mythical beasts. At the foot of the endless frieze more than two thousand elephants march in the same direction, all different in detail of action and trappings, some with mahouts; next come the mythical lionlike beasts some call leogriffs and some *shardulas;* scrollwork with tiny figures of birds and beasts, gods and goddesses singing and dancing; next horses and riders with fine gear, boots and weapons; scrollwork with episodes from Hindu legend; *Ramayana* scenes; and finally mythical birds and animals set within terrestrial foliage.

In the West we are accustomed to 'studio' works: Rubens for instance cannot be credited with more than a small fraction of the large canvases commissioned from his studio. Such a tradition may have existed at Dvarasamudra, but to a much lesser extent, for the vivacity and elegance of thousands of details seem spontaneous yet deeply felt and supremely achieved with an expressive confidence born of a master-guild system known for instance in German cities like Nuremberg·or Italian cities like Florence. Close your eyes and imagine the tap of hammer and chisel made by bronzed men, lithe, small and slim, head

Halebid. Hoysaleshwara Temple. Details of Hoysala sculpture

swathed in moist cloths against fierce summer heat. Above them, tapping on scaffolding platforms of bound wooden scaffolding, masters would work on half-lifesize figures of Hindu gods and goddesses, full-face, framed by pillars and canopy, with subservients very much smaller, one on each side, and all in relief high enough to cast almost human shadows. Erotic scenes run the gamut of human emotion, which is all we can know of divine emotion.

While Belur's extravagant beauty reigns inside, that of Halebid shines outside. Arjuna holds his bow above his head, drawing attention to his opulent pyramidal headdress; his jewels glitter in the sun, the moving shadows lending a vibrant depth of the relief and 'colour' to the monochrome carving, the whole protected from heavy rains by overhanging eaves. With a single arrow the great hero Rama pierces seven trees. A haloed dancer with rich necklace and fine anklets is accompanied by two tiny drummers.

Within the conjoined mandapams columns have been lathe-turned or carved with many facets. Brackets are adorned with the same breed of dancer and musician as we found at Belur, but they seem even more graceful in their pinnacle of sound and movement.

The doorways themselves are of no great interest, being plain rectangles. Of the four entrances, two to each temple, only those on the south and southeast are complete. A great dvarapala or doorkeeper stands left and right in the tribhanga attitude, that is with head, body and legs at three different angles in a posture familiar from Indian dance. The doorkeepers are costumed extravagantly, with jewels and daunting symbols of office set inside a foliated, arched aureole. Above and between them, somewhat shadowy beneath straight over-hanging eaves, is a twelve-foot frieze centred on Shiva dancing the tandava, accompanied by musicians on drum and cymbal.

The shrines may be visited to see the almost featureless lingam-yoni focus of worship that marks the temple out for Shiva's domain.

Outside the archaeological museum a colossal Jain figure without its original hands towers naked between two fine columns, over the surrounding trees and bushes. The museum itself is closed on Fridays, but even then you can see in its grounds a dancing Shiva, a seated Ganesha, and a rounded sculpture of King Hoysala, founder of the dynasty, overcoming the leogriff to claim the kingdom, a St George slaying the dragon transposed under Karnatakan blue skies.

Somnathpur

Buses for the Hoysala temples of Somnathpur leave Mysore for both Bannur and Narsipur: whichever you choose requires a change of bus, and both inter-changes are crowded village market squares. From Narsipur I bought a one-rupee ticket for the 10-km ride to Somnathpur, and I somehow pushed and squeezed through the standing throng in the gangway to the door by yelling 'shukria, shukria' ('thanks, thanks') in an effort to persuade the driver not to continue his journey with me on board. A nurse from Hannover called Bettina alighted with me, equally anxious to see the magnificent Hoysala temples dated 1268, created at the expense of Narasimha III's general Somanatha. The rest of Somnathpur dozed in the warm afternoon sun. A monkey tilted its head inquisitively at me from a whitewashed wall. Bullocks ambled like lords almighty along paths of beaten earth, red like burnished copper. A snake wound its cautious length along a field-edge. Storks clattered beaks officiously like town criers. I sipped Gold Spot bought from a hole in the wall, where a vendor celebrated the provision of electricity not only by keeping beverages cold in his fridge, but also by lighting his single naked bulb, waggling above my head in a slight breeze.

The wondrous Kesava Temple may be your foretaste of Hoysala splendours at Belur and Halebid, but Hoysala architecture has less celebrated masterpieces also beginning in the late 10th century at Kukkanur near Gadag, at Lakkandi, Ittagi and Kuruvatti. Mughal architecture has come to be regarded in the West as the Indian type *par excellence*, due to its own qualities, the advocacy of powerful connoisseurs less familiar with Deccani work, and because most visi-tors to India see only the north. But Hoysala builders preferred a dark stone of much finer grain, often chlorite, to the great sandstone blocks chosen by early Chalukya builders at Aihole or Pattadakal. The aim was to enable sculptors to work in fine detail to almost miniature standards, and for column shafts to withstand turning on a lathe, resulting in an ivory-like polish.

The great rectangular exterior wall has a single gateway to the east with an open portico and an inscription recording the temple's foundation by Somana-tha, a high official and general in the service of King Narasimha III (1254–91), a name indicating Vaishnavite affiliations.

The rectangular courtyard is inset with sixty-four *cellae* attuned to the pro-portions of the temple and its three shrines so carefully that one feels filled

Somnathpur. Kesava Temple

with serenity, especially as the temple is seldom visited and usually quiet.

'Kesava', dedicatee of the temple, is the 'long-haired one', or Krishna, himself an incarnation of Vishnu: life-size bronze figures show him playing the flute, and Janardhana, another incarnation of Vishnu, adorning south and north shrines respectively. Krishna in particular is a masterpiece of fully rounded carving, both arms sumptuously braceleted and his brow brightly jewelled. The Venugopala in the west shrine is recent. Corbelled ceilings make a riot of lobes and pendants.

The shrines and mandapam stand on a raised plinth that seems to begin to elevate Kesava Temple heavenward. Each of the three symmetrical shrines has a stelliform exterior belying a circular plan but reflecting the outer edges of the dignified platform. The towers rise pyramidally with an abundance of elegant carvings filling almost every space with that horror vacui that we note in Chandella sculpture at Khajuraho four centuries earlier.

The lower friezes contain elephant processions, ducks and devils, horses with riders, epic or Purana scenes. The higher friezes are devoted to divinities, usually Vishnu with his consorts, each figure magnificently arrayed in draped costumes, glittering jewels and often crowned: depending on the time of day the reliefs seem to give off scent, music and colour. They are so shaped and angled as to move with the flitting sunshine; the dancing scenes cavort with grace. Half-closed eyes will quicken the movement, increase the pulse-beat, raise the temperature. Above head-height, the figural friezes soar out of view to become as vague as birds in flight, so binoculars are advised. You can just make out roof-shapes and graceful pots, with seated gods and goddesses at intervals like the ladder of a Hindu *Paradiso*, though Dante was only three years old when Somnathpur's Kesava temple first filled the sky. The sculptors, not so bashful as their counterparts in the supreme French Gothic cathedrals, have left their names on image-pedestals: Chameya, Bhameya, Mallathamma. I rejoiced too in the exquisite lathe-turned shafts that seem as delicate as timber, yet last as long as diamond. A canteen nearby provided tea and cakes on that hot January afternoon, and the beautifully-maintained garden drowsed below a pair of chasing giant butterflies.

On the Narsipur side of the village I had glimpsed in the fields a smaller temple, called Panchalingam or 'Five Lingas' after the shrines to Shiva aligned in granite. Plants grow through an abandoned temple that villagers say was built as a memorial to Somanatha and his family. Three galleries of columns are round except for one square at the end. The lingam plinths inside the cells remain, but their lingams are missing. The whole is contemporary with the Kesava Temple close by, but simpler, less ornate as befits a work intended in homage to a man, and smaller. An inscription in Old Kannada on a monument shows lingam worship with a Nandi bull.

I waited for the evening bus back to Mysore, seated crosslegged like any villager, back from the road far enough to avoid dust from passing vehicles yet near enough to be able to rush for the bus. I tried to buy a bunch of five bananas from a stall-holder, but he refused. 'No good, sir!' he explained, pointing at the bananas. Could he have been standing by, waiting for them to ripen? A cockerel vaunted his prowess in the distance. A boy cycled past with a sack of rice as pillion. A woman tending two babies winnowed rice grains with a rhythmic sway of her arms. As the sun descended into the far fields, a barefoot elder black as soot in an off-white vest and black shorts shook his head in disapproval at the passing world, and cracked knuckles angrily, his white beard bristling. Little Chandrashekhar, in the sixth grade, begged 'one rupee, hello mister, one school pen' until shooed away by two dignified women with sharp teeth bearing firewood on their heads. General Somanatha would have recognised the village seven hundred years on.

Srirangapatnam

Just as the river Kaveri graciously divides into two streams at Shivasamudram, and crashes towards the plains of Tamil Nadu down the falls Gagana Chukki and Bara Chukki, so it divides into two streams 15 km north of Mysore, curling around the island which has burrowed its way into English history as Seringapatam, a corruption of Srirangapatnam.

The name means the town of Lord Ranganatha, a manifestation of Lord Vishnu, whose temple was commissioned in 894 by the Ganga overlord Tirumalaya. According to local stories, a brother of the Hoysala King Vishnuvardhana, whom we have met at Belur, founded a settlement that arose around the ancient temple.

I caught the bus no. 125 marked S. R. Patna which tooted and barged its way through cattle and unheeding cyclists past St Philomena's neo-Gothic church mocking in pseudo-European antiquarianism Mysore's overweening blue skies. The bus finally creaked in at 9.40, after amazing halts at almost every street corner, shouts from the bustling, joking conductor, and oaths from the apoplectic driver as he shaved cars, carts and lorries but never actually hit anyone head one, due no doubt to an image of Lakshmi above his windscreen and luck beyond compare.

On alighting beneath banyans in S. R. Patna square, which is a main stop on the highway to Bangalore, I was accosted by a tongawalla named Sideya, his skin burned mahogany and his skeletal arms waving at his aged, weary horse overdue for retirement pastures. After fierce and defiant haggling with this impresario, I settled for Rs 10 to be driven to Daria Daulat and the mausolea of Haidar Ali and Tipu Sultan, a figure doubled as the horse sagged beneath Sideya's whip.

I mean no disrespect to Mysore when suggesting that SRP is infinitely more inviting to the historically-minded. The Mysore palaces have little but grandiose rhetoric to recommend them, whereas the monuments at SRP are not only earlier, and more evocative of daring times, but far more beautiful.

Dariat Daulat is a summer palace and garden of immense charm, and its museum tells (in part) much of the tale of the Muslims of southern Karnataka.

At Geetha Book House, K. R. Circle, I had bought B. Sheik Ali's *Tipu Sultan: a study in diplomacy and confrontation* (Mysore, 1982), a distinguished and cogent appraisal of Tipu Sultan's importance as the most formidable enemy the British had to face in India. Tipu declared that living like a lion for a day was preferable to living like a jackal for a hundred years, and he felt nothing but contempt for local rulers who achieved a marriage of convenience with the British in exchange for nominal suzerainty. He urged Indian rulers to unite in order to remove the British, who exploited the old maxim of 'divide and rule', but they proved recalcitrant, and he was compelled to seek assistance from the French (Europeans should fight against Europeans just as the British forced

163

Indians to fight Indians), as well as from the Turks and the Afghans. Napoleon showed every sympathy to Tipu, and the Maratha leader Peshwa Madhava Rao I could be relied upon to harass the British throughout the south.

In the first Mysore War of 1766, the Marathas from present-day Maharashtra, and the Nizam of Hyderabad of present-day Andhra Pradesh, allied themselves with the British against Tipu's father Haidar Ali, who had made Mysore a Muslim sultanate. Haidar Ali bought off the Marathas, persuaded Hyderabad to remain outside the conflict, and single-handedly took on the British, whom he defeated and required to sign the Treaty of Madras in 1769, by which the British were obliged to send aid if he were again attacked by the Marathas. A few months later the Maratha leader Madhava Rao returned from the north with forces to humble Haidar, who naturally invoked the Treaty of Madras, but the British ignored their obligation under the treaty, playing the Great Game of matching one adversary against another, and seized Mahé, a French possession on the Malabar coast. In 1780, having paid off the Marathas in the Second Mysore War Haidar overcame the British and took prisoners whom he held in some cases until 1784, and in others till 1799, but lost an engagement at Porto Novo in 1781. Haidar died in 1782 after twenty-one years as head of state, and was succeeded by his son Tipu, who retained his father's Brahman adviser Purniah, that same chief minister who would be retained by the British as adviser to the young Krishnaraja Wadiyar from the age of 5 to attainment of majority in 1811.

Purniah is considered by scholars such as Mildred Archer to be the subject of a shimmering painting by Thomas Hickey (1801) now in the Yale Center for British Art: a vivid likeness in a pose familiar from Van Dyck set among classical elements such as the goddess of justice and a gleaming Hellenic column.

Tipu's burning ambition was to drive the British out from the state of Mysore, but in 1791 Lord Cornwallis took control of Bangalore and marched on SRP during the Third Mysore War of 1790–2. Without adequate supplies, the British retreated, only to return victorious in 1792 and impose the humiliating Peace of 1792 on Tipu. The idea was to isolate Tipu by an alliance with the Nizam of Hyderabad and the Marathas, but this time the Marathas proved refractory. Tipu now tried to increase contacts with the French, and despatched an embassy to Mauritius to obtain French aid against the British; they agreed and did actually send a small force at a time when the British feared the menace of Napoleon in Europe. So Wellesley declared war and in the Fourth Mysore War of 1798–9 the British achieved not only final victory, but the death of Tipu, the destruction of SRP, and the restoration of a Hindu dynasty likely to remain docile.

So the monuments we shall see date almost exclusively to the second half of the 18th century, when the Hindu ascendancy switched to a Muslim ascendancy. The 'Wealth of the Sea', as Daria Daulat signifies in Urdu, is an ample garden laid out on the south bank of the north branch of the Kaveri, with a splendid low wooden summer palace accessible down a cypress avenue where fountains play in a long pool. The palace, now a museum, is raised on a square stone platform five feet high bearing a broad verandah with eight columns on each side painted during my visit a gaudy red, contrasting with the gaudy green shutters to keep out intrusive sunlight. A small hall in the upper floor, reached by carefully concealed staircases, once served as Tipu's private reception room.

The west wall has battle murals of Polilur, showing Haidar and Tipu leading their forces on elephant-back in 1780, their victory over Colonel Baillie counting as possibly the worst British defeat in India, with 36 European officers killed out of 86, and 3,820 prisoners taken, of whom 508 were European. Baillie himself was taken captive and spent years in the dungeons at SRP. The caption describes how Baillie 'sits in the palanquin with his fingers on his lips in dismay.' The Nizam's general is painted above a cow and a boar, reflecting Tipu's bitter aphorism that his tardy ally had arrived like a cow but fled like a boar.

The east walls are decorated with panels showing durbars of Tipu's contemporaries, among them the Hindu Rani of Chittor, the Raja of Tanjore, and the Raja of Benares. The museum also displays prints and drawings of Tipu's family, most of whom are buried at Vellore in Tamil Nadu. Chairs, chaise-longue and divan from Tipu's period give the weird impression that he might return from campaign at any moment: here is a map to illustrate all his two dozen forts from Gooty in the north to Palghat in the south, and Mangalore in the west to Sholinghur near Vellore in the east, where Sir Eyre Coote defeated Haidar Ali in 1781. His dozen mints spread from Dharwar in the north to Dindigul in the south. In London's Victoria and Albert Museum the new Nehru Gallery of Indian Art shows the mechanised toy called Tipu's Tiger, his war helmet and his cuirass, so that even in Europe his renown lingers on.

Before leaving Daria Daulat note the crown-domed dovecots so similar to the tall twin minarets in the town's Friday Mosque. Sideya the tongawalla now demanded thrice the agreed fare for continuing in midday heat to the mausoleum, but I quietly said 'no' and continued on foot. Coping with the extremes of weather in India may be trying, but the benefits of not cocooning oneself from the real world of India are indisputable, such as the chance to see the Roman Catholic Church of Our Lady of the Immaculate Conception founded in 1800 by the Abbé J. A. Dubois, author of the indispensable though comically prejudiced *Hindu Manners, Customs and Ceremonies*. Dubois worked in India from 1792 to 1823 as a Christian missionary of that rare breed who recognises 'the absolute necessity of gaining their confidence,' as Dubois wrote of his Indian hosts. 'I adopted their style of clothing and studied their customs and methods of life in order to become exactly like them. I even went so far as to avoid any display of repugnance to the majority of their peculiar prejudices.' Dubois left France in 1792 under the auspices of the Missions Étrangères and spent some time in what is now Tamil Nadu, attached to the Pondicherry Mission. Tipu Sultan is known not to have persecuted a single priest, though he did convert 1,800 Christians to Islam. After his death, many of these 'lost sheep' were brought back to Christianity, and the permanent Roman Catholic church and mission were set up. Dubois was a pioneer of vaccination against smallpox in Mysore and organised farming colonies to improve the lot of the poor peasant.

At the crossroads left to the Fig Gardens I chose right to 'Gumbaz', Urdu for mausoleum. Set in a charming garden called Lal Bagh, the tombs are found two hundred metres from the site of Haidar Ali's Lalbagh Palace, dismantled by British officers. Some of the timbers can be seen in St Stephen's Church and others in Holy Trinity, both in Ooty. Tipu laid out the grounds in 1794, and he was buried here in 1799 in a mausoleum he had built for his illustrious father and his family. An elegant square cream building with an onion dome

Srirangapatnam. Tipu Sultan's mausoleum for his father Haidar Ali

and polished black basalt pillars supporting a balcony, and a minareted square upper floor, the mausoleum is open daily from 8 to 6.30, and is conscientiously maintained. The ebony and ivory doors were given by Lord Dalhousie in 1855.

In the centre the tomb of Haidar Ali is draped as a mark of respect and sprinkled with flower petals. It is flanked by a dark-canopied tomb of his consort Fakhr an-Nisa Saidani Begum (east) and the tiger-pattern-covered tomb of the great Tipu, considered by Muslims a holy martyr. The British buried him with full military honours amid a thunderstorm in which two officers were killed by lightning, a fact doubtless relayed to each generation of worshippers as an omen of divine wrath. The British – probably for quite different reasons – resited the capital of the state at Mysore, and the garrison later at Bangalore.

I had hoped to visit the adjacent mosque, but no amount of gentle remonstration would induce any caretakers to look for the key. So I set off back along the road to the fort, knowing that a much greater mosque awaited me there.

The Fort

In Arabic, the root *jm'* denotes a meeting or congregation, so that a Friday or Jum'a Mosque is the principal mosque in town, where the communal prayers take place on the Muslim holy day. The imam will read out notices, offer significant prayers and guidance, and lead the faithful in such matters as holy war, exhortations to give alms, to go on the pilgrimage, and to observe Quranic precepts. The Friday Mosque in the fort at SRP was deserted and ghostly, even my steps soundless as I had of course removed my shoes outside. The hall has

166

Srirangapatnam. Bangalore Gate, near Friday Mosque

a mihrab on its western wall like a small room, and foil arches in a Mughal manner, and is dated from stone inscriptions to 1787, the story being that Tipu played near the grounds of the early 18th-century Hanuman Temple here as a boy, with his father was no more than a young officer in the Mysore army. A faqir approached the lad and predicted a great future for him, claiming as his reward for the augury that he should raze the Hindu temple and build instead a mosque to the glory of Allah. All happened as predicted, so Tipu set up this fine mosque, with twin minarets each allowing access to the top by a winding staircase. During my last visit the steps were blocked and access denied; according to a ghafir because the structure was no longer safe. In the front portico's shadow, an imam was teaching the Qur'an by rote, his white-clad pupils rocking back and forth in the customary attempt to learn more easily by a steady rhythm of chant and motion. The grave is that of the Diwan of Haidar, Mir Muhammad Sadak, notorious for proclivity to torture.

The British made Tipu out to be a fanatical Muslim, but he left undisturbed not only the Vijayanagar-period Gangadhareshwara temple north-east of the palace harem enclosure, and the Narasimha temple, but also the great Dravidian-style temple to Sri Ranganatha with which the capital of Haidar and Tipu has always been identified. Local lore has it that the nucleus of Sri Ranganatha is of 894, but the earliest inscription on the sanctum's south basement cornice records that the Hoysala ruler Ballala II gave grants in about 1200 for the sanctum, or garbha-griha; the forward projection, or sukha-nasika ('nasika' meaning German *Nase*, English *nose*); and the many granite pillars with round and stellate Hoysala forms. As I looked into the cella forbidden to non-Hindus

167

from the external navaranga or pillared pavilion, I tried to make out the great image of Vishnu on the serpent Ananta who raises his hood to shield his master's head. The river-goddess Kaveri and the local rishi Gautama are depicted significantly tiny by his legs. If you can't see the whole of Sri Ranganatha's image, then you can circumambulate outside the cella in semidarkness, returning to the navaranga with its twin dvarapalas or doorkeepers. Plain ceilings and beams support the evidence of inscriptions that much has occurred since Hoysala times, including the emplacement of a Lakshmi as Ranganayaki of obvious Vijayanagar date, as opposed to the more refined Gopalakrishna in a shrine to the west, quite similar to that in Somnathpur. East of the pillared court a late Vijayanagar frontal mandapam reuses some Hoysala columns: the whole temple is like a stone palimpsest for architectural detectives to unravel.

Due north, by the outer wall just above the Kaveri are the dungeons of bitter memory where British prisoners standing in water were kept in chains, their arms crossed, for years. The dungeons are brick-vaulted and measure about 100' × 40'.

Tipu's original palace was dismantled on Colonel Wellesley's orders in 1807; it stood close to Sri Ranganatha temple, and its destruction was an act of idiotic vandalism.

Four km from SRP is the Ranganathittu bird sanctuary, on an island in the Kaveri. Take a tonga from the village to the entrance of the sanctuary, then a boatride. Look for bottle-shaped nests of mud above the river, where Indian cliff swallows have colonised, the flesh-coloured bill of the cattle egret, the yellow bill of the intermediate egret, and the blackbilled little egret. The red eyes of black-and-white night herons peer at your boat cautiously, at dusk when fox bats come back to hang upside down from branches too high for predators. You will possibly see a marsh crocodile sunning himself on a rock or slipping away, thieflike, to hunt freshwater fish.

Twenty minutes by train out of Mysore Junction or 20 km by road is the station at Krishnarajasagar for the Kaveri dam, terraced gardens flatteringly named Brindaban after Krishna's mythical paradise 9 km from Mathura in North India. This Brindaban is floodlit every night, and there is a comfortable western-type hotel called Krishnarajasagar, as well as a much cheaper Tourist Home with attached bathroom, if you don't require airconditioning. The great artificial lake is a convenient spot to relax after a strenuous journey.

The Slow Bus to Nagarhole
Mysore Central Bus Station is intended only for Kannadigas: timetables and destinations are printed only in Kannada and, as usual, I relied on the presence of an English-speaker to steer me through the day. Inspectors and conductors normally speak enough English, but they are rushed off their feet, attending to illiterate enquirers from villages or to foreign pests like myself, and I missed the 12.30 direct bus to Nagarhole through Birunani, because an inspector forgot to indicate its arrival. It takes only 3 hours for 100 km, whereas the slow 1.30 bus via Hunsur takes 5½ hours. As usual, I had ample compensation for delay because the country bus showed me much more of South Kodagu (the British called it 'Coorg') than I could otherwise have seen, and the variety of passengers, farmers and schoolgirls, grannies and coffee-labourers, made an absorbing

study of facial types, clothes and manners. I stocked up with bananas, Spencer's fruit loaf, and a bottle of Bisleri mineral water. A Tibetan monk got on a bus to Madikeri ('Mercara' in British lore) which would drop him off near the resettlement centre and monastery of Rabgayling, near Hunsur.

Within half an hour we had ascended into the hills of Kodagu, reaching Hutagalli at 1.55 along roads steadily emptier as we drove into Hullenahalli by 2.10. Trekkers and climbers will assure you that spirits rise with altitude. Credit is due to awesome vistas, purer air, and the physical satisfaction of achieving higher ground. That is how I felt, leaving Mysore plain for the mountains of Kodagu.

The Kodavas who live here are now administered as citizens of Karnataka, but until 1956 Kodagu remained an independent princely state. In 1804, during the rule of Virarajendra Wadiyar, Kodagu consisted of its present hilly area, and another below the Western Ghats, including Sullia-Amara and Puttur. When the British annexed Kodagu in 1834, they separated lowland Kodagu and merged it with South Kannara, leaving an area sixty miles north to south, and forty miles east to west. Its inhabitants differ markedly from those of the rest of Karnataka and adjoining Kerala, with their own language and customs, a pro-British inclination heightened by memories of Haidar Ali's incursions in 1773 and Tipu Sultan's in 1785, when he took several families as prisoners and forcibly converted them to Islam. The vexed question of *The Coorgs and their Origins* has been tackled by M.P. and Ponnamma Cariappa ('amma' means 'mother' and 'appa' father) in their 1981 book, and by many others, who have suggested that the Kodavas derive from Kadambas, Arabs, hill tribesfolk, Rajputs, Kurds, Aryans, Kurus, Scythians and Dravidians. The solution seems to be that they arrived in several waves beginning in the 6th century B.C. from hundreds of villages in north and north-west India, notably from Kashmir, Himachal Pradesh, Gujarat, Rajasthan and Madhya Pradesh, explaining why they are taller and lighter-skinned than surrounding South Indian peoples, with a martial history owing something to the honour system and traditions of Rajput kshatriyas.

As most of the undulating countryside is situated above 4000 ft a.s.l., the climate is Kashmiri, likened by some to a tropical Switzerland or Scottish Highlands. Like Highlanders too they are martial, and have a thousand extended families like septs or clans who descend from common ancestors, but traditionally marry outside the family. No class or caste distinctions exist, except of course among families who have immigrated into Kodagu more recently, and even those tend to wear the European clothes assumed by the vast majority.

At Rangainakoppalu a tidal wave of women and children crushed on to the bus, so that most seats were occupied twice or thrice, with women, older children and babies among the scattering of menfolk: the bus had to stop while the conductor issued fresh tickets. I was offered a slice of jackfruit by a small party of women chattering on the floor. We stopped again at the brickmaking village of Mukannahalli, where women were filling water-bowls from a tap; like every other village it has its arrack shop for the sale of potent liquor. Three o'clock saw us pull into Hunsur bus station, and the customary pandemonium as passengers trying to alight fought with those trying to embark: they never realise that it cannot be done: the bus filled like a balloon to accommodate twice as many passengers as before, and I could swear it sighed and sank down a couple of inches. All signs were in Kannada or English; I thought pessimistically of the All-Indian hope for Hindi as a national language. A 'Forest Checking Gate' was passed at 3.30 and at 4.15 the National Park barrier, with bamboo thickets on both sides. The Balmany coffee estate spread emerald green bushes below shade trees clustered with pepper creepers like ivy, then we entered the straggling village of Tithimathi, where tailors plied their sewing-machines in the open air, facing the traffic, and reached Gonikopal at 4.50, with its 'Perfect Kushion Work' and coffee collecting depôt. Charming young Kodava beauties flounced on to the bus, their long lustrous straight black hair regaled with strings of flowers. One smiled at me in unaffected wonder, and I could not help repeating under my breath the immortal fragment attributed to the Greek lyric poet Archilochos, who spent time on a campaign in Thrace around 650 B.C.:

> ékhousa thallón myrsínes etérpeto
> rhodés te kalón ánthos,
> e de oi kome
> ómous kateskíaze kai metáphrena

which one might render, 'she toyed with a myrtle, and one fresh rose; her cascading hair darkened down her shoulders and her back.'

An auto-rickshaw bore the legend 'Truth is God, Sound Horn', possibly not in that order. I saw a mosque on the main square, having passed a Muslim graveyard en route. Roses festooned the route to Ponnampet, where mango orchards hung heavy with luscious fruit, and white coffee blossoms mimicked snow. At Hudikeri (5.20) I put on my jacket against cool winds, and my last memory of the dusk was of rice-terraces in the background, and hibiscus below swaying palms by the road. I took a warming tea at Kutta village (6.10) as the guest of the conductor, whose brother greeted me: 'this is the only chance we have to chat, because he goes back to Mysore at 6 tomorrow morning'. One by one the passengers dropped off the darkening bus, until at 6.50 I was dropped by the Range Forest Office. It had closed for the day, but I had booked a cottage with the Deputy Conservator of Forests, Wildlife Preservation, Ashokpuram, Mysore (tel. 21159) and my roomboy Selvaraj hovered to carry my suitcase on his head, and lead me along the night path to my isolated cottage, which he unlocked. He revealed a sitting-room with sofa and table, a dining-room with a table and four chairs, a bathroom with both Western and squat toilets, a cold-water shower (facilities he amplified with a bucket of hot water for a shave), and a spacious double bedroom equipped with mosquito nets.

He made the bed and bowed: 'vegetarian meals only, sir, rice, chapatis.' I assented enthusiastically, having eaten only a small fruit loaf and four bananas since breakfast. He padded off to bring my tiffin-carrier, while I drew the curtains, and pulled down an astonished lizard with my hand. She blinked, stood rapt still in a careful impression of a brooch, then skeltered off quicker than a squirrel can twitch his whiskers. After my vegetarian spread, I edged silently out of my cottage, anxious not to disturb the universe. Clear skies over Kodagu sparkled with stars, honouring a crescent moon far above a road that

170

peters out into jungle. I switched on my torch and glimpsed one pair of green eyes, then another, a third, fourth, fifth, all turned towards me like planets around the sun. I stroked the torchlight gently round to reveal the flanks of a herd of seven spotted deer. I felt elated, then relaxed when I realised that tigers could hardly roam in the vicinity without frightening these deer.

Back in the cottage, I sheltered from mosquitoes under my net and shone my torch on a park map, showing Nagarhole ('Snake River', from one of the six streams that wind through the park) at the northwest fringe of the park. Eastward is Karapura, where Kabini River Lodge provides year-round accommodation and coracle rides before breakfast. The best seasons at Nagarhole are Winter (November to February) and Summer (March to May), because the June-September monsoon season can be too wet for comfort.

Next morning my alarm shattered pre-dawn silence at 5.30 and I walked across to the Range Forest Office for a jeep-drive through the jungle at 6, but Indians lodged in a dormitory rose late and we didn't get away until 6.50. Hill tribes inhabit the park: Hakki Pikki (Bird-Trappers), Jenu Kurubas (Honey-Gatherers) and Yeravas. The jeep-driver stopped for photographs every time we noticed wandering or grazing animals: an Indian bison, peahens, langurs in the trees, timid sambhar, several herds of spotted deer, a wild boar, Blyth's mynah, a red-vented bulbul, but regrettably no leopard or tiger.

After an exciting hour's drive, I met K. M. Chinnappa, the Range Forest Officer. Wildlife conservation is perennially controversial in India, from the populist approach of Periyar who offer rides on tame elephants, to Mr Chinnappa's own restrictive view that human beings should be limited in numbers and

Nagarhole National Park. Herd of spotted deer

171

activities in the interest of animals, birds and plants. 'We risk damaging the very environment that we are paid to protect,' he pointed out. 'We must avoid building more cottages, more dormitories, and keep out anyone with tape recorders and transistors. Ignorant people sing and shout, not thinking of the effect on shy wildlife. And can you believe, a reporter once came from Bombay to visit the park wearing a *red shirt!*' I smiled understandingly, relieved that I had chosen an all-beige outfit for the trip.

Selvaraj brought my tiffin-carrier with breakfast and a flask of black coffee. Rhesus monkeys swung noisily overhead, sensing titbits. I consulted T. N. A. Perumal's *Photographing Wildlife in India*, and noted his advice as coming from the heart: 'Avoid being placed in the middle of a herd of elephants'. Tiptoeing spotted deer gave away their presence by the rustle of leaves underfoot.

I tipped Selvaraj for his solicitude, and caught the private Shiva Prakash bus for Madikeri at 9.40, the sun already warming the seats as we dropped neatly-uniformed boys at St Mary's Convent School in Kutta, then the driver stopped outside K. P. Ibrahim Haji's general stores to watch a fierce argument between two gesticulating men in express-speed Kannada while a crowd gathered in silent judgment below a mandala of a million buzzing gnats.

Madikeri

We traversed Glenlorna Estate at Hudikeri, Ponnampet, and the Coffee Demonstration Farm at Gonikopal. Near the Mamatha Picture Palace an ice-lolly man was dispensing wares from a tea chest with a sliding panel set on top of his bike. The driver alighted at Virajpet for a tea and idli sambar, at a café where three auto-rickshaws were parked: 'Life is a Music', 'St Joseph' and 'Sri Ganesh'. The breathtaking climax of one's approach to Madikeri is twenty minutes of shimmeringly green fields and trees, amid intimate mountains that seem both closely accessible, fruitful in their yield and yet tantalising, like the earth goddess fecundated after monsoon.

At the bus station I hailed an auto-rickshaw which in a few minutes had assaulted the ridge of Madikeri and deposited me in a room at the Valley View Hotel overlooking the precipitous valley visible from Raja's Seat, and from the opposite side the prosperous hill-station's red-tiled roofs and the reflecting tank of the Omkareshwara Temple dedicated to Lord Shiva commissioned by Linga Rajendra in 1820.

After an excellent lunch of sweetcorn soup, chicken fried rice, and a pot of coffee, I sauntered along the road down to the town centre by way of Raja's Seat garden, the pavilion itself no more than an uninspired square stone belvedere with a comically plebeian red-tiled titfer, reputedly the vantage point of past Kodagu kings. Below a curve in the road, the stout fort, boasting three sturdy stone gates to repel invaders, cradles the palace of Linga Rajendra Wadiyar (1812), whose mausoleum (and that of Dodda Vira Rajendra and their queens) is to be found on the other side of Madikeri, recognisable by gilded domes. These are among the most famous rulers of the Haleri dynasty, who were the first family to govern the whole of Kodagu (1600–1834). Madhu Raja I, the third of his line, created the first mud fort in Madikeri, and it is thought that the town derives its name from his. Dodda Vira (1780–1809) went mad in his last years and executed many of his relatives (the *Coorg Gazetteer* tells us);

having no son he left his kingdom to a ten-year-old daughter. In 1811 her uncle Linga Raja II usurped the throne and ruled unscrupulously until 1820, being succeeded by his son Vira Raja II called Chikka Vira, who massacred his relatives in the manner of Dodda Vira, and was deposed in 1834 by the British, who carted him off to Benares; he died in 1859. Lt.-Col. J. S. Fraser, in the name of the Governor-General, called the Kodagu leaders to a meeting at Kushalnagar (subsequently named Fraserpet in his honour) in 1834, and requested them 'to express their wishes . . . in regard to the form of government which they desired', learning that they wanted to be governed by the laws applied elsewhere in the British East India Company's lands and subsequently hoisting the Union flag over the Lingayat dynasty's fort. The *Mysore Gazetteer* grandly claims that during the peaceful period from 1834 to 1947, the British 'built this state from a small loose-knit feudal principality into a prosperous and well-administered unit.'

The fort, roughly hexagonal, is defended by a steep glacis to the north and a ditch in front. Its walls are preserved, and within them are a palace converted into administrative offices of the Deputy Commissioner and his staff, an arsenal also used now for offices, and St Mark's Church now a Government Museum (9–5, closed Mondays), with one chapel blasphemously dedicated to Field Marshal K. M. Cariappa, including his portrait and memorabilia. Two plaques record the death of British servicemen from Kodagu in the World Wars: those who gave their lives in 1939–45 included W. A. Davies of Bullacadoo Estate, E. C. B. Harper of Whaddon, G. A. Parsons of Dalquarren, and A. W. Sprott of Haleri, which was the capital of Kodagu before Madikeri. Victorian stained glass commemorated Rev. A. Fennell, 'who was chiefly instrumental in erecting this church in 1856' and died in 1897. Four 11th-century Jain tirthankars from Bettagare stand naked and inward, unlike the vibrant 15th-century Durga and Vishnu from Virajpet. Three interesting cult deities reveal persistent animism as in most mountainous areas, like a pair of metal boar masks. The 18th century is represented by a dagger and a fine Lakshmi hanging lamp, strange bedfellows in this British Protestant church. I was kindly invited into the offices to view wall-paintings of 1821 showing the Maharaja Vira Raja II, a pair of elephants, horse and lion. The first floor housed the royal zenana, or harem, with a balcony illusionistically supported by a pair of rearing white fairground horses. Stone steps are flanked by low balustrades which incorporate the bodies of a pair of falling lions, viewed laterally. Viewed frontally, they have elephants' trunks to symbolise the victory of elephant over lion. I entered the rabbit-warren offices, and enquired of the Statistics Office about the population census of 1991.

'In 1981, the population of Madikeri town was 24,724; the taluq 117,726, and the whole of Kodagu district 461,888. The final figures will not appear for some years, but you can multiply those numbers by 120% to get the picture.' The public library, next to the museum, offered little that was new, exhorting 'Serene Silence Please! Have Respect for Thought!' The District Prison close by the second gateway looked dark and drear: what else should one expect? Two massive dark grey stone elephants stood by the wall, a monument set up by the crazed Vira Raja II, who used to be serenaded at dawn by his favourite trumpeting elephants. One day he asked not to be woken at dawn, but his mahouts never received the message, and in fury Vira Raja had both mahouts

Madikeri. Former Royal Palace, now offices

and elephants put to death. On feeling remorse, he ordered statues to be erected – to the elephants.

On my last evening in Madikeri I decided to call at the North Coorg Club, founded in the late 19th century as a refuge for British coffee-planters who wanted to spend some time among their kind. It is now open to women, like the affiliated Bamboo Club (for South Coorg), and the Belur Club in Somwarpet (North Coorg), but the Cosmopolitan Club in Madikeri remains resolutely stag in membership.

Though a non-member, I strolled into the deserted North Coorg Club and found a bar-tender. 'Hullo,' called a voice from the phone booth, and within ten minutes I had become a guest, awash with hospitality, of Sunil Ganapathy, who farms at Hutti to the north. Like all coffee-growers, he mixes his crops: coffee-bushes low to the ground, shade-trees like red cedar and white cedar welcoming pepper, figs, and oranges. He grows on the same plantation *arabica*, the best coffee for percolators, and *robusta*, a lower quality for instant coffee.

Ancestral property having been divided, acreage now averages no more than twenty to thirty, which is why there are no coffee barons on the scale of oil barons.

Local coffee producers have been hit by the dissolution of the International Coffee Organisation in New York, which regulated a quota of million bags for each producer, such as Brazil, Guatemala, Papua New Guinea and Kenya. Now the market is free, and Indian growers have suffered because the national Coffee Board at Bangalore has fixed an artificially low rate and after negotiations an action committee called up collecting depôts to close down two

174

weeks before, to protest against actions by Coffee Board. Sunil showed me the figures: the planter is paid Rs 13,000 a tonne up to Rs 17,000, while the Board fixes a retail price of Rs 44,000 to RS 62,000 depending on quality. Coffee-growers view this disparity as exploitatively large. 'With sixty acres you need a minimum of 30 permanent labourers working 7.30–3.30 without a break. In the third week of May the pre-monsoon spraying, manuring, clearing, and new planting take place, and in September-October the post-monsoon spraying and manuring needs to be done. Throughout the year scuffling (removing weeds) is essential and pests have to be sought and eradicated: the white steam-borer *arabica* and the short hole-borer in *robusta*. The berry borer hit Sri Lanka badly, then parts of Kerala and Tamil Nadu, and it is expected to penetrate Karnataka in two to three years. Nothing of the crop can be saved: every berry has to be destroyed, including those on the ground.'

The North Coorg Club (B. Arun Biddappa Hon. Sec.) currently has 263 members, many of them also members of Mercara Downs Golf Club and Kodagu Vidyalaya Tennis Club. The billiard-table was made in the 1920s by John W. Roberts (Madras) Ltd., but the most popular pastime is cards. A locked library on the closed verandah looks desultory: *Seasons of Passion* by Danielle Steel, and *The Final Diagnosis* by Arthur Hailey, all paperback donations. Residential quarters for members needing to spend the night in Madikeri consist of two rooms, one double- and one triple-bedded, at Rs 75 and 100 respectively.

Next morning I took a local bus 36 km southwest to Bhagamandala, where a Keralan-style many-roofed temple, Sri Bhagandeshwara, commemorates the confluence of the sacred Kaveri river ('Ganges of the South') with the streams Kanike and Sujyothi. Temple rites and regulations here and at the Sri Subramanyam temple are Keralan in usage, as they are at Talakaveri, the source of the river. Once a year, when the Sun enters Libra 'notified fairly in advance every year as per astrological calculations by the authority of the Coorg Temple Funds Management Committee,' the river is said to bubble up at Talakaveri's small well a metre square in the hills 9 km from Bhagamandala. Thousands of pilgrims come to bathe on this day, usually around mid-October, and priests sprinkle pots of holy water on the surrounding crowds. It is a season of light rains, which are believed to augur well for the coming year. I never saw any foreigners during my visit to Coorg in January, yet I cannot imagine a more relaxing, fascinating and historic region for Americans or Australians intent on experiencing an aspect of authentic India. As Hilton Brown, a district magistrate, wrote in the 1920s, 'we could solace ourselves with the water meadows of Fraserpet, or climb to the windswept grass plateau of the Brahmagiris, where the sambhar walk in open solitude; and in the end descend into Malabar by the Saratabbi Falls, which are four hundred feet high, and the great gorge of the Barapole river, which must surely be as fine a piece of scenery as there is on Earth.'

Mangalore

Rs 22.50 (just over US $1.00 or UK£0.67) paid for a ticket on a four-hour bus ride across western Kodagu, down the spectacular Western Ghats, and across the coastal plain via Kannur to Mangalore. We passed the Cardamom Research Centre at Appangala, the Glencoorg estate, a cocoa nursery, and hairpin bends down to rubber plantations round Sampaje, where a fresh driver took over. Sparse traffic eased our progress through Kulchar and Sullia, with Cadbury's Cocoa Collection Centre and huge carts of grapes and watermelons; crowds of country folk bartered and shopped. Beyond Aryapu's sawmills we entered the town of Puttur, with its Mai de Deus Roman Catholic Church reminding me of Portuguese penetration from their coastal enclaves. Now the bus broke into a run, instead of a jog, aimed across the Netravati plain, over the railway bridge, and stopped only to pick up passengers stranded from the collision of their own bus with a contorted lorry that lay on its side. 'The driver is absconding', a favourite laconic ending to news tales of road accidents, occurred again to my mind. After Kannur's idyllic padi-fields we tooted into the hullabaloo of Mangalore bus station. Ravenous as a young kestrel, I dumped my case at the left-luggage office and steered towards Famous Restaurant and Fast Food, where the proprietor obligingly put a Hindi rock-and-roll cassette on the instant I sat down so we could not hear ourselves speak over the crowded menu. 'Pomfret', I decided. 'You want fat rice or thin rice?' I gazed at him in my usual amazement. 'Fat?' I suggested. He shook his head in total accord.

The most significant temple in Mangalore is named for Sri Manjunatha, an aspect of Shiva, but reminiscences of other cult worship include a lingam of the Natha Panth Hindu sect, and Buddhist images, including sword-wielding Manjusri, destroying falsehood, and a teaching Buddha, both of the 11th century. A bronze Avalokiteshvara, Lord of the Worlds, dated 968, is of exceptional quality, in extraordinary contrast to the wooden-wheeled temple carts, say, or the Keralan-style tiled roof above a low screen wall, or lavish silver doors, beyond which there is 'no entrance except to archakans', that is to priests of the shrine. A frog stared at another world in the 'snake' pool, as I tiptoed past.

Ibn Battuta called at Manjarur in 1324, noting, 'This is the town at which most of the merchants from Persia and Yemen disembark, and pepper and ginger are very abundant . . . There is a colony of about 400 Muslims there, living in a suburb alongside the town. Conflicts frequently break out between them and the (Hindu) townspeople, but the Sultan makes peace between them on account of his need of the merchants.' In 1514, Duarte Barbosa observed that it was 'a very large town inhabited by Moors and Gentiles who shipped rice and pepper to Aden', so the Portuguese determined to take Mangalore. Vasco da Gama first blockaded the entrance to the river Netravati in 1524, and the Portuguese seized the town two years later, but ruled through a client whose family was recognised as legitimate by Vijayanagar. It was not until 1670 that the Portuguese established a factory here, re-established in 1714 after having been burnt by the Arabs. The fort built (1739–54) by Basavappa Nayak of the Ikkeri dynasty was demolished in 1794 by Tipu Sultan. Even now 20% of Mangalore folk are Roman Catholic; Milagres Church is one of India's oldest, and the Chapel of St Aloysius on Bavte Gudda ('Flag Hill') displays frescoes by the 19th-century Italian Jesuit Antonio Moscheni.

The Government Museum is named for Shrimati Bai Mirajkar who died in 1944, and the museum was donated by her sons in 1955. Captions are only in Kannada, so a local guide will help to explain the small Hindu bronze images, mainly of the 15th–18th centuries, together with excellent 18th-century wild boars, elephant and horse. The paintings, such as 'Brindaban Gardens' by N.

Mangalore. Decorated temple car at the 10th-century Sri Manjunatha

Hanumesh, are of no great value: the best works are in stone: a 16th-century Nayak-style Royal Lady and Warriors from Naravi (east of Mudbidri), and a magical Jain tirthankar in Hoysala style and a 13th-century Saraswati, both from Barkur. The 1st floor's claim to distinction has nothing to do with geological specimens or stuffed animals, but a 17th-century Nepalese Vajrasattva.

Tipu Sultan's Battery is a low battlemented redoubt on the shore, so picturesquely sited that you might guiltily expect it to have been placed for photogenic purposes, beside flat-bottomed ferry boats, some with bedsheet-sails, and hollowed canoes. An industrial chimney, still now, prods the blue sky, mocked by herons in the water and parrots in the palms.

But Mangalore is synonymous with cashews, being the leading cashew-port in the world, and I was invited for a briefing by Mr G. V. Narayana, of the Cashew Development Corporation. Cashews are native to Brazil, and were diffused in Africa and Asia by the Portuguese in the mid–16th century. The

Mangalore. Ferry-boat leaving the beach by Tipu Sultan's Battery

tree, evergreen and about 6–10 metres tall, has an economic life of 30–40 years, yielding 50 kg per hectare in the 4th year up to 1000 kg per hectare in the 10th. Its habitat is the coastal tropical belt up to 600 metres, but in India this reaches a height of 1000 metres a.s.l. There is a National Cashew Research Centre at Puttur, Karnataka, which specialises in breeding high-yield nuts. The bigger the nut, in general, the more valuable. Of the 18 recognised varieties, the largest fetches Rs 220 a kg, and the smallest Rs 40 a kg, too expensive for the average Indian, so the key is the export market. Sales are so good that demand will probably always exceed supply. Of every kg of cashew crops, 25% represents the kernel, 25% the oil, and 50% the husk, all of which can be utilised: the nuts for eating, of course, the oil for paint-industry lubricants, and the husk as boiler-fuel. Cashews are attacked by stem-borers, and tea mosquitoes attack flowers and leaves, but treatment by spray is quite effective, and small farmers choosing high-yield varieties such as Ullal I and II can be assured of a good income. Ninety per cent of India's cashews are grown in Kerala, but other states increasing yields include Karnataka, Andhra Pradesh, Orissa and Goa.

Mr Narayana kindly arranged for me to visit the Achal Industries Cashew Factory in New Mangalore, a huge industrial area 12 km from the old town along a modern highway with views of the port and prosperity. Achal gives employees (almost all women) free transportation across a catchment area of 20 square km. Raw cashews are procured from March to May, dried for two days, roasted for 45 minutes, left overnight, and cooled for a day; they are then cut, shelled (against anacardic acide the shellers have to grease their hands with castor oil), and oil is extracted from the shell, sieved and stored in tanks for use in varnishes and epoxy resins. After drying, the husk is removed, leaving the white kernel, which is cooled for a day. It is then peeled by hand, graded by colour and size, cooled again to reduce breakage, weighed and packed in hermetically-sealed tins.

In Mangalore I was invited by a Muslim to watch his family rolling cheroots. Most of the dried tobacco leaves or 'beedis' come from Madhya Pradesh, and are acquired by local contractors, some in Vellore and other Tamil Nadu towns, but most in Mangalore's hinterland called Dakshina Kannada, where over 300,000 beedi rollers can average up to 750 beedis a day, earning Rs 14.3 a day from the contractor, who then takes the beedis to the sorting-house, and is paid commission. Around 200 million cheroots are made in Dakshina Kannada every day, and sold in packs of 25 for only Rs 1.5. They are prepared by wives and daughters in between household chores, and constitute a welcome if meagre supplement to the family income.

One of the eccentricities of Indian travel is that to reach Bombay by rail from Mangalore, a distance of some 991 km, you have to journey 2,041, starting *southward*. There are a couple of flights a day, but these are generally overbooked, and the main road link is the slow and busy Highway 17 through Goa, the average speed on this highway having declined from 50 kph to 30 kph over the last decade. The British never completed the Panvel-Mangalore link, and after Independence the Indian Government viewed the line as a second priority. But Konkan now survives mainly on a money-order economy, with male wage-earners in Bombay factories and females as domestics. North Konkan near Bombay is being industrialised, and a new rail network is planned to run parallel with the existing road network, destined for upgrading; a new major port between Bombay and Goa will further energise the region. Meantime, I see that a fresh steamer Mangalore-Bombay will take scarcely longer than the present rail trip.

Mudbidri

Deceptively, Mudbidri town centre could be anywhere in South Kannara, but if you take a quick rickshaw from Nishmitha Towers Boarding and Lodging, just short of the bus stand, you will arrive at a quiet, historic and contemplative Jain district with a 17th-century Chettiar Palace set behind the Sri Chandranath Swami Tribhuvana Tilara foundation, or *basti*, called 'The 1000-Pillar Temple' by the same token that the Arabs call the *Arabian Nights* '1001 Nights'.

Just before you reach the Chandranath Basti, you see on the left a Jain math or monastery, where a Hindi-English-Kannada illustrated booklet on Mudbidri can be bought. Though it has no map, you can find your way around by pointing to the headings in Kannada which correspond to the same numbered temples in English. As well as 18 bastis, there are tombs or *samadhis*.

The Chettiar Palace is still inhabited by descendants of the royal family which ruled Tulu Nadu region from 1160 to 1867; the building dates from the 17th century, and if asked nicely at reasonable hours the owners will let you examine the beautiful woodcarving in the Audience Hall.

Mr Adiraj, Supervisor of the Jain Math, told me that the population of the town exceeds 20,000, but Jains are in a small minority of some 60 families, with a further 400 in surrounding villages, living mainly from such crops as

Mudbidri. Jain festival

180

Mudbidri. Façade of the 'Thousand-Pillar Temple'

rice, cashews, coconuts and vegetables. He showed me *The Jaina Path of Purification* (1979) by his brother-in-law Padmanabh S. Jaini. 'Not less than 75 visitors are coming per day here from North India,' he claimed, though I saw only a handful as it happened during my morning's tour of the eighteen temples. They are superintended by His Holiness Swasti Sri Bhattaraka Charukeerthi Panditacharyavarya Swamiji, a chubby white-garbed figure crosslegged on his ample throne, with a peacock-feather fan and reflecting spectacles. Jain Math is itself a temple, with its sanctum enclosing a shrine to Lord Parshvanatha.

Chandranath basti close by was begun in 1430 and we have a date of 1463 for Bhairadevi mandapam on massive pillars at the front, succeeded by mandapams called Chitradevi, Namaskara, Tirthankara, Lakshmi, Sukhanashi and Garbhagriha, the last next to Samavasarana mandapam, where devotees worship Lord Chandraprabha. No two pillars are identical, and if you want to explore the cosmic world of the Jains, this makes a good beginning. See the giraffe carved on the base, and the Chinese dragon indicating that Jain merchants were familiar with Africa and China in the 15th century.

Temples and houses mingle in Mudbidri's Jainpet, as in any mediaeval town. A Pre-University College for Jain pupils allows them to study among fellow-believers. Chola Setty Temple is a living temple, with a tall free-standing pillar or manastambha among living and waving palms; its antechamber has four lathe-turned pillars and an elegantly simple ceiling. In Mahadeva Setty Temple the black stone Adinatha in kayotsarga posture was being adored by a woman outside the sanctum, while within an old priest, naked but for a loincloth, officiated and rang two bells to call his Lord's attention. A crow craaked displeasure at the unfairness of existence amid the rustling palms. Vikrama Setty Temple, with 24 bronze tirthankars, stood devoid of worshippers, but a young priest, chanting beautifully, anointed the black granite image of Lord Adinatha, ringing a bell and wafting incense around the sanctum lit uniformly by little bulbs. In these precious moments of ritual intensity, scent and chant, flickering light and spreading dark, I realised why I came to India. The living faith, strange as death, isolates me like an Eskimo in Zanskar.

The oldest temple in Mudbidri is the Guru or Siddhanta basti dedicated to Lord Parshvanatha, whose smooth black granite image must be one of the masterpieces of Jain sculpture, two climbing, entwining cobras forming a protective hood and back: it is dated to 714 A.D., but the outer throne is as recent as 1538.

Venur and Karkal
Buses will take you to Venur for its 1604 Lord Bahubali, the two-storeyed Santishvara Jain basti and many other Jain structures, and Dharmasthala, with its 1973 image of Lord Bahubali and Jain temples, as well as Hindu pilgrimage sites. Alternatively, you can travel north to Karkal (1500 Jains) by frequent public bus doing the Udupi circuit. While still under starter's orders at Mudbidri bus stand, my bus was invaded by an ice cream seller, a news vendor offering the Kannada press, and a blind man with two wooden clappers, his claw-like hands insistently beseeching from seat to seat. The journey of only 18 km is made with the same solemn purpose that one would undertake a pilgrimage, with tiffin carrier and shopping bag. On the half-hour route you traverse Jainpet

Karkal. 'Four-faced Basti' seen across a ricefield

suburb, Belvai village, and Kudremuth National Park. On arrival, a young student called Ananth Murthy chatted with me over tea and masala dosa, and we explored Karkal together by auto-rickshaw: as in Mudbidri, its modern village sprang up beside the Jain district, Hindus outnumbering the diminishing Jain minority. There's no left luggage office for Karkal's open-air bus stand, so I deposited my case at Hotel Swagath, whose name means 'Welcome' and headed for the monolithic image of Lord Bahubali, around 13 metres tall and dating to 1432, visible on its hilltop from afar. It is one of the local imitations of the 10th-century Bahubali at Sravana Belgola. There is no associated temple at present, merely a stone perimeter, so to explore the world of Karkal Jains one needs to cross paths betwixt rice fields to such as the 'Four-Countenance' or Chaturmukha Temple named for four black images of tirthankars. Grey stone tiles replace traditional small red tiles of the Mangalore type, above finely carved white-gray pillars. We overheard villagers speaking the local Tulu dialect as we entered the Jain Math, with figures of the tirthankar Lord Chandranath and the goddess Kushmandini. The morning's *Hindu*, picked up at a newsstand, said that the State Government expected to hand over Nagarhole National Park to the Taj Group on a fifteen-year lease.

I collected my case, bade farewell to Ananth, and boarded the 3.30 bus for Manipal and Udupi, arriving one hour later. I stayed at Malpe, a beach area five km from Udupi, but if you prefer lively urban scenes you could choose the downtown Kalpana Lodge Hotel on Upendra Baug or the Mallika on K. M. Marg. The nearest airport and railhead are at Mangalore, 60 km due south.

Udupi

The name of Udupi (wrongly spelt 'Udipi' in many books) is indissolubly connected with the name of Sri Madhvacharya, a Hindu philosopher-saint born in 1197, according to H. N. Raghavendrachar or in 1238, according to the official local guidebook. Sri Shankara promulgated the concept of non-duality or *dvaita*, the difference between the supreme soul or Sri Hari, and individual souls, and between individual souls and inert matter, between one individual soul and another and so on. The world is real, according to Madhva, and individual souls trapped in the cycle of birth and death may obtain liberation by devotion to Hari and virtuous deeds. Madhva installed an image of Sri Krishna in Udupi, and passed sannyasa to eight of his disciples, each of whom founded a monastery in Udupi and officiated at the shrine of Sri Krishna in turn, originally in a two-month rotation but now in a two-year rotation, marked by the Paryaya Mahotsava or 'Handing Over Festival', occurring in even-numbered years (1994, 1996 and so on) on 17 or 18 January. The incoming abbot undertakes a pilgrimage two months before Paryaya, and returns to Udupi one week beforehand, when he is greeted on the outskirts and taken in procession to Car Street, and pays homage to the deities of Chandreshwar, Ananthasana and Sri Krishna Math. On reaching his own ceremonially decorated monastery, he receives gifts of rice, cash, fruit and vegetables from rich wellwishers, and is invited in turn to feasts by each of the other seven abbots as a sign of respect and solidarity. He reciprocates by inviting them to the festival, with a procession beginning at Jodukatte (near the taluq headquarters) and taking a route through Koladapet and Tenkapet to Car Street and Sri Krishna Math, where the outgoing abbot receives him, he washes hands and feet, worships his deity, offers prayers to Sri Mukhyaprana, and takes a seat on Sri Madhvacharya's throne. All the abbots then go to Badagumalige and take their seat on a throne made of puffed rice before a public durbar with invited guests. The ceremony concludes with the presentation of keys to the incoming abbot, and the procession of abbots who lead the outgoing swami back to his own math.

Realising the historical and religious significance of Sri Krishna monastery is essential because the math itself is relatively modest in size. It has no traditional front door, but a window from which worshippers may view the idol without entering, beneath a small gopuram. The main entrance on the south side is situated to the left of a holy bathing tank called Madhvasarovar, into which a pilgrim assured me that water from the Ganges flowed once every ten years. A sign reads 'Spitting and Using of Soap Prohibited.' Again, I appeared to be the only western visitor, as though Udupi has for some reason eluded those fascinated with other Hindu centres. Yet of course this very absence of non-Hindus quickens the pulse and enlivens the scene. How often one has wished away Japanese cameras from Taj Mahal or German accents from Amber Palace? Here the sounds are the liquid silver of Kannada, the bubbling stream of Tamil, and the swift coursing of Malayalam, mingling with the sharper edges of Hindi and Marathi.

The garbha-griha door is kept closed except for the annual replacement of padi sheaves on Vijayadashami Day. To the left of the northern door into the sanctum is an idol of the saint Madhvacharya. It is said that some lamps burning

Udupi

beside the idol of Sri Krishna were lit by Madhvacharya himself and have never since been allowed to go out. One shrine is signed 'Please remove your shirt before entering'. On the northern side of the math stands the chauki or dining-hall, where the abbots take their daily meal with invited guests; above this another dining hall prepares food for more invited guests, and east of the chauki is a general dining hall where uninvited brahmins may eat; north of this is an idol of Subrahmanya and the Vasanta Mahal courtyard with a pavilion at its northern end. Here public lectures and dramas are arranged; during my visit seven seated priests, dressed in vivid orange, were in turn addressing a packed audience in Kannada.

The great temple square of Udupi has at its centre the ancient temple of Sri Ananthasana. If you enter the garbha-griha, or sanctum, north of the central mandapam you will be shown the place where Sri Madhvacharya is said to have vanished from sight while discoursing to his disciples. Facing Sri Ananthasana is the temple of Chandramulishvar. You can now perambulate the rectangle known as Car Street from the temple cars or chariots drawn around it during festivals. There are half-a-dozen other monasteries off Car Street, but the important eight as founded by Sri Madhvacharya's disciples are the Sode, Puthige and Adamar on the southern side; the Pejawar and Palimar on the western; the Krishnapur and Shirur on the northern; and the Kaniyur on the eastern. They do not look in the least like Christian or Buddhist monasteries: Sri Puthige could almost be a patrician mansion in New England, with its upper-floor verandah, sloping tiled roof, and slender neo-classical columns.

The present abbot or pontiff of Sri Puthige Math, the twenty-seventh in line, is Sri Sugunendra Tirtha, born in 1962, whose first turn for Paryaya occured in 1976–8.

A cow meandered purposefully into a monastery nearby. Mr P. Srinivas explained to me in the Janatha Co-op Bank on Car Street about his bank's unique Shashwatha Seva deposit scheme, which passes seva money permanently to Sri Krishna Temple when so authorised.

If you don't want to arise at 4 a.m. at the conch-blowing and nagari-beating outside the math premises, then try to attend the great service or Mahapuja performed by the current Paryaya abbot, offering sandal paste, tulasi, and flowers to Lord Krishna while reciting the Brahmasutra and other texts, followed by the presentation to the deity of cooked rice, sweets, coconuts, plantains, and betel leaves, after which the abbot retires to allow Sri Madhvacharya in turn to make the offerings to the god. Meanwhile drums, pipes and bhajan songs accompany the ritual and two shots are fired, signalling to the residents in the area that the puja is being completed and that they may now take their food.

Bhatkal and Jog Falls

The coastal road from Udupi to Bhatkal (in the absence of that long-awaited Konkan Railway) is the only real transport artery and both sides of the road are dotted with straggling villages and cafés for casual trade. Hotels are sparse, so in Bhatkal they are often full by nightfall: the Seema Lodge had no vacancies, so I trudged by moonlight to Vaibhav Lodge, where a sweaty room without a shower was offered at Rs 45, and at the non-vegetarian Hotel Kubera in the same complex I found a passable meal among hard drinkers, their tipples including whisky, brandy and beer. Traffic outside the open window poured endlessly past, and conversations in bedrooms on each side of mine, and apparently in the corridor too, made sleep impossible when the fan was turned off; when it was turned on, its whoosh and creak, rattle and whoosh made sleep almost as unlikely as a pig on a spit. Night lurched round as slowly as a pig on a spit.

Next day dawned bright and burnished, silver in the air, and gold in the sun. I asked for a tomato omelette and tea in my room ('plain omelette is not available'), packed, and strolled to the bus station for that glorious drive up the Western Ghats to Jog Falls. Nobody at Bhatkal bus stand speaks English, and signs are only in Kannada. I sat pensively on a stone bench next to a bearded belching pilgrim in a dirty salmon-pink robe who rummaged in a white linen shoulder-bag. A turbaned peasant, his hands borrowed from a millennial tree-trunk, muttered in Kannada to his lungi-clad, white-bearded companion, both wearing ancient chappals on their feet. Khaki-uniformed conductors slouched in their office doorway, keeping bus schedules a carefully guarded secret. As every bus dislodged its passengers who struggled to get off through a teeming mass of pushers, I enquired 'Jog Falls?', until a bespectacled man with a fresh white short-sleeved shirt and razor-pressed flannels gesticulated towards a dilapidated new entrant, dusty, muddy, with two broken windows and three more missing. 'Not direct bus Jog Falls', he confessed, 'direct bus left six o'clock, this circuit bus.'

Within fifteen minutes, the aching bus was puffing its toxic way up into the

Jog Falls, during the dry season

fertile, magical Western Ghats, with a change of viewpoint at every bend. Numerous women and children alighted and ascended at lane-ends, but in the forested heights their rural cottages lay hidden from public view. After an hour's laborious ascent, we considered ourselves aloft: the lines of green wooded hills curled and lapped around us like seawaves, each sloping rush-roofed shack impoverished in the wealth of nature. The first extensive village, Kogar, is two hours out of Bhatkal, and a few padi terraces lurk huddled in the landscape's generous curves, but the crops hereabouts are mainly vegetables, grown in opportunistic plots wrested from spreading undergrowth. I gazed openmouthed in admiration at my neighbour, a grizzled countryman of sixty summers, snoring deeply and contentedly up all the hairpin bends, beyond realisation of the bumping, swerving and tooting of the aged bus. Women fetched water in brass pots by Aralgod, and terraced housing at Kargal looked idyllic, from a distance. We finally emerged at Jog Falls village three hours from Bhatkal, at 12.10. I checked on the next departure for Sirsi (3 p.m.), then chose an omelette with bread at a shack, where a whole pineapple was cut into slices for dessert. The Government-owned Sharavathi Tourist Home looked comfortable and very cheap, with a suite for Rs 75, or about U$4, including a shower-room, mosquito nets, and a sitting-room with a view across to the falls. I sped down the steps for a swim at the foot of the falls, yet still had time for the easy ten-minute walk round the main road to the head of the falls, stepping over rocks to the precipice, taking advantage of the dry season. During the monsoon such an exploit would be impossible, and the views are correspondingly more dramatic, but each season has its splendour at Jog.

The Sharavati river crashes nearly nine hundred feet down four main channels named King, Queen, Rocket and Roarer. No Niagara, perhaps, but in this magnificent setting, wild and unspoilt by all but the merest semblance of tourism facilities, Jog Falls have the uncultivated grandeur of African waterfalls.

Back in the village square, a conductor was yelling 'Shimoga Shimoga Shimoga', which like the Sharavati at Jog has its own wildlife sanctuary nearby, a 16th-century Nayak palace now a museum, and a charming Hoysala shrine in the ruined fort. I took the Sirsi bus for my destination lay north, at Mundgod, accessible on the Sirsi-Hubli road. At Siddapur village, a plateau with wide vistas made a backdrop for neat girls in white blouses and blue skirts leaving the Government Pre-University College.

A leper entered the bus at Kansur, and extended his deformed hands to each passenger, deftly sloping his elbow to lodge each successive coin neatly in its crook.

Two hours out of Jog we arrived in Sirsi (57 km) where a cacophonous bus station had invoked the God Pandemonium's presence: he had deigned to spread his influence over the crowds, which scurried around like anxious rats in a trap. I managed to scramble onto the second bus to Hubli, among eighteen standing, then a youth offered me his seat at the behest of an angry middle-aged man who seemed to exert some influence, real or spurious.

Mundgod and the Tibetan Colony
Ten minutes before Mundgod our bus stopped with a puncture, to the driver's patient, silent, fury. We lounged around in the gathering darkness, comparing

notes on the Gulf War then in progress, Muslims in the group generally siding with Iraq, the rest siding with the Coalition. Approaching Mundgod, I asked to be set down at the turn-off for the Tibetan Colony, and there I encountered a monk haggling for fruit and vegetables in the market. Lobsang Chophel Tsulkhang had been to Hubli to have his portrait of His Holiness the Dalai Lama framed, and I helped him load it onto an auto-rickshaw.

'Are you from Drepung Loseling?' I enquired. 'Yes', he smiled, his youthful face glowing, 'how did you know?' The answer was that monks from the Tibetan colony at Mundgod, and specifically from Drepung Loseling, had visited Cambridge in 1989, and I had enjoyed the spectacle of their music, chanting, and vigorous monastic debate. Tibetan civilisation is one of the world's oldest and richest, but has been ravaged almost to extinction since the Chinese Communists invaded Tibet in 1959. Drepung Monastery was founded near Lhasa in 1416 by Jamyang Choje, and since has acted as a focal point for Tibetan religion, traditional education, and culture, including art and music. Drepung's reputation in Tibet and among its offshoot cultures in twenty-five neighbouring kingdoms of Central Asia attracted more than 10,000 monks, and its affiliated Loseling Dratsang a further 8,000, constituting the largest and most vital monastic culture in the world. When the Chinese began their systematic destruction of Tibetan Buddhism, exacerbated by the cynically misnamed 'Cultural Revolution' of 1969, monks and nuns fled from Tibet across its southern border into India, where they were welcomed by India and housed in refugee camps at Buxa, West Bengal. In 1971, the community was invited to Karnataka and given 142 acres outside Mundgod, then adequate for the 216 monks who successfully reestablished the monastery. Since then the monastic population of Drepung, Ganden and Tsera monasteries has risen to 2,700, and the total number of Tibetan refugees to more than 10,000. Mao Zedong insisted that the State is entitled to use all dictatorial weapons at its disposal to suppress its enemies: in this case they 'enemies' are all the Tibetan people who want to be free. Amnesty International has documented the torture of women as well as men, but refugees continue risk life and liberty by fleeing across the Tibetan snows in the depths of winter, when they are less likely to be seen and shot by Chinese border guards.

Lobsang Chophel came to Mundgod at the age of 12 in 1976, but his parents remain in Lhasa. His slim hands trembled slightly as he told how he eluded Chinese border guards, armed as they are to shoot down refugees on sight. His parents did not dare to leave Lhasa, but the boy and his few companions headed south from Lhasa with scanty provisions to keep them alive, but not too many to arouse suspicion, first keeping to the main tracks then at nightfall concealing themselves in the homes of sympathisers. At dawn they risked their lives on dangerous slopes where Chinese patrols made only rare reconnaissance, and slipped into freedom and safety after enduring hardships of freezing cold, near-starvation, and hazardous snowfields. He has his own home now, with electricity but no toilet or running water, a sloping roof of bamboo branches and a hard board bed netted against mosquitoes. For furniture, there is a table with 2 suitcases, a table and two chairs, wall-niches for candles, a kerosene stove, and shelves crammed with Tibetan books, snaps of his family and friends now dwarfed by the new smiling, serene portrait of His Holiness. A partitioned room just inside the front door has a table with a wash-basin, towel and soap, and hooks for monastic robes. After preparing buttered tea and breaking off a piece of unsalted monastic bread for me, Chophel asked if I would like to see a monastic debate. I enthusiastically agreed. The low-lit room was packed with a sea of crosslegged maroon-garbed monks, focussing their attention on a leaping, twisting shaven-headed master firing theological questions at a row of six crosslegged monks wearing the tufted semi-circular Yellow Hats that give this monastic sect its name. As the teacher came to a conclusion, contradicting the pupil's humble response, he brought one rigid palm across the other in a thunderclap all the more resonant because he would be moving from one foot to another, unnerving his antagonist by swift pirouettes to emphasise his swift turn of argument. His triumph in debate would be stressed by a surge of laughter from the assembly, under the sober gaze of the Abbot, seated behind the row of interrogated students. The atmosphere was tense like that in any debating chamber, from India's Lok Sabha to the Oxford Union. It broke up suddenly at 8.50 p.m., after the master had bowed before the Abbot and taken his leave. We followed the buzzing monks to Drepalden Tashi Gomang, where youngsters in maroon mimicked the claps and dialogue of their elders, the 'master' often clowning in parody. Older monks were reciting sacred texts in the dark: I felt transported to fifteenth-century Lhasa, the hubbub gradually settling like a hive of drowsy bees as the night drifted on. Lobsang Chophel unlocked his little home again, showed me the squat toilet in a building opposite, offered me soap and a hand-towel at his wash-basin, and put on a kettle for more buttered tea, with monastic bread and a packet of biscuits. Hot, sweating, bronchitic, queasy: I had never been so happy in my life, and finally fell asleep, after apologising to Chophel for my persistent cough.

At six in the morning, Chophel whispered, 'Do you want to go to puja?' and I sleepily concurred. In the faint dawn light I followed him to Drepung's small loseling or prayer-hall, where eighteen monks, nine on each side of a low breakfast table, chanted in two or three parts the low, stentorian, music of lamaist incantation, a sound like no other, ethereal, rhythmically interwoven, like volcanic rumblings written by Wagner for such a Wotan as Hans Hotter. I was apportioned a mat beside a wall, where I sat with my legs obediently crossed and my eyes closed in ecstasy to memorise the bass-baritone melody. Prayers over at seven, acolytes half-bowed brought tea made with clarified butter and handed round to each of us a small loaf of unsalted bread. Some monks dunked their bread into their tea, others sipped then ate, in total silence. At 7.15 the acolytes returned to collect cups and plates, and the chanting resumed. Lobsang Chophel invited me to leave with him, and we returned to his house amid birdsong and a few roaming dogs.

I packed quickly and visited the office, where the Abbot's secretary, an abacus behind him, gave me more buttered tea and bread, gazing abstractedly at two suitcases marked 'Free Tibet', while sparrows on the windowsill engaged in a pert debate of their own. Girls in white blouses cycled past, belled oxen were led down the dusty road, and the day's activities yawned into existence. Venerable Dakpa Topgyal, a monk-interpreter, showed me the Library, with a reading room and department for research and translation. The monastery school begun in 1980 has 200 pupils aged from 10 to 18, who study academic

Mundgod. Tibetan monks at Drepung Loseling

subjects and Tibetan Buddhism before leaving to commence higher Buddhist learning. The hospital, permanently underfunded and understaffed, deals primarily with TB, ulcers, mental problems, cancer, and illness caused by blood pressure and blood-sugar deficiency. Dakpa visited Tibet in 1985 and tried to take in Tibetan books printed at their own press in Mundgod, but all the books were confiscated by the Chinese authorities. By contrast, the Indian authorities have shown nothing but support, co-operation, tolerance for the refugees, who of course emerge from Tibet with no money or possessions, yet have to be supported by the monastery, who give them work and food but no wages.

The Tibetan colony urgently needs more funds for its school, hospital, drinking water-supply, orphanage, and agricultural bore-wells. Donations – however small – should be sent to the Abbot, Drepung Loseling, P.O. Tibetan Colony, Mundgod, Karnataka, India 581411; in Europe, funds may be channelled through the Tibet Foundation, 43 New Oxford St., London WC1A 1BH.

On leaving, the Abbot presented me with a white scarf, offered from upturned palms. 'It is a sign,' murmured the interpreter, 'that you will return one day.' 'I shall return,' I assured the Abbot, 'but to a Free Tibet, when monks and refugees will be rebuilding their monasteries and homes.'

Vijayanagar
Between Mundgod and Hubli the bus takes one hour, and at Hubli you have the choice of road or rail to Gadag and Hospet for the magnificent remains of the Vijayanagar Empire at Hampi.

You might choose to spend the night at Gadag, a cotton town, for its Hindu temples both within the town and at nearby Lakkandi, 13 km to the southeast. Lakkandi's biggest temple is a Jain basti near the small museum, but many Hindu temples are scattered throughout the town, all constructed in the late 11th or 12th centuries in Late Chalukya style in schist.

But all of central Karnataka focuses on the massive capital of Vijayanagar, which I shall call by its modern name of Hampi for convenience. The rail station is at Hospet, where the Malligi Tourist Home provides very cheap accommodation and two restaurants, one outdoors. You can hire a taxi here for half a day or a whole day, or rickshaws or bicycles. *Always* wear a hat, for there is virtually no shelter. Unless you intend to spend a week here, it is essential to have your own transport, for the archaeological site covers thirty square km, with over five hundred monuments. For those in an unreasonable hurry, a morning could be set aside for the sacred area, including the Virupaksha complex, while the same afternoon could be spent in the royal area, including the Lotus Mahal, Elephant Stables, Palace and Ceremonial Platform, ending at the Archaeological Museum in Kamalapuram close by.

The following account is designed for those spending two days or more in the great zone, which reminds one of Ostia, perhaps, or Persepolis, in the quality and range of monuments that survive an empire's destruction. As usual, an ideal beginning would be the site museum, signed 'Please don't sleep on the lawn,' where D. Devakunjari's authoritative *Hampi* (2nd ed., 1983) can be purchased for a pittance. It has the best map, 16 plates, and a useful summary of each major monument. One of the museum's four rooms is devoted to excavations at Hampi, still in progress every year. Prehistoric finds could be expected close to the perennial Tungabhadra river, and they are both Neolithic and Chalcolithic in date, but the main surprise of Hampi to the unsuspecting traveller is the cyclopean boulder-landscape, as if giants in a fight had torn down mountains bodily and hurled the pieces at each other, shattering granite into brown, gold, pinkish, blackened, grey or purplish hues and bruises, changing colour with the evanescent light almost like tangible rainbows. The Tungabhadra divided the old capital of Anegondi from the new Pampa, known by the early 13th century as Hampi. Anegondi was the base – if not always the capital – of the Sangama dynasty from 1327 to 1340, following which they zigzagged among five other bases from Sringeri (1346) to Hosappattana (1355), before settling at Vijayanagar in the 1360s. Their spectacular expansion reflected in architectural grandeur their military conquests and religious aspirations until the empire reached its broadest expanse in 1509–42 under Krishnadevaraya and Achyutaraya of the Tuluva dynasty. The empire was destroyed by the allied Muslim Sultans on 23 January 1565 during the so-called 'Battle of Talikota', which H. K. Sherwani has located not at that village (from which the armies pressed southward according to all accounts) but twelve miles south of the Krishna, possibly at Banhatti (15° 53′ N, 76° 18′ E). So we are viewing the remains of two centuries of hectic, purposive building, where an empire creates a capital intended to demonstrate its secular power, and its devotion to Hindu deities.

Since the Muslim conquerors were as always iconoclastic, the museum is not as rich as it might have been, for most images were smashed to pieces or damaged, leaving a splendid Garuda Holding Naga, a flute-playing Venugopal, and stone Hanuman and Garuda, all of the 16th century, and contemporary weapons from Anegondi including a tiny shield. Shaivite dvarapalas greet visitors to the first gallery, but we have an uneasy feeling that they are unrepresentative, that most of their accomplices are lost, an impression corroborated by small bronzes, dated to the 18th century, long after the glory had departed. Then again, we shall not find at Hampi the aesthetic excitement of Hoysala sculpture, but the delusions of eternity that led rulers here as at Hamadan to create seven concentric walls, as though bricks and boulders could defy the passage of time. The empire grew wealthy on spice trade to the south, cotton trade to the south-east, on clearing timber forests for agriculture, on land taxes levied against tributary peoples, and hydraulic works improving irrigation.

While Europe was undergoing the Baroque vision exemplified by Bernini in the south and Rubens in the north, the Deccan experienced the final flowering of Dravidian architecture and sculpture, bearing within it the seeds of decadence, the blight of imitation.

Anegondi
To find the original nucleus of Vijayanagar I chose to start on the north bank of the Tungabhadra, at the village of Anegondi, which served as the empire's capital from around 1336 to 1368, that is beginning with the reign of Harihara I, first of the seven Sangama sovereigns, a dynasty that ended with the death

Anegondi. Sri Ranganatha temple

of Virupaksha II in 1485. Anegondi's monuments clearly antedate Harihara, however: the river-bank has temples as early as the 10th–11th centuries.

I took a taxi from Hospet bisecting the royal centre at Hampi and aiming due north from the Shiva Temple to the gate in the walls called Talarigattu, after the riverbank village. There I alighted for a crossing by coracle, a round rush-basket paddled by a ferryman. It is tarred at the base to make it waterproof, but none of the coracles I saw stayed dry, and three had been overturned for fresh treatment. I crossed with three local villagers, and a talkative pilgrim from Harpanahalli in the far south of Karnataka called Mr Gabiappa, garrulous as a parrot, small and sturdy, walnut-brown, with deepset dancing brown eyes, and a rough stubble that defies burning. As a visitor himself, he delighted in showing me the treasures of Anegondi, from banana plantations including

Tungabhadra river between Anegondi and Hampi. A motor-cyclist about to cross by coracle

delicately-carved princely summer pavilions, to the temple chariot and the temple to Sri Ranganatha not far from the defensive walls, where the majority of the villagers worship. A mosque in the lee of the walls serves some of the Muslim minority (400 or so) while a mosque near the southern perimeter serves the rest. There are only about ten Christian families.

Vishnu, Anegondi's presiding deity, is worshipped both as Ranganatha (Reclining on the Serpent) and as Venkateshwara (Lord of the Seven Hills). Men from a distant village come in late January or early February to make lifesize images of gods and horses for the April chariot festival. They were creating a bamboo frame independently for the body and each limb, then covering the infrastructure with gum and sawdust before placing plaster and cloth, coating the outer layer with white lime, then painting them in gaudy colours.

Mr Gabiappa took me to the home of Rama Deva Raya, a descendant of Krishna Deva Rayalu (d. 1872), who greeted me warmly: I was in the presence of a scion of a line going back to Timma, Iswara, Narasimha, Rajas of Anegondi generations before the loss of Talikota to the Muslim Deccan Federation. He was dressed simply in white, and spoke quietly, with dignity. His uncle, Sri Krishna Deva Raya (1946–66) had been succeeded by his wife Rani Lal Kumari. She adopted her husband's brother's son Achyuta Deva Raya as future raja and he, a company director in Hospet, succeeded on her death in 1984. Rani Lal Kumari died on the day that Indira Gandhi was assassinated: both deserved and were given enormous respect in their own right, quite apart from their position. Rama Deva Raya showed me the buttermilk room with its store of brass and copper pots last used when the royal family fed hundreds of retainers and relatives, next to a room for food preparation where female relatives ate. Other palace areas predating Vijayanagar have been identified in Anegondi: one lay below the present Sri Aurobindo ashram. Chipmunks flew like quicksilver around Anegondi: I counted twelve, but they might all have been the same frantic chipmunk.

Hampi

'Don't pay the two rupees they try to charge,' called out Mr Gabiappa, as the coracle rode the waters back to the south bank, 'the ferry is free, paid by the Raja.'

My taxi dropped me from the ferry at the nearest sacred complex: Sri Vitthala temple, a great 16th-century ensemble in a rectangular court, with a granite chariot honouring Garuda, its wheels once turning but now unhappily cemented down. Kannada Vitthala (so named to distinguish it from its more famous counterpart at Pandharpur in Maharashtra) is set within a fortress-like wall of granite blocks with three gopurams: at north, east and south. The shrine itself lacks a cult image, and may safely be ignored: the splendour lies in the stepped eastern mandapam called Dolotsava Mandapam, or 'Hall of Musical Pillars', from the small range of sounds produced by tapping columns, a property of the rock, not of the sculptor. Neglecting this trivial aspect of the pavilion, we can concentrate on the fine carving on the sixty pillars, and on the elephants flanking the balustrade. Vishnu appears as a boar and in all his other incarnations. The moulded basement again possesses friezes of elephants, lions and

HAMPI AND ITS ENVIRONS

1 — ½ — c — 1 Kilometre

1 — ½ — 1 Mile

N

NARAHARI BRIN

RUINED BRIDGE

SIVA TEMPL

PURANDARA DASARA MANDAPAM

VITTHALA TE

KINGS BALANCE

RAMA TEMPLE

KODANDARAMA TEMPLE

VIRUPAKSHA TEMPLE

HAMPI

SOOLAI BAZAAR

HEMAKUTAM TEMPLES

NANDI

GANESA (LARGER) IMAGE

GANESA (SMALLER) IMAGE

MATANGA PARVATAM

E MOSQUE

ACHYUTA-RAYA TEMPLE

KRISHNA TEMPLE

IMAGE OF NARASIMHA

KRISHNAPURAM

LARGE LINGA (SIVA TEMPLE)

SARASVATI TEMPLE

VISHNU TE

CHANDIKESVARA TEMPLE

UDDHANA VIRABHADRA TEMPLE

ZANANA

ELEPHANT STABLES

RANGA TEMPLE

HAZARA-RAMA TEMPLE

UNDERGROUND TEMPLE

DANAIKS ENCLOSURE

KING'S AUDIENCE-HALL

MAHANAVAMI DIBBA

MINT

OCTAGONAL

SARASVATI TEMP

GANIGITT

BHI

SIVA TEMPLE

KADIRAMPURAM

QUEENS BATH

CHANDRASEKHARA TE

MOSQUES

TRAVELLERS BUNGALOW

ARCHAEOLOGICAL OFFIC

VIRABHADRA TEMPLE

KAMALAPURAM

BASAVANNA TEMPLE

NAGARESVARA

HANUMAN TEMPLE

FORT

TO HOSPET

BARMAPPA TEMPLE

KAMALAPURAM TANK

Map of Hampi

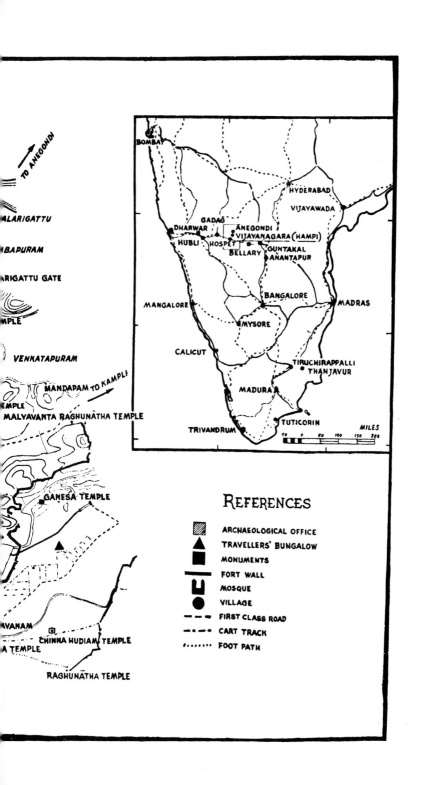

TO ANEGONDI

ALARIGATTU

BAPURAM

ARIGATTU GATE

MPLE

VENKATAPURAM

MANDAPAM TO KAMPLI

EMPLE
MALYAVANTA RAGHUNATHA TEMPLE

GANESA TEMPLE

AVANAM
CHINNA HUDIAM TEMPLE
A TEMPLE

RAGHUNATHA TEMPLE

BOMBAY

HYDERABAD

VIJAYAWADA

GADAG
DHARWAR   ANEGONDI
HUBLI   VIJAYANAGARA (HAMPI)
        HOSPET
        BELLARY   GUNTAKAL
                ANANTAPUR

                BANGALORE

MANGALORE   MADRAS

        MYSORE

CALICUT

        TIRUCHIRAPPALLI
        THANJAVUR

    MADURA

                MILES
TRIVANDRUM   TUTICORIN   50 0 50 100 150 200

REFERENCES

ARCHAEOLOGICAL OFFICE

TRAVELLERS' BUNGALOW

MONUMENTS

FORT WALL

MOSQUE

VILLAGE

FIRST CLASS ROAD

CART TRACK

FOOT PATH

Hampi. Temple car in the Sri Ranganatha temple complex

horses. Piers are in the form of animals with riders, while the ceilings have conventional medallions, geometric designs and foliage: the whole is impressive, except when compared with the greatness of Hoysala work we have seen at Belur and Halebid.

As I strolled northwest from Sri Vitthala to the isolated Shiva temple, along an empty, ruined bazaar, I was reminded of Pompei's Via dell' Abbondanza or the Leptis Magna suq. Within, the sculptures of Hanuman and Shiva are uneroded.

The taxi drove up to the eastern limit of Hampi: the Raghunatha or Rama temple on Malyavanta hill. On coming close, I found the complete gopuram unobtrusively supported within and at the front. Unlike Sri Vitthala, this is an active temple: in the sanctum I found Hanuman, Lakshman, Rama and Sita all crowned and wrapped in silver, though the white bathroom-tiled floor tended to detract from the aura of sanctity. The temple garden, aflush with bright red oleanders, seemed to be walled like a fortress, and indeed this must have been defended as such in time of strife. The date must be 16th century, to judge by sculpted pillars in the contemporary Kalyana Mandapam.

Continuing with sacred buildings, I asked the driver to continue across the royal centre to Hemakuta Hill, sacred to Shiva since the 10th century, and fortified in the 14th, with Ganesha idols, a scaffolded Krishna temple commissioned by Krishna Deva Raya in 1513 to celebrate victories in Orissa, and the same monarch's massive four-armed Narasimha protected by a seven-headed serpent (1528), 6.7 metres tall and carved within a makana torana. The

198

figure once bore a figure of Lakshmi on its left thigh, but this was smashed to fragments.

The temple of Virupaksha or Pampapati, meaning Shiva as the consort of the local river goddess Pampa, antedates the Vijayanagar Empire, being recorded from the 13th century, but it suffered continual restoration and renewal until the 17th century. It is still active today, as the gangs of tame monkeys prove. Domingos Paes, a Portuguese who saw Hampi in 1520–2, refers in awe to the great straight bazaar street ending at the west with Virupaksha and at the east with the hill overlooking Achyutapura on the other side, with its own majestic street culminating in Tiruvengalanatha Temple (1534). 'A very beautiful street of the most lovely houses', noted Paes, 'with verandahs and arcades, sheltering the pilgrims who come here, and including houses for the aristocracy; the king has a palace in this street, where he resides when visiting the temple.' This from a man familiar with the glories of Lisbon!

Look first for two pre-Vijayanagar shrines (to Pampa herself and to Bhubaneshvari, or Parvati as World Sovereign) in the north colonnade, with columns and ceilings carved in the familiar Late Chalukya mode. The main temple has a lingam in the sanctum, and a mandapam which though later is its best feature: a five-aisled hall of 38 pillars made in 1510 at the expense of Krishna Deva Raya (1509–29) of the Tuluva dynasty. Every April the chariot festival draws throngs to Virupaksha for a ceremony dating back to the 14th century.

The chariot street has lost its aristocratic patrons nowadays: baskets, cold drinks, and a variety of hats against sunstroke are set out to tempt those foreigners (mainly English-speaking youngsters with backpacks and blisters) who have penetrated this far into remote India. Framed Hindu oleographs, ripe bananas, ice-creams, Udupi meals and nan-sandwiches are offered, but I sank gratefully into a chair at the Aspiration Stores where good Mr Guthi had assembled the best range of books about India for a hundred miles in any direction. Settar's *Hampi*, Deva's *Temples of North India* and Tandon's *Jaina Shrines in India* all exchanged hands. He also sells soft drinks and products from the Sri Aurobindo community.

Virupaksha is open only from 8 to 12.30 and 3 to 6.30, so in the middle of the day your best plan is to visit the royal centre, which never closes. I was distressed by the chaining of an elephant in the cloister, and felt that a belief in the sanctity of all living creatures must encompass elephants as well as roaming dogs and keen-eyed monkeys. A horrendous stagnant, green and slimy tank beside and below the main court wall looks as though it has never been cleaned.

At the end of Hampi bazaar you climb up Matanga Hill for a glorious view down to the 16th-century Tiruvengalanatha Temple, a grandiose chariot street, and round the corner at the northwest the Kodandarama ('Bowbearing Rama') Temple, alleged to be on the very place where Rama crowned Sugriva, monkey-king.

The time has now come to explore Vijayanagar metropolis, planned possibly by Harihara I from his modest capital at Anegondi, but mentioned for the first time in 1557, when Bukka I ascended the throne; by 1368 it is recorded as 'the new capital'. Desolate and dejected now in its sudden ruin at the hands of the Deccan Federation's Muslim victors, Hampi must be seen primarily by the mind's eye, using fragments and sherds of the dead city as our guide. The royal nucleus was protected by several circuits of defensive walls, including royal temples, and as many as thirty palaces. The underground temple (now the abode of frogs cavorting in slime left from scant rainfall) was a private royal chapel centred on a shrine that may even be 14th century. Eastward lie palaces, pavilions and halls, with a great open area dominated even now by the so-called Mahanavami Dibba, a platform from which the king viewed the nine-day festival of Navaratri. Longhurst's *Hampi Ruins* says that this throne platform 'represents the remains of the magnificent pavilion in which was placed the wonderful throne of gold and gems used by the sovereign. . . . when all the chiefs, nobles, and captains had to assemble at Vijayanagar to pay their rents and do homage to the King.' With throne and pavilion vanished, what remains – as at Persepolis – is a series of reliefs of parading soldiers, camels from Rajasthan, horses and elephants, merchants with mules, sportsmen, courtesans, dancers and musicians.

In this same durbar enclosure elaborate waterworks include drains, aqueducts, sluices, troughs, tanks often lined with plaster, and canals, the most impressive being the so-called Pushkarini, or stepped tank recently excavated. To the northwest of the durbar area is a 15th-century royal chapel devoted to Lord Rama, locally known as Hazara Rama, 'A Thousand Ramas', for its external friezes in three rows and internal friezes in six rows, depicting scenes from the *Ramayana*, though often out of sequence. On the outside King Dasaratha is shown in court at the outset on the bottom row, which culminates in

Hampi. Mahanavami Dibba. Corner of a durbar panel on the side of the podium

Rama's exile with Sita from the court. The middle row shows them in forest exile, Ravana's capture of Sita, and Hanuman's pursuit. The upper row finds Hanuman in Sri Lanka and concludes with Rama's coronation.

The square hall has four pillars with carvings of the first quality, reminiscent of Hoysala inspiration, including Ganesha and Krishna playing the flute, with other incarnations of Vishnu: note the superb high-relief horse and vivacious Hanuman.

The last great zone at Hampi is known as the Zenana enclosure, like most other names here unscholarly but familiar. Heightened interest is aroused by the mingling of Hindu and Islamic styles, as Vijayanagar comes to terms with the aesthetics of its Muslim rivals. Deva Raya II (1422–46) showed affection and tolerance towards Muslims at his court, hiring up to ten thousand Muslim horsemen and providing them with their own mosques, and taking from their building practice both dome and arch, so that the flatroofed mosque in the Moorish quarters retains its Hindu element, and the domed and arched Elephant Stables look Islamic. Moreover, the charming Lotus Mahal, with stucco details typical of Islamic Gulbarga, stands on a plinth like any Hindu temple. And to stress this two-way influence, it is no accident that Aurangzeb's Badshahi Mosque at Lahore (1674) displays many features in the earlier Elephant Stables here at Hampi.

I can testify that the open Lotus Mahal offers a breeze and shade on upper and lower floors even in the height of summer, with vantage points over the whole of the enclosure. The very sturdiness of these twenty-four colossal pillars guarantees broad shade, with overhanging eaves to cast yet more shadows, and tiny windows on the upper floor to screen out bright midday sun.

The great Elephant Stables in the open courtyard next to the Lotus Mahal enclosure lie at right angles to a rectangular building known as the Guards' Barracks. The courtyard fronting both may have served as a parade ground. There are ten domed chambers, each accommodating one elephant, and a central staircase leading to upper pavilions, where the view is again impressive. Each cell is connected to the next by a door large enough for an attendant; the elephants were chained by each foot to the ground, and by neck and back to teak beams in the ceiling.

Other points which should not be missed on the way from the Mahavanami Platform to Kamalapuram are a temple to Chandrashekhar (fine, low reliefs of Hanuman) and adjacent 'Queen's Bath', which may well have served as a recreation pool for the royal zenana; and east of these the early Ganagitti temple of 1385 identifiable as Jain from its lamp-pillar inscribed on its shaft. But then you could explore the tombs at Kadirampuram, the 'Noblemen's Quarters' and so-called 'Danayak Enclosure' in the royal centre; the Mallikarjuna Temple at Malpannagudi and the Anantasayanagudi temple, both just east of the road between Hospet and Hampi. That there is nowhere like Hampi in the world is a solemn fact, as there is nowhere like Angkor Wat, or Nefta. I closed my eyes, remembering Abdurrazzaq's observation that in 1442 Vijayanagar was 'extremely large and thickly populated, with a King possessing greatness and sovereignty to the highest degree, his dominions extending from Serendib (nowadays Sri Lanka) to Gulbarga, and from Bengal to Malabar.'

I was invited to the private home of Raja Achyuta Deva Raya, Anegondi

House, Hospet. He owns iron-ore mines and, unlike many former princes, has had nothing to do with politics since being adopted as her heir by Rani Lal Kumari. 'We have had no statesmen in India since 1967: all is done on the basis of expediency, and there is no visionary able to see our situation clearly as a whole.' He shares the pessimistic view enunciated by V. S. Naipaul in *India: a Million Mutinies Now* (1990), where the host of problems facing free individuals each braced to further his own interests (Sikh against Government; Muslim against Hindu; caste against caste) seem insoluble and incline the land to chaos. For years, I too thought India would collapse into communism or anarchy, but as time goes on I am more and more impressed by the impulse to compromise, which refuses to take differences of opinion to violent conclusions. There are riots, there are demonstrations, there are strikes: but these are all facets of a pluralist society dedicated to free speech and a free press, with parliamentary democracy and a long tradition of discussion. Japan's homogeneous society has never had to suffer these strains; China's minorities have never enjoyed such freedom; Pakistan's drift towards Islamic fundamentalism leads inevitably to authoritarian controls. Of all the great Asian powers, India possesses probably the greatest inner resilience and ability to assimilate complex change.

Badami

The leisurely Guntakal Express takes four hours to travel between Hampi and Badami, but does not involve a change at Gadag, though most other trains do. Some of the way is green and fertile, but elswhere only fitful patches of scrub and bush lighten leonine brown with dabs of dusty green. Yoked oxen plough wide fields, and cows graze absentmindedly close to the track in the knowledge that a hooter's whoo-whoo will warn it of impending doom just in time. You can find a two-minute omelette on Gadag platform, then watch ploughmen encourage their teams boustrophedon, veering in predestined pattern on God's ironing-board, the Deccan plateau.

Northern Karnataka's interminable plains and flat scrub, parched like a giant brown tongue from Gadag to Bijapur, would not provoke your attention unless you tried to prise out for scrutiny every lazy buffalo, each hardy family huddled for comfort under the pitiless blue dome. But sometimes clouds emerge to pit against your tedium: in your working life you cannot watch them, but now is a precious opportunity to cultivate their intricacy, to gamble on their speed and massing, their infinitesimal gradations of tone and shade, how sometimes the train will race them, and win or lose, but never exactly match their pace, like two pedestrians parallel on a pavement. Sometimes a rare red glow illuminates them as a master scribe might doodle on the margin of a vellum page. Just as a flaming coal fire induces in the mind strange pictures of hell or nightmare, so Karnataka's billowing clouds invoke visions of heaven or dream, as if the Hindu god Varuna (the Greek Ouranos) were idly showing denizens of earth what he might do if he chose, if earthlings warranted a moment of his eternity.

It almost seems an anti-climax to reach Badami: at first. The auto-rickshaw or tonga from the station 4 km to the town passes through flat fields along a shady avenue of neem trees. The bus from Hospet will drop you in the town

Badami. Town, seen from the caves

centre, from which it is a five-minute walk to the rather run-down Hotel Mayura Chalukya, which I was assured by K. Anandachar, the tourism promoter, would be refurbished post haste.

Old Badami centres on an artificial lake called Agastya Tirtha, which collects water running off both mountain slopes. On the south side, Hindu and Jain caves made at the behest of King Mangalesa (598–610) lead up to the south fort. On the north side, a Lower Shivalaya temple leads beyond the north fort to an Upper Shivalaya temple. The lake is encircled by fascinating temples, including the Yellamma and Jambulinga to the west and, clockwise beyond the Archaeological Museum, two Bhutanatha temple groups.

Vatapi became the Chalukya dynasty's capital in the time of Pulakesin I (*c.* 535–66), whose son Kiritavarman I (567–98) added temples and palaces. His brother Mangalesa then created the temple complex and populated the village as a source of service to the temples. The Pallava monarch Narasimhavarman defeated Pulakesin II, and devastated Badami, which never recovered its former glory and has remained a rural town of purely historic interest ever since. Its position is extravagantly beautiful wherever you look, from a precipitous pair of forts across the wide valley, down into Agastya Tirtha, with its gently curving steps, or down into the white Sahara-like rooftops of the market town numbering some 15,000 souls.

An easy climb from the little tonga square with café and fruit-stalls leads up to Cave 1, hewn in friable red sandstone. It is important to see Badami before the later Early Chalukya sites at Aihole, Mahakuta and Pattadakal, to observe the chronological development of the style, influenced at Badami by Pallava craftsmen from Kanchipuram. Features to note include ornate door frames, or *pithas*, an octagonal shikhara, plinth mouldings, and the projecting roof or sukhanasa over the ardhamandapam.

Cave 1 antedates 578, and is probably the first to have been carved. Like Caves 2–3, Cave 1 has steps leading to a simple colonnaded verandah, a pillared hall and a square sanctum hollowed in the central back wall. The exterior seems wilfully plain: only the interior excites the senses. Column shafts have been delicately carved with cushion capitals and medallions around foliage and figures. The ceiling motifs include flying amorous couples, Shiva with Parvati, and a coiled serpent god: we know that the ceiling of Cave 3 was painted, and can assume that the other caves were painted likewise, but have no evidence. It is the great sculptures, surviving virtually intact, which are the glory of Badami. Harihara with Parvati at the left of the verandah; standing Shiva at the right, and eighteen-armed Shiva on the rockface nearby, the last especially a miracle of uncluttered motion in high relief, his left foot raised on tiptoe, his right foot solid on the ground, both knees bent as if about to be launched into frenzied action. The hall's eight columns are in the Elephanta style. The verandah has a frieze of ganas, or comic dwarf attendants on Shiva.

Cave 2, roughly contemporary, is situated higher in the sandstone hill, and was dedicated to Vishnu. On the left the figure portrayed is Varaha, or Vishnu as a boar; on the right, Vishnu as a dwarf or Trivikrama, of immense dimensions, with one foot mastering Earth and his other the sky. A frieze depicts Vishnu in his incarnation as Lord Krishna. Fine ceiling panels include a lotus with sixteen fish around it, and a four-armed Vishnu riding Garuda.

Cave 3, dated 578, has a façade seventy feet wide, and shows ganas on the plinth frieze. Its large size, sculptural complexity and high artistry, and elaboration of brackets and other architectural features, make it a highlight of Deccani art, as well as a virtual encyclopaedia of sixth-century costume, jewellery and hairstyles: take for example the amorous couples or girls below trees who form brackets on the outer row. The ceiling in the mandapam is carved with flying guardians of the eight directions governed by Lord Brahma. A high-relief Vishnu with the serpent, or Narayan, is a masterpiece on the left of the porch; on the right is Narasimha (Vishnu as man-lion). Side panels on the left depict Varaha and Standing Vishnu; on the right, Harihara and Trivikrama.

Cave 4 is a Jain Cave started in the 6th century, and completed certainly after the other three. Left of the verandah, the tirthankar Parshvanatha can be identified by the serpents at his feet; a seated Mahavira appears in the shrine. Steps lead up from these cave temples to a defensible position known as the South Fort.

The north fort rises above a stairway just east of the 7th-century lower Shivalaya temple of which very little survives. At the top of the hill, overlooking Agastya Tirtha, the Upper Shivalaya is considered the first structural temple of the Early Chalukyas, about 610 A.D. A Vaishnavite foundation, it has sculptures of Krishna lifting the mountain (south side), subduing the serpent (west side), and Vishnu as Narasimha (north side), as well as Krishnalila scenes and gana-friezes that we have come to expect as Badami. Even more dramatically situated, Malegitti Shivalaya overlooks the town, and seems to be balanced on a great boulder. In a marvellous state of conservation for its

Badami. Cave 3. Verandah colonnade, with Sri Vishnu protected by the serpent king

thirteen centuries, it has a small square porch, an elaborate square mandapam with pierced stone windows, and a sanctuary covered by an octagonal dome. External figures portray Shiva (south side) and Vishnu (north).

The Archaeological Museum (closed on Fridays) overlooks lush lawns, a charming view over the dammed lake, and Shiva's bulls at the entrance to welcome you to two small rooms. The front door's double-sided makana torana dates from the 11th century, which is very late for Badami! More tiny dancing dwarves enliven the museum, where the Curator, R. S. Kulkarni, showed me on a map how far the Early Chalukya empire had extended beyond the limits of the Later Chalukya dynasty's grasp. Eighth-century matrikas of no great interest proved yet again how limited and repetitive Hindu iconography became, making Christian images seem almost varied and sophisticated by contrast. In the forecourt, only a 7th-century Vishnu and 9th-century hero stones made any artistic impact, but then throughout the centuries many movable treasures from all over India have been stolen or sold.

At the eastern end of Agastya Tirtha two Shaivite temples glorify the Lord as Bhutanatha, or God of Souls. One shrine is of 7th-century or Early Chalukyan age, but all the rest are 11th-century or Late Chalukya additions. Shiva leans back in the unusual pose of Bhutanatha in the cella, angry and intimidating. Behind these shrines a well-worn cattle track leads to boulders where incarnations of Vishnu and a Jain figure on a throne are carved.

I strolled back into the bazaar as the sun was descending, and a rosy glow spread over Badami's sandstone gorge. I enquired of insistent children the way to the Early Chalukya temple dedicated to Jambulinga, or Shiva as Lord of the Jambu Tree, and in the gathering dusk just made out ceiling figures of Brahma, Vishnu, and Shiva with Parvati. 'Pen, pen your country, one rupee', shrieked the infants, as I followed a buffalo herd home. A bull suddenly felt frisky and mounted a female buffalo, to the amusement of women at their doorsteps. The ubiquitous stench of dung floated through the blue-brown-pink evening, and I bought biros at Iqbal General Stores for all the children who had found me the 11th-century Yellamma temple, elegant and fine as a freshly-baked cake.

Back at the Chalukya Hotel I found no electricity in the bathroom, so shaved by torchlight; then electricity in the bedroom suddenly gave out, so I couldn't see to bat mosquitoes, I drew the curtains for privacy and out dropped a lizard, A roomboy brought tomato soup, egg noodles, and black coffee, with a candle to see by. I winked at the lizard, who chomped gleefully on fresh mosquitoes.

Aihole
The delight of Aihole is the variety and complexity of early Chalukya temples to 757 A.D., Rashtrakuta architecture from 757 to 973, and Later Chalukya work up to 1198, not to mention traces of pre-Chalukya plinths and foundations pointing to the importance of the site from ancient times. The earliest temples include Gowda (dedicated to Bhagavati) and Ladkhan dated by L. K. Srinivasan to the mid-sixth century, and by G. Michell to the 7th or even eighth. These are preceded by the Shaivite Ravala Phadi Cave (late 6th century), a Hindu temple comparable with those at Badami, with splendid guardian figures, an intricate ceiling with makaras and other figures round a central lotus, and reliefs

of Varaha and Durga in the cella's antechamber, Shiva holding Ganga, and others in the mandapam, and, in the north chamber, matrikas or mother-goddesses, Shiva dancing with Parvati, and Ganesha: the figural style is more nervous, refined, slender than at Badami. Another cave temple, of Buddhist origin, is partly structural with a portico in front, and double-storeyed. Dated to the 6th century, it clearly precedes an impressive Jain temple dated 634 and ascribed to King Pulakesin II. Apparently ruined, it bears signs of not having ever been completed, and the superstructure, 16-columned porch and hall extension are all later. A superb Jain tirthankar is seated in the sanctum; another can be seen in the Badami museum.

Almost fifty religious buildings are scattered outside Aihole proper, and fifty or so within the township limits, so it is as well to buy the cheap *Glorious Aihole* booklet available locally with a map showing 24 main sights. The central complex near the bus stand is enclosed by an oval wall with bastions and gates, and is dominated by the misnamed 'Durga' temple of the 7th century, which may have been dedicated to Vishnu or Surya, but certainly has a plan based on earlier Buddhist chaitya halls, with an apse, ambulatory, three-aisled columned mandapam, and porch columns elaborately carved with gems, garlands and medallions. It is a masterpiece of Early Chalukya sculptural art, with a strangely high layered plinth, a sequence of ganas and foilage on basement friezes, and full-length niche deities of exuberant vigour, especially a svelte Shiva with Nandi, a bold Varaha, and a Mahisha-Mardini in which Durga lacks only one leg and a few arms as she conquers the buffalo demon. The tower is a tasteless

Aihole. 7th-century Gaudar Gudi, near Ladakhan temple, with a newly-exca-vated tank in the foreground

later addition. Nearby, a 7th-century Hindu temple known as Surya Narayana has a later idol of Surya in the sanctum, and a lotus ornament on the doorway.

South of this complex are four temples designated the Konti group, two of Early Chalukya times, and two from Rashtrakuta times. The northwest temple has splendid low reliefs of three-faced Brahma with a leg drawn up horizontally on a double lotus, and the other bent at the knee and extended towards the floor; and of a radiant Vishnu protected by the naga-king. South again, and on an axis with the 'Durga' temple to the north and Meguti to the east stands the late 7th-century Huchchappayya Math, with amorous couples on columns, and vivacious ceiling panels: see the bearded figures flying around three-faced Brahma on his goose!

At the back of the 'Durga' temple is a two-room and courtyard Archaeological Museum (10–5, closed on Fridays) with a fine 7th-century Ambika, Dvarapala, and Saptamatrikas. The rest of the site is open every day from sunrise to sunset, and in its peace and harmony seems to be a million miles from anywhere, though it is only 46 km from Badami, and accessible by frequent bus. Chipmunks rove much as their ancestors did, cocks crow, and the village thrives in its own quiet way: I watched a wheelwright at work, then took the road out in the direction Bagalkot for the late 6th-century Jain temple carved with images of Parshvanatha, Mahavira, and Adinatha's son Bahubali, whom some consider a tirthankar though he does not appear in the official sequence.

Pattadakal

Just as Aihole (Aivalli on some maps) is known in the ancient inscriptions as Aryapura, so Pattadakal (Ptolemy's 'Petrigal') appears as Raktapura, or 'red town'. It lies 17 km from Aihole on the road back to Mahakuta (15 km) and Badami (a further 14 km) and constitutes a close-packed complex of royal temples facing east towards the river Malaprabha.

Though the site reached its zenith of power and fame in the 8th century under the Early Chalukya King Vikramaditya II (735–45) and his queens, there is an experimental air to the main complex because it comprises both northern and southern (or Nagara and Dravida) architectural styles, the former represented by the Kadasiddheshvara and Jambulinga temples to the north of the site, the Kashi Vishveshvara temple in the middle, and the Papanatha temple to the south.

Outside the main enclosure with its manicured gardens generously watered by the Archaeological Survey of India, Papanatha temple has a sanctuary tower which exemplifies the central-western Indian style, and dates from around 680–690. Southern Indian in feel are the pilaster-makaras and parapet. Niches on the exterior preserve scenes from the *Mahabharata* and *Ramayana*, but the finest craftsmen worked on girls, guardians and couples on columns in the porch. The sanctum has a covered ambulatory behind two axial halls, the first being a vestibule or antarala, and the second a projecting open portico. As well as elaborate doorways at mandapam and sanctuary, fine carvings (such as Shiva Nataraja) ornament ceiling panels.

The enclosure itself should be seen from north to south, beginning with the two small 8th-century Shaivite northern-style temples of Kadasiddheshvara and Jambulinga, the one with a sadly-eroded Shiva and Parvati, the other with a

Pattadakal. Sculptural detail from Papanatha temple

Pattadakal. (Left to right) Galganatha, Sangameshvara, and Papanatha temples

Shiva Nataraja. The 8th-century Galganatha temple is relatively large, and contemporary with monuments at Alampur, now in Andhra Pradesh, on the banks of the Tungabhadra. Though unfinished, it possesses a charming curved tower and a memorable carved panel of Shiva conquering Andhaka. Next is Vijayeshwara temple, named for King Vijayaditya (696–733) and hence possibly the oldest structure in this enclosure; it was renamed Sangameshvara in honour of Lord Shiva, but never finished, as the panels show. Here is the flower of south Indian style: walls receding and projecting by the use of pilasters, a complex parapet, and a many-storeyed tower. Look for Shiva Nataraja and Ugra Narasimha sculptures on the external wall. Kashi Vishvanatha is a work of the later 8th century, in central and partly western style, slightly at an angle to the majestic Mallikarjuna temple, like its even greater companion, the Virupaksha, funded by two consorts of Vikramaditya II to celebrate Chalukya triumph over the Pallava armies of Kanchipuram. Both are Shaivite, with a lingam in each sanctum, and both have columned mandapams, with Nandi pavilions facing the shrine. Reconciliation with Vaishnavism was achieved by portraying Krishnalila on the pillars of Mallikarjuna, for instance, and Vishnu with Durga, and Vishnu as Trivikrama on Virupaksha panels. Brahma and Surya also appear on porch-ceiling panels in Virupaksha, the most magnificent of all Pattadakal constructions, with inscriptions in Old Kannada around the walls. It is incidentally an active shrine, so be careful to remove your shoes before entering.

Off the road back towards Mahakuta and Badami, look for a Jain temple of

Rashtrakuta age (early 10th century?), its mandapam trumpeting with high relief elephants, its gate decorated with makaras, and a lovely view across sunflower fields to the Hindu complex from the roof reached by stone steps.

Mahakuta

The map published by the Karnataka State Tourism Development Corporation unaccountably omits Mahakuta, which is an active place of worship today, and has been since Early Chalukya times, in the 7th century. It represents a phase between Badami and Pattadakal, and is thus a precious link in our understanding of both. The main complex consists of four temples with entrances at the east served by a large central tank, and there is a fifth Shaivite temple called Naganatha about 2 km away.

The two middle temples in the main enclosure are Mahalinga and Sangameshvara, intimate with porches proportionate to their shrines, and niches bearing sculptures of deities. The principal temple is that devoted to the Shiva of Mahakuta, or Mahakuteshvara, with a lingam in the sanctum, surmounted by a storeyed tower with an octagonal domed roof. The later porch leads into a three-aisled mandapam. The best carvings are on the basement frieze. A slightly later temple to Mallikarjuna, another aspect of Shiva, corresponds roughly to the position and conformation of Mahakuteshvara. Its high point is a trio of ceiling panels: Shiva with Parvati, Brahma, and flying couples with lotuses.

Bijapur

One of those enchanted milieux, like Lacock, Ghadames and Rothenburg, Bijapur seems in retrospect an invention, like Calvino's fabulous Venice in *Le Città Invisibili*. Each is sufficiently far from a major city to be left to its own devices, identified only by cognoscenti with enough time to let sorcery penetrate their subconscious. I dream of Yazd a dozen times a year, yet I have explored the tiny city only once. On my telephone pad I have doodled Machu Picchu's terraces while listening in boredom, but I climbed those heights on only one occasion, as the jungle below shrieked and babbled in perpetual riot.

Bijapur spins such a skein of wonderment, such a tale of lost dynasties, that I pinch myself here and now to make sure I am not dreaming.

'Vijayapura' began as a Hindu 'City of Victory' founded by the Kalyani Chalukyans in the 10th century, but came under Muslim influence as early as the 13th century, falling under the control of regent Yusuf Adil Khan, appointed Governor in 1481 by Muhammad III, then Bahmani Sultan of Bidar. Yusuf, a son of the Ottoman Sultan Mehmet II, declared independence from Bidar in 1489 to found the Adil Shahi dynasty, a line which united with other Deccani rulers to overthrow Vijayanagar in 1565 and ended only with Aurangzeb's conquest in 1686. The population nowadays exceeds 150,000, but there are so many intriguing and outstanding Islamic monuments that the good folk of Bijapur seem to fall away from your view like playing cards in *Alice*. I recommend a week in Bijapur, for the atmosphere is unique, and the opportunity to relive the seventeenth century is given to few. I admit I was high on fatigue, starvation (suffering from diarrhoea I could drink copiously but eat nothing) and the adrenalin that comes from exploring a city so strange that it sings in my ear like Shahrazad in Harun al-Rashid's. But Bijapur has trodden that fine tightrope: neither demolishing buildings to replace them with others far inferior, nor 'restoring' them in a taste so vulgar or garish that the original cannot be visualised. During my visit I saw no non-Indians, so I delved into the city much like Kipling's Kim, though without his need for disguise. Uncommercialised, untainted, Bijapur welcomed me to shall we say 1646, in Asar Mahal, or 1659, in Gol Gunbad. In a very real sense, I am still there.

Because Bijapur stands in a plain with no natural rock defences, Yusuf Khan and his successors from 1490 onwards had to create a solid defensive moated wall (roughly oval in plan, extending for a circumference of ten km), with three strong gates on the west (Makkah, Zahrapur and Shahpur), two on the east (Padshahpur and Alipur), and one each on north and south (Bahmani and Fatih), with insignificant intermediate postern gates, locally called *didis*. Within these fortifications which protected the population in time of siege, the rulers appointed a vast *qila* or citadel, as in Delhi or Agra, which are similarly flat. Though much of the citadel has vanished to make room for later works, the main walls are almost intact, and during a circumambulation you will come to a variety of *burjes*, or bastions, with cannon intact: the Landa Kasab gun on the bastion of the same name at the south, near Fatih Gate; the Upari Burj of 1583, with two guns strapped together; and the Lion Bastion (Burj-i Sherza 1671) just north of Zahrapur Gate at the west, with the 'Lord of the Battlefield' cannon that created notorious carnage at the Battle of Talikota when the Vijayanagar Empire fell. You will also notice tanks, cisterns, canals, and baths throughout the city, fed by waterpipes from both south and north; rainfall is both sparse and infrequent in the Deccan, and measures for its conservation have always been crucial.

Asar Mahal, called Asar-i Sharif from its reputation as a repository for two airs from the Prophet's beard, was once a Hall of Justice (1646, in the time of Muhammad Adil Shah), but now you remove your shoes before entering. Storks gaze regretfully into the stagnant tank, wondering when the next frog will emerge, if ever. The tank is signed 'Danger: Deep Waters. Avoid Water Edge', and the door of the mahal itself instructs 'Out of Bounds for Females'. Four teak columns extending up two storeys are painted livid green, like the tank algae. From the open verandah I watched green and yellow parrots swoop and chatter. The voluble, persistant chowkidar fumbled and clanked with keys, leaving me in no doubt as to the favour he was doing me by opening the rooms, one with fifteen niches painted with flowers in bowls in a remarkably good state of preservation. Elsewhere, paintings have not survived well in Bijapur, where the leading painters thrived from the late 16th century to the 1680s. You will see some examples at Kumatgi, a pleasure-resort 16 km to the east, but the major work surviving is a portrait of Ibrahim Adil Shah II (1580–1620) in the Bikaner Collection, painted about 1600. For the story of the Bijapur school, see *Deccani Painting* (1983) by Mark Zebrowski.

A bridge now ruined led from Asar Mahal into the citadel, to Anand Mahal (1589), which may once have been a royal residence and now, haphazardly converted, is closed to the public as the present home of the Assistant Commissioner. Two old mosques lie north and south of Anand Mahal. The former must have been a Jain temple, but was converted to a mosque while reusing pillars from this or other local Hindu and Jain temples: one pillar is dated 1320, and only the inner door has Islamic workmanship. The latter employs stones from a Jain temple, and seventy pillars, many from pre-Muslim shrines. The Makkah Mosque dates from the last Adilshahi years: the reign of Ali II (1656–72), but it replaces an earlier mosque whose minarets remain. The 'Elephant Stables' are so called because high walls may have been intended to provide shade for jumbos, but this is not certain. West of the southern old mosque is the 'Granary', so-called from the large amount of grain found here during excavations, with the 'Chini Mahal', so-called because of the china sherds discovered during excavations. Nowadays divided into offices, it may have served a similar administrative function in early Adilshahi days, possibly even under Yusuf (1489–1510). The Sat Manzil ('Seven Storeys') northwest of the 'Granary' quadrangle is a palace amply provided with water-pipes and cisterns even in the walls. Ibrahim Adil Shah II built the Sat Manzil in 1583, though it rises now only five storeys high, and his successor Muhammad commissioned court painters to depict royal scenes, including a portrait of himself and his favourite courtesan Rambha. The frescoes have been vandalised over the centuries, but in 1854 James Bird identified the sultan 'seated on a cushion near which are laid a sitar, a basket of flowers, and a Persian book. The expression on his countenance is that of good nature and much kindness of disposition, virtues for which he is yet celebrated . . .' You can obtain a fine aerial view from here, more revealing than that from the top of Gol Gunbad because so much more central.

Gagan Mahal (1561) was one of the earliest enterprises of Ali Adil Shah I (1557–80), even before he extended the city walls and strengthened the citadel. Its clear function was as a durbar hall, with a majestic central arch flanked by two minor arches. At this period the 'Heavenly Palace' would have been built substantially of wood, as regards the carved window frames and four massive pillars supporting the upper apartments which no longer survive. It probably also served as a royal residence before Sat Manzil was erected close by, and it served Aurangzeb's vengeance in 1686, when he accepted here the surrender of Sikandar Adil Shah, chained in silver.

My favourite building in Bijapur is none of these, but the exquisite Jal Mandir, a little water-pavillon in the form of a paper 'tabut' (called a *ta'ziya* in northern India), which is a model of Husain's tomb at Karbala in Iraq carried in procession during Muharram celebrations. What a shame that the tank surrounding Jal Mandir should be dry, now, when it would be a simple matter to keep the water supply running. Like most other monuments, Jal Mandir was built in the local brown basalt which can look dull in a plain broad wall, but in glittering sunshine, highly intricate carving and deeply recessed porches and copings can produce dramatic effects as at Jal Mandir.

Near Jal Mandir two dozen schoolchildren parroted 'What is your name?' with the identical flawed accent, showing that the old habit of rote-learning still flourishes in India's educational system. These people of North Kannara, blackhaired, darkskinned, browneyed, fit easily into mediaeval patterns of thought consonant with their surroundings, as sacred cows plod between banana stalls and women in fabulous tribal bangles tinkle past. A small lockable tin hut, devoted it seems to the repair of cricket bats judging by a man's concentrated work outside, bears a tin plate reading 'We bank with the Bank of

Bijapur. Jal Mandir, a water pavilion

Mysore.'

I asked for the Masjid Begum Malaika Jahan, and was taken by a snub-nosed lad of twelve in red shorts to a gem, again with unrestored dry tank, with a delicate tracery on the parapet between two slender minarets and a perfectly-proportioned dome above a triple arch. It was made in 1586–7 for a wife of his by Ibrahim II, who was also responsible for Taj Bauri (1620), the tomb-mosque complex or 'Rauza' named Ibrahim Rauza (1626), the Haidar Burj (1583), and the buildings at his intended new capital based at Torvi, 6–7 km west of Bijapur. Twenty thousand workmen started work at 'Nauraspur', but before the walls could be finished Malik Ambar leading the Nizam Shah's forces razed the nascent city in 1624.

Mehtar Mahal dates to the period of Ibrahim II, deriving its name from the 'mehtar' or ayatollah called Gadai who had accompanied Ali Adil Shah I (1557–80) on a state visit to Vijayanagar and had received such generous presents that he was able to construct not only the mosque, but also a gateway so ornate that it looked like the gate to a palace, or 'mahal', completed around 1620. The mosque itself is tiny, with twin minarets anorexic in proportion to the triple-arched façade. The plump, riotously decorated gateway, by contrast, has two boldly projecting minarets in front of a tall tower, and splendid brackets below tiny windowed balconies. Especially striking is a pair of miniature minarets pricking the sky between the principal pair. Nearby, Andu Masjid is one of the two twin-storeyed mosques in Bijapur, the other being Afzal Khan's (1653) at Afzalpur, west of the city. The ground floor of Andu Masjid (1608) was probably intended as a dormitory for visiting pilgrims, leaving the upper floor as the mosque proper, with an egg-shaped or 'Andu' dome and minaret-caps, rather than the traditional onion-shaped domes. The workmanship of masonry in arch and bracket is notably fine.

Eastward from Mehtar Mahal, a right turn brings you to Hazrat Sayyid Ali Shahid's mosque (c. 1565), unusual for its large waggon-vaulted roof, with an elaborate façade flanked by slim minarets, carefully recessed moulding at the arches and fine stucco medallions in the spandrels. The sayyid's tomb is adjacent. Rejoining the main road, the next buildings to the east are Yusuf Adil Shahi's former Friday Mosque, predating 1510, and the grand Friday Mosque begun by Ali I in 1565 and completed in 1686 by the addition of Aurangzeb's eastern gateway. The gilded mihrab, protected by a canopy which may be pulled back, dates from the time of Muhammad Adil Shahi. The prayer-hall has forty-five square bays divided into five aisles, and gives the impression of stolidity, rather than the frivolous carving and decorative brackets recalled from Ali Shahi's mosque or the Mehtar gateway. Its huge onion dome soaring between a parapet and the Islamic crescent is in perfect harmony with the remainder of the building, as are the arches round the fountained courtyard.

The great authority on Bijapur, Henry Cousens, refers to the 'restful massive-ness' of the Friday Mosque, the largest mosque built in the Deccan before 1577. All that is lacking are the twin minarets that should have been raised at the ends of the eastern wall. Aurangzeb the zealot must be debited with erasing the likenesses of human beings in frescoes, oils, water-colours and sculptures, and it is recorded that in 1818 the Raja of Satara scraped the paintings left at Asar Mahal and Sat Manzil for gold-leaf that he wanted to melt down. After the Peshwas had taken Bijapur from the Nizam of Hyderabad in 1760, they removed carved woodwork for their own mansions in Maharashtra, and Bijapur gradually diminished to a small city of ten thousand, concentrated in this area around the Friday Mosque, Shahpur and Zahrapur.

I walked from the Friday Mosque to Mustafa Khan's mosque, which stands on a raised platform with one principal arch and elongated arches, whitewashed between brown basalt side pillars. Above the prayer hall, a dome is set on a parapet with two small minarets. Locally, they call it 'Ek-chip-ka Masjid' because of 'one chip' of stone incorporated into the southwest corner. Mustafa Khan's ruined palace recalls the general whose diplomacy led to that temporary unification of four Muslim kingdoms against Vijayanagar in 1665. It is an easy stroll from here to the mausoleum of Sultan Muhammad Adil Shah, who died in 1656. Built in 1659, it was intended to outshine the mausoleum of his father Ibrahim at the other side of Bijapur, and to show in spirited masculinity the opposite dimension of the Bijapuri style which is exemplified by the light and feminine lines of Ibrahim Rauza. Nothing could be simpler than this huge cube, with a single hemispherical dome, and four octagonal domed towers.

With a greater internal space than the Roman Pantheon, it is overtaken in the size of its dome only by S. Pietro in Vaticano. To the west is a fine mosque, and below the dome rest Muhammad himself in the entrance, his youngest wife and his son Ali II (1656–72), and his Hindu mistress Rambha, his daughter, and his eldest wife.

Four winding staircases lead to the upper storeys, but only one is kept open: that to the left of the main entrance. Schoolchildren who climb to the 'whispering' gallery create such a deafening din that at 11.05 it sounded like tormented souls in hell; but if you go at six in the morning, the first hour of the twelve-hour day should be quiet enough for you to test the remarkable acoustic qualities of the dome. A match struck on one side of the gallery can be heard 124 feet away on the other, as can a whispered 'Muhammad Adil Shah' or a single footfall. The view from the roof at the base of the dome is memorable.

A music-gallery or naqqar-khana just in front of Gol Gunbad was never finished (minarets should have soared up beyond the roof level) but has been transformed into a museum. On the upper floor, carpets, coins, pottery, weapons and paintings are displayed. The lower floor is devoted to inscriptions and sculpture, with many 14th-century Jain tirthankars, 7th–8th century hero stones, and a fine 18th-century Virabhadra.

I took a tonga through the crowded city centre from Gol Gunbad to Ibrahim Rauza (1626), west of the city walls, where Ibrahim Adil Shah II is buried with his queen and other members of his family. The architect was Malik Sandal, who also created a water tank which he named for Ibrahim's wife and Muhammad's mother, Taj Sultana: it is known as Taj Bauri or Baudi, and can be found just within the city walls south of Makkah gate. Legend would have it that Malik Sandal's words on his own Ibrahim Rauza ran: 'At the beauty of this structure, Paradise stood amazed'. The imprudent Sandal designed the enclosure as a tomb and mosque for Taj Sultana, but Sultan Ibrahim died first. Delicately feminine, the mosque's façade has five equal arches, perforated parapets, and two series of minarets: four which roughly repeat the height of

Bijapur. Ibrahim Rauza. Side of the mausoleum, seen from the mosque

the terrace; and tiny reproductions in perfect scale. A feature found elsewhere in Karnataka is the virtuoso carving of heavy stone chains and pendants hanging below the cornice, all from a single block of stone.

The mausoleum is surrounded by a colonnaded verandah with a compartmentalised ceiling inlaid with arabesques and floral decorations, though most of the gold and lapis lazuli has disappeared. The chamber is fittingly dark, each tomb being raised on a separate plinth, lit only by natural sunlight slipping through the perforated stone windows, with wooden shutters below and three open doors. The mausoleum shelters the remains (from west to east) of Sultan Sulaiman and Darwish Padshah (two sons of Ibrahim), his daughter Zahra Sultana, Ibrahim himself, his mother Hajji Bada Sahiba, and Taj Sultana. The hanging ceiling of 40 feet square comprises stone slabs apparently held edge to edge by the strength and durability of the mortar but I believe iron clamps are also used. Narrow stairways lead to a chamber in the dome. The pillars in the corridor are Hindu in style, and certain decorative features such as lotuses, wheels, and even crosses testify to the religious toleration practised during the Adil Shahi period. Palms all around and neat gardens do credit to staff of the Archaeological Survey of India.

I turned back inside the city walls to find Malik Sandal's Taj Bauri (1620), now used as magnificent dhobi ghats, with plenty of water for saried women to slap the laundry with, against the worn steps. Nearby the Jod Gunbad ('Twin Tombs') is a public garden with tended lawns. There are in fact three tombs, and the two major tombs are completely different. The smallest, architecturally the most distinguished, honours Sidi Rahan, a minister under Muhammad Adil Shah, with a splendid raised dome and the usual four corner minarets with miniatures. The square mausoleum commemorates a Muslim teacher of Khawas Khan, called Abdurrazzaq Qadir. The octagonal mausoleum shelters the remains of a general, Khan Muhammad, and his son, Khawas Khan, prime minister to Sikandar Adil Shah (1672–86).

Retracing my steps to Taj Bauri by the Makkah Gate, I turned north to Chand Bauri (1579), named for Chand Bibi, queen of Ali Adil Shah I. This is a smaller tank than Taj Bauri, without the long porticoed ranges that the latter afforded travellers as accommodation. The idgah nearby is one of those Makkah-facing walls with an open space in front, often with more than one niche but always with a mihrab in the centre. In his otherwise authoritative *Bidar* (1947), Yazdani asserts that 'idgahs are always constructed outside the town in Muslim countries', yet as close as Bijapur he could have found an idgah well within the city walls. Westward are the Sikandar Rauza, an unostentatious tomb of the last Adil Shahi Sultan (1672–86), the Bukhara Masjid, happily no longer used as a post office, and the tomb and mosque of that most honoured citizen of Bijapur, the architect Malik Sandal.

For half an hour I wandered in the K. C. Market, finding 'Red Tooth Powder', a show by transvestites and an entertainer with both arms amputated, a loudspeaker van for Congress (I) and an altercation between cyclists who had each demanded and taken right of way. Pretending I was not lost, I eventually came out by St Anne's Roman Catholic Church opposite Hotel Tourist and

Bijapur. Bazaar, with (centre) transvestite performer

218

the District Central Library, where I asked directions to Bara Kaman, the local name for Ali Adil Shah II's mausoleum. Open to the sky, the unfinished tomb would obviously have outshone Ibrahim Rauza and Gol Gunbad, in that line of royal emulation, but the enterprise came to the same end as most megalomaniac projects, and all we can see now is a public garden with a noble base and a series of undressed brown basalt stone arches, looking for all the world like Fountains Abbey near Ripon, the largest monastic ruin in England, after the despoliation of its roof and much of its walling for Fountains Hall. The tomb of Ali is the centrepiece of fifteen graves.

Then I sat at an open-dust café sipping Bisleri Club Soda while coughing from pulverous clouds: we have had no rain for months in Bijapur.

Gulbarga

It is four hours by bus from Bijapur to Gulbarga, and I was nonplussed to be advised by the hotel receptionist at the Mayura Adil Shahi that I should on no account go to the bus station because of 'riots, police, broken heads'. I pointed out mildly that I had just passed the bus station, but had seen no sign of trouble whatsoever. Though both towns are on a rail line, it is not the same one, and everyone travels the 145 km by bus, via Devar Hippargi, Sindgi, Almel and Afzalpur.

I spent most of the time talking to a civil servant in telecommunications from Gulbarga who works in Bidar. He described the tensions in the new University of Gulbarga between higher and lower caste students. The Law Faculty Dean, Dr J. S. Patil, had spoken out against alleged atrocities of lower-caste students, and was thought to be mobilising upper-class students against them. He was assaulted by ten students, suffered multiple fractures and classes were boycotted, with closure of some shops, businesses and hotels for one day.

From Gulbarga bus station I took an auto-rickshaw to Hotel Pariwar, on the long Station Road; one dines next door at the Hotel Kamakshi. Much quieter is the Hotel Bahmani in a public garden, opened as a 'tourist home' in 1966, where I met the friendly, informative manager, H. T. Ratnakar.

I couldn't find a town plan at a bookstall in the bazaar or at the station, so I called on Superintendent G. B. Chabbi at the Station Bazaar police station. The sweating walls bore the slogans 'Police is for the People' and 'We respect those who respect law.' Various policemen and passers-by, booksellers and hotel staff, replied to my appeal for a map to find my own way around town, 'Auto rickshaw will take you there', 'We are not having map', 'At rail station you will find map painted on wall', 'Nobody is asking', 'Not available', and 'What for you are wanting map?'. Superintendent Chabbi admitted he didn't have a map of Gulbarga but in a genuine desire to be helpful promised to find one before tomorrow, if I could get to Brahmapur police station early enough. The following day, however, he had not traced one, I found no postcards, and could buy no guide, even in the Tourist Office at Hotel Bahmani.

Before the Islamic Conquest, Gulbarga was ruled by the Kakatiya dynasty of Warangal, now in Andhra Pradesh. It was taken by Ulugh Khan (crowned as Muhammad bin Tughlaq) in the 14th century and as Ahsanabad it became the founding capital of the Bahmani dynasty in 1347. The Adil Shahis took the city in 1504 and kept it, despite a brief resurgence by Amir Barid in 1514, until

1657, when it fell to those all-conquering Mughals. Most monuments date from the century and a half of Bahmani hegemony, and can be seen in three main complexes from west to east. First are the Bahmani Sultans' Tombs, south of the Junaidi Dargah and Shah Bazar Mosque. Second, to the southeast, is the fort with the Friday Mosque. The modern town is situated between the fort and the last historic complex: the Haft Gunbad, then east are the Gisudiraz Dargah and the Mujarrad Dargah. Like Bijapur and Bidar, the city is set so far from defensive mountains that strong walls proved essential to prolonged occupation. Moreover, the sultans continually extended themselves and their armies by wars of expansion, into Goa on the west, into the Vijayanagar empire to the south, and into Gujarat in the north.

The dynasty was founded by Hasan Gangu, who took the title Ala ud-Din Bahman Shah, but it was Muhammad I (1358–75) who established the dynasty on a permanent footing, dividing the government into civil, judicial and military departments, and the territory into four provinces based in Ahsanabad/Gulbarga, Bidar (then called Muhammabad), Berar and Daulatabad. The great days of Gulbarga came to an end in 1424, when Sultan Shihab ad-Din Ahmad I decided to transfer the capital to Bidar. One of the chief reasons for the fall of the Bahmani empire was perpetual strife between the *dakhnis* or older colonists and the *afaqis* or new settlers, since the administration had always welcomed the immigration of Persians and other Muslim foreigners into Deccan as military allies against Hindu (and other Muslim) antagonists.

The first necessity was a strong walled fort. Raja Gulchand's original fortifications were strengthened by Ala ud-Din, with double walls 16 metres thick fifteen towers, and a moat up to thirty metres wide. It is worth remembering when we go to Bidar fort that those walls are Bahmani too, though the *town* walls were Barid Shahi works.

Within the great fort, most of the edifices have been razed almost to nothing, except for the Citadel with a great cannon nearly eight metres long, and the marvellous Friday Mosque, started in 1367 by a Persian from Qazvin called Rafi bin Shams bin Mansur, but probably completed in the early 15th century. Its uniqueness in India stems from the fact that its pillared hall is completely domed over, allowing natural illumination only from open side aisles and the central dome's clerestory. One dome covers the mihrab, four others the corners and seventy-five the rest. This pattern would not be repeated (though two in Delhi are partly covered) because many of the congregation would not have been able to view the minbar, or pulpit. In shape and size, Gulbarga's Friday Mosque resembles the Great Mosque at Cordova, though it has suffered none of the latter's grotesque alterations.

Abandoned, derelict, the fort is in no sense protected, and the stagnant moat has a foul stench. People live inside the fort, in shanties, as they do at Bidar. As if to counteract the brooding Islamic presence of the Friday Mosque, a temple outside the walls is dedicated to Sri Sharana Basaveshvara, with a festival lasting a fortnight in March-April. A double row of squatting beggars awaits pious paisa from arriving pilgrims. The low multi-arched mandapam is dark, but gives on to a tall round gopuram, not at all like the broad-based gopurams of Tamil Nadu, but slender-based on a square parapet. The crowds of worshippers, obviously in from the villages, chattered excitedly, one queue

Gulbarga. Fort area. Friday Mosque

for men, and one for women and children. Film music played loud over the speakers while devotional works in Kannada were perused but not bought on one stall; other stalls purveyed garlands, coconuts, and Shiva lingam models to the faithful.

North of the fort is the 14th-century Shah Bazar Mosque, a left turn leading to the dargah of Shaikh Siraj-ud-Din Junaidi, religious teacher to Ala ud-Din Bahman Shah, and hence of 14th-century date, though the great gateway with twin minarets was added by Yusuf Adil Shah in the late 15th century.

South of the dargah and west of the fort is the group of early Bahmani tombs, including those of Ala ud-Din (1358), Muhammad I (1375), and Muhammad II (1397). The two rulers between Muhammad I and Muhammad II are buried in the Haft Gunbad complex. The western tombs are in the Tughlaq style; single square domed chambers with small corner miniature minarets, low domes and inward sloping walls. As one might expect, the two earlier Bahmani sultans are interred in Tughlaq-style single tombs at Haft Gunbad, but the later Bahmanis have more elaborate tombs there. That of Daud I (1378) is one of the rare double-chambered tombs in India. The Zafar Khan Ghazi tomb of 1313 in Tribeni, West Bengal, was originally a madrasah or religious school, and outside Gulbarga they are virtually unknown. The exteriors are plain, but new engaged jamb colonnettes at the entrance may signify Hindu influence or at least the Indo-Islamic style of Delhi's Alai Darwaza. The interior of Daud's tomb is vigorously decorated, with incised stucco, colonnettes, cusped arches, and corbelling. Ala ud-Din Mujahid (1378) is also buried here, but the best of the Haft Gunbad series is that of Taj ud-Din Firuz Bahmani, who died in 1422; it has jali-type windows, typical engaged jamb colonnettes, and excellent stucco. It is double-storeyed, like the Chor Gunbad (1420) on high ground west of the city, which has corner chhatris and a fine stucco-embellished interior. The Haft Gunbad are forlorn, perhaps technically guarded but in fact desecrated within as cricket pitches by local boys who mark wickets on the walls.

By contrast there is a buzz of activity in the Chishtiyyah mosque, dargah, and sarai or living quarters named for Khwaja (this is the 'Hoja' of Turkish lore) Bandahnawaz Gisudiraz, who died in 1422 as a reputed centenarian. His name was actually Muhammad al-Husaini, but he is called 'bandah nawaz', meaning 'a comfort to others' and 'gisudiraz' meaning 'long-haired'. As a boy in Delhi, Muhammad had felt the urge to study with the Chishti Sufi mystic Nizam-ud-Din Aulia, but Aulia died in 1325 and so Muhammad and his elder brother studied under Aulia's successor Nasr-ud-Din Mahmud. On the latter's death, Muhammad was named shaikh of the community where he laboured for 44 years before predicting the downfall of Delhi and moving to Daulatabad. We have seen the tomb of Shaikh Siraj-ud-Din Junaidi in Gulbarga; after his death, Sultan Taj-ud-Din Firuz Shah Bahmani sought a new religious guide and, despite the fact that Chishti practice forbade contact with royal families, Gisudiraz could not avoid meeting the ruling Bahmanis. Firuz Shah showed him favours, and his brother Ahmad Wali Bahmani (1422–36) regularly visited the monastery to seek guidance and solace. Then, desolate at his mentor's passing, he constructed the great tomb at Gulbarga and it has been suggested that one of his reasons for moving to Muhammadabad – as he called present-day Bidar – was in distress at the gap left by the saint's demise in Gulbarga; moreover, the name Muhammad would have recalled not only that of the Prophet (salla Allahu alayhi wa sallam) but also that of Bandah Nawaz, his own comfort before coming to the throne.

The language of the dargah nowadays is Urdu, we have an Arabic commentary in the India Office Library, London, and he read Sanskrit (at least the *Mahabharata*), but the language of most of his writings is Persian. They fall into two categories: works for novices and students of Sufi mysticism, concentrating on ethics and practices; and spiritual masterpieces such as *Asmar al-asrar*, recently edited by the specialist scholar S. A. Husain. Of course his stress on a student's love and attendance towards his *pir* or guru is heretical to orthodox Muslims, who reject any mediation between the Muslim and Allah, but Gisudiraz states that absolute contemplation at the heart of religion cannot be achieved without the help of a spiritual guide. The dargah was enlarged over the next two centuries with tombs of the pious and the aristocratic who sought merit by burial near Bandah Nawaz. Buildings had been freshly whitewashed, and I mingled happily with crowds of pilgrims hanging out their laundry from numbered lodgings, dipping their hands into a communal meal on the ground, and browsing in the first-floor library with manuscript firmans framed on the walls. 'Beware of Thieves and Pickpockets' warned a sign. The two-storeyed tomb of Gisudiraz, divided into arched recesses, has a fine painted dome with silver calligraphy. Worshippers knelt and pressed their hands and foreheads towards the shrine. A canopy protects the tomb from birdmess. Elsewhere, I roamed from shrine to tomb to madrasah, as if transported to

*Gulbarga. Darga of Hazrat Khwaja Banda Nawaz Gisudiraz. Inner courtyard,
with 17th-century arch*

mediaeval days. Afzal Khan's mosque in the southern court dates to Adil Shahi
times – the late 16th century. Companion tombs, square beneath low domes,
and with recessed arches, to honour Shah Habibullah Husaini and Matwali
Husaini, glitter in the sun when seen from the tomb of Shah Yadallah Husaini.

Parched with thirst, I walked until I came to Hotel Roshan, but even they
had no cold drinks, so I took hot tea in their crowded room in Muslim Chowk,
off Dargah Road.

Tea is of course the universal panacea throughout India, refreshing the weary
traveller with milk and sugar. Beside a pavement book-cart I came across The
Bingi Tea Company, and sampled different textures, flavours, colours and sizes
of tealeaf with the enthusiastic proprietor. The most expensive was his large-
leaf Bingi Special, followed by 'Suprime Dust', Calcutta Tea Company Leaf,
Colombo Mixture, Family Mixture, Shalimar Dust and Hotel Dust. The lowest
grade of all was Janata Tea.

Bidar
It's a three-hour bus trip from Gulbarga to Bidar via Homnabad because,
although both are on railway lines, there is no rail connection between the two
without contortions of the timetable beside which Houdini would appear a
beginner.

Bidar is now a small town of 20,000 or so, as opposed to the 180,000 of

Gulbarga, but its historical and architectural significance is even greater, for it possesses Bahmani monuments such as royal tombs, and also Barid Shahi monuments from the succeeding dynasty, which lasted from 1492 to 1609, including royal tombs.

From the 10th century to the 12th, Bidar was ruled from the Chalukya capital of Kalyani, 57 km west of Bidar, which succumbed to the Kakatiya dynasty of Warangal, the incumbents when besieged and captured by Ulugh Khan in 1322. A general seized the town in 1347 for the Bahmani dynasty, which moved its capital here from Gulbarga in 1424.

The Bahmanis embellished their new centre until 1487, when they were replaced by the Barid Shahi dynasty. Ibrahim Adil Shah of Bijapur seized Bidar in 1619. Aurangzeb conquered Bidar in 1656 and for some time it was known as Zafarabad. The Nizam of Hyderabad took Bidar from the Mughals in 1724, and it stayed within Hyderabad's sphere of influence until 1956, when – with Gulbarga and Bijapur – it formed part of the great new state of Karnataka.

The four sequences to visit Bidar begin with the Fort, continue to the Old Town, then Ashtur for Bahmani Tombs, and end with the New Town and Barid Shahi Tombs on Udgir Road.

The great fort enlarged and strengthened by Ahmad I (1426–32) stands on Hindu foundations, but now has a circumference of nearly 10 km, above a 300 metre cliff on the east and north, and a triple moat on west and south. The fort is made of trapstone and the soft, porous local laterite with a limonitic surface. Muhammad Shah Bahmani added many of the features within the fort, and Ali Barid Shah mounted guns and cannon on the battlements. The main entrance is from the old town to the south, though one has to imagine the moat outside the outer gate, which has since been filled in, once defended by an old gate with a barbican leading to a drawbridge. The Sharza Darwaza is so-called from the tigers carved on its façade from the Shia belief that representations of Ali as Asad Ullah al-Ghalib would protect a fort from attack. Sharza Darwaza bears an inscription dating it to the reign of Mahmud Shah Bahmani in 1503, and above it is a naqqar-khana or musicians' gallery. A great space for up to two and a half thousand soldiers divides Sharza Darwaza from the even more massive Gunbad Darwaza of 1429, with later bastions. A huge banyan tree fills the view from the small door within Gunbad Darwaza: in spring it is full of birds and those langur monkeys affectionately called Hanuman from their supposed divine ancestry. The Rangin Mahal or 'Coloured Palace' dates from a coup against Mahmud Shah in 1487, when the assailed monarch judged it prudent to have rooms close to the great Gunbad Darwaza; Ali Barid Shahi later added mother-of-pearl inlay to the granite and carved wood. The diminishing size of royal apartments gives a vivid feeling for the decline of Bahmani power. Opposite Rangin Mahal is a suite of offices, one of which houses the District Malaria Officer.

Military planes regularly roared overhead as I headed for the royal baths, now adapted as a small museum (8–1; 2–5 daily). The Curator, Mr J. Nageshwar Rao, showed me stone age tools from Raichur district, and stone sculptures (including a door-guardian) from the Kakatiya period before the Bahmanids. A head of Vishnu, a Shiva Nataraja, and a Shiva with Kubera and Parvati stand out. Huge locks indicate the scale of Bidar Fort, one of the most Persian of Deccani cities, with its elegantly detailed ceramic tiles counterbalanced by

Bidar. Fort. Gunbad Darwaza

the need for stout defence.

The humble museum faces vestiges of a once-beautiful Lal Bagh or Red Garden, its western side entirely occupied by the magnificent Solah Khamb mosque of 1327, so-called from the sixteen columns in the middle of its prayer-hall. An inscription gives the building's date as 827 A. H. = 1423–4 A. D. during the viceroyalty of Prince Muhammad, son of Ahmad I (1422–36), so it is the earliest Muslim building in Bidar. It is plain, austere, and in its series of nineteen uniform arches could be considered monotonous by comparison with later Muslim buildings in the city. Its most pleasing features are squinches, struts, and a high clerestory with windows of lovely jali-work round the dome.

The southern flank of Lal Bagh is filled by Tarkash Mahal and Gagan Mahal as part of the zenana enclosure; 'Tarkash' denotes a 'Turkish' wife of the sultan, but it may have been copied from a Tarkash Mahal in Golconda (Andhra Pradesh), just as we find a Gagan Mahal in Bijapur. Though the roofs have fallen, most walls still retain their niches where women would have kept perfumes, ointments and china. Climbing up to the ruined roof of Gagan Mahal, one can see domes and arches nearby, and the fantastic Iranian-style skyline of Bidar old town.

The first major edifice west of the zenana enclosure is the Diwan-i Am, or Public Audience Hall, with steps of hornblende, a black polished stone used at Bidar also for lintels, friezes and pillars, and tilework (regrettably damaged or lost to a great extent) of obvious quality where it can be discerned. North of Diwan-i Am is the outer court of a building conventionally known as the Throne Palace, but in my view almost certainly the Palace and Private Audience

Hall or Diwan-i Khas of the sultan, with palace baths in the southwest quarter and a throne room in the centre of the southern range. It was built for Ahmad I by Persian architects, almost certainly with Hindu artisans. To the west is a steep stairway down to the so-called Lowlands! This is a natural valley in the fort precincts still inhabited today. Goats graze among water buffalo as if they were in river meadows instead of a massively-defensible fortress. An Indian family roared up in their Ambassador car: the man smiled at me and asked where I was from: 'Cambridge? Ah, I was at Corpus in the 1960s, engineering y'know'. He was on holiday from Bombay. It is a long, breathtakingly rewarding walk beside the walls from the royal pavilion, including an octagonal room (it is *not* an octagonal pavilion, as Yazdani would have it) between the palace and the edge of the plateau dropping to the Lowlands. You can see the Thousand Cells (Hazar Kothri), actually seven in number, hewn underground in such a way as to posit the existence of hundreds more, honeycombing porous laterite, an impression boosted by the existence of a subterranean passage nearly seven feet wide and at least ninety feet long, ending at the moat, for a secret, safe and sudden escape.

A circumambulation of the fort walls brings you – clockwise – to the Karnataka Gate, Kala Burj, Lal Burj, Petla Burj and the Kalyani Gate, Kalyani Burj, the Delhi Gate and a double moat as far as the old fort in the northwest corner, Kalmadgi Gate, Mandu Gate, and back to the main entrance via the large powder magazine which is of course set well apart from the walls, barracks, and royal enclosures.

Bidar Old Town

I took a cycle rickshaw to the mausoleum of Hazrat Abu 'l-Fath Shamsuddin Muhammad al-Qadiri called Multani from his father's Iranian birthplace. Before I could enter, I was hauled almost bodily into the Junaid Unani Pharmacy of Shifa Khana Sofia by Hakim Muhyuddin, a portly, jovial pharmacist who gestured broadly to his remedies with the confident grin of Donizetti's Dr Dulcamara. We drank tea while he produced balsam after medication for every ailment known and some which may still be on the drawing-board. How can you praise such hospitable hosts, without seeming fulsome? He had ten minutes to spare, perhaps, so what better than to welcome a foreigner? He showed me the modest tomb of a saint who has a myriad followers even today. Some earlier followers are buried in a cemetery within the enclosure. Muhammad, called Multani Padshah, was born in 1457 and died in 1529, after enjoying the patronage of successive sultans of Bidar.

The mausoleum seems to have suffered many repairs, of which the latest date to 1923. His tomb is draped under a wooden canopy, and incense burns perpetually in a lampstand. The tomb of his father Shaikh Ibrahim and his mother are located at the back. Everyone looked delighted that I had come, and insisted on shaking my hand before I left.

The Bahmanids cultivated the company of religious men, and invited many to found monasteries in the old town of Bidar. Such a monastery is known locally as a khanqah, in North Africa as a *zawia*, in Iraq as a *ribat*, 'and in Turkey as a *tekke*, though of course the Christian word 'monastery' is a misnomer for the congregation of Muslim mystics, usually belonging to a dervish or Sufi order. They normally incorporated prayer-rooms and accommodation for individual mystics and their many disciples. The original Syrian and Egyptian khanqahs were sumptuously built and decorated under official patronage, but Indian Muslims had to be content with more modest dwellings, as here at Bidar. The map indicates the position of many khanqahs in the east of the old walled town, starting near the Chaubara with that of Shah Abu 'l-Faid and ending to the north with that of Minnatullah Bi near Dulhan Darwaza.

In the west, the Khanqah of Hazrat Nur Samnani on Siddiq Talim Road does not enclose the saint's tomb, which can be found on the edge of the plateau 2 miles south-east of the tomb. Instead, it has a mosque room with three arches, and a meditation- and teaching-hall for disciples with a cell for the leader's private contemplation at the back.

The crux of the walled town (though not its centre) is a cylindrical watchtower known as the Chaubara (*chau* denoting all four directions in both Hindi and Farsi; and *bara* meaning a house in Hindi, and a fortified place in Farsi. So the meaning is a fortified house (in this case for sentinels, occupying niches in the arched niches) where lookout could be maintained throughout daylight hours, and an eye kept out for fires at night: an effective early warning system and aid to public order. It dates to Bahmani days, though local tradition assumes an earlier Hindu tower on the site.

Just to the south, off Chaubara Road, stands the Friday Mosque (1430), with a high domed ceiling and lantern-shaped vaults that resemble those of the Zaituna Mosque in Tunis. Barid Shahi alterations and additions include characteristic chain and pendant motif.

Long, low and white, it reminds me of the Friday Mosque in the fort in Gulbarga, though here worship is active. Cells in the courtyard flanks are occupied: I was invited into one by an engineering student born in Hyderabad. I passed silent Muslim women in black purdah, only their eyes showing, and entered his room, with a bed, chair, table and fan. I sat on the bed while the B.B.C. World Service crackled its distant voices from Bush House to Bidar. 'This way I have English guests every day', he told me, pouring black tea from a black kettle on the kerosene stove hissing under the table.

To find bidri ware, there is nowhere more appropriate than Siddiq Talim Road in Bidar itself. A genre of damascened metalwork, in which engraved and inlaid silver designs are made on an alloy of lead, copper, zinc, and sometimes tin, then blackened, and highly polished, bidri ware is first recorded in Bidar (whence its name) in the 17th century, though examples are known from craftsmen in Bombay, Surat, Jaipur, Lucknow, Patna, Benares and Calcutta, and the Victoria and Albert shows specimens from Murshidabad (west Bengal) and Purnea (Bihar). Bidri ware has been used for a variety of functions, from domestic bowls and vases to hookahs, pan boxes used for the widespread habit of betel-chewing, and weights to anchor mats and carpets, to cigars and cigarette-boxes, and ashtrays. A regrettable recent tendency is to produce tasteless junk for the mass market, though even such wall plaques with dancers or astrological signs are not cheap.

I talked to Shah Rasheed Ahmad Qadri of Novel Bidri Craft, 2–1–65/2 Siddiq Talim Road, who had just finished a splendid traditional vase. About a foot high, it was priced at Rs 1,200, or roughly US$80. More complex goblets fetch

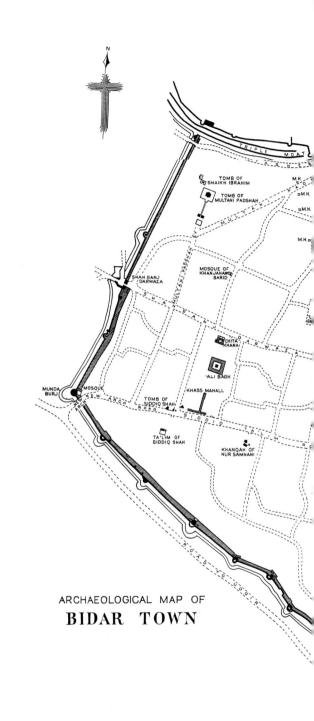

ARCHAEOLOGICAL MAP OF
BIDAR TOWN

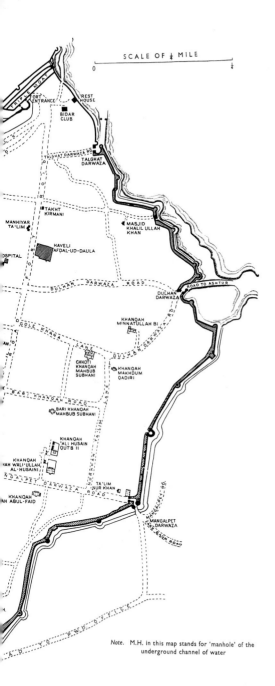

SCALE OF ¼ MILE

FORT ENTRANCE
REST HOUSE
BIDAR CLUB
TALGHAT DARWAZA RD.
TALGHAT DARWAZA
TAKHT KIRMANI
MANHIYAR TA'LIM
MASJID KHALIL ULLAH KHAN
HAVELI AFDAL-UD-DAULA
HOSPITAL
DULHAN DARWAZA ROAD
ROAD TO ASHTUR
DULHAN DARWAZA
KHANQAH MINNATULLAH BI
GOLE KHANA LANE
DULHAN DARWAZA
CHHOTI KHANQAH MAHBUB SUBHANI
KHANQAH MAKHDUM QADIRI
BARI KHANQAH ROAD
BARI KHANQAH MAHBUB SUBHANI
KHANQAH 'ALI HUSAIN QUTB II
KHANQAH SHAH WALI 'ULLAH AL-HUSAINI
TA'LIM NUR KHAN
KHANQAH SHAH ABUL-FAID
MANGALPET DARWAZA ROAD
TA'LIM NUR KHAN
MANGALPET DARWAZA
BAGH ROAD
RD. TO PWD OFFICE
ABAD

Note. M.H. in this map stands for 'manhole' of the
underground channel of water

up to Rs 3,500, and there is no limit to the ingenuity of the craftsman, whose technique was in danger of dying out earlier in the 20th century. There is even a Bidriware Cooperative Society in Hyderabad, the nearest major city.

Almost at the centre of Old Bidar stands the city's most graceful, most nearly Persian building, the madrasah of Mahmud Gawan, prime minister to Muhammad Bahmani III (1463–82).

We have noted magnificent examples of Persian architecture in the Takht-Mahal and Rangin Mahal within the fort, but neither comes within hailing distance of the proportions and elegance of Mahmud's madrasah, which unquestionably profited from designers and even engineers of Iranian provenance. Gawan himself came from Gilan, and under the enlightened patronage of Bahmani sultans anxious to vie with their Persian contemporaries in art, learning and architecture, determined to found a religious school as distinguished as the Khargird madrasah near Mashhad and the Ulugh Beg madrasah in Samarqand. Gawan, himself a linguist and mathematician, not only procured the designers for his Bidar madrasah, but hired scientists, philosophers and divines, and also equipped its library reputed to contain three thousand manuscripts, a colossal acquisition for a relatively obscure Indian town. The building started in 1472 and was soon completed, but its wreckage today is due to its use by Aurangzeb's occupying army as a powder magazine, for the obvious happened when gunpowder was accidentally touched off; lightning also struck half its frontage and half its southern wing. The Public Works Department has coped manfully with difficult decisions about conjectural restoration and, if the result is not altogether successful, at least it is safe to roam; clean enough of débris to observe its finer points.

Rectangular in shape, the madrasah is approached by two successive terraces, each four feet high, giving a noble aspect to the impressive walls. The outer arch must have spanned seven metres, double the inner arch span, and the height to the apex of the outer arch would have been 15 metres from the floor. A dome of Samarqand type would have graced the portico, as such domes grace projections in south, north and west wings. Best-preserved are the minaret at the northern end of the façade and its adjoining walls, but I cannot dispute Sir John Marshall's contention that the building 'depends entirely on its surface treatment for the effect for which its walls are specially prepared.'

Tiles are the glory of Isfahan, and tiles would be the fame of Bidar, if only they had been preserved or properly restored, but in their absence one must evolve a dream of lost tiles to complete the shattered reality. Azure on glittering white, sea-green and maroon, lapis lazuli and again turquoise or ultramarine. Persian tilemakers and designers toy with other colours, but their obsession is with the radiance of blue, of Heaven, of aquamarine. Fragments of these hues, damaged and faded, hint at their original splendour.

Halfway between the madrasah and the fort entrance, on the other side of Fort Road, stands a distinguished building much victimised by the passage of time. It is called Takht-i Kirmani, because it contains the couch or 'throne' of the Muslim mystic and saint Hazrat Khalil Ullah from Kirman in Iran. He immigrated to Bidar at the invitation of Ahmad I in 1431, and the building may have been specially designed for him in the 1430s: it is certainly Bahmani, for the Hindu *rudraksha* beads on the border of the arch-head could only be

Bidar. Madrasah of Mahmud Gawan

ascribed to Hindu craftsmen working for the early Bidar-based Bahmanids, whereas the spandrel medallions are Muslim. The main arch is flanked by two smaller arches one above the other, both left and right, with lovely recessed façades. I was invited inside by a chowkidar who had been summoned by a knot of urchins begging for paisa and pencils.

Within, the arched hall has a wooden tiger, and a proudly-enthroned wooden couch carved and gilded in contemporary Persian style, protected by a canopy of cloth from dust and bird-droppings. What protects the couch from destruction and the hall from demolition is the reverence felt for the couch, which is put on public display between the hours of 8 and midnight during the Muslim month of Muharram. The chowkidar said regretfully that the town used to be 75% Muslim, but the percentage has dropped over the decades to 55%.

The Bahmani Tombs, Ashtur

After leaving Bidar's Barid Shahi town walls by Dulhan Darwaza en route for the tiny village of Ashtur, 2½ km distant, outlined against the horizon we see the chaukhandi of Hazrat Khalil Ullah. 'Chaukhandi' is a Hindi compound meaning four storeys, but this two-storey tomb never stood higher: its name derives from the extra flights of steps you ascend to pay your respects to the saint-adviser to Sultan Ala ud-Din II whose Persian architect was clearly responsible for this octagonal gem. The Sultan's own mausoleum (1458) is the most distinguished of these eight royal tombs, with five recessed, pointed-arched niches on each side. The Bidari style of Bahmanid architecture emerges as flattened, less plastic here and in say Takht Mahal than the Gulbarga style of the previous generation, as exemplified by the Firuz Shah tomb. Ala ud-Din Ahmad II (1436–58) was a monarch devoted to Iranian culture, so his tomb was originally painted within and tiled without, but almost all vestiges have disappeared, leaving a misleadingly blank appearance. What remains indicates that the tiles must have been selected from the range blue, green, and yellow on a white background. Parrots whirred their bright colours inside as if in consolation. The decorative panels were bordered by black stone margins, which recur on the wall-edges, and often were ingeniously carved. The square base of the building and its dome have practically the same dimensions as those of his father's museum, but the parapet is trefoiled, not arch-figured. The interior has been seriously damaged over the centuries by neglect and vandalism; even the sarcophagus has had to be rebuilt by the Public Works Department.

The next most impressive tomb at Ashtur is that of Ala ud-Din's father Shihab ud-Din Ahmad I, ninth Bahmani sovereign but the first to move to Bidar, four years after his accession in Gulbarga in 1422. It was he who paid homage to the saint Hazrat Banda Nawaz Gisudiraz of Gulbarga, after whose death he sought guidance from the Kirmani pir Shah Nimat Ullah. Not wishing to leave Kirman, Nimat Ullah, dispatched his grandson. Ahmad I accepted this deputy and indeed appears to have supported Sunnis at one stage of his life, Shias at another, and Sufis at a third: certainly we have evidence in his inscriptions and tomb to support the theory that, like Akbar himself, Ahmad sought a reconciliation of all sects and religions, affirming the majesty of the One God. His mausoleum is a masterpiece of sombre majesty, with the typical Late

Bahmani arch, stilted above the haunch, and wonderful calligraphy including two *shajras* quoted and translated in Ghulam Yazdani's fundamental *Bidar* (1947). The name of the painter Shukr Ullah of Qazvin is also shown, evidence if any were still needed that Persian artists were employed. Bats nested comfortably near all ledges. Two minor tombs nearby may be those of Ahmad I's wife and a son, though we have no proof.

Sultan Humayun the Cruel (1458–61) has reaped the rewards of his barbarity: lightning struck his tomb open like a cracked egg. Built of black trap masonry laid in lime, the tomb has upper spongybrick courses in the dome suggested by Hindu artisians who knew from Warangal that the upper part of domes should be built as lightweight as possible. Then come two incomplete tombs: Nizam ud-Din Ahmad III, who ruled from the age of eight in 1461 to the age of ten, with his mother as Regent; and his brother Shams ud-Din Muhammad III, who also ruled as his mother's puppet from the age of nine (1463) for nineteen years. Next comes the tomb of Malika-i Jahan ('Queen of the World'), so called because of her influence over her husband Humayun and his two sons, though her tomb is deferentially smaller than all three. Her dome has an external circumference of 124 feet, and the walls are nearly 31 feet high from ground level.

Mahmud Shah reigned from the age of 12 (1482) for 36 years, but during his minority a Council of Regents led by Qasim Barid, founder of the Barid dynasty, continued to undermine royal authority and civil unity. Seeing the example of his uncle Nizam Shah Ahmad III and his father Shams ud-Din Muhammad III, he obviously wanted to ensure that his tomb would be finished, so emulated the example of earlier sultans such as Ahmad I and Ala ud-Din Ahmad II by creating a square tomb with a fine dome and walls sloping inward to counteract the thrust of the great dome. The effect of the triple rows of arched niches is to lighten the façades, but there are no magnificent paintings or external tilework.

Mahmud's successors were puppet-rulers under the control of Amir Barid: Ahmad IV and Ala ud-Din, placed on the throne in 1518 and 1521 respectively. Their tombs are to the south of Mahmud's while in a line with his are tombs of the last pathetic monarchs in the fading Bahmanid line: Wali Ullah (1523–6) and Kalim Ullah (1526–7). These are contemptuously small, with conical domes that look meagre in Ashtur's majesty. Amir Barid had Wali Ullah murdered, and would have done the same to Kalim Ullah, had this wretch not fled to Bijapur, and finally to Ahmadnagar, where he died. So ended the Bahmani dynasty, and so began the Barid Shah line.

The Barid Shah Tombs

If you stay at Hotel Bidar International, you are living on the Udgir road which continues out of town towards the Barid Shah necropolis bisected by the modern road. (Barid is stressed on the second syllable like bar*ee*d, the Arabic for courier or 'post', not like b*aa*rid, the Arabic for 'cold'.) The office of royal courier was probably held by an ancestor of the dynasty.

Great credit is due to the Archaeological Survey of India for clearing the necropolis of intrusive local farmers, who had ploughed up original gardens and even paths, and for maintaining these magnificent tombs. Just as the

Bahmani tombs of Bidar represent one stage in the evolution from the Bahmani tombs of Gulbarga, so the Baridi tombs here show another. At Ashtur, royal tombs are grouped close together; here, they are spaced in the Iranian style, each to be observed on its own terms, without reference to any other. Chronologically, the first of the Baridi tombs – on the Chidri road – is that of the minister Qasim Barid, *éminence grise* behind Mahmud Shah Bahmani. He died in 1504 and is ironically commemorated by the same kind of conical dome that derogates from two puppet kings at Ashtur. His son Amir Barid added murderous ruthlessness to his family's inheritance, manipulating four consecutive young Bahmani 'monarchs' to doom or exile while he maintained effective control over the state. Nevertheless, his tomb remains incomplete, though it is imposing, on a platform raised high enough for even his hubris. The walls are eleven feet thick, by no means beyond the Bahmanid scale, but the dome was never erected. His temporary tomb is flanked by those of two wives. He died suddenly while at Daulatabad in 1542, and was succeeded by his son Ali (1542–79), who completed his own tomb with sculptured granite, lavish plasterwork, and calligraphic and floral tiling, the whole offering a vision much lighter than the tombs of Qasim and Amir. The tomb had an enclosure wall, gardens, and entrances from all four cardinal points, though the north entrance is no longer apparent. Travellers who like connections and disjunctions will enjoy charming windows in the upper storey reminiscent of Moorish Spain, and brackets deriving from Hindu temples of the 12th century and even earlier. And while we appreciate features proceeding from Bahmani aesthetics, the

Bidar. Barid Shahi tomb complex. Tomb of Qasim Barid II (right) and an unnamed scion (left)

architect has daringly left the tomb open to light, air, the four winds, and whispers of eternity, contrasting with the traditionally tenebrous Bahmani interiors. Ali Barid seems to be asking what is so sombre about death: is it not the promise of Allah's heaven, with houris, cool fountains, and gardens always red with roses, emerald-green with watered lawns?

On the platform southwest of the tomb are 67 tombs belonging to Ali's concubines, given by vassals anxious to curry favour with the Deccani ruler. They came not only from India, Afghanistan and Persia, but even we are told in the records from Circassia and Georgia. To the northwest is a mosque, and a cistern supplied from a well by an aqueduct.

The incomplete tomb of Ali's son Ibrahim (1580–6) and his two wives echoes the design of his father's, and stands opposite the mausoleum of Qasim Barid II (1586–9) and his consort, across the Udgir road. This is the larger of two similar tombs; that of Qasim Barid II is exquisitely proportioned with twin arches top and bottom flanking the tall central arch, which is capped by a delicate design of a lozenge shape and two smaller panels, the whole square base being surmounted by a trefoil patterned parapet and a dome which must have looked magnificent from a distance when tiled in blue on white. The court of the mausoleum adjoins the back wall of an idgah, constructed to face Makkah al-Mukarrimah. It has a mihrab in the middle of its seven niches, the whole eloquently rounded off at each end by cylindrical towers like those of the early Delhi Sultanate, and possibly even attributable to the same masons. If you follow a road from the idgah to the north edge of the plateau, you will come to a pleasing tomb open on all four sides on a small square platform, near an associated mosque. For some reason this is conventionally known as the 'barber's tomb'.

Bidar has many other monuments worth attention: underground water canals at Naubad and in Bidar itself similar to the *qanat* of Oman and like them deriving from Iranian prototypes; a Black Mosque of 1694 (ask for Kali Masjid), and a cave temple to Narasimha.

Kalyani

West of Bidar – even less frequented and thus even more authentic in its architecture and traditions – lies the Later Chalukya capital called Kalyani. In the tenth century it was reputed to surpass 'in beauty and splendour all the cities of the world.' The triple fortified walls are located in a depression so that they are glimpsed only when one is nearly upon them. The middle wall seems to be the first, and of Hindu origin, whereas those concentric within and without display Islamic tendencies. The dynasty, which ruled from Kalyani from 973 to 1198, treated the temple as the focal point of its enterprise, reflecting in soft chlorite schist stone the arts of wood and ivory carving throughout northern Karnataka from Belgaum in the northwest to Bidar, Gulbarga and east to Raichur.

Wherever you travel in Karnataka – and I have had no chance to cover the gold mines at Kolar or the Hindu religious centre at Sringeri – the land and its people present a hundred thousand facets, inexhaustible as the Earth itself, and alive with colour, music, warmth and beauty.

In the bus to Kalyani nobody knew me: nobody for thousands of miles in any direction would recognise me. I experienced the dizzying, half-guilty vagueness of partial recollection. Who am I anyway? Pi-dog or Martian, Bodhisattva or Dali's Narcissus? A figure of speech or a figure of fun? Those shards of split personalities that make up my tenuous curriculum vitae I dandled in my mind, mingling hard facts, softer facts, and artful misinterpretations that wander through the brain like souls in Dante's Limbo, semiphantasmal, semicorporeal. That is why reading history is so satisfying for dreamers in time, and geography for dreamers of place: from a few embryonic suggestions of war or expedition can flow embodied characters with whom one can identify or clash in one's imagination. Agastya in Tamil Nadu, Aurangzeb at Daulatabad, Vasco da Gama in Old Goa: each can become a transposition of oneself into another social or mythic mode, like R. K. Narayan's Mysore guide, or the emancipated Indulekha in O. Chandu Menon's Malayalam novel of 1889. Because India is a country more diverse than any except perhaps Indonesia, Brazil or China, one can listen to a thousand unspoken stories of love or vengeance, sanctity or conquest in traversing Bharat even for a few weeks; and this whether one's bias is to music or sculpture, landscape or voices.

USEFUL INFORMATION

When to Come

Bombay's best months coincide with Europe's winter: December to March, but even then very high humidity can make you wish overpoweringly to take a cool shower and change your clothes at least four times a day. The mean annual temperature vacillates about 80°F but May turns one's temperament sullen and heated in a damp heat of 95°F, longing for the first day of the yearly monsoon. Whatever the season, sea breezes can offer respite, and the spread of aircon-ditioning in recent years has alleviated some of the stress exacerbated by constant increases in traffic, population, pollution, and jerry-building. The old *chawls* or tenements are crowded to the walls with six, seven, or eight sleeping to a room, and at any season holding a perfumed handkerchief to your face is sensible if your nose is sensitive.

In July it is not uncommon for the streets to be flooded with monsoon rains, making any normal life difficult verging on the unspeakable.

Aurangabad (for Ajanta, Ellora and Daulatabad) starts to get hotter than Bombay in March and only cools off somewhat towards July. Like Pune, it experiences much drier heat than Bombay.

Bangalore's fairly even temperature throughout the year is pleasantest in December and January, like Mysore, Mercara and Mangalore.

Here are the average *maximum* temperatures in degrees centigrade of these four cities in recent years.

	J	F	M	A	M	J	J	A	S	O	N	D
Aurangabad	30	32	36	38	40	35	29	29	30	31	30	29
Bangalore	28	30	33	33	34	31	28	28	29	28	27	28
Bombay	30	31	32	33	33	32	31	30	30	32	32	31
Pune	32	33	36	38	36	32	29	29	30	32	32	31

The hill-stations of Mahabaleshwar, Lonavla, and Matheran, achieve their high season when Bombay and Pune are intolerably hot, and during school holidays, festival weekends, and Christmas to New Year. If you have a choice, travel in December before Christmas, or in January and February well after New Year.

In Bangalore, the *rainfall* is highest in October, with lesser precipitation in May-September. In Maharashtra, by contrast, the rainiest months are June-September, with a peak in July, and virtually no rain from December to March. Of course these are averages, and some years – for example in Rajasthan for the seven years until 1989 – there is no rain at all in parts of India.

How to Come

International airlines fly direct to Bombay without the need to connect, and it is worth paying a little extra if necessary to avoid the internal congestion, delays and cancellations plaguing domestic air travel. Indian Airlines currently operates connections from Bombay to Aurangabad, Pune and Bangalore, of the destinations covered in this book.

I cannot honestly recommend travelling anywhere on domestic air routes in India, except if you have to cut short your journey for illness or lack of funds. Every moment spent at ground level in the highly efficient road and rail networks will be amply repaid: removing oneself from the hustle and wonder seems to be quite contrary. Why else did we come?

Rail travel is for the connoisseur of nostalgia, steam trains making their heavy, arduous way across vast tracts of Deccani desert (Gadag to Bijapur) or the straight run from Mysore to Bangalore. The Deccan Express leaves Bombay at 6.45 a.m. and arrives at Pune about 11.15; the faster Deccan Queen leaves Bombay at 5.15 p.m. and reaches Pune at 8.45 p.m. The plane takes only 30 minutes, but the traffic in Bombay may delay you, the pilot, or both, on the way to Santa Cruz airport in Bombay. Trains in Maharashtra fan out from Bombay: north to Surat (Gujarat), southeast to Pune, Miraj and Belgaum (for Goa), and east from Pune to Sholapur and from Bombay to Nasik and Manmad for Ahmadnagar and Aurangabad. An eastern line travels to Nagpur from Jalgaon and another to Nander from Aurangabad. These lines don't cover the coastline down to Ratnagiri, or Ajanta, or a whole region east of Ahmadnagar.

The serious traveller is thus dependent on the splendid bus services, statal and private. They are faster, more frequent, more reliable, cheaper, and cover many more localities than the rail network. After arrival by bus, you can find a hotel close to the bus stand or within easy reach by rickshaw. Local and statal bus companies also offer local city sightseeing tours and longer regional tours. Most offer the same itinerary for similar prices, but ask at a couple of offices to make sure by comparison that the price-range is correct.

Bombay, though overcrowded at most seasons and most hours of the day, has a large efficient communications network: just avoid the peak periods around 9 a.m. and 5 p.m. if at all possible. The red double-decker buses which remind you of those in London cover all major city routes and are safe as well as very cheap. The chief train route is Churchgate – Bombay Central – Dadar, with intermediate stops. This too is very cheap. Walking in Bombay is without question one of the world's most exciting experiences if you can stand the intensity of noise, colour, beseeching by beggars, the 'Eve-teasing' by which frustrated Indian men ogle and touch unaccompanied women, and the smells and occasionally appalling sights which tend to leave ineradicable memories in the North American or European traveller.

If you want to get anywhere relatively quickly, then a taxi is the answer. *Always* fix the rate to your destination well in advance by asking the fare, reducing it, then accepting a figure between. Auto-rickshaws will be much cheaper over the same distance. The more comfortable tourist taxis often have English-speaking drivers and airconditioning and, as well as hourly rates, you can negotiate for daily or longer rates.

On arrival at the airport, ignore the touts and head for a kiosk near the exit door selling tickets for taxis at fixed prices. If in transit, a half-hourly bus will take you the 4 km to the domestic airport of Santa Cruz (and vice versa). If you are in charge of your own airport arrangements, remember to reconfirm a return booking on arrival, be at the airport two hours before take-off even though the check-in counters open shortly before departure, to get your luggage in a queue (most flights are overbooked), and remember the domestic flight tax (currently Rs 30 each flight).

Domestic air travel is by Air India on a few major internal routes such as Bombay-Delhi, chiefly by Indian Airlines, and some routes are plied by Vayudoot, such as Bombay-Pune-Goa and Bombay-Aurangabad. If you have a foreign passport you must buy your tickets in foreign currency. Discount arrangements vary from time to time, but Indian Airlines currently operate a 21-day fare called 'Discover India', unlimited except that you may stop over at each city served only once; a 14-day fare called 'Tour India' offering no more than six flights, and a regional system of 7-day fares offering no more than four flights in any one region which, in the case of the western region, includes Bombay, Aurangabad, Nagpur, Nasik, Pune, and in Karnataka both Belgaum and Mangalore.

Indrail passes are really only useful if you are spending most of your time on a train, which rules out those discovering the real India – which you do by bus and on foot. You can make seat reservations free of charge with such a pass. Passes can be bought in Bombay either at Victoria Terminus or Churchgate, and reservations can be made from your own country up to six months in advance. Agents include Hariworld Travels Inc., 30 Rockefeller Plaza, Shop al, North Mezzanine, New York, N.Y. 10112; Hariworld Travels Inc., Royal York Hotel, 100 Front St West., Arcade Level, Toronto, Ont., M5J 1E3; S.D. Enterprises Ltd., 21 York House, Empire Way, Wembley, HA9 0PA; and Adventure World Pty Ltd., 37 York St., Sydney, New South Wales, Australia. Pay special attention to your luggage on trains, and of course hold on to such valuable items as passport, money, tickets, credit cards and travellers' cheques, details of all of which (including numbers) should be copied out and retained in one or more different places.

Accommodation

Maharashtra
Bombay, for hotel-fanciers the world over, is synonymous with the Taj Mahal Intercontinental, a splendiferous way to open or close your Indian travels with a fanfare of luxury. At last a hot bath! Luckily for those on a lower budget, cheaper hotels at all price levels can be found in the same district, within easy suitcase-carrying distance of the Gateway of India. Mid-price are hotels along Garden Road and Ramchandani Marg, among them the Ascot, Garden and Godwin, and the Strand, Shelly's and the Sea Palace. This zone, called Colaba, is crowded with low-price lodgings, such as the Oliver, a seedy joint where I spent a mosquito-infested night once in 1990 for fifty rupees, or about three dollars.

In the Marine Drive area, try the Astoria, 4 Jamshedji Tara Road, or the Sea Green Hotel, 145 Marine Drive, or Norman's Guest House. The choice narrows rapidly as the day advances, for most flights arrive at Bombay International Airport in the night, and hotels tend to be booked up well before noon.

At Nariman Point stands the Oberoi Towers, as expensive as Taj, while at Land's End in Bandra you can find the Welcomgroup's Searock Hotel. A typically soulless but efficient airport hotel is the Centaur; like the cheaper Airport Plaza it has a swimming pool. Juhu Beach has a number of fairly expensive hotels, particularly the well-situated Ramada Palm Grove, Holiday Inn and Sun-n-Sand, and for a novelty (if you stayed at the Aurobindo Ashram near Pondicherry) you might care to sample a night at the Iskcon Ashram, run by the International Society for Krishna Consciousness. If you arrive at Bombay Central bus or rail station, the expensive hotel Sahil nearby is most convenient.

Hill stations beckon after the heat and humidity of Bombay. At **Matheran** try the Regal, Royal or Divadkar, all near the rail station, or the Laxmi Hotel or nearby Central. At **Mahabaleshwar** I enjoyed the Grand for its prize-winning gardens, but you have a wide selection of lodgings, such as the Frederick, Dina and Dreamland, the last-named with only vegetarian cuisine. **Lonavla** is distinguished by the delightful yet low-priced Pitale Boarding House, with a verandah, preferable to the Purohit, Dinesh and Girikunj. **Khandala**'s de luxe establishment is the Duke's Retreat; for the budget-conscious there is always the Mount View.

Pune has few mid-price inns. The Amir is near the rail station and the Blue Diamond close to Osho Commune if you want air-conditioned accommodation. Cheap places near the rail station include the National and the Green.

Ahmadnagar's best lodgings are at the Ashoka Tourist Hotel. **Aurangabad**'s choice is between the Aurangabad Ashok, in town but quite some way from the bazaar, and the two outside the town on the road to the airport: the Ajanta Ambassador and the Rama International, both first-rate, with Western food. Ellora and Ajanta are far enough from Aurangabad to warrant a night at each; **Ellora**'s hotel is the Kailasa, with a reasonable restaurant; **Ajanta**'s is the State Travellers' Lodge, but to savour Indian life near Ajanta, stay at the government Holiday Resort in Fardapur, or the Travellers' Bungalow there. The only Indians at the caves are guides, tourists or touts, and just when you thought you were getting to grips with the mental worlds of Hinayana Buddhism and Mahayana, Fardapur tips the balance back towards contemporary complexities.

In **Satara**, there is no good hotel; if you want to steer clear of the options around the noisy bus station, there is the noisy Hotel Monark, with rooms off the full-volume TV in the central lobby.

Kolhapur has splendid choices: the Opal, the friendly Pearl (though Woodlands Restaurant's unnerving sign 'Leftovers not to be carried away' made me wonder if I should be frisked by a bouncer for fragments of toast), and for those who can afford it the regal Shalini Palace Ashok Hotel, on the quiet, serene, Rankala Lake, where boating can be arranged by the Irrigation Department. Budget hotels include the Samrat, Lisham, Tourist, Opal or Tapasya.

Karnataka
The Mayura chain of hotels owned by the Karnataka State Tourism Corporation offers a generally reliable and economical standard of accommodation, the

best-located being the Valley View in **Madikeri**, with its panorama of the valley to one side and the town on the other. The rest of the Mayura inns are at **Badami** (the Chalukya), **Belur** (Velapuri), **Bidar** (Barid Shahi), **Dandeli** (Dandeli), **Gulbarga** (Bahmani), **Hospet** (the Vijayanagar sited near Tungabhadra Dam), **Krishnarajasagar** (Kaveri), **Mangalore** (Nethravathi), **Mysore** (Hoysala), **Nandi Hills** (Pinetops), and **Srirangapatnam** (Riverview).

Bangalore is a convenient stop on the way between Vijayanagar and Mysore or Madras. Try the Cauvery Continental on Cunningham Road near the Cantonment Railway Station, or hotels in the Gandhi Road district (M G Road is the local abbreviation) such as the Ajanta, the Brindavan or the Kamadhenu. The best of the top-grade hotels is the West End, on Racecourse Road, where the stars of the film based on Forster's *Passage to India* spent relaxing evenings and nights. Discreet and charming, it is a place to take tea away from the jostling hordes in Chickpet and Kempegowda.

A similar aura clings to the Lalita Mahal Palace Hotel in **Mysore**, one of the Ashok chain, but whereas the Bangalore Ashok is near the centre, both the Lalita Mahal and Mysore's other fine choice, the Rajendra Vilas on Chamundi Hill, are situated well outside. For a central location in Mysore I selected the Hotel Siddhartha at 73 Government Guest House Road, near the long-distance Central Bus Station. Its restaurant is vegetarian, so I dined at the Hotel Sandesh across the square. To stay near the rail station, try Hotel Metropole, 5 Jhansi Lakshmi Bai Road. Out of town at **Mangalore** I like the Summer Sands Beach Resort (Ullal) but if you need to stay in the city, try Moti Mahal Hotel on Fahnir Road. Give a thought to overnighting at a beach resort between Mangalore and Goa: I enjoyed the Tourist Bungalow at **Udupi**, handy for the Krishna temple with a large tank, in the heart of a Hindu pilgrimage zone.

Belur and **Halebid** have government-run Tourist Cottages close to the temples, and **Sravana Belagola** has an equally convenient Guest House, just beside the temple area.

Central Karnataka is under-visited, because it is relatively inaccessible. The nearest airport to **Badami**, for example is 192 km away at Belgaum. So the chances are you'll need to stay at Badami, accessible by rail south from Bijapur and north from Gadag (on the Hubli-Hospet line for Hampi) and by road. You might be lucky to get in at the Hotel Mayura Chalukya, PWD Complex on Ramdurg Road, but the chances are you'll have to put up with the Sri Mahakuteshwar Lodge on Station Road (bring your own lock and key). **Aihole** offers a passable Tourist Bungalow, but you strike gold in **Bijapur** with the Hotel Mayura Adil Shahi on Anand Mahal Road near the citadel. Its annexe was an Ashok Travellers' Lodge and is the second-best lodging.

Hampi is still badly off for hotels, despite its growing popularity as the site of the capital city Vijayanagar. The nearest rooms are 3 km away, at Kamalapuram, in the Inspection Bungalow or the Power House Guest House, but these are liable to be full up, so it is as well to know about the Malligi Tourist Home, Bellary Road, **Hospet** (13 km from Hampi) and the Mayura Vijayanagara Hotel at Tungabhadra Dam (17 km from Hampi).

Stranded at **Hubli** overnight, head for the Hotel Ajanta, near the rail station. **Bidar** has the Bidar International and the best accommodation in **Gulbarga** is the **Pariwar**, with a restaurant in the same compound.

Restaurants

Anyone accustomed to the difficulty of finding a rural Spanish restaurant open before about nine at night might well wonder about mealtimes in India. But the fact is that food is available almost everywhere at most times of day, from a very early breakfast suited to those about to begin long journeys to dinner lasting beyond midnight. American-style 24-hour coffee shops are spreading fast. You will have a choice of continental, American or Indian-style breakfast, often with a buffet to allow a mixed choice. You may not like the thin milk, but at least it will be safe, or you can ask for a milk-powder sachet in a top-class restaurant.

Lunch begins at noon in Bombay and ends about three. Dinner begins at 7.00 or 7.30, but snack-bars and wayside stalls provide sustenance of amazing variety and very low cost. If you want alcohol, remember that some states such as Maharashtra had – and probably still has though changes are rumoured – partial prohibition, which means that you can buy alcohol only with a liquor permit obtainable either abroad, from embassies or tourist offices, or in Bombay from Sahar Airport or the Taj Mahal Intercontinental Hotel. Imported liquor is very much dearer than Indian wines and spirits.

Restaurants offering the local cuisine of Maharashtra will specialise in vegetables, wheat and rice: try the pav bhaji, a concoction of mixed vegetables. Gujarati food is recommendable in Bombay, especially at the Chetana, 34 Dubash Marg, which also offers Rajasthani food: it is located opposite the Jehangir Art Gallery and Prince of Wales Museum, and has a bookshop at the back with a range of religious and philosophical titles. I like partaking of Parsi food in Bombay, with its powerful individual heritage. If the Piccolo on Modi Street is closed (Saturdays and Sundays), you can try the marinated mutton at the Landmark at 35 Hughes Road (now Patkar Marg), which closes on Mondays, or Bombay A–1, 7 Proctor Road by Grant Road Junction, with Mughlai and Chinese alternatives. North Indian food is very popular, and can be found in all the big hotels, but much more cheaply at the Copper Chimney behind the Prince of Wales Museum, on Rampart Row. South Indian vegetarian meals are widely available and cheap. Goanese and Karnataka food (Mangalore-style) can be found at the New Martin Hotel, 21 Glamour House, Strand Road in Colaba. While in Bandra try the Searock Hotel's seafood restaurant at Land's End, for which a booking is necessary. All restaurants in Bombay of course are less crowded at weekends, when you should avoid major tourist spots like Elephanta, beaches, or parks in favour of architectural tours: central Bombay is relatively deserted on Sundays.

Restaurants elsewhere in Maharashtra tend to depend on food locally available, usually seasonal. Near the coast, I recommend fish (though not shellfish of course). If you can avoid meat, and stick to rice, varieties of bread, and cooked vegetables without a great deal of chili or spices, try to do so.

In Karnataka, the bigger cities such as Bangalore have reliable Chinese restaurants. In Mangalore and Udupi, the fish is first rate, though dearer than plate meals. Everywhere you will find prices amazingly low by western standards.

Passports and Visas

Every visitor to India must have a passport, with a visa for India (tourism or business), and special permits for any restricted areas you hope to visit. There are no restricted areas in Maharashtra or Karnataka. Allow two weeks for your visa, after obtaining the visa form and supplying (currently) three passport photographs with the fee, which has recently been reduced. In the U.S.A. the Embassy is at 2107 Massachusetts Avenue, N.W., Washington, D.C., 20008, and there is a Consul-General at 3 East 64th St., New York, N.Y. 10021. In Britain, send passport, visa, photos and fee to your travel agent or direct to the High Commission for India, India House, Aldwych, London, WC2. In France, the Indian Embassy is at 15 rue Alfred Dehodencq, 75016 Paris. To be safe, I take with me photocopies of the first three pages of my passport and Indian visa, and keep them with my travellers' cheque numbers in a place distinct from passport and cheques.

Customs and Currency

To pay for accommodation, unless you are a member of a prepaid group, you must pay in rupees obtained by changing currency or travellers' cheques within India. This is simplified by the fact that many of the bigger hotels will change money for you and give you the necessary receipt, enabling you to pay your bill and, even more significant, to change money back on leaving the country. Don't try to change money illegally: it is not worth the risk of getting caught and those who do either get caught by tricksters or find that, at best, they have made a few per cent over the authorised rate. Hotels display the daily rate of exchange in dollars, sterling, Deutschmarks and a few other leading currencies, and anyone who has tried to change money at an Indian bank will know what a boon and blessing the hotels' service will be. But not all hotels will change money, and few hotels will change more than a couple of hundred dollars' worth on any one day: you cannot insist. Keep your receipts in different places, so that in case of loss or theft you have at least one receipt to show.

It is prohibited to carry Indian currency into or out of India, so a mixture of cash (small quantities) and travellers' cheques (the bulk) in easily convertible currencies should be carried in a variety of places, such as a waist-belt or a neck-pouch. I have a hip pocket sewn up at the back and opened inside; ladies carry a bag in front of them or sew an inside pocket inside a skirt or jeans. Backpackers should never put money in a backpack, where it is neither visible nor secure. Replenish your small change each morning from your hidden store, when you take your malaria pills.

The currency throughout India is the rupee, divided into one hundred paise. Coins are minted in denominations of 5, 10, 20, 25 and 50 paise and one and two rupees, and notes are printed in denominations of one rupee, 2, 5, 10, 20, 50, 100 and 500. Take care of the notes, for it is quite common for a shopkeeper or hotel or restaurant to refuse a note if it is torn on one or more edges. Holes caused by staples on the interior of the note are normally not a problem. Tipping in small denominations oils the slow machinery of travel throughout India: few are exempt from this golden rule.

As a rule of thumb, one avoids giving money to beggars, but produces one- or two-rupee notes for services actually rendered, like a small boy showing you to the correct bus in a crowded bus station in Madurai, or a station porter finding you a sleeping berth in the train from Bangalore to Trivandrum when all hope seemed lost forever. The 18 hour-trip can seem a very long night indeed without one.

Small change, I emphasise here, is very hard to come by, and you should take very chance to change larger notes into smaller denominations. ALWAYS KEEP IN RESERVE YOUR AIRPORT DEPARTURE TAX, which in 1991 was Rs 300.

Customs searches entering and leaving India have in my experience always been conducted perfunctorily, simply, and scrupulously; you are treated neither like a leper nor a mafioso. As usual, you may bring in 200 cigarettes and spirits (up to 0.95 litres), but remember that many states in India have introduced Prohibition.

Goods to be declared in the red channel on arriving at an international airport in India include any weapons, dutiable goods, high-value articles, or foreign exchange worth in excess of the equivalent of US$1,000.00. You have to fill in a form declaration the description and value of your baggage contents. The Tourist Baggage Re-Export form should be produced with listed articles at the port of departure, including such items as expensive personal jewellery, cameras, binoculars, radios and tape recorders.

On departure, you may export goods to a maximum value of Rs. 20,000, *except that* gold articles may not exceed Rs. 2,000 in value, silver Rs. 200, and non-gold precious stones and jewellery may not exceed Rs. 15,000. You may not import ivory, animal skins, antiques, and gold items such as ingots, bullion or coins. Moreover, if you have spent more than ninety days in India, you need an income-tax clearance certificate from the foreign section of the Income Tax office in Madras, Bombay, or your city of departure elsewhere.

Health

Travellers have always experienced trials and tribulations of the digestive system when visiting a new country, and this is as true of India as anywhere else. You take precautions, therefore, to minimise risks. Never drink the water or use it to clean your teeth: there is a wide range of reputable mineral waters which you can order in restaurants or, in light plastic bottles, carry with you. I am never without a 'sticky bag', with sun-cream and water bottle, as well as my clean bag with camera, spare film, books and maps. Together these will fit unobtrusively into a cheap, tough Indian shopping bag found in any bazaar which can quickly be replaced if damaged or lost. Some people use Sterotabs with ordinary water, but sterilizing tablets can never be 100% sure, whereas the mineral water is, in my experience, completely safe.

Avoid the temptation of 'going native' with food, and keep as far as possible to your normal diet. This has become much easier with the spread of international-style hotels in Bombay, Pune, Bangalore and Mysore, and hill stations popular with foreigners such as Mahabaleshwar. Familiar ingredients may be found everywhere, but Western India is astonishingly fertile, rice is abundant everywhere, and various kinds of bread can be found. An omelette is a safe standby, and potatoes are sometimes available. Most Indian restaurants are well accustomed to the more sensitive Western palate and stomach, and often reduce the amount of chili or curry when serving foreigners. If in doubt, make your wishes clear to the waiter: 'no chili!' Buffets are even more helpfully divided into Western and Indian-style counters.

Toilets exist everywhere tourists are expected, such as major sights, palaces, forts and museums. You may have to use a squat-type toilet, and you will usually have to provide your own toilet-paper, but more lavatories are being adapted to Western use as tourism spreads geographically and upwards into the de luxe category. You do not have to stay in a given hotel, or eat in a given restaurant, to use the facilities.

Injections needed for India vary from time and time and must be checked well before departure with your local doctor to allow time for the full course prescribed. British Airways, 65–75 Regent St., London W1 can advise if you have no medical registration. It is safe to assume that you need protection against cholera, hepatitis, polio, tetanus and typhoid, as well as of course malaria. Current suggestions for precautions against malaria include Paludrine (two daily) and Nivaquine (two weekly) but your doctor is in the best position to advise. Dehydration, sunstroke and exposure are all dangers to those travelling in South India, so make sure your head is covered out of doors, and your neck and face should be protected with your usual lotions. I have found locally-prepared coconut oil very effective against sunburn: it is cheap and emanates a pleasant odour, but it *is* greasy. *Take everything with you,* because not all chemists carry all preparations, and you will normally not want to waste precious time gallivanting for all-night drug-stores.

It is virtually impossible to prevent all stomach problems, because your system is not accustomed to the new conditions and it consequently rebels. Take as little alcohol as possible, eat in moderation, and be prepared to take pills such as Streptotriad, unless you are sensitive to sulphonamide. After diarrhoea or vomiting, avoid eating anything at all for twenty-four hours, rest as much as possible, and keep drinking weak tea or mineral water to avoid dehydration. Imodium works well, but may take up to a day to work.

After taking a shower or bath, rub or spray anti-insect protection on exposed areas of your body. Mosquito coils, lit before you go to bed, generally last long enough to dampen the ardour of biters in the dark. Remember to shut windows or put up screens before you sleep.

A universal bath-plug is a great boon in all but five-star hotels, but *do* remember to take it away with you when you dry yourself. If you have no plug, saturated toilet-paper stuffed into the hole will retain water as long as you need it. I always take to India my own shampoo sachets, toothpaste and shaving kit, hand-towel and soap in a soapdish. Most hotels will provide a towel and soap if asked, but service is often so slow that – on arriving in a new hotel after midnight – you often do not want to wait for it.

In a hot, tropical and often humid climate, even small cuts can turn septic quickly, so keep antiseptic cream and a choice of three or four dressings to prevent minor accidents becoming major.

Clothing

Take as little as possible, but remember that nights in hill stations such as Matheran or Mahabaleshwar can be cold and, if you intend to travel in buses or trains by night, an anorak can double as a pillow. Increased pollution makes a face mask desirable on long road journeys, and within Bombay. On long journeys I wear an airfilled cushion (obtainable at major airports before departure) on my shoulders to take the weight off my head and reduce wear and tear on my neck muscles (and bruising) caused by bumping, braking, and jerking.

Speaking the Languages
Readers familiar with my previous travel guides may recall my opinions that learning one or more of the local languages will repay the effort in proportion to the effort. Sadly, this does not apply to Westerm India, where you stand a grave risk of offending somebody by trying to speak a regional language. It is assumed that, in avoiding English, you consider your acquaintance ignorant, uneducated, stupid, or from a lower class, and this is – as elsewhere in India – thought to be offensive. Furthermore, Kannada is not widely spoken outside Karnataka, and Marathi seldom used outside Bombay and Maharashtra, so when you stray into Andhra Pradesh from Bidar, or into Gujarat from Bombay, all is lost. Even in country areas, any crowd can easily summon someone who can understand and speak English, and will gain prestige in the community by so doing. In the cities, many people you meet will have studied in an English-medium school from a very early age.

For those tempted into the delightful world of Kannada (or another of the lilting Dravidian tongues of South India), language cassettes and grammars are available from reputable language institutes. Marathi tapes can also be found. But there is little to be gained from such manuals as *Marathi Pravesh* by B. V. Keluskar, with practice sentences such as 'Grandmother! The cats hold the young ones with the mouth' and 'Uncle paternal! See how the elephant catches a thing with the trunk.' M. Mallikarjuna's *Self Kannada-Teacher* offers English idioms in the style of 'He has the art of the getting grapes from throns', 'I was at the shop of a ninth part of a man', and 'Once in life the time and tide knocks the door of every one.'

Holidays and Festivals
Hindu festivals are fixed in accordance with the Vikramaditya calendar based on lunar months which begin with the full moon, and intercalate a thirteenth month of the year every thirty months to ensure the months stay consonant with the seasons. As years of the Vikramaditya era are often quoted in books or on monuments, you need to remember that these years are 57 or 58 years *ahead* of the Christian calendar. The India Government has officially sanctioned a third type of era, Shak, which is 77 or 78 years *behind* the Christian era.

You are never far in time or place from an Indian festival: Christian, Muslim, Hindu or Parsi: it is virtually impossible to weave your way around them. So make the best of celebrations that may block your bus or fill the pavements and immerse yourself in what happens.

Bombay celebrates Republic Day on 26 January, and in February-March the spring rites of Holi, when coloured powders will be squirted over you at a distance or daubed on your clothes and head at close quarters. Wear your old clothes for this exuberant period. This is around the period of the one-day Mahashivratri Festival, in honour of Lord Shiva, when processions to Hindu temples can be seen. Gudi Padva in March-April begins the Maharashtran New

Year; Parsis have their own ceremony deriving from Iran: the Nowruz. This is the season for the Jain festival of the birthday of the last tirthankar, Mahavira, and the Hindu festival celebrating the birth of Lord Rama, as well as the Christian Good Friday and Easter Day . . . Muslim festivals move throughout the lunar calendar, so check with your nearest mosque or reference library when the end of Ramadan is due (the Id-ul-Fitr is celebrated at the end of it) and the dates of the first of Muharram, and Id-ul-Adha. April 13 is an official holiday for the official New Year. August 15 is Indian Independence Day, and a national holiday. A special Bombay festival is dedicated to the elephant-headed god Ganesha. Dussehra (September-October) marks nine nights of dedication to the mother goddess or Devi of the Hindus, with ten days of music, dance, and drama. October 2 is Gandhi's birthday. Diwali comes three to four weeks after Dussehra, and for about ten days thereafter you can visit fairs and welcome the new financial year with offerings to Lakshmi, goddess of wealth.

December 25 is a holiday for Christians.

Books and Maps

Your local tourist office will supply you with maps of Bombay, Bangalore, Mysore, and Pune, and smaller cities are mapped in *The City Atlas of India* published by Tamilnad in Madras, covering also Ahmadabad, Aurangabad, and Mahabaleshwar. Other maps of smaller towns will be found in the indispensable *Penguin Guide to the Monuments of India* (2 vols., Penguin Books, 1989), of which volume 1 by George Michell covers Buddhist, Jain and Hindu sites, and volume 2 by Philip Davies deals with Islamic, Rajput and European works. A good general map, such as the Nelles *India* or the 1:4,000,000 *Indian Subcontinent*, is of course necessary.

Indian books, often produced on low-quality paper with poor illustrations, are invariably good value. I am thinking of S. Settar's *Hampi* (Kala Yatra, Bangalore); the series of handbooks by the Archaeological Survey of India such as *Ajanta*; and Hanumantrao Kaujalgi's *A Visit to Bijapur* (Kaujalgi, Bangalore). For Bombay, the best general account in Gillian Tindall's *City of Gold* (Temple Smith, 1982). For the story of Maharashtra's hinterland, I recommend R. V. Nadkarni's *The rise and fall of the Maratha Empire* (Popular Prakashan, Bombay, 1966), and a good general introduction to Karnataka is I. M. Muthanna's *History of modern Karnataka* (Sterling, New Delhi, 1980). These are for the general reader: for those wishing to delve more deeply, the new edition of the *Cambridge History of India* now being revised in many volumes has recently included Burton Stein's thoughtful *Vijayanagar*.

One final suggestion. Karnataka and Maharashtra are still so inadequately documented, despite their obvious appeal, that most details of places and buildings, bazaars and people that you would wish to recall on returning home are unillustrated and unmentioned in the above books and guides. There is a widespread lack of information about India everywhere you go, as I note in my cautionary tale about trying to find a good town plan of Gulbarga. So take plenty of pens and paper, plus more films than you think you will need, for the wondrous days ahead of you. Everything you see is memorable, from water buffalo and spices, to temple sculpture and coffee plantations, sparkling in perpetual sunshine. The wide expanse of Maharashtra and Karnataka will seduce the voluptuary in you, and exhilarate the connoisseur.

Chronologies

Islamic Dynasties in Maharashtra

Imad Shahi Sultans of Berar

Fathallah	1490
Ala ad-Din	1504
Darya	1529
Burhan	1562
Tufal	1568–77

Nizam Shahi Sultans of Ahmadnagar

Ahmad	1490
Burhan I	1509
Husain I	1553
Murtaza I	1565
Miran Husain	1586
Ismail	1589
Burhan II	1591
Ibrahim	1595
Bahadur	1596
Ahmad II	1596
Murtaza II	1603
Husain II	1630–3

The Five Great Maratha Dynasties

Bhonslas

Shivaji	1674
Shambhuji	1680
Raja Ram	1689
Tara Bai	1700
Shahu	1708
Ram Raja	1749
Shahu II	1777
Pratap Singh	1818
Shahaji	1839–48

Peshwas

Balaji Vishwanath	1714

Baji Rao I	1721
Balaji Baji Rao	1740
Madhava Rao Ballal	1761
Narayan Rao	1772
Raghunath Rao	1773
Madhava Narayan Rao	1774
Baji Rao II	1795–1818

Gaekwars

Pilaji	1721
Damaji II	1732
Govind Rao	1768
Sayaji Rao I	1771
Fateh Singh	1771
Manaji	1789
Govind Rao	1793
Anand Rao	1800
Sayaji Rao II	1818
Ganpat Rao	1847
Khande Rao	1856
Malhar Rao	1870
Sayaji Rao III	1875

Holkars

Malhar Rao	1728
Ahalya Bai	1765
Tukoji I	1795
Jaswant Rao I	1798
Malhar Rao II	1811
Hari Rao	1834
Tukoji Rao II	1843
Jaswant Rao II	1926-

Scindias

Madhava Rao	1761
Daulat Rao	1794
Jankoji Rao	1827
Jayaji Rao	1843
Madhava Rao II	1886
Jivaji Rao	1925

Dynasties of Karnataka

The Hoysala Dynasty

Hoysala	1006
Nripikama	1022
Vinayaditya	1047

Bettiga, later called Vishnuvardhana	1100
Narasimha I	1152
Ballala II	1173
Narasimha II	1220
Someshvara	1233
Narasimha III	1254
Ballala II	1291–1342

The Bahmani Dynasty

Ala ud-Din Hassan Bahman Shah	1347
Muhammad I	1358
Ala ud-Din Mujahid	1375
Da'ud I	1378
Muhammad II	1378
Ghiyas ud-Din Tahamtan	1397
Shams ud-Din Da'ud II	1397
Tadi ud-Din Fairuz	1397

The above made their capital at Gulbarga, calling it Ahsanabad. The following made their capital at Bidar, calling it Muhammadabad.

Shihab ud-Din Ahmad I	1422
Ala ud-Din Ahmad II	1436
Ala ud-din Humayun	1458
Nizam ud-Din Ahmad III	1461
Shams ud-Din Muhammad III	1463
Shihab ud-Din Mahmud	1482
Ahmad IV	1518
Ala ud-Din	1521
Waliallah	1523
Kalimallah	1526

The Barid Shahis of Bidar

Qasim Barid	1487
Amir bin Qasim	1503
Ali bin Amir	1543
Ibrahim	1579
Qasim II	1586
Mirza Ali	1601
Ali II	1609

The Adil Shahi Dynasty of Bijapur

Yusuf Adil Shah	1489
Isma'il bin Yusuf	1510
Mallu bin Isma'il	1534
Ibrahim bin Ismail I	1535
Ali bin Ibrahim I	1557

Ibrahim bin Tahmasp II	1579
Muhammad bin Ibrahim	1626
Ali bin Muhammad II	1656
Iskandar bin Ali	1672

Rulers of Mysore and Srirangapatnam

Adi Yaduraya Wadiyar	1399
Hiriya Bettada Chamaraja Wadiyar	1423–29
Thimaraja Wadiyar I	1478
Hiriya Bettada Chamaraja III	1513
Thimaraja Wadiyar II	1553
Bola Chamaraja Wadiyar IV	1572
Bettada Chamaraja Wadiyar	1576
Raja Wadiyar I	1578
Chamaraja Wadiyar VI	1617

now no longer feudatory lord of the Vijayanagar Empire

Raja Wadiyar II	1637
Ranadhira Kanthirava Narasaraja	1638
Dodda Devaraja Wadiyar	1659
Chikkadevaraja Wadiyar	1673
Kanthirava Maharaja Wadiyar	1704
Dodda Krishnaraja Wadiyar	1714
Chamaraja Wadiyar VII	1732
Krishnaraja Wadiyar II	1734
Haidar Ali	1761–82
Tipu Sultan	1782–99
Krishnaraja Wadiyar III	1799
British administration of Mysore	1831–81
Chamaraja Wadiyar X	1881
Krishnaraja Wadiyar IV	1895
Jayachamaraja Wadiyar	1940–7 (d. 1974)

The present scion of the Wadiyar House is Srikantadatta
Narasimharaja, but the former State of Mysore now forms
a part of the State of Karnataka, so the Wadiyar family's
ruling position is now symbolic

Index

Bankot, 42, 67
Bannerghatta National Park, 126
Bannur, 160
Bara Kaman, 219, 251
Barapole river, 175
Barbosa, Duarte, 176
Barid Shah dynasty, 85, 219–20, 224, 227, 233–5
Barkur, 178
Baroda, 31
Basavangudi, 127
Basavanna, 135
Basavappa, 176
Basaveshvara, 135
Bassein, 4, 20, 40–1
bazaars, 61, 22–7, 71, 143, 218
beauty, female, 170
Bedsa, 48, 51, 53, 122
beedis, 179
Begg, J., 27
beggars, 37–8, 243
Belbagh, Pune, 58
Belfrage, S., 61
Belgaum, 235, 238–9
Bellary, 124
Belur, 152–6
Belvai, 183
Bence-Jones, M., 10
Bendre, D. R., 138
Berar, 85–6, 220, 249
Berkson, C., 90
Berlin (Staatliche Museen), 86–7
Bettiga, 157
Bhabha family, 7, 10, 12
Bhadrabahu, 146–7
Bhagamandala, 175
Bhagavadgita, 43
Bhaja, 48–52, 122
bhakti movement, 9–10
Bhameya, 162
Bharata, 148–52
Bharatiya Janata Party, 158
Bhil tribe, 96
Bhima river, 83–5
Bhoj, 78
Bhoj II, 83
Bhokardah, 79
Bhonsla dynasty, 56, 73, 249
Bhujbal, V. P., 64–5
Bhuleshwar, 1
Bhumaka, 43
Bhushi lake, 48
Bibi-ka Maqbara, 88
bicycles, 192
Bidar, 73, 85, 113, 211, 220, 222–35, 251

customs, 243–4
cycle rickshaws, 226

education, 46
Edwardes, Michael, 88
Eknath, 84
Elephanta, 1, 8, 16, 38–9, 94, 110, 124, 204, 242
elephants, 140–1, 172–3
elephant stables, Hampi, 201
Ellora, 19–20, 43, 49, 87, 91–2, 94, 96, 104–11, 124, 237
Elphinstone, *Lord*, 11, 48, 57, 69
Elphinstone Circle, 4, 6
Elphinstone College, 29
embassies, 243
Emerson, W., 24
Eve-teasing, 238
Exodus Expeditions, vi

Fa Hsien, 101
Fardapur, 97
Fennell, A., 173
Fergusson, *Lady*, 10
Fergusson, James, 96
festivals, 246–7
films, 17, 82, 122, 132
Firishta, 85–6
FitzGerald, *Sir* S., 57
Flora Fountain, 5, 14, 27
Folk Art Museum, Mysore, 143
forests, 134. *See also* under the names of individual forests, *e.g.* Nagarhole
Forster, E. M., 104–110
forts. *See under* the names of individual forts, *e.g.* Pratapgarh
fortune-tellers, 132
Franciscans, 10
Fraser, J. S., 173
Fraser, Stuart, 81
Fraserpet, 173, 175
French in India, 76, 164
Frere, *Sir* Bartle, 4–7, 11, 27, 29, 46, 57
Fritchley, E. W., 143
Fuller, J. A., 26, 28, 35

Gabiappa, *Mr*, 194–5
Gadag, 191–2, 202, 238, 241
Gaekwar dynasty, 250
Gama, Vasco da, 176
Ganapathy, Sunil, 174–5
Gandhara, 119
Gandharan sculpture, 15–16, 18, 131
Gandhi, I., 18, 64
Gandhi, K., 58
Gandhi, M. K., 12–13, 20, 31, 46, 58, 73, 81, 119, 247
Gandhi, R., 76
Gandhi, S., 18
Ganesh(a), 11, 39, 56–7, 127
Ganga, Ganges, 39, 118–9, 184
Gangachari, 147

Ganga dynasty, 124, 163
Gangu, Hasan, 220
gardens, Bangalore, 126–7; Bombay, 6, 13; Pune, 58–9
Gateway of India, 7–9
Gawan, Mahmud, 113, 230–1
Gayatri, 70
Gharapuri. *See* Elephanta
Gisudiraz, *Khwaja* Bandahnawaz, 220, 222–3, 232
Godavari, 119, 122
Golconda, 85
golf, 73
Gol Gunbad, 216
Gonikopal, 170, 172
Gooty, 165
Gopalgarh, 42
Gorakshar, *Sri* Sadashiv, 18
Goregaon, 8
Goswami, S. B. S., 20
Goswamy, R., 116
Govardhana, 147
Government Museum, Bangalore, 126, 130–1; Madikeri, 173; Mangalore, 176
Governors of Bombay, 10–11. *See also* under the names of individual governors, *e.g.*
    Frere, *Sir* Bartle
Govindraj, 132
Grant, *Sir* Robert, 57
Great Hindu Congress, 118
Gudalur, 133
Gujarat, 4, 33, 43
Gulbarga, 73, 124, 201, 219–23, 232, 234–5, 251
Gulchand, 220
Gullekayi Ajji, 148–50
Gundlupet, 134
Gupta art, 130
Gupta era, 98
Guthi, T. T., vi, 199
Gymkhana, Bombay, 27, 34; Mahabaleshwar, 71

Haft Gunbad, 221–2
Haidar Ali, 126–7, 141, 152, 163–7, 169
Haji Ali tomb, 16–17
Haldenkar, S. L., 142
Halebid, 153, 155–60
Haleri dynasty, 172–3
Hallur, 124
Hampi, 191–202. *See also* Vijayanagar
handicrafts, 24, 56, 58–9, 132, 143
Hanuman, 58, 120
Hanumesh, N., 178
Hardinge, *Capt.*, 6
Hardwar, 118
Harihara I, 153, 193, 199
Harishena, 96–7, 101, 103
Harle, J. C., 108
Harpanahalli, 194

Harper, E. C. B., 173
Hasan, Malik, 85
Hassan, 152
Hastinapura, 141
Hatkamba, 67
Hawkins, J., 4
Haywood, *Sir* Arthur, 46
Hazardinari, Kafur, 113
health, 244–5
Heimann, B., 157
Hemmige, 124
Hickey, Thomas, 164
Hindi, 184
Hindus and Hinduism, 4, 6, 13–14, 20–2, 27, 33, 56, 83–5, 90–7, 104–11, 116, 118–21,
    126–7, 135, 142, 146, 148, 153, 156–62, 167–8, 176, 182, 184–6, 192, 196–211, 220–1,
    246–7
Hole Narsipur, 152
Holi, 246
holidays, 246–7
Holkar dynasty, 250
honey, 71
horseracing, 14, 131, 142
horseriding, 73
Hosappattana, 192
Hospet, 192, 202
hotels, 239–241; Ahmadnagar, 87, 240; Aihole, 241; Ajanta, 240; Aurangabad, 89, 240;
    Badami, 203, 206, 241; Belur, 241; Bhatkal, 186; Bidar, 233, 241; Bijapur, 219, 241;
    Bombay, 7, 10, 22, 239–40; Dandeli, 241; Ellora, 104, 240; Fardapur, 240; Gulbarga,
    219, 241; Halebid, 241; Hampi, 241; Hassan, 152–3; Hospet, 192, 241; Hubli, 241;
    Jog Falls, 188; Karapura, 171; Karkal, 183; Khandala, 240; Kolhapur, 82, 240;
    Krishnarajasagar, 168, 241; Lonavla, 240; Madikeri, 172, 241; Mahabaleshwar, 71,
    73, 240; Mangalore, 241; Matheran, 48, 240; Mudbidri, 180; Mysore, 134, 140, 143,
    145, 241; Nandi Hills, 241; Nasik, 122; Pune, 54, 240; Sholapur, 65–6; Sravana
    Belagola, 241; Srirangapatnam, 241; Udupi, 183, 241
Hoysala art, 130, 142, 146–7, 153–62, 167, 178, 188, 193, 198, 201, 250–1
Hubli, 188, 191
Hudikeri, 170, 172
Hullamaya, 146
Hullenahalli, 169
Humayun, 233
Hunsur, 168–9
hunting, 70
Husain I of Ahmadnagar, 86
Husain, S. A., 222
Husain, Shaikh, vi, 54–9
Hutagalli, 169
Hutti, 174
Hyderabad, 230. *See also* Nizam of Hyderabad

Ibn Battuta, 176
Ibrahim Adil Shah II of Bijapur, 86, 212, 215, 224
Ibrahim Rauza, 215–7
idgahs, 218, 235

languages, 246. *See also* under the names of individual languages, *e.g.* Marathi

Murtaza I, 86
Murtaza II, 87
Murthy, Ananth, 183
museums. *See under* the names of individual museums, *e.g.* Tribal Cultural Museum,
   Pune
music in Bangalore, 132; Bombay, 12, 24
Muslims and Islam, 4, 6, 16–17, 27, 40, 64, 124, 126, 142, 163, 165–7, 189, 192–3, 195,
   199, 201, 211–4, 222–35, 247. *See also* mosques
Muthanna, I. M., 247
Muzaffar, Baba Shah, 89
Mysore, 124, 130–45, 166, 168, 237–8, 244, 247, 252
Mysore State, 124, 142
Mysore Wars, 164

Nadkarni, R. V., 247
Nadurrattanam, 132
Nagaraju, Y., 139–41
Nagarhole National Park, 133, 168–72, 183
Nageshwar Rao, J., 224
Nagpur, vii, 46, 238
Nahapana, 43
Naipaul, V. S., 202
Nallur (T.N.), 16
Nander, 238
Nandi Hills, 126
Nandy, Pritish, 116
Narasimha (God), 198–9
Narasimha I, 153, 156
Narasimha III, 160
Narasimhaswamy, K. S., 138
Narasimhavarman, 203
Naravi, 198
Narayan, R. K., 134–5
Narayana, G. V., vi, 178–9
Narayanpur, 15
Narayan Rao, 56
Nargis, 17
Narsipur, H. *See* Hole Narsipur
Narsipur, T., 124, 160, 162
Nasik, 79, 91, 100, 118–23, 239
Nasir Jang, 112
National Centre for Performing Arts, Bombay, 10
National Maritime Museum, Bombay, 38
Naukonda Palace, Aurangabad, 88
Nauraspur, 215
Nayak dynasty, 178, 188
Nehru, *Pandit* J., 74, 116–7, 119, 158
Nepali art, 142, 178
Neral, 46–7
Netravati river, 176
Nevasa, 79
New Mangalore, 179
New Palace Museum, Kolhapur, 81
Nizam of Hyderabad, 164–5, 216, 224

Nizam Shahi dynasty, 85–7, 115, 249
Nizam ud-Din Aulia, 112, 227
Nizam ul-Mulk Asaf Jah I, 112
Nocil, 67

Oberoi Towers Hotel, 10, 22
Old Woman's Island, Bombay, 1, 7
Osho Commune, Pune, 59–63
Oxenden, *Sir* G., 6

Padmadurga, 42
Padmavati, 150
Paes, Domingos, 199
Pahari art, 15
painting, 15, 86–7, 96–103, 165, 177–8, 212
Paithan, 43, 79, 84
Pala dynasty, 16
Palghat, 165
Pallava dynasty, 16, 43, 203
Pampa (author), 135
Pampa (place). *See* Hampi
Pampa (river goddess), 199
Panchgani, 69, 71, 76
Pandharpur, 83–5, 195
Pandya dynasty, 43, 153
Panhala, 78, 83
Panvel, 42, 179
Parell, 1, 10–11
parks, national, 18. *See also* under the names of individual parks, *e.g.* Nagarhole
Parsis. *See* Zoroastrians and Zoroastrianism
Parsons, G. A., 173
Parthia and Parthians, 18
Parvati, 1, 17, 39, 74, 105–6, 108, 199
passports, 242–3
Patalishwar, 54–5
Patil, C., 138
Patradevi, 67
Pattadakal, 108, 160, 203, 208–11
Paunar, 79
Pauni, 79
Pawar, Nandi, 54
Peerbhoy, A. H. A., 48
Pendse, S. M., 67–8
pepper, 174, 176
Periyar, 171
permits, 243
Perumal, T. N. A., 172
Peshwa dynasty, 46, 56–7, 59, 122, 216, 249–50
Pestonji family, 26
Petit family, 57
Petrigal. *See* Pattadakal
Phule (formerly Crawford) Market, Bombay, 6

Phule (formerly Ray) Market, Pune, 58
Phule Museum, Pune, 56
Piklihal, 124
Pitalkhora, 15, 51, 79, 122
planetarium, Bombay, 12
Poladpur, 68
police, 219
Polilur, 165
Pondicherry (T.N.), 165
Ponnampet, 170, 172
Poona. *See* Pune
population of Bombay, 37
Porto Novo, 164
Portuguese in India, 4, 40–2, 85, 176, 178, 199
Potters' Bridge, Pune, 54
Pottinger, E., 6
Prabhu, Pryagji, 77–8
Prabhupada, *H.D.G.* A.C.B.S., 20–1
Prakash, 79
Prasad, *Dr* Rajendra, 119
Pratapgarh, 69, 73–6
Prayag (Allahabad), 118
prehistory, 124
Prince of Wales Museum, Bombay, 14–16, 30, 152
Prohibition, 244
Protestants and Protestantism, 6, 27, 173
Pugin, A., 35
Pulakesin I, 203
Pulakesin II, 203, 206
Pune, 30, 33, 54–63, 70–1, 86, 116, 237–40, 244, 247
puppets, 59
Purandhar, 73
Purniah, 164
Puttappa, K. V., 135–8
Puttur, 169, 176, 179

Qadri, Shah Rasheed Ahmad, 227
Qutb Shahi dynasty of Golconda, 115

Rabgayling, 169
Rabi'a, *Begum*, 88
Raeside, Ian, 67
Rafi bin Shams bin Mansur, 220
Raghavendrachar, H. N., 184
Raichur, 124, 224, 235
railways, 7, 26–7, 30, 46–8, 63–5, 132, 179, 202, 238–9
rainfall, 237
Raja Ram, 70, 79
Rajaram II of Kolhapur, 81
Rajaram, C. P., 130
Raj Bhavan, Bombay, 10
Rajgarh, 74
Rajmachi fort, 48

198, 202–11. *See also* under the names of museums, *e.g.* Prince of Wales, *and* locations of sculpture, *e.g.* Karkal

Tithimathi, 170
toilets, 245
tombs. *See under* the persons commemorated, *e.g.* Bibi-ka Maqbara; and under the location of tombs, *e.g.* Bidar
tongas, 163–6
Topgyal, Dakpa, vi, 190–1
Torvi, 215
Town Hall, Bombay, 4
Town Hall Museum, Kolhapur, 81
toys, 59
Traikutaka dynasty, 38
trains, 7, 26–7, 30, 46–8, 63–5, 132, 202, 238–9
transmigration of souls, 57
travel agents, 239
Tribal Cultural Museum, Pune, 58
tribes, 58–9, 171
Trimbak, P., 77
Trombay, 7
Trubshawe, J., 27, 57
Tsulkhang, Lobsang Chophel, 189–90
Tughlaq, Ghiyas ud-Din Muhammad bin, 113
Tughlaq, Muhammad bin, 46, 54, 113–5, 219
Tukaram, 82
Tuljapur, 74
Tuluva dynasty, 192
Tungabhadra river, 192–4, 211

Udipi. *See* Udupi
Udupi, 183–6
Ujjain, 118, 147
Ulsoor, 126
Ulugh Khan. *See* Tughlaq, Muhammad bin
Underi, 42
Universities of Bombay, 13, 29–30; Pune, 57
Unwalla, J., 31
Upanishads, 118–9
Updike, John, vi, 61–2
Urdu language, 222

Vakataka dynasty, 15, 43, 96, 98, 101, 123
Vani, S. V., 38
Varahadeva, 96–7
Varma, Raja, 141
Varma, Ravi, 140–2
Varuna, 39, 202
Vasai. *See* Bassein
Vatapi. *See* Badami
Vathar, 71
Vayudoot Airlines, 239
Vedas, 20–2, 74–5, 119
Velapura, 153
Vellore (T.N.), 165
Venkatappa Art Gallery, Bangalore, 130–1
Venur, 182